HUMAN BY DAY, ZETA BY NIGHT

A Dramatic Account of Greys Incarnating as Humans

by
Judy Carroll

Wild Flower Press
An Imprint of Granite Publishing
P.O. Box 1429
Columbus, NC 28722

Library of Congress Cataloging-in-Publication Data

Carroll, Judy, 1952-
Human by Day, Zeta by Night:
A Dramatic Account of Greys Incarnating as Humans
/ by Judy Carroll.
p. cm. -- (Zeta series ; v. 2)
ISBN 978-0-926524-71-2
1. Human-alien encounters--Drama. 2. Alien abduction--Drama.
3. Shape shifting--Drama. 4. Life on other planets--Drama.
5. Australia--Drama. I. Title.
PR9619.4.C38H86 2010
0822'.92--dc22
2010024237

Manuscript Editor: Brian L. Crissey
Cover Design: Pamela Meyer

Printed in the United State of America

Address all inquiries to:
Wild Flower Press
An Imprint of Granite Publishing
P.O. Box 1429
Columbus, NC 28722

http://GranitePublishing.us

DEDICATION

I dedicate this book to my Zeta Family — my beloved Guides
and Teachers — for your Lessons, Love and Light, as well as your
endless patience, compassion and encouragement.
Thank you for helping me to learn and to grow, which
in turn is enabling me to help my fellow humans.
Love does indeed conquer all!

ACKNOWLEDGEMENTS

I would like to acknowledge and thank the folks at
Wild Flower Press for their support and belief in the messages conveyed
through this book. As a publishing company renowned for its commitment to
Truth, their agreement to publish this "fictional" story has been an
unusual and controversial step for them to take.

Also, a special acknowledgement for my dearest friend and
spiritual sister, Helene Kaye, her husband Gary, and their two beautiful children,
Kira and Ben, whose amazing experiences, patience, dedication and love have
made this book possible. I love and thank you all,
more than mere words can ever express.

Human by Day, Zeta by Night is presented as a
docudrama, based firmly upon our non-fiction book
The Zeta Message — Connecting All Beings in Oneness,
co-authored by fellow experiencer, Helene Kaye.

TABLE OF CONTENTS

FACT

Tens if not hundreds of thousands of perfectly sane, normal human beings are being regularly taken on board extraterrestrial (ET) space craft for the purpose of medical examinations, probes and genetic procedures. These people, popularly referred to as abductees, contactees, or experiencers, cover a broad cross-section of the world community and all age groups.

The ETs involved are usually the small, thin-bodied, large-headed ones with black almond-shaped eyes known as the Greys, although other types, some very human in appearance, have also been reported. The encounter experience often begins with the person waking in the night to find a number of entities (usually three) in the bedroom. They are then whisked mysteriously out of the house through locked doors and closed windows, and the next moment find themselves on board an ET disc, lying on an examination table in a clinic-like room. A medical examination is then carried out on them, which often involves the removal of tissue samples, the placing of an implant into some part of their body, and sometimes a gynecological procedure of some sort.

If the situation becomes too painful or frightening, an "anesthetic" is administered, simply by one of the ETs placing their hands on the head of the human guest. When it is over, the person is returned safely to bed, occasionally waking the next morning to such anomalies as pajamas on back to front, inside out or folded neatly beside them, unexplainable bleeding or body marks, often in the shape of a triangle, and more rarely, awakening in the wrong bed, or even the wrong house.

Some have conscious or semi-conscious recollection of their encounter experiences, some do not, but this phenomenon, along with the UFOs which have been seen, reported and investigated over a period of many years, is gaining more and more credence. In fact hardly a day goes by without at least one sighting of a UFO or an "alien abduction" report somewhere on the planet. Many popular books have been written on ETs and abductions, but up until the present time, most literature on the subject has naturally been written from the human viewpoint. Now it is time for the ETs themselves to have a say on the subject.

1 ▶ RECONNAISSANCE

Our discs skimmed the sandy surface of the planet, travelling at a steady and moderate speed of only a few hundred kilometers per hour. This was a reconnaissance flight, so my fellow crew members and I had left the safety of our space station to venture forth in two of our smaller, more compact discs to carry out our mission. We were operating on a lower frequency band of the electromagnetic scale, which meant we were visible to any Earthling eyes that happened to be scanning the night sky, but with the storm that had been raging for the last half hour or so, that was not very likely. This was not a thickly populated area of the planet, and most of the inhabitants would be tucked up safe and sound in their beds anyway, so we felt fairly secure that our presence would not be noticed.

We were probably appearing as blips on the radar screens at the local Air Force Base, which was a bit of a worry, but even if they sent one of their planes up to investigate and intercept us, we would soon make our escape. Compared to our discs even the very latest fighter planes of Earth are slow and cumbersome, and we can easily out-maneuver them. We knew exactly what their capabilities were, because we'd been monitoring them for years, positioning our data-gathering plasma balls close to their wingtips during the last major war to ensure a regular supply of information on the technological progress of the military forces of Planet Earth. These plasma balls are actually living, sentient thought forms created as extensions of our own minds. They appear to Earthling eyes as balls of light and have been known by human pilots as "foo fighters."

On this mission my "twin soul" Ashka and I were piloting our disc, along with three other crew members. Ashka and I are close friends, sharing a very similar energy signature, so we often work together in this way. Our discs are not powered by fuel-driven rockets, or engines of any sort for that matter. They are motivated solely by the pure, naturally occurring energy that is the driving force behind the entire universe. They are designed to access this cosmic energy directly through the hands and mind focus of the crew.

To put it simply, we ourselves are the conduit for the power, and the disc is an extension of us in that we are linked to it and to each other by thought processes alone. This energy flows into and through our bodies, which act as conductors, and is directed into the disc, which is intimately linked into our energy and nervous systems through our hands when they are placed on the control panel. Direction and speed are governed solely by our minds, and so the disc can potentially travel at the speed of our thoughts, thus transcending time and space. The disc is a living entity of which we are the brain and nervous system. The disc itself is "attuned" to the energy signature of each individual crew member, and will respond only to our touch.

Our people, known on Earth as "Zeta Reticulans" or "Greys" because of the color of the bodies we sometimes use, are visiting your planet as a rescue team, to assist in the awakening of Earth human consciousness to higher and deeper levels of awareness. The name we call ourselves may be translated into the physical languages of Earth as Family, or Guardians, and where we come from is Home, or Realm. We have experienced lives in many different star systems including your own, but we have now evolved to a point where we are no longer trapped in the physical universe. We moved beyond that state eons ago.

We are not physical beings but rather pure soul essence, and we are caretakers of life-force energy within the universe. In order to carry out our role of guardianship on physical planets such as Earth, we sometimes must utilize physical bodies, or "containers," as we call them. These may be biological, artificial, or even a bit of both, depending upon the work we are carrying out at the time. The artificial containers have caused some Earth-plane investigators to conclude that we are robots, but the truth is, Earth humans are in general far more "programmed robots" than we are!

Having evolved past the psychological or karmic need for physical form, we operate in total oneness as a Group Soul Consciousness. As Guardians, we are able to consciously access many different dimensional planes, and those beings known on Earth as "Angels" are very highly evolved members of our group. Beings like Ashka and me, who have not yet attained this advanced frequency level, are referred to as helpers, or workers of the Angels. Earth humans have given us many different labels — Zetas, Greys, Visitors and ETs, which are all fine as far as we are concerned. What we do not like to be called is "Aliens," for the immortal soul consciousness that we are, you are also, so in the greater reality we are all One.

Part of our mission on this particular flight was to investigate certain electromagnetic anomalies that had been picked up in the area by another crew during a previous reconnaissance sweep. A fact that most people on Earth are blissfully unaware of is that electromagnetic "traps" or "fences," have been set up deliberately in certain areas of the planet. How they came to be, who set them up in the first place and why, is a whole story in itself, and it is one of the main reasons why we Guardians are coming here to Earth at this time. Unfortunately some of these traps are still active and can be triggered by the right atmospheric conditions. They themselves affect atmospheric conditions as well.

These are the areas of your planet where people and even planes and ships can disappear in the blink of an eye if they accidentally enter the force field. They are also quite dangerous in that they can cause major disturbances in the weather patterns, as evidenced by the raging storm through which we flew that night. In fact it was taking the combined concentration of all of us to keep the disc steady and on track. Telepathic communication from the other disc indicated that they were having trouble as well.

A sudden, split-second frantic warning from them jolted through our minds, followed by dead silence, then a bolt of lightning set off by a solid object coming into contact with an electromagnetic fence hit us full-on, short-circuiting our energy system. A massive explosion threw me sideways as the control panel disintegrated in a shower of sparks, and spiraling and spinning out of control, our disc nose-dived into the hard and unforgiving terrain of the planet below.

Everything around me was still and silent as death. Time lost all meaning as I lay half conscious in the tangled wreckage, but then a feeble, pain-wracked mind reached out to me, making me aware that at least one of the others was still alive. Thank goodness I was not alone on this dangerous and primitive planet! Slowly disentangling myself from a twisted mass of fiber-optic cables, I crawled out from under part of the control panel that had caved in on top of me and went in search of survivors.

Being in the almost completely artificial body that is standard equipment for disc pilots, I had no physical injuries as such. The electric shock caused by the lightning strike on the disc had left me feeling rather disoriented and slightly dizzy, but apart from that I was okay. The planetary atmosphere was not a problem either. An immortal spiritual soul essence does not need air to breathe, and neither does the container/body that we use to carry out physical-plane activities. Inhabiting this body, I needed neither food nor water, and that is why we generally use such containers for space travel. But unfortunately the others weren't so well equipped.

As well as being a reconnaissance mission, our venture had also been experimental in nature. The other crew members, including Ashka, had been in biological containers, with the intention of testing them out in the extremely heavy atmospheric conditions of Planet Earth. Our plan had been to land the disc in a remote area where they could step outside briefly to check their potential for survival, but still remain close to the disc, if anything went wrong. We had not, however, been prepared for a crash.

"Alarca, Alarca! Over here! Please help me! I can't move!" It was Ashka, and she was pinned under the side of the disc that had collapsed inwards under the impact of the crash. I got to her as fast as I could, and somehow managed to lift the tangled metal up and off her body, but it was obvious she was badly injured; then I saw the others, their physical containers well and truly dead and beyond my help. At least I knew they would all be safely home by now.

Turning my attention back to Ashka, I lifted her container gently and carried it outside. It was still dark, but our eyes adapted to night vision. Nevertheless, in the heavy atmosphere of Earth it was hard to move about, so it took some effort to help Ashka and then to get back to the disc for a first-aid kit. By the time I returned to her side, it was obvious by the injuries she had sustained there was nothing much that could be done for her. It was clear that her biological body was struggling to survive.

"Oh, Alarca, I am so sorry! I'm not going to be able to stay here much longer, but I don't want to leave you here on your own!" A thin, grey, four-fingered hand reached feebly for mine and she gasped in pain as her rapidly weakening thoughts telepathed into my mind.

"Ashka, it's all right!" I cried, holding her hand in both of mine to enable her to draw on the maximum amount of energy to ease and hasten her release from the pain of her badly damaged container. "Please, just let go! Go home with the others! I'll be fine." I wanted to take her in my arms, but dared not because of the severity of her injuries. Instead of comforting her, I would only cause her more pain.

Car headlights swept the area as a convoy of military vehicles arrived on the scene. Coarse, loud human speech assaulted our senses and lights blinded me as a group of large uniformed Earthlings descended upon us. I wanted to run, but I could not leave Ashka alone and at their mercy, but when I looked back at her again, I knew her container was uninhabited.

Struggling to my feet, fighting against the heavy gravity of the planet, I tried to get back into the disc, but a shot fired at my body weakened me further, causing me to almost black out. A half dozen pairs of strange, stubby, five-fingered hands grabbed and secured me, dragging my semi-conscious body over to a waiting vehicle. Frantic activity, lights and sounds assailed my senses. I could not comprehend these sounds on a physical level, but I knew it was human speech, and I was at least able to register the strong emotion being generated. Then I was lifted, none too gently, and pushed into the opening at the back of the vehicle. The door was slammed shut as I sank onto the floor.

As a senior pilot of the Realm, my duty was to remain calm and to consider my options. The choice was mine, whether to step free of the container right now and return home, or whether to stay a little longer to see what information I could gather, if any. I made my decision.

2 ▶ DESTINATION EARTH

"Oh *no*, Sothis!" I protested across the room to the Elder standing impassively opposite me. "Do I really *have* to? I've just spent a whole *three* weeks down there as their 'prisoner,' gathering as much information as possible before abandoning my container to return home. Can't I just resume my duties as a disc pilot?"

"Come now, Alarca," he replied calmly, drilling into the very core of my being with a dispassionate glare from huge, pale blue, implacable eyes — the eyes of an ancient Elder. "It will be an *adventure* for you. After all, you've been piloting discs from one end of the physical universe to the other for many millennia; surely you could do with a change. And besides, I get the distinct feeling you and Ashka have been doing this work for so long that the pair of you are getting just a wee bit careless. I mean it's understandable when an Earth human pilot accidentally flies into one of the Controllers' energy screens and crashes or else completely disappears into a parallel time-line, but really and truly, a Guardian of the Realm Forces should know better — especially ones of your and Ashka's experience."

The atmosphere hung heavy in the room as he paused a moment to ensure that the seriousness of our "little accident" was fully appreciated before continuing: "I've just finished examining the de-briefing notes from your time spent as a 'guest' of the Earth authorities, and frankly Alarca, this information disturbs me. We've been maintaining a fairly low level of surveillance on this planet for some time now, but it's obvious from your firsthand observations that *much* more active intervention is required down there, especially now that they have developed this 'atom bomb' they are so proud of. If they are not awakened to higher conscious awareness soon, there will *be* no humanity left on that planet to re-awaken — in fact there will be no planet!

"Now Alarca, with this in mind, you should be more than willing to be re-assigned to alternative duties, this time down there to live among them for the short span of a human lifetime in a fully biological container. Part of your duties will be ambassadorial and diplomatic, and you will report back to us here at headquarters on a regular basis, but your main work will entail teaching Earth humans to become more consciously aware of soul energy, to assist in their awakening process.

"We will also be bringing more Earth humans up onto the discs for re-adjustments and balancing of their energy systems to enable the necessary genetic upgrading to be carried out in preparation for the up-coming energy shift. A major part of the project will also be focusing on those several thousand members of our own lost patrol who are still caught up down there in a state of amnesia. These ones need to have their spiritual heritage restored to them as soon as possible so they can be brought home."

"But Sothis, must I go and *live* down there? I haven't used a fully biological container in *millennia*! It's only the very *youngest* evolved humans in the universe that use those bodies! They're so weak and vulnerable, and — and *messy*! Do I *have* to?"

"Alarca, somebody has to do it, and you're the one who has been there most recently and experienced the energy first-hand. Anyway, others will be sent to help you, and Ashka has already agreed to be assigned duties down there because of your close connection. In fact it will be a real 'family project!' And besides, it won't be *that* bad. Remember there are certain advantages in occupying a biological container. Just think — you'll be able to really enjoy eating *food*, and all sorts of other physical human activities. It will be quite *fun*! And by the way, speaking of Ashka's planned incarnation into physical Earth human form; I feel you also would be better off incarnating into a female container."

"*What*! Oh no! *No way*! Please, Sothis, don't ask me to do *that*! Not a *female* container! You *know* how we never managed to properly adjust the reproductive system to the point of perfect, painless working order when we were assisting in their development? And the plumbing! It seems to break down in so many of the containers once they reach the 50-year mark.

"And anyway," I stubbornly persisted, "why do I have to reincarnate into an Earthling container? Why can't I be born into one of the hybrid containers that we're producing out of our inter-species breeding program that has been started with the Earth humans? After all, being half and half they're much closer to us in vibrational frequency, so surely it would make things easier."

"No, Alarca, that won't do at all. Because of the nature of the work we need to carry out with Earth humans, it is most important for you to fully integrate the experience of actually *being* one of them. In this way you will be of invaluable assistance to us in our interaction with them in the future. As you well know, this is an area where we are having great difficulties that need to be ironed out if we ever hope to interact with them in a more open way."

"Well, yes, you do have a good point there," I reluctantly admitted, "but I still don't see why I have to incarnate into a *female* container. Planet Earth does not seem such a good place to be born a female. In fact it appears to me that they are looked upon very much as second-class citizens. I really and truly feel, considering the work I am expected to carry out, that a male body would be a much more sensible way to go."

"Nonsense, Alarca!" the Elder firmly replied, cutting off all objections. "You know as well as I do that a male body would be out of the question. Even though we are more evolved, we still must tend towards one polarity or the other, and ours is towards the creative, feminine yin polarity, as opposed to the more aggressive and physically inclined masculine yang polarity that is so prevalent on Earth. After all, part of our job *is* to try to balance out their energy systems a bit more. Anyway Alarca, really and truly, you surely cannot in all honesty see yourself, an intrinsic part of the Guardian Consciousness, decked out in a large, muscular, testosterone-charged male body, running around a sports field, kicking the life out of a poor, innocent little leather ball, can you?"

Shaking his head in profound amusement at the mere thought, he went on: "Oh, no, no Alarca, my dear friend, that would not do at all. You will be much better off and safer as a female, and besides, it is definitely more in keeping with the nurturing role of us Guardians, so no more arguments."

"But Sothis, I still protested, "what about procreating in a fully biological container? You know our people don't reproduce themselves as humans do. I mean to say! The *pain*! And the *mess*! And the *blood*! How am I *ever* going to get on? I'll never manage to procreate in a primitive Earthling body! Please don't ask me to reproduce. Please."

"Alarca, you will not be expected to physically reproduce as an Earth human. In fact if you do you'll jeopardize the entire mission. You are going to the Earth Plane as a spiritual parent and teacher, which will be quite enough for you to handle. You will have neither time nor energy for physical motherhood. Besides, Ashka wants to have a go at Earth human motherhood, which will be fine in her case, as she plans to work with the hybrid children up here and with the Star Children on Earth, but your case is different — you have other work to do."

"Well, that's a relief!"

"Alarca, I never expected you to reproduce. All I am asking, and note that I say *asking*, not ordering, is that you return to the Earth Plane, in human female form to try to reach out across the incredible abyss of misunderstanding and fear, to enable the Earth humans to more clearly understand just who and what we are, what we are about, and also what they *themselves* are, to set them free from the influence of the Controllers.

"Oh, is that all?"

He smiled in feeling my total bewilderment and soothingly calmed me. Just remember you will not be alone. And after all, once they access this deeper understanding, the mind control being used against them will be nullified completely. The survival of the planet and every living creature on it depends entirely upon Earth humans accessing this clearer awareness of self. Please Alarca will you do this for us, your soul family, and for our human children?"

The sad desperation in the Elder's words washed over and through me. What else could I do? There was no more to be said. I wasn't being ordered, but the wisdom of the Elders and the importance of our work always have a way of being very convincing. I knew Sothis was right. And besides, I wouldn't be alone.

3 ▶ FAMILY PLANNING

Most of my time was spent with the Elders in prolonged discussion, planning and preparation in order to master as much as I possibly could about existence as a female human on the Earth plane, however, hard as I tried, I could not shake off the feelings of apprehension. It was the idea of having to use a vulnerable biological container that was really worrying me. A hundred times I nearly backed down, and came up with just as many valid and perfectly logical excuses as to why I did not need this Earth plane experience, but each time the realization of how desperately our intervention was needed on Earth came back to haunt me.

With the time-line of 2012 fast approaching, the spiritual evolution of Earth's inhabitants to a higher level of conscious awareness is vital, but with the influence of the Controllers still so strong, this process is not proceeding as it should. We'd thought that they had been defeated long ago and their force fields destroyed, but the fate of our surveillance discs was proof that this was not so. It was obvious that our assistance was needed to try to locate and dismantle the remainder of this system, in order to allow the population of Earth to move on to where they need to be. The more I thought about this sad state of affairs, the stronger I felt the need to help Earth humans before they destroy themselves, their beautiful planet and affect the greater universe. Yet apprehension kept surfacing in my mind.

When I met with my Teacher Maris to discuss the details of our plan, he immediately sensed my state of disquiet, and suggested we share a few moments of quiet contemplation, and so we took a little time just sitting together, our minds linked as one in peace and calmness, before he turned to me: "Now then Alarca, let's get down to the business of your impending physical, Earthly incarnation. We must begin to make plans, for a suitable family for you, and a time and place for your birth. Have you given the matter any thought?"

"Any thought!" I telepathed back at him a little more forcefully than intended. "In the name of the Great Oneness, Maris, it fills my every waking moment!"

He smiled gently and continued, quite unruffled by my outburst. "Let's hear your ideas then."

With a sigh of resignation I turned to face him. "My thoughts on the matter are that if I really *have* to carry out this mission, and as a Guardian of the Realm I know that it is my duty to do so, then it is vitally important that I make contact with the Earthlings on their own terms, in order to give myself the best possible chance of success." He nodded in agreement and waited patiently for me to continue.

"As Sothis has told me," I went on, "I am returning to the Earth Plane primarily as a spiritual teacher, and also as an ambassador of our people, whom the Earthlings think of with much fear and trembling as 'aliens,' or 'Greys.' With this in mind, I need to be reborn into a very specific astrological time frame which will bring about those influences most conducive to the personality traits and particular abilities I will require to best carry out this work as a teacher and ambassador.

"Also the fact that I am a Guardian must be taken into consideration if I am to enter the physical dimension of Planet Earth with the least amount of difficulty, so my birth will need to be as close as possible to one of the solstices, when the interdimensional portals are at their weakest. The last thing that I want to have to worry about is getting caught up in and affected by one of the astral-plane force fields. That doesn't even bear thinking about!" I added with a shudder.

"Well now, Alarca, you certainly have been putting some very constructive thoughts and planning into your mission, and yes, it is most definitely a good idea for you to make your entry at the time of the solstice. After all, your main reason for this mission is to assist humans to wake up and remember, so you don't want your own soul awareness to be adversely affected during the process of entry into the lower physical dimensions. You need to bring that knowledge in with you.

"And as for the astrological time frame for your birth," he added, "you are quite correct. This is a vital point to consider, as it will affect your whole life, outlook and personality as an Earth Human. In this regard, there are three important criteria for you to meet. The first is that you must have good communication skills, because it has been this lack of communication between our two species that has caused all the problems so far. This fear and misunderstanding that needs to be addressed can only be overcome through communication and dialogue.

"What we are finding is that when we take Earthlings on board our ships it is well-nigh impossible to communicate, for they are usually terrified in the totally alien environment and see us in the worst possible light. Approaching them in their dream-state does not work well either, because again they see us as frightening, nightmare figures, or else they have forgotten the meeting by the time they wake up. The second trait you will need to cultivate is a confident and reasonably outgoing personality, which I can tell you now, is not going to be easy after the experience you had in your fleeting contact with Earthlings after your crash. I know that you have a deep-seated aversion to aggressive human behavior, so you will need to work hard on cultivating confidence and calmness in your mind to overcome this obstacle.

"The third and extremely important personality trait you will need for this mission is groundedness, which is a *most* necessary commodity for a spiritual teacher. In this field on Earth there is a serious lack of proper grounding, with many who tend towards spiritual development spending their entire lives walking around with their heads in the clouds, caught up in astral plane webs of fancy woven by the Controllers to create delusions of ego and fear. This is also a serious problem which needs to be overcome, as it causes a huge block to their spiritual awakening, and, after all, it is their spiritual awakening that we are concerned with, first and foremost. Are you in agreement with all of this, Alarca?"

I barely had time to nod before he continued: "Now, as to your impending family, I have given this much thought. I feel a settled, stable environment will be the best, to provide you with the security, support and finely balanced outlook you will need for the difficult task which lies ahead of you. You certainly do not need the psychological problems which can result from a traumatic childhood. I feel you need to be born into an English-speaking culture, because this is a very widely spoken language on Planet Earth, and will enable you to reach more people with your message."

He paused a moment in deep thought, then suddenly his huge, black eyes lit up in excitement. "I know what we can do! I've just thought of a *brilliant* way to break down your barriers of communication even more, and also to overcome the myriad difficulties you will face as an interdimensional Guardian trying to adapt to a biological human body. You could be born into a *multi-cultural* family! That's it! We need to introduce some *exotic* bloodlines somehow — maybe some sort of *tribal* culture. Now just be quiet for a minute and let me think.

"Ah, I know! How about Native American? They are tribal societies who speak English, and probably Spanish as well when you get down among the tribes of New Mexico, you know, Pueblos and Hopis. There you go Alarca — we could find a nice Hopi family for you to be born into. They also have a very deep respect and understanding of our Star Nations as well, which would be a bonus."

"Oh no, *please!*" I cried, "*Any*where but America!" The very thought of being reborn anywhere near the scene of the crash made me feel awful, and if a "Grey" can possibly turn pale, I did at that moment.

"Alarca, Alarca, it's all right. Calm yourself. I was only thinking of how good a fit Native Americans would be, but I can see the area would not suit you. We'll think of something else. We sat in silence until his mind processes nearly overwhelmed the room.

"Wait a minute!" he exclaimed excitedly, almost knocking me backwards with the force of his thought waves. "I *have* it! Why didn't I think of this before?"

"What, tell me!"

"Alarca, listen! Which group of tribal people live in countries all over the world, and are considered extremely mysterious and exotic by most other humans on Planet Earth because they are perceived as being strange and different?"

I looked at him blankly and shook my head in confusion. "I'm sorry Maris, you've lost me completely."

"The Romanies, Alarca! The ones that Earth humans call 'Gypsies!' That is the answer to our problem. We'll find an English-speaking Romany family for you. That way those big, black eyes of yours won't look out of place."

I caught Maris's excitement. Perhaps it wasn't going to be so bad incarnating as an Earth human after all. From what I could recall of our history, the original Romany people who emerged mysteriously out of Northern India were actually a small group of our own people from a base we'd established in that area many millennia ago. This base had come under a major attack by the Controllers, which had resulted in all of our personnel being permanently trapped in biological Earth human bodies. Ever since that time many of them have remained in a state of almost total amnesia, unable to remember who or what they really are and cruelly cut off from the Guardian Consciousness. Over the millennia we tried to reach them with a number of failed rescue attempts. This was the "lost patrol" that Sothis had spoken of, and I knew very well that part of my work on Earth was going to be connected to this important mission of search and rescue. Yes, a Romany family would be perfect for me. They really would be "family" in the truest sense.

It wasn't long before Maris called me to meet with him again. As soon as I came into his presence, I knew by the aura of satisfaction that emanated from him that he had been successful in finding a suitable family for me.

"Yes, Alarca, indeed we have," he answered. "This couple we have chosen is perfect and meets all our requirements and more. The country in which they reside is located in the southern hemisphere of the planet, so your birth will be timed to coincide with their mid-summer solstice. The potential mother was born in this country, so her native language is English, and her husband, who is of Spanish descent, migrated there when he was quite young.

"We have succeeded admirably in introducing a bit of exotica into your human bloodline. Both your Earth parents are from a Romany background, so you shouldn't have much trouble relating to them, or them to you. They are both kind and gentle folk, descended from our own people, and they badly want a daughter, so you can't ask for more than that."

"Well, yes, Maris," I replied, "it does all sound very promising, so what country is it?"

"Australia!" he answered, looking very pleased with himself. You can't get much further away from the location of your last unpleasant Earthly experience than that now, can you?"

My whole aura lit up with relief. "Oh, yes, that *is* good news! And if I remember rightly I had a very positive and enjoyable Earth-plane experience there eons ago. Wasn't that ancient land once part of Lemuria? I'm sure I've worked there both as a teacher and a healer."

"Yes, Alarca, indeed you have, many millennia ago, so I take it that you are agreeable to these plans? Remember, the circumstances of this birth are your choice, but once you decide and the seed is planted, I don't want you changing your mind at the last minute and disappointing this family. You are already a glint in your potential father's eye, in fact they have been trying unsuccessfully for some time to start a family, so if you decide to go ahead with them, we'll get things started immediately."

"Well," I replied, taking a deep breath, "it's now or never, I suppose, so let's get on with it."

4 ▶ TAKING THE PLUNGE

It was "all systems go" in the intensive preparation that followed my decision to accept physical birth into the family that had been selected for me. The Source was tapped into and the creative energies of the universe were brought into play, permitting conception to take place. Although it was not necessary for me to be continually present within the tiny form that was to be my Earth human body, I did have to make visits on a fairly regular basis during the gestation period, to familiarize myself with things and also to begin melding with it on an energy level.

The physical form of an unborn baby, just like a sleeping human, can be likened to a car parked at the side of the road with its engine running, while the driver temporarily leaves to carry out business elsewhere. What many Earth humans have lost touch with is the fact that they are immortal, non-physical soul essences inhabiting a physical body for a biological life experience. They are *not* a physical body with a soul floating around somewhere. The physical body is nothing more than a vehicle of which you, the eternal spiritual soul essence, are the driver. This is the main reason why we, the Guardians, are here at this time. It is to awaken humankind to the fact that your true nature is spiritual and therefore far more than just a physical body.

When the physical body is safely asleep in bed at night, or in the mother's womb, its spirit is free to come and go at will, just like a driver who parks his car and gets out to shop. His absence will only be brief, so he leaves the engine running, idly ticking over, until he returns. Although the engine is running, the car cannot go anywhere on its own. It cannot drive itself, but must await the return of the driver to release the brake and select the appropriate gear to move on. However, just occasionally the spirit forgets to put the "hand brake" on, and the "vehicle" goes sleepwalking all on its own.

It is the experiences of the spirit, set free from the limiting confines of the physical body, which are remembered on waking as dreams. That is why during your dream state you can freely move backwards and forwards in time, and meet again with those who have stepped permanently from their physical vehicles. That is really what death is — the driver simply stepping out of the vehicle and not returning to keep it maintained and fueled. It cannot keep going on its own without the driver's care, and so eventually it ceases to function.

During the nine months of Earth-time in which my mother-to-be carried my new physical body within her own, I spent much time with the Elders, discussing the life and work that lay ahead. It was agreed that my formative years could be well spent, gradually accustoming myself to the Earth human body and all that it entailed, slowly getting used to the different energy frequency, and learning all I could about what it meant to be a female human on Planet Earth. Once I reached maturity, I would then be able to step smoothly into my role of teacher and ambassador for our people, working quietly and surreptitiously with as many humans as possible, all of whom would be blissfully unaware of the ET presence among them, giving them a little push-along in the right direction.

Even with all our careful preparations, there were still risks involved which the Elders made clear to me, the main one of which was my final approach to the physical plane at the time of birth. Coming from higher planes of spirit in which we Guardians dwell, I had to enter through the portals of the astral plane. It was during this final birthing process, when it became necessary for my immortal spiritual essence to become fully conscious as an Earth human, that I would be most at risk of becoming ensnared in the illusions of this dimension.

As the time of the solstice approached, I began shifting my mind focus from our Realm and centering myself more fully in the physical. This meant spending more time in the tiny unborn body and less time in the freedom of spirit. I cannot pretend to say I wasn't a wee bit concerned; in fact lying there all curled up in the fetal position as my quarters became more and more cramped, I was, to use one of my very favorite human expressions, "as nervous as a long-tailed cat in a room full of rocking chairs."

All too soon the moment of birth was upon me. The long, dark tunnel to the physical Earth plane was opening up before me and I was being drawn inexorably through towards the bright light at the end. If I was to retain my fully empowered Guardian consciousness it was most important not to experience fear. The astral plane "traps" are triggered by the energy of fear, so it was this emotion that had to be controlled, but as I passed through, memories of the crash came flooding back. Probing, clutching alien hands were once again pulling me from my place of warmth and protection.

Grasped by my feet and held dangling in mid-air, I gasped in terror, and then a wrenching, jarring, shuddering sensation tore through my entire system, as if gears were being changed without the aid of a clutch. I sent out a frantic call to the Elders for help, but it was too late, nothing could be done for me. All memory and awareness of who I was, where I had come from, and why I was here was wiped from my consciousness, my mind short-circuited by the energy portal through which I was pulled. Time lost all meaning as consciousness became totally absorbed in the need for food and warmth, and the security of my mother's arms. This was the totality of my world.

Like all human babies, I was to spend much of my time asleep, and it was during these periods that I would become aware of other minds reaching out towards me with messages of reassurance, gently reminding me of something that I could not quite grasp. Accompanying these messages were images of strange-looking, grayish-skinned beings with enormous, black eyes into which I yearned to lose myself. Then the pangs of hunger or some other discomfort would awaken me, causing me to scream in frustration as the memories of the eyes and the minds behind them retreated from my consciousness, leaving me with a deep sense of loss and bewilderment.

What failed to boost my confidence in my new container were the conversations I sometimes managed to pick up on, not so much the physical speech, but rather the telepathic content. My parents, like most proud new parents, thought that I was wonderful, but others were not so blinded by parental enthusiasm.

"Oh, my goodness me!" an unrecognized, high-pitched and extremely irritating *voice* remarked, "What a strange-looking little thing she is! I mean to say — just *look* at her eyes!"

"Well, yes," the warmly comforting voice of my mother answered, "I suppose they are strange and a little large, but I'm sure she'll grow into them eventually."

"That's where she mostly takes after my side of the family," the familiar voice of the one who was my father interjected proudly. "So many Spanish Gypsies have those dark, rather slanted eyes. Some look quite oriental. If you ask me, I think her eyes are her best feature."

"By the way," the *voice* went on, "what name have you given her?"

"This is something we've talked about for weeks," my mother answered. "We had several different ones picked out, but none of them seemed to suit her. Then a day or two after she was born, while I was nursing her, this really strange name just came into my mind. I actually heard it being spoken softly into my ear three times. It's definitely not a family name and I don't think I've ever heard it before. Perhaps it's the secret name that is traditionally given to Romany children, and if that's the case, it can only be revealed to her and no one else. Just in case it is we've had to compromise, and have decided to call her Ali."

"That's nice!" the *voice* chirped, all gleeful curiosity. "This secret name business sounds fascinating. What's the reason behind it?"

"Well," my father answered quietly, "the sound of a person's true name carries much power and magic, and if it is known to someone who wishes to do that person harm, it can be used against them in a detrimental way — not physically but rather on an energy level, so the true name is never revealed, not even to close friends."

"Oh!" said the *voice* with a touch of annoyance, "so you're not going to tell me what it is. I bet I can guess anyway! It's Alison, isn't it?"

"No," my mother replied, a veil of secrecy closing over her face, "it is not."

My early years in human form were lived in an old and rambling house of many rooms which nestled comfortably in the very midst of a huge and half-wild garden inhabited by numerous nature spirits, birds and insects, and presided over by Greypuss, a Cat Person of many parts and talents. This magical garden comprised about five acres or more of native flora, including a majestic stand of fine ironbarks and bloodwoods, as well as a wide and colorful variety of exotics such as several large and spreading poincianas which delighted the eye each summer with their display of brilliant, blood-red blossoms, and purple-flowering jacarandas which evoked mixed feelings in the minds of all Australian school children, with the delicate, bell-shaped blooms making their appearance in November, the time for end-of-year exams. Shaded pathways meandered beneath garden arches and trellises festooned with climbing jasmine, its white, waxen, star-shaped flowers like perfumed snowflakes against a backdrop of small, shiny dark-green leaves.

The family which had been selected for me by mutual agreement between myself and the Elders were good people, easy-going and tolerant of the strange little creature that had come among them. Although forgotten on the conscious level, we had all been a close and loving group many millennia ago, so on a soul level I felt safe and secure with this family.

While the ins and outs of my growing human body were strange and unfamiliar to me, conversing with animals was not, and so Greypuss was my very special friend. A large, smoky-gray cat with a thick, soft coat trimmed in silver tones, and eyes like deep pools of liquid gold, she was my protector, my ever-faithful companion, and the willing receptacle of my most intimate thoughts and secrets.

One morning, with nothing better to do, I sought out Puss's company to ask her some very deep and meaningful questions. She was a wise old cat who never failed to get me back on track with a few telepathic words of good advice when they were needed, but today it was not so much advice I was after, but rather answers to things that puzzled me.

After searching the garden I finally found her in a patch of winter sunlight, grooming her fine coat with the usual sense of thoroughness, concentration and precision that she always devoted to this particular task.

"Greypuss," I asked, squatting down beside her on the grass, "why is it that others cannot converse with animals and see the colors around all living things? Can't everybody do that?"

"They can, child, they can indeed," she purred, giving the very end of a long, sleek, silver-tipped tail a quick and final flick with a pink and roughened tongue. "It is just that they don't bother to develop these abilities. You may have noticed how most humans prefer to spend their days in idle chatter — chatter about the neighbors, chatter about the weather, chatter about next year's holiday or last night's dinner — the tongues never stop flapping! Now if they would learn to be more like cats, keeping their tongues busy in a more constructive and cleansing way which would in turn enable them to meditate at the same time, there is no end to what they would be capable of perceiving and understanding.

"You see child," she went on patiently, "if one wishes to progress spiritually in life, then one must learn silence, and the art of listening. Too many humans indulge in endless chatter, desperately trying to fill the empty void within, putting their point across and broadcasting their personal thoughts and ideas to the world in general, who on the whole aren't interested anyway, being distracted completely by their own thoughts, worries and ideas.

"It is only by cultivating peace, calmness and stillness and so allowing the quiet voice within to be heard, that any progress can be made or wisdom attained. Talking endlessly is easy — it is the art of listening that is more difficult to acquire.

"Why do you think we were venerated in ancient Egypt, and actively encouraged to make our homes within the temple precincts? It was because cats are a physical manifestation of the art of meditation. This is why we have come to dwell among the Earth humans — to teach them to reach within through silence, peace and relaxation. We embody this very concept, and we are a living example for them to follow. This understanding is the only way they will ever get to perceive the still, small voice within, and it is our special gift to humankind. Those humans who do not like cats are often the very ones who cannot bring themselves to look deeply within."

"You know, Greypuss, I've never thought of cats in that way — of them being teachers I mean. Are all animals put on Earth in order to carry out teaching?"

"Well, yes, I suppose you could say that," she replied. "Humans would certainly learn a lot by observing and listening to animals more closely. Trees and rocks too make excellent teachers, you know, because they have been around on this planet for a very long time. Reptiles also, are extremely ancient and knowledgeable — and they make a good be-tween-meals snack as well!" she added, with a knowing wink and a flick of the tail.

5 ▶ AUNT MELILA'S WISDOM

An ancient and important link shared by our family was music and dance, which filled our home and every day of our lives with harmony and joy. My mother had been a professional dancer before she married, and my Spanish Gypsy father came from a large family of dancers, singers and musicians. Whenever friends came to visit, the evening inevitably ended in music and dance, and many a night I fell asleep to the sound of guitars, castanets, and the beautiful *cante jondo*, the "deep song" of the Spanish Gypsies. There was one family friend in particular who had the most wonderful voice, untrained except for many years of singing his heart out as he labored in the fields of his native country. His *cante jondo* never failed to bring tears to the eyes of everyone who heard him, but to me, his voice was a lullaby, sending me to sleep with its sweetness.

In our Romany culture children are very special. They are never made to feel as if they're in the way or a nuisance, and they are encouraged from an early age to take an active role in all the affairs of the family. In this way I found it perfectly natural to dance. Everybody else did, whether they were good or bad, so I did too. I apparently showed a natural talent for it from the time I could walk, and so I was encouraged even more, and the result was that by the age of seven, I understood and could follow the rather complex *compas*, the timing of flamenco music, far better than I could understand or follow the boring arithmetic we were taught in school.

In this happy home environment, there were really only two clouds over-shadowing my childhood. The main one was school, which I loathed and detested beyond description. How often I begged and pleaded with my parents to give up their settled lifestyle and take to the roads in the traditional Romany fashion. In that way I hoped to avoid school and have the time to get on with the important things in life — like dancing, and playing with the cat. Every morning it was the same routine, with monotonous regularity — my mother calling down the hallway, "Ali, get up! You'll be late for school!"

No answer.

Ten minutes later — "Ali, hurry up! Your breakfast is getting cold!"

Fifteen minutes later — "Yuk, I can't eat this, it's gone all cold!"

Mother (close to exasperation), "Well, whose fault is that? It was hot when I first called you. Hurry now or you'll be late."

"I don't want to go to school. I feel sick!"

"You didn't look sick five minutes ago when you were playing with Greypuss!"

Then my father would intervene, ever patient, calmly pointing out to me, "Ali, if you don't go to school you'll never learn to read, and you know how much you like stories and books. Just think — if you go to school, someday you'll be able to read any book you like. Surely that makes it worth the effort! Come on, hurry up and I'll give you a ride on my way to work." And so I would be cunningly cajoled into yet another day of academic drudgery.

The second cloud on my horizon was not quite so tangible. Try as I might, I could not put aside the strange feelings of disquiet that came upon me so often. It was an awareness which hovered on the very outer edges of my mind — a half-buried memory which, the harder I tried to retrieve it, the further it retreated from my consciousness. Sometimes it felt like there were two brains inside my head, each one competing with the other for the upper hand.

This sense of disquiet drove me on many occasions to escape through my bedroom window at night, moving carefully and quietly so as not to wake my parents sleeping peacefully in the next room – simply to watch the stars. On warm summer nights my greatest pleasure was to lie on my back out in the garden, looking up into the heavens. The sight of those stars, seemingly close enough for me to reach out and touch them, stirred emotions and strange yearnings way beyond my childhood comprehension.

One evening as I sat with the family watching a TV news broadcast, a report came on covering a war-torn area in Africa that struck at my core. Heart-rending scenes of starving, malnourished children were graphically depicted, alongside even worse scenes of people wounded or killed in the fighting when entire villages were set upon by armed troops. Immediately after this report, another was shown, obviously to introduce a happier perspective into the program, of a family in America who had been fortunate enough to win a major lottery. This time, children were shown playing happily in a large swimming pool on the grounds of a luxury home, while the adult members of the lucky family sat by watching, sipping tall glasses of champagne and obviously enjoying the good life.

"That isn't fair!" I protested angrily. "Why is it that those poor little children in Africa are born into such a dreadful life, of war and starvation, a life from which they have little or no chance of escaping, and those other ones in America have everything their hearts desire, just because they were lucky enough to win a lottery? The nuns at school talk so much of God's goodness, but God cannot be good to allow such unfairness! How could tiny little children be bad enough to be punished in such an awful way? Why are some born into terrible conditions like that, and others are born so lucky? I don't think there is a God, otherwise it wouldn't be that way!"

"Anna, Juan!" Aunt Malila's voice piped up from the depths of the comfortable and over-stuffed rocking chair in which she had been snoozing. "I really do think it's high time we spoke a few home truths to Ali. She has been exposed enough to Christianity at the convent. She now needs to learn more about the beliefs and teachings of her own people, and to be given the sacred knowledge that we used to pass on to our children around the campfire in the evenings. We may no longer be living a traditional life-style, but this is no excuse. She is old enough now to be told, especially as she is asking such questions."

My parents looked at each other, then my father went to turn the TV off, before coming back to sit beside me. I felt a sense of excitement, wondering what mysterious revelations were about to be imparted. "Ali Cat," my father put his arm around me, giving me a hug, "Aunt Malila is right. I know much of what the nuns teach you at school is correct. In fact overall, the education they give you is excellent, otherwise we wouldn't have sent you to a convent school, but you must understand that even though they are nuns and priests, they do not know everything, even when it comes to the subject of God."

"But how can that be?" I queried. "Surely nuns and priests must know more about God than anyone else."

My father sighed and shook his head. "That is what one would assume," he agreed, "but the truth of the matter is, many of them are limited in their knowledge — after all, it was only a few hundred years ago that they insisted the Earth was flat, and that it was the center of the universe. You see, Ali, people in general are too ready to place limitations upon everything, particularly those things that they cannot possibly fully understand, like God for instance. In fact, it seems to me that the less understanding there is, the more limitations they need to impose as a buffer against their own insecurities and lack of knowledge. All you need do is to look at how desperately they try to prove God's existence in their own terms, by limiting His omninature to the little pettinesses of human nature by ascribing to Him the very human vices of anger, jealousy, bigotry and intolerance. It seems to me that if a person cannot fit the largeness of a concept into the tiny pigeon-hole of their mind, then they cut it down to size to make it fit, losing much of value in the process, which is a great pity indeed."

"Ali," my mother added, "you only have to look at the way many people think of us, the Romanies, or any other foreign cultural group for that matter. They label us in a completely inaccurate and stereotyped way to fit in with their own limited concepts of what Gypsies should be, what we should look like and how we should act, and more often than not these stereotypes are totally wrong, as you well know. If they would only try to move past these barriers that they have created in their minds regarding us, this in turn would open them up to a very rich and diverse culture that could perhaps prove beneficial within their own lives."

"Exactly, Anna," my father put in. "You are so right! And this," he added, turning to me, "brings us right back to what you were talking about before, Ali Cat — those so-called 'truths' you're so rigidly taught at the convent in regards to the concept of God and His fairness, or lack of it, towards humans.

"The Romanies left the country of India hundreds of years ago to travel throughout the world. There are many legends concerning our exodus, but none of them are completely accurate. The real truth of our origins is held secret and sacred by only certain Tribal Elders, but we do know that much time was spent in the northern part of India before we ventured forth. This is why so many of us follow the belief systems of India, all of which are based on the concept of reincarnation — that is, the rebirth of the soul into many varied physical lives."

At these words a deeply familiar chord began to reverberate inside me, accompanied by the recognition of the fact that I knew this already, but how? My parents had never mentioned such a thing before, so where did this recognition come from? The family was pleased by my obvious reaction of interest, but as usual, words of warning came first, before any exciting revelations.

"Now, Ali," said Mother, "We have never discussed any of this with you before, because we worried that you would unthinkingly speak of it at school, and that would not do. For one thing it would be disrespectful to talk of such matters at a Catholic convent. Most Catholics don't believe in reincarnation, and you must learn first and foremost to respect the beliefs of others, and never ever try to impose your beliefs onto another person. The other reason we haven't brought it up is that we didn't want to confuse you with concepts so very different from those taught to you by the nuns; however, the truth is, reincarnation was taught and fully accepted by the Church right up until nearly 400 years after the death of Jesus, so really, it is not at all contrary to the original Christian doctrine."

"Ali," Aunt Malila spoke up from her chair in the corner, "you are now old enough to be told of these mystery teachings which are held sacred by our people, and also by many millions of others the world over

— teachings on the subject of the birth and rebirth of the soul over many lifetimes in its seemingly endless struggle to escape the Wheel of Karma. These teachings will clarify and answer many questions for you and will hopefully provide you with a more mature, loving and compassionate way of dealing with those around you.

"Now, child," she went on, "please don't make me use these old legs of mine any more than I have to. Come over here and sit down close to me. I well remember my grandmother sitting beside the campfire on many a cold and frosty night, under a sky ablaze with stars, with the rest of the tribe grouped companionably around her, listening to her words of wisdom. My goodness that brings back some fond memories! Among our people it is the solemn duty of the *Phuri Dai*, the Old Mother of the tribe, to pass on spiritual teachings to the young folk, and so, as the 'Old Mother' of this family I shall do the honors."

Aunt Malila leaned back in her ancient rocking chair, waiting patiently for us to settle ourselves comfortably at her feet. As she closed her eyes, collecting her thoughts, I saw a very distinct change come over her. Gone was the little old lady who often dithered about the place, forgetting where she'd put her shawl or her glasses, or whether she'd taken her herbal tea. In her place I clearly perceived a wise, proud and venerable Elder, an honored repository of vast mysteries and great knowledge, and so I sat waiting in her presence, as quietly and patiently as my parents.

"Now Ali!" she suddenly turned in my direction, black, gimlet-like eyes boring into me. "I want you to just stop for a moment to consider the idea of eternity. You are now what? Ten years old? Think back upon your childhood, as far back as you can recall. Do you remember when you were nearly three-years-old, and we went on that lovely holiday to the beach?"

"Oh, yes, Aunt Malila. I can remember that, but only just. It seems like so very long ago."

"There now, child," she replied, "that was but seven years ago, and yet to you it seems like such a long time, an eternity even! But eternity is far, far longer than seven years. In fact, multiply your seven years by seventy million, and you still have only a moment in eternity." Aunt Malila paused, allowing the full import of this notion to sink in, but it really was beyond me. To my child's mind the concept of eternity was unthinkable.

"Ask yourself this, Ali," she then went on. "How could an average, ordinary person, anybody you know, possibly be good enough or bad enough in one short lifetime to warrant spending eternity in either heaven or hell? Just think about the length of eternity compared to the usual three score years and ten of a human lifetime. Admittedly you do very occasionally come across someone who seems to be a living saint, or else the devil himself incarnate, but these are exceptions rather than the rule. Most humans are just average folk, neither very good nor very bad.

"Now I want you to think about those poor little mites you saw on the TV news. They are normal, ordinary children, with parents and families just like you, and in fact you don't even have to go so far as to compare them to those other lucky ones in America whose family won all that money. Oh no, Ali. You could just as easily compare them to yourself. Here you are, a happy, healthy 10-year-old child, part of a secure and loving family, born into a country at peace, not war, a country where everyone is free to follow their heart's desire, where everyone has a chance, where it is a right, not a privilege to gain an education and earn a living, and to live in security and freedom. Why are you, and all the others like you, permitted to do this, whereas those other children are not? The truth is, for them, they would consider themselves fortunate to have one decent meal a day, let alone all the luxuries you and other children here in this lucky country have.

"Looked at in the way the church teaches, this situation would be grossly unfair. On one hand they preach and speak of a merciful and loving God, but on the other hand they accept such apparent injustices as 'God's will'! I really do wish they would make up their minds. Is their God merciful and loving, or is He a one-eyed tyrant? He cannot be both! If you truly believe that humans have only one life, then how can such things be justified — that one person is born into the lap of luxury, with everything in life that they could possibly want, while another is born into a slum, perhaps blind or crippled, and struggling every single day of their life just to exist? Indeed, without the balancing effect of reincarnation and its associated karma, it would be grossly unfair. Tell me child, how do the nuns explain these inequalities in the world?"

"This is what really puzzles me," I answered. "They don't, apart from insisting it is God's will. They teach us so many other things about religion. like how to recite our prayers, and what to do and say in Mass, and we get into big trouble if we don't know our catechism and the Ten Commandments, but none of this explains why some have so much and others so little, through no fault of their own.

"And something else that I don't understand," I went on, determined to take full advantage of the situation. "If God is supposed to be so good, kind and merciful, then why does He allow terrible things to happen to people? For instance, why does He let little babies die before they have a chance to grow up? And what about that girl at school last year who was run over by a car and will never walk again? Not to mention the awful things that happen in wars like that one in Africa."

"Well, Ali Cat, these questions are in the minds of many others too, and this is exactly how most people react, blaming God when such things occur, for they do not understand the truth. You see child, it is not a matter of God allowing this or that. We knowingly choose our fate for each lifetime before we are even born, and everything that happens to us is for a reason, even the death of a child. Everything happens according to karmic law, which goes hand in hand with reincarnation.

"Do you know Ali, that there are several references to karmic law in the Bible if you know what to look for? For example: 'As you sow, so shall you reap'; and 'He who lives by the sword shall die by the sword.' Another well-known passage which is puzzling unless you realize that it refers to both reincarnation and karma is: 'the sins of the father (past life) shall be visited upon the son (present life).' This is why one must be careful in everything that one does or says. Karma is sometimes referred to as cause and effect, and is the result of a good or bad act performed in one lifetime which is carried through into a subsequent lifetime."

"Aunt Malila," I put in, "is that where the Golden Rule comes from? 'Do unto others as you would have them do unto you.'"

"Yes, child," she smiled, "that is exactly the basis of the Golden Rule, which is an extremely valid and most sensible rule for life. And in fact Anna," she said, turning to my mother, "don't you remember me telling you that when you were Ali's age?"

"Yes, Malila," my mother replied, "I certainly do, and it has stood me in good stead all my life."

Aunt Malila nodded in pleasure, happy in the knowledge that her wise words had been proven correct in at least one life. Settling herself more comfortably, she then continued: "In order to grow, learn and purify yourself spiritually, you must return many times to physical existence, to be exposed to a variety of situations and experiences. For example, in one life you may be born to be someone important, a king, or a president of a country, to have the opportunity to learn to handle responsibility and power. In the next life you may come back as a beggar, to master the lessons of humility and poverty. One life may bless you with great riches; another may bring pain and loss.

"In one round of existence you may take the life of another, but then in a subsequent life you will either find yourself the unwilling victim of such a crime, or will perhaps give your own life to save that of your former victim. Even if you think you are terribly clever and smart because you have gotten away with your crime and avoided the long arm of the law on Earth, there will be no escaping karmic law. Everyone must pay in the end for their sins, be they large or small.

"In some lives a soul may manifest as a black or dark-skinned person living perhaps in the country of Africa or India, then in the next as a fair-skinned European. In one life we may be Asian, and in another an Eskimo or an Australian. Sometimes we are born male and sometimes female. In one life we may choose to be Catholic, and in the next a Protestant, a Jew, a Moslem or even an atheist. It is only by experiencing life from all these different angles that a soul is able to achieve a balanced point of view.

"Ali, the most important thing for you to understand is that you are a soul temporarily inhabiting a physical body for the span of a lifetime. You are *not* a physical body with a soul floating around somewhere. You are a spirit, and therefore eternal, so you can survive the deaths of many different physical shells which, being physical, must eventually wear out, like an old suit of clothing."

"So, Aunt Malila," I ventured to ask, "what you are saying is that the physical body is like a container for the soul?"

"Well yes, Ali!" she replied. "That is a rather strange term to use, but yes, you are quite right. The physical body is simply an outer covering. In your true form, your soul form, there are none of the divisions such as gender, nationality, creed or color that seem so very important upon the physical plane. These are, in reality, simply an illusion. If you like, they could be compared to the costume and make-up worn by an actor in a film or stage production. You put them on when you come to Earth to play your 'role' in the physical body, the role you have chosen to suit the learning experiences you need to have in the coming life. They are then removed at the end of that life when you return home to spirit, just as an actor removes his costume and make-up after the performance and goes back to being himself."

This idea of us actually being souls temporarily housed in a physical body really fascinated me and made so much sense. The way the nuns at school taught about the soul made it sound like it was an organ of the body, like a liver or a kidney. They spoke about keeping our heart and soul pure, and of how the soul could become stained with sin and of how we must cleanse it, as if it were a separate part of us that needed to be removed every so often and given a good scrub, like a set of false teeth! But if we *are* souls, how incredible! And how much easier to grasp the concept of immortality! And, if that is truly the case, then at the end of each life, of course, we would be able to step out of our old, tired and worn-out physical body and into another new one.

Then another thought occurred to me — surely the same would apply if our physical body was damaged beyond repair. In that case you would be able to get a new one too!

This then led me on to further speculation. I wondered if by any chance these new revelations held the key to the strange dreams I'd been experiencing on a regular basis. This was certainly worth thinking deeply about. Pleading tiredness, I thanked Aunt Malila warmly for her fascinating teachings, kissed everyone good night and headed for bed. I really did need some time to myself to consider all of this.

6 ▶ AN ALIEN IN SCHOOL

T hese dreams had been regularly disturbing my sleep for as long as I could remember, and after Aunt Malila's teaching on reincarnation, I couldn't help but wonder if they were actual events from past lives that had really happened to me. I'd come to think of them as my "alien" dreams, and they always left me with a sense of disquiet. While in them, they didn't seem at all like dreams, but rather real happenings. In them, I found myself on board a strange craft that travelled at incredibly high speed, and in the company of weird-looking beings who, in the course of the dream, I looked upon quite comfortably as "family." I was aware of being very much one of them, sharing the same physical characteristics of small, spindly body, large head, long, thin triangular-shaped face, huge, black enamel-like eyes slanting upwards at the outer corners, grayish-colored skin, and hands with only three or four long fingers. When I was in the company of these others, we often seemed to be carrying out some type of extremely important work, but what it was exactly I could never recall on waking.

Sometimes these dreams had a more frightening twist. They would begin as usual on the fast-moving craft, but then suddenly they would become a nightmare when we would find ourselves hurtling forward, spinning and flipping over, going faster and faster. The more effort we put into trying to right ourselves, the more we seemed to lose control. If luck was on my side, I would wake at this point, heart racing and body trembling, but more often, worse was to follow — a jarring, shattering impact, confusion, darkness, and then — horror of horrors — strange, clutching alien hands would drag me from tangled wreckage, seemingly oblivious to my distress. I would be woken by my own screams, and one of my parents would rush in to comfort me in their arms until the overwhelming emotions subsided and I calmed down enough to sleep again.

There were other dreams too which were, in their own way, even more unsettling, reaching as they did into my conscious day-to-day life. One involved a school friend named Jenny, who arrived for class one Monday morning in tears, because her older brother Tom had been diagnosed with a serious illness. Jenny and I were good friends, so I felt very upset at the news, because I also knew Tom fairly well. The whole class joined together after school to say a rosary for his recovery.

The next morning I awoke with a clear memory of having experienced one of my "alien" dreams. It began just like the other ones, travelling in the craft with my weird-looking companions, but the next moment found three of us in a strange bedroom. A young man who seemed quite familiar to me at the time lay on the bed, and I was aware of us do-ing something to him, but on waking I could not recall who this person was. The harder I tried to think, the farther his image receded from my conscious mind.

Jenny was very quiet and withdrawn for the rest of the week. She didn't seem to want to talk any more about her brother, so we let her be, but each day the nuns led us in prayer for his recovery.

It was during lunch hour on the following Friday that Jenny ap-proached me. "Ali, can you come over to the church for a few minutes? I need to talk in private." So saying, she headed off towards the small, covered walkway that led directly into the church from the school ve-randa. Stepping into the quiet interior, our senses were immediately soothed by the sweet perfume of the red carnations and pure white arum lilies that were arranged in vases upon the main altar, as well as on the two smaller side altars, which held statues of the Virgin Mary and Saint Joseph. The whole atmosphere of the church was also permeated with the distinctive and ever-present aroma of incense, which was burned regu-larly at every Mass.

Dipping our fingers in the holy water font at the door, hastily crossing ourselves and dropping in quick genuflection in front of the main altar, we headed for the small Chapel of Our Lady, a partly en-closed area set aside in the front right-hand corner of the church. We made ourselves comfortable in a back pew, and then Jenny hesitated a few seconds before turning to me with a strange look in her eyes.

"Ali, something really weird happened to Tom the other night, and I've just got to talk to somebody about it. I don't know why, but it's you I feel I need to tell — maybe because I trust you and know you won't go blabbing to the others."

"Course I wouldn't, Jen." I assured her. "Whatever you want to say is safe with me, I promise."

Jenny looked carefully around the church to make absolutely certain we were alone before going on: "Ali, Tom was visited by *aliens* last Monday night!"

Just for a moment I thought she was joking, but I knew immedi-ately by her face that she wasn't. Besides, she would not make such a joke with her brother so ill; and then the dream, which by then I'd forgot-ten, flashed back into my mind and with it the clear memory of a very distinctive piece of furniture against the opposite wall to where the young man lay on the bed. Suddenly I knew exactly who he was.

Jenny was looking at me with a worried expression. "Ali Cat," she said, leaning forward. "Are you okay? You've gone as white as a ghost! I'm sorry — I didn't mean to scare you."

"No, no Jen, it's all right, I — I'm fine. Come on, tell me about Tom. *Who* visited him? Is he okay?"

"Oh, God, Ali, it was really weird! It happened last Monday night, after I told all of you about Tom being so sick. The next morning he woke up remembering a 'dream' from the night before in which three strange little alien-looking beings came into his room. He was really scared, and he tried to fight them off, but they told him not to be frightened, that they were there to help him, and then two of them held him down hard on the bed while the third one gave him some sort of injection, telling him it was to make him better.

"Mom wouldn't believe him at first and kept insisting it was only a silly dream, but then he rolled up the sleeve of his pajama top and showed us the mark of an injection on his arm! Poor mom nearly fainted. She's a nurse, so she knows what an injection mark looks like. What do you think of it? Do you reckon we're all crazy?"

I hastily assured her that I didn't think any such thing, and that maybe it was possible. After all, there were sometimes reports in the news of UFOs, and strangely enough a number of them had been seen recently in our area. One of these local reports had even involved an alien abduction a couple of months back.

"Anyway Jen," I pointed out, "they didn't hurt Tom, and they did tell him that the injection was to make him better, so if it works I guess that's the main thing."

"Yes, I suppose," she agreed. "Let's hope so anyway. Ali, are you sure you're okay? You still look a bit strange."

"Honestly Jen, I'm fine, but I hope no weird little aliens decide to visit me! Come on, we'd better go or we'll be late for class and Sister Mary Angela will murder us! Oh, God, that's right! It's History — *yuk!*"

For the rest of the day I kept getting into trouble for not paying attention to my lessons, but I could not get out of my mind the memory of Tom lying on the bed. And did he really have that unusual chest of drawers against the wall opposite his bed? I could still see it so clearly.

A week or so later, Jenny came to school bursting with excitement and relief — Tom was going to be okay. His full recovery would probably take a while, but he was going to be fine. Their doctor was totally amazed, and the nuns declared it a miracle brought about by prayer, but I wondered if maybe something else was involved as well.

It was Jenny's birthday at the end of the month, and along with some of her other school friends, I was invited to her party. It was to be a double celebration, for Tom's recovery as well as for his sister's eleventh birthday.

"Aha!" I thought to myself. "At last I'll be able to find out if it really was Tom's room I visited that night."

It was all I could do to contain my curiosity the afternoon of the party. I had a plan worked out, and just hoped that the family were not in the habit of closing their bedroom doors during the day. At the first possible opportunity, I excused myself to go to the bathroom. As luck would have it, it was situated at the end of the hallway, so the journey involved walking past all three bedrooms. All that was needed was a quick peek in each.

The parents' room was easy to find, being the largest of the three and containing a double bed. Jenny's too was obvious, from the pretty little rosebuds on the wallpaper, the pink tubular frame bed, and the family of dolls arranged neatly on the matching dressing table. Looking around to make sure no one was following me, I peeked through the open doorway of Tom's room — and nearly passed out on the spot. All the anticipation in the world could not have prepared me for the sight of the distinctive chest of drawers, standing in exactly the same position as I remembered from my dream. It was obviously antique, with deeply carved woodwork and heavy brass knobs on each of the three drawers — not the sort of furniture you would see in every home. And the pattern on the bedspread was familiar to me as well; in fact the sight of it brought a clearer memory of the "dream" to the conscious level of my mind. I even knew exactly where I'd been standing, and the thoughts that had passed through my head at the time.

Not sure whether to laugh or cry, I suddenly felt totally overwhelmed by the whole thing. I did not want to know — it was all too strange. Turning from the doorway I went back to the party in a vain attempt to lose myself in the celebrations until my father arrived at 5:00 to take me home.

Unfortunately for my peace of mind, this was not going to be the one and only weird experience for that year. About a month or so later I again awoke with a clear dream memory of one of the girls at school. Patricia was a bit of a "case," coming as she did from a very dysfunctional family — an unhappy situation which expressed itself in teasing and trouble-making behavior on her part. We all felt sorry for her, but because of the way she acted she was not popular. If ever there was trouble in class, Patricia was never far away.

All I could recall of the dream was that I had turned around and found myself standing at the foot of Patricia's bed, and she had woken up and screamed in fright. It was the sound of her scream that woke me, back safe and sound in my own bed.

The next day she came up behind me in the school playground, calling out: "Hey Ali! Do you know *what?* You're *weird*! Where's your flying saucer parked? Hey everyone, did you know Ali Cat's an *alien*!"

There was a small group of girls who tagged along with Patricia, at least at those times when they weren't fighting with each other, and now they joined her in ganging up on me. "Come on Pat," they all giggled, "tell us something we don't know! Course she's weird! She's a Gypo, isn't she? Watch out, she'll pick your pockets!"

"Nah," sneered Patricia, "being an alien is even worse than being a Gypo!" A vicious look came into her eyes as she turned on me. She reminded me of a cornered animal that was ready to fight. "What were you doing in my room last night?" she hissed.

"What are you talking about?" I replied as calmly as I could, trying to keep out of my voice any hint that I remembered the dream. "You're the one who's weird, Patricia, not me. What would I be doing in your room anyway? I don't even know where you live."

"You're a lying bitch!" she snarled. "You were there and you know it. I woke up and you were standing at the foot of my bed, with your back to me. You turned around so I could see it was you, and then your face changed! You turned into one of those horrible, ugly aliens with gray skin and a long, thin face, and you had great, big, huge, black bug eyes. That's it! You looked just like some kind of nasty insect! Then you went to touch my feet with your hands! YUK! They were weird and horrible too — long and thin with only four fingers. Eww! You're disgusting! Just stay away from me! Don't you come anywhere near me!"

Belying her words, Patricia came at me, hands raised to attack. Taking a step back, I caught a glimpse out of the corner of my eye of somebody approaching very fast. By the long, flowing, black garb I assumed it was a nun coming to my rescue. Patricia stopped mid-stride, leveled one last malevolent glare in my direction, then turned on her heel and stalked off, followed closely by her "cheer squad." I turned around, fully expecting to see a nun, but there was nobody there. What was going on? Maybe Patricia was right! Maybe I *was* weird!

7 ▶ NOT ALL THAT DIFFERENT

I hoped sincerely that the whole incident would soon be forgotten, and that Patricia and her gang would have found someone else to pick on, but no such luck. The moment I stepped outside the school gate they came after me, taunting me with their chants and jeers, and throwing stones at me. By the time I reached home I was close to tears.

"Ali," my mother put a comforting arm around me, "what's the matter? Have those girls at school been teasing you again? Do you want me to go and talk to Mother Bernadette about it?"

"Oh, no, please, not that! They all think I'm weird enough without having my parents running to Mother Superior and complaining. It's not fair! Why do we have to be Romany anyway? Why couldn't we be an ordinary *gajo* family, then maybe I'd be able to fit in better, and be accepted by the others. As it is they treat me as if I've just arrived from some other planet, complete with four eyes and green skin! Why do we have to be so different?"

"But Ali Cat, we're not all that different. What makes you say that?"

"Not different!" I cried, staring at her in disbelief. "Don't try to tell me that all the others at school can see auras and energy, and understand the language of animals! And then there are those weird dreams I keep having! If that's not 'different' then I'd like to know what is!"

"Look, Ali, that has nothing to do with you being Romany, and I must admit that, yes, in that regard you are a little different, even for one of us. When you were younger we used to think it was just an over-active imagination, but now I know that there really is something unusual with you. But what's the point of getting upset about it? You have these abilities, so you must just learn to accept them, and as I've told you before, try not to talk about it at school. You know what the others are like and how they tease you."

"But I *didn't!* It's *not fair!* All I want is to be able to fit in and to be like everyone else. It wasn't so bad when I was younger, but now I realize myself how strange I am, even compared to my own family, and I don't understand why! Why won't these stupid abilities and dreams just go away so I can be like everyone else? I don't *want* to be this way! I wish I'd never been born!"

By this time I was crying my eyes out, and again my mother put her arms around me, stroking my hair to comfort me. "Ali Cat, come over here and sit down, we need to talk." She led me over to the couch and sat beside me, still holding me tightly. "Look, Ali, there is something

I really need to talk to you about — something that may help you to come to terms with these 'abilities' you have, and the strange dreams as well.

"It all goes back to when I very first became pregnant with you. I too experienced a very strange dream. Now the funny thing is that I'd forgotten it completely until you began having yours, then suddenly it all came back to me, clear as a bell. What reminded me was the one you have of being on board a fast-moving craft, because that is exactly where I was in my dream too, and while there I was handed a baby — a girl-child. I couldn't see who gave her to me, but I felt a sense that it was the child's 'true mother,' and that she was giving the little one over into my care, and the understanding was that this was a very special child. The whole event was surrounded by a feeling of great love and nurturing.

"Something I was acutely aware of when this baby was placed in my arms was that she was different — not physically but rather more, how can I say, on an energy level. Yes, that's it, her energy pattern was different, but at the same time it felt good and positive, and I was aware of a sense of great responsibility in being given her care.

"Right throughout the nine months of the pregnancy I could feel this motherly 'presence' around me, watching over us both. Then a couple of nights after you were born, I again experienced a dream in which the Mother came to me. She seemed relieved that the birth had taken place and that you were safe and sound. It was then that I was given what I understood to be your true name. I had great difficulty in hearing it exactly, because it was conveyed in the strangest voice. In fact it didn't sound like a human voice at all, but more like the whisper of the wind in the trees. It sounded like 'Alar,' but there was more to it, another syllable on the end. This is why I called you Ali, because it was close enough to the name that was given, but not exactly, so it was safe to use.

"I'm sorry I can't tell you exactly what the true name is, but I feel that when the time is right you'll know. So there you are Ali Cat. I can't explain this any more clearly because I really don't understand it myself, but I just want you to know that your birth was not accidental or for no reason. In fact, I feel you have something very special and important to do with your life, and these abilities you have are a part of it. You know we love you very much, and will always be there for you whenever you need us."

I felt more tears welling in my eyes, and I threw my arms around her, holding her tightly. "I'm sorry!" I cried, "I'm so sorry! I love you too and I really didn't mean that about wishing I'd never been born. It's just that I get so frustrated sometimes because I know there's something important that I *have* to remember, but it won't come to me no matter how hard I try to think of it!

"And now while you were telling me all of this, I felt like my head was going to burst with the effort of trying to remember. And you know something else that is really weird?" I went on. "How is it that I have all these strange abilities that others don't have, but when it comes to doing ordinary 'physical' things, things like cooking and sewing, and playing games at school, that everybody else just takes for granted, I'm completely hopeless, almost as if I'm all fingers, or all thumbs. In fact, it's almost like I have trouble getting my physical body together. Do you suppose there's a connection here somewhere?"

"Goodness me, Ali Cat," my mother laughed, giving me a cuddle. "Who knows? Maybe you come from some strange and highly advanced race of alien beings who have long since moved away from the need for physical bodies and such mundane activities as cooking, sewing and playing tennis. I suppose that would explain your questionable abilities in the kitchen and on the sports field."

"Wow!" I exclaimed, "That would be funny, wouldn't it? I'd better not mention that at school, especially around Patricia. Hey! Maybe she's right — maybe I really do have some strange, alien body hidden away just below the surface of my human body, just like she said I did when I mysteriously appeared in her room that night."

My mother and I sat looking at each other, neither quite knowing what to say, then she broke the spell by jumping up from the couch in an uncalled-for flurry of nervous haste and brisk efficiency.

"Come on then, Ali Cat! Let's have another go at teaching you how to cook dinner!"

8 ▶ MAKING SOUL CONNECTIONS

It was on one of my favorite walks through the bush land bordering our property when I decided to make a detour down a rough and rutted track that I had not previously explored. The time of day was perfect for adventure — early morning, with the dew sparkling on blades of grass like myriad diamonds, and tiny, scintillating flashes of life-force energy glinting and gleaming in swirling fragments of golden light around every leaf and branch, every tree and bush. I was filled with gladness and gratitude for the gift of this deeper way of seeing, and of being able to sense so intensely the vital forces of nature all around me.

I rounded a bend in the track and came upon a clearing in which was parked an old and battered but brightly painted caravan of the type Gypsies favor. An old woman with the dark and weather-beaten features of the travelling folk was sitting under the shade of a tree, weaving a small basket out of lengths of dried grass. She looked up as I approached, smiling a warm and friendly greeting.

"Good day to you, child. I see there is no need to ask if you are well this fine morning. You are all lit up like a Christmas tree. Have you been off dancing with the spirits of nature?"

My mouth dropped open in surprise, and it was several moments before I could collect my thoughts enough to answer: "Yes, I have, but how can you tell? I thought I was the only one who seemed to be aware of such things. Can you really see my aura and the Nature Spirits?"

"Oh, goodness me, yes child! Even easier than I can see you, now that my old eyes are beginning to fail. Some of our people have this gift or ability, not all mind you, but certainly those few who can trace their soul lineage back to that small group of us who first came to this planet long ago. Come and sit here beside me, and I'll tell you, on one condition, that you don't breathe a word of this to others. It is part of our sacred, secret lore that not even many of our own people know of, as it is only passed down to certain ones. Do you understand and promise me this?"

"Yes, of course I promise! As I've found out from my own experiences, no one would believe me anyway, so your secret teachings are quite safe with me. But you don't even know me. Why are you telling me these things?"

"Because, child, I can see by the energy and colors surrounding you that you have a great deal of inner knowledge that you have not as yet been able to tap into, and this forgetfulness is causing you to feel a sense of deep loss and disquiet. I can also see that you are here on this planet to carry out certain work. I sense a deep and ancient link between us, and I feel that if you can come to understand a little more of who you are and where you came from, it will be helpful to you. I have my suspicions ... but only time will tell.

"Now come and sit down, child. You're Ali, right?"

"Yes."

"Ok, Ali. It's good to meet you. I'm Mara."

She waited patiently for me to settle myself beside her, then continued: "Our people travelled here long, long ago as part of a group known as the Guardians, who came to Earth in order to help humans wake up to a higher level of soul awareness. These humans had been trapped in mortal bodies back in the time of Atlantis and had not been able to evolve spiritually to higher realms. As far as we knew, the ones who had perpetrated this cruelty had moved on, and so we set up our little community inside a mountain cave in the northern part of India to get on with our appointed task of making things right again."

My eyes widened in wonder, and Mara asked if I understood. I nodded my head, so she continued.

"Unbeknown to us, the negative group still had a base close by, and soon we came under attack. They were determined to stop the Earth humans from progressing any further, desiring to keep them in a state of ignorance and forgetfulness in order to make slaves of them. We did our very best to protect our charges, but there were only a few thousand of us — not nearly enough to hold out against the other group.

"Our teaching tells us that these negative ones have a magical weapon which has the effect of trapping a person's soul inside the physical body. The soul then forgets its true state of immortality and becomes imprisoned, never able to move on to higher realms beyond the illusions of the astral plane.

"This terrible weapon was used to defeat our own people, and so we too became trapped on Earth along with our human charges, but because we are of the Guardian Race, we managed to retain a little of the higher knowledge. A very few of us, like myself, have even regained much of the memory of who and what we truly are.

"For many millennia our people remained, trapped and forgetful, in the underground place, until eventually a small group of us managed to find our way out. Since then we have wandered on the face of Planet Earth, refugees from elsewhere and without a land to call our own. Whenever we make an attempt to settle somewhere, the dark forces of fear and superstition eventually intervene, forever seeking us out and moving us on, seeming to sense at some deep level that certain ones of us hold the key — the sacred knowledge from the dawn of time which would enable humanity to escape the bonds of ignorance and forgetful-ness.

"Rescue missions have been attempted, but they too have fallen victim to the traps set in place by the negative forces and became en-snared in a state of amnesia. However, I have lately been seeing certain signs and portents that others are now returning from higher realms to lend their assistance. We have waited patiently for them, guarding the ancient knowledge as best we could, and trying our hardest to preserve the sense of magic and sacredness that has almost disappeared from the face of the Earth, buried beneath layers of fear-induced cynicism and superstition.

"Earth humans have forgotten that it's more important to have great spirit and imagination than great intellect and power. We miss our ancient family deeply, and the spiritual unfolding of all Earth humans has been blocked since their departure."

The old woman's eyes filled with tears as she spoke of the lost family, and I too found my vision blurring and a lump rising in my throat that would not go away. Her talk of work needing to be completed on Planet Earth was stirring something deep inside me, and for a fleeting moment I had a vivid recollection of a blinding, wrenching crash, intense pain and fear, then blackness. Then I found the old woman bending over me, her eyes full of concern.

"Are you all right, little one? You've gone as white as a ghost." She placed her hand on my shoulder and I felt warmth and strength pass from her hand through my whole being, instantly making me feel better. I didn't want to move. I wished I could just stay forever, drawing on this beautiful energy.

Then another figure appeared, walking briskly along the dirt track leading to the campsite. I immediately recognized him as a boy from school. He was a year older, and, even though he was always kind to me, we had never really gotten to know each other.

"Hello, Ali!" he called out in friendly greeting, "What are you doing here? I didn't know you lived close by or that you knew my grandmother."

"Your grandmother!" I exclaimed, looking at the old woman in surprise. "I didn't know you were Romany! Why haven't you ever said so?"

"Why bother!" he answered glumly, "You know how the other kids at school would carry on if they knew. As far as I'm concerned, the less they know the better. Look at the way they tease you all the time. I don't want to cop that. It's bad enough having a foreign name, but if they find out I'm a Gypsy too, and that I live in a caravan with my Granny, that would be way too much for their limited minds to handle!"

"Paco!" the old woman scolded, "How many times do I have to tell you? They are young souls who do not know any better. Since your dear parents died and you have come to live with me, how often have I explained these things to you? They are children in both body and mind, and with most of them, even when their bodies grow to adulthood, their minds remain immature, so we must be tolerant and not reciprocate in anger. Two negatives do not make a positive, you know that! This is a lesson you especially must learn if you wish to become a priest, as you say you do. If a priest cannot practice tolerance and understanding, then who can?"

Paco sighed and sat down beside me. "Yes, Granny, you're right, and I'm sorry I got angry, especially in front of Ali, who is our guest. Please don't let me interrupt. What were you talking about?"

"Ali and I have been speaking of ages long past," the old woman answered, and then turned to me. "Ali, do you have any questions?"

"Yes, please," I answered. "Could you explain something for me? You spoke of being able to see the Nature Spirits, as I can. Are these the Guardians you are talking about? Are they the same beings?"

"In a way, yes, for they too are of a higher, finer realm than the physical plane, and they are also caretakers of energy. The role of the nature spirits is to take care of the mineral, plant and animal kingdoms, whereas the Guardians of whom I speak work more with human energy. In times gone by, when mortal man was more innocent and less technologically minded, on those occasions when one of them was taken by the Guardians, as still happens now, by the way, they believed that they had been transported to fairyland, because the wonder of what they saw and experienced on their journey was way beyond their comprehension.

"For the Guardians, time runs differently, so the human 'abductee' would find to their amazement that hours and sometimes even days had passed, whereas to them only moments seemed to have gone by before they were returned safely to their home and bed. Sometimes they carried no memory at all of what had befallen them, but awoke to find strange marks upon their bodies seemingly inflicted by the 'Fairy Folk.' Often too they experienced a great fear which could not be explained, or else a deep sense of loss and sadness, which caused others to believe they had been bewitched.

"You see," she went on, "it was exactly the same experience then that those who are taken on board the UFOs are having now, but it is simply the Guardians continuing to carry out their work with humans."

As she spoke I sat entranced, for her words stirred strange feelings inside me that I could not quite manage to express. Then the moment passed as Paco interrupted my train of thought with a question of his own. "Granny," he asked, "are these Guardians the Angels that we are taught about at school?"

"Yes, sort of," she answered him. "Probably more like assistants to the Angels. Angels are of a higher dimension, but all of these various ones work together like a grid system, filtering the sacred energy of the Source down through the levels so that it can be safely accessed by humans and other physical creatures, to assist in their growth and evolution. In the ancient Indian language of Sanskrit upon which our own Romany language is based, the word Deva is used to describe these ones. It translates simply as Shining One, and those humans who have had experiences with the beings of these finer dimensions will know that they often appear as a shining orb of light. Why, it is from this word 'Deva,' that our Romany word for God — Devlesa, is derived. It certainly has nothing whatsoever to do with the devil, as some folk have believed in the past, even going so far as to accuse us of devil worship because of it!

"The Guardians are indeed a very ancient race of beings whose origin goes back way beyond that of the human race of Planet Earth, or possibly any other planets for that matter. Depending upon the sort of work they are carrying out, they do sometimes manifest upon the physical plane and can even take their place among us, looking like any other human. They work with energy, assisting first in the initial process of creation, then, as each being grows and evolves, the Guardians are responsible for assisting the transmutation of the soul energy of that being to higher and higher levels of spiritual awakening.

"For eons past they were present in the universe, nurturing and watching, adjusting and assisting in the process of growth and development on many planets. Since the time of Atlantis not many of them have elected to manifest on Earth as physical beings, but have preferred to stay hidden in the finer dimensions, still close enough to keep an eye on our progress, but far enough removed to be protected from the disharmonies and imbalances which have befallen this planet since the interference which brought about the Fall of Man. They are interdimensional as well as extraterrestrial beings, which explains the strange and intangible nature of the contacts humans have had with them.

"What many down here fail to understand, or perhaps have forgotten, is that true evolution takes place on the soul level through reincarnation. This is a natural path of spiritual growth, but on Earth this flow has been disrupted and blocked for many people. My sense tells me that it is now time for the Guardians to intervene — to bring things back into balance and wake the humans up before they destroy themselves and their planet with their technology and lack of soul awareness."

Then I just had to ask, "Mara, my family was talking to me about reincarnation only the other day. Can you tell me, have we shared past lives with the family we have in this life?"

"Oh, yes, Ali, most definitely! Often the family we're born into in the present life is actually part of what could be referred to as our 'soul family,' with whom we have shared many lives, and are intimately connected to on an energy level."

"What do you mean? I don't quite understand."

"Well, child, to put it simply, everybody, whether in physical or spirit form, is part of a 'soul family,' which can span several dimensions. This is why sometimes when you meet up with someone for the first time, you feel an instant rapport with that person, and you may even see yourself reflected in them. Some people refer to this experience as linking with their 'soul mate,' which simply means that they are part of the same soul family."

"But what is it that makes people part of the same soul family?" I wanted to know. "What makes them so similar?"

"It's a matter of vibrational, or energy frequencies," Mara explained. "Tell me, child, do you learn about such things as radio and TV wave lengths at school, and how each station broadcasts on a particular frequency band of its own?"

"Yes, we've been taught a bit about that."

"Well," she went on, "to put it simply, each radio and TV station broadcasts on its own unique frequency band. That is why each station has its own identification or 'call sign' if you like, made up of certain letters and numbers, so listeners can know where it is on the dial, and differentiate between the various frequencies. In this way you can choose the station you wish to tune into.

"For example, one station may be broadcasting a program of classical music, and others may be presenting a news report, a sports program, or whatever, all at exactly the same time, but they don't impinge upon each other because of the fact that they are broadcasting on *different* frequency bands, whereas members of the same soul family operate on *similar* frequency bands. People, like radio stations, all have their own unique energy wavelengths, but some are more similar than others. When you have several operating on similar wavelengths, you have a soul family. Do you understand what I'm saying?"

"Sort of, but you said before about soul families spanning different dimensions. If that's the case, how can they vibrate on similar wavelengths? Aunt Malila once told me about ghosts, and how they vibrate at a higher frequency than people in physical bodies. She explained how that's why they can pass straight through closed doors and solid walls, and why most often we can't see them."

"Ah! That is quite easy to answer, Ali. You do know about different octaves in music, don't you?"

"Yes, of course."

"Well then, let's say for argument's sake that all the members of a particular soul family vibrate more or less to a certain musical note, for example the note of B. They can't be exactly the same as each other, but one might resonate to B major, another to B minor, and a third to B flat. These three are all occupying physical bodies on Earth, so they are all vibrating within the same octave.

"However, there are other members of this same soul family living in different dimensions, maybe in spirit, or else part of a more highly, or less evolved race of beings on another planet. These ones would also be resonating with the musical note of B, but are on a higher or lower octave, and in this way are in total harmony with their fellow soul family members on Planet Earth. Thus we have a soul family spanning two or more dimensions, all resonating nicely and compatibly with each other. This of course is rather over-simplified, but hopefully it will help to answer your question."

"Yes, Mara, thank you, but I do have just one more. You said before that you could sense a deep and ancient link between us. Does that mean we are part of the same soul family?"

"Well now, Ali, let's see if we can link in more deeply so we can find out. I'll hold my hands out palms up, and you place your hands just slightly above them, palms down, and we'll wait quietly for a few minutes to see if we can tune in to each other."

Mara sat in front of me with her eyes closed in deep concentration. Only seconds passed before I became aware of a strange sensation in the center of my forehead, just above my eyebrows. Suddenly a beam of bright, white light, almost like a laser, passed from the front of my forehead into hers, and as this happened, a wave of freezing cold passed through me and out of my palms. Mara's eyes opened, and for a moment she stared at me, or rather it seemed that she stared *into* me, and then tears began coursing down her cheeks. Not quite fully aware of what I was doing, I lowered my palms onto hers and gripped her hands in mine. As our fingers closed together a tremor ran through both of us, and the next moment I found myself crying as I had never cried in my whole life. I felt silly and embarrassed because I didn't know why I was crying, but then Mara gathered me into her arms, my face pressed against her shoulder, while over and over she kept repeating the words, "Welcome! Welcome my dear one! Welcome back!"

After several minutes she released me, and still holding my hands tightly in hers, she began to speak: "My dear friend, I know there is deep confusion within you and that you do not understand who or what you are, but many things will soon be revealed that will make the way clearer. You definitely have important work to carry out in the future, and the path will not be easy, for the burden you have chosen to carry will at times weigh heavily upon you."

"Mara," I cried, my voice still unsteady from the profound experience which had taken place between us. "I'm scared! There are just too many strange things going on with me, and I'm only a child! I don't know what to do! My mother too spoke of a dream she had concerning important work I am to carry out someday, but I can't! I'm afraid!"

"Hush, little one, and be still," she replied gently, stroking my cheek. "You will come to a deeper understanding when the time is right, and not before. You wish to know of the connection between us — we are as One. We three share one soul. And very soon you will be contacted by another who is also part of this soul, one who is of a higher dimension but still connected to us. This one is very wise and will give you further teaching and guidance.

"Also, my grandson Paco here is your spiritual brother. As you probably know already, Ali, there is a tradition among the Romany Folk that where a strong link exists between two people, a link at soul level, the bond between them is even deeper than a physical blood tie. This spiritual relationship between two people is as sacred and binding as marriage and must be respected always. Paco understands this, and as such will always stand beside you as your brother and protector. I believe that someday his duty will be to act as a bridge for you, between yourself and others, assisting you in your work."

Through all of this, Paco had sat watching, mystified, puzzled, and I think a little embarrassed, but then he smiled and reached out, taking my hand in his. "It's okay Ali, don't worry — I'm honored to be your brother, and I'll always help you if I can and be there for you. There's no need to be scared."

"Paco is right, Ali," Mara reassured me. "There is nothing to fear in life except fear itself."

9 ▶ NIGHT VISITOR

I woke in the early morning hours after my 13th birthday. For a few moments I lay there, acutely aware of something strange going on but not knowing what. Was I awake or asleep? Then two realizations hit me at once — I could not move a muscle in my whole body… and somebody, or something, was standing in the corner of the room watching me. Straining every fiber of my being, I somehow managed to move my eyes just enough so I could see… then I wished with my whole heart that I hadn't! I tried to scream, to cry out to my parents sleeping peacefully on the other side of the wall, but no sound came out of my mouth. I was yelling my head off, but it was all inside me. Just as in the worst nightmare, nothing was coming out, and still I couldn't move.

What stood there in the corner was definitely not human. Towering above me in height, it was dressed in black from head to toe so that only the hands and part of the face were visible. From its shoulders hung a long, flowing cape, and a wide-brimmed black hat was pulled down so that I could only see the lower half of the face, but that was quite enough! A note of bizarre incongruity was struck by a pretty blue hatband decorated with a feather of the same color.

What I could see of the "face" appeared to be long and triangular in shape, and the skin was of a darkish gray color, slightly wrinkled around the mouth. The mouth and nose were in the same position as on a human face, but they were very small, in fact almost vestigial. The eyes were not visible, hidden as they were by the lowered brim of the hat, but that was fine by me — I really didn't want to see any more.

Then, horror of horrors, the "thing," whatever it was, began moving towards me in a strange puppet-like way. This horrified me even more, because I'd always had an inexplicable aversion to dolls and puppets. It then extended its hand, which was of the same dark gray color as its face, with four extremely long, thin fingers that were slightly rounded on the tips. One of these fingers appeared to work like a human thumb, in opposition to the other three so that the hand could grasp objects. And, God Almighty, that was exactly what it seemed about to do, as it reached slowly and inexorably towards my throat….

But no, the hand lay gently on my head, and immediately I felt calmer. The same healing energy flowed from this hand as I'd felt from Mara — warm, tingly, loving energy that washed over me, soothing my fear and releasing my body's paralysis.

Then the being spoke to me. Its lips did not move, but I clearly heard a deep, authoritative, but not unkindly, voice resonating inside my head.

"Please, little one, do not fear me. I shall not harm you. Can you not feel my love?"

"Y-yes," I stammered, "but you look so weird … Wh-who are you?"

"I am the one your friend Mara spoke of, the one who would be coming from higher up to give you further guidance. I am your teacher, Maris."

My mind went back to that day several months ago, when Paco and I had questioned Mara about soul families. I'd completely forgotten her prediction of another coming to me who was also a part of our soul family. But why did he have to look so scary? Why couldn't he be some-one more beautiful, like an angel for instance?

The flicker of a smile played about the lower part of his face as he picked up on my thoughts. "Ah, little one," the words came to me. "If we looked like that, people down here would never understand that outer appearances do not always count for everything! Please do not be afraid of me. I am here to help you."

"Help me with what?" I frowned, struggling to sit up. I felt con-fused and still rather nervous about this strange-looking being, despite the energy that flowed from his hand.

"The path which lies ahead of you," he answered.

"What path?" I persisted, my curiosity increasing and now start-ing to replace fear.

"The one you have chosen as your life's work," he patiently re-plied.

"But I don't know what that is!" I cried. "I keep being told of this work I'm supposed to do, but I *haven't* chosen it, and no one will tell me what it is, anyway! All they ever say is how important and *difficult* it will be. I'm only 13, and I am having enough trouble with school, with-out having to do this rotten work they keep going on about. Why does everything have to be so hard?" I grumbled.

"Be still, child, and listen to me," he replied. "At the current time, you must experience some difficulties and suffering upon the physical plane, for this is the only way you can truly grow and become strong in spirit. If your life was always easy, always happy, with every-thing going the way you wanted it — you would remain undeveloped and untried.

"Just as a precious gem stone must be rubbed hard and polished before its true beauty can shine forth," he went on, "so too must the soul be rubbed and refined by adversity. Your helpers and guides in spirit may protect you to a point, but at the same time it would not be right, in fact it would be unkind of us to shield you from every pain and difficulty in your life, for then you would never have the chance to evolve. This is so important for you to understand!"

When he had finished speaking, he sat down beside me, at the same time reaching up slowly and pushing the hat back off his face so that I could see him properly. Once his features were fully revealed, I found myself looking into the most incredible pair of eyes that could be imagined — huge, black, almond-shaped and slanting upwards at the outer corners; they completely dominated the whole face. Although these eyes made him look even stranger and totally alien, somehow I felt reassured by them, for in their liquid depths shone a light of infinite love and wisdom. It was at that moment, looking into his eyes, that something stirred deep inside me — a memory? A dream? Where had I seen those eyes before? Of course! In the strange dreams I'd been experiencing. But where did these dreams come from? It was further back than that — the dreams were only a part of something that had gone before, something that flickered on the very edge of my mind.

Maris sat there patiently, watching my mental struggle, my vain attempt to dredge up whatever it was from the deepest recesses of my consciousness. Again he reached towards me, placing one of his long, thin, gray fingers on my forehead in the space between and a little above my eyebrows. Then he pushed, so hard and so suddenly that I cried out in pain and fright and felt myself fall backwards. It was as if a needle had been thrust into my head.

I was falling and spinning — a loud, roaring, buzzing sound ringing in my head — blackness all around — hurtling through space — totally disoriented. My companions and I being thrown around inside the disc like so many broken dolls, our bodies bouncing against each other and against the walls. Desperately, we tried to grab hold of something, anything, to stop the falling and the spinning....

Then the horrible, nauseous spinning sensation stopped as I fell towards him, and the warm, enveloping folds of his cape closed around me as I hugged him tightly, tears flowing freely in sheer relief, never wanting to ever let go of him again. Our minds melded on the deepest, most intimate level and total love, accord and understanding passed wordlessly between us, flowing back and forth with no barriers, no façades, no sense of separateness. We were as One.

His arms enfolded me — not clutching alien arms with strange five-fingered hands dragging me out of the wreckage of our disc, but rather long, familiar arms — the arms of an Elder of my own people, my beloved teacher, Maris, embracing me.

"So, Alarca, my little one! You recognize me at last!" The sound of my true name being spoken by my beloved Teacher brought on another flood of tears, which I made no attempt whatever to control. I'd never been one to shed tears easily, but in Maris' presence, I melted completely.

My God, how could I have forgotten? Of course that was who I was. All the lost memories of being a Guardian, and of the crash, my subsequent rebirth into a human body, and the all-important work we were here to carry out came flooding back into my mind, so much that I felt my poor head would burst.

I leaned back against the pillows to look at him. Not having the same musculature in their faces as humans, and especially those in fully artificial bodies, Guardians cannot show much emotion through facial expression, but Maris's eyes and the energy radiating from him said it all — he was literally glowing with joy and relief.

"Welcome back, my child!" He leaned forward and took both my hands in his, holding them tightly. "It is *so good* to have you back! As an Elder of our people, and your own teacher, I look upon you as a much cherished part of me. I know that what you have been through since your birth into human form has not been easy, and all along I have carried the burden of responsibility that I was one of those who sent you forth in the first place. However, the positive side is that you could not have had a better opportunity to understand intimately just what it means to be born upon this planet, confined to the three-dimensional existence of human form. As we all know in the greater reality, there really *are* no accidents or mistakes, only opportunities for learning!

"I do know that after the crash of your disc, you set out upon this mission with many doubts in your mind and an understandable wariness of Earthlings, but hopefully now you can see exactly what the poor things are up against. I believe that from this point on you will be able to proceed with your mission in a state of greater compassion and deeper empathy with the human condition and the circumstances which make them as they are. Am I right?"

"Oh, Maris," I replied, shaking my head, "you are so right! You would not believe how limiting it is to be human. The true awareness that they are immortal, spiritual beings has been totally destroyed in so many of them. It's no wonder they are so caught up in the pursuit of material possessions and badly distracted by the emotions and demands of everyday life on Planet Earth.

"For many of them these very things that keep them sane and functioning also unfortunately cause them to become entangled and trapped in a vicious circle by blocking their perception of, and appreciation for, the finer, simpler things that really matter, like tranquility, and joyfulness, and the pure, unconditional love that would enable them to rise above the grossness of material existence."

Maris's eyes smiled gently at me. "Yes, Alarca, your understanding has indeed opened up to the plight of Earth humans. Too many of them care more for the body than they care for the spirit, and in this way they *become* the body and lose the way of the spirit. They have forgotten that spiritual awareness and soul consciousness is the true essence of self.

"And perhaps now, after the awful fright you suffered on seeing me standing in the corner of your room, you will also have a better understanding of the fear humans experience during what they perceive to be 'alien abductions,' when we take them on board the discs for examination purposes and for the genetic work that is so vital if they are to continue as a viable species.

"My goodness me," he chuckled, shaking his head, "you should have seen the look on your face when I reached out my hand towards you! What did you think I was going to do, strangle you?"

"Well," I hedged in embarrassment, "you did seem to be going for my throat! I wonder if that's where the scary human legends of vampires come from. If it's just garbled memories of our people making their nightly rounds, maybe we need a different approach, because you really scared me when you did that!"

"This is where much of your work needs to be focused, Alarca, dressed as you are in human form, the Earthlings can relate to you without fear. You have a lot to teach them — and us as well, it seems! That is an interesting point you have brought up there, about considering a different approach. As you well know, we try to communicate, to tell them not to fear, but so often the barrier of terror and the cocoon of emotion in which they wrap themselves are almost impenetrable. I was able to reach you through your fear because you are one of us on the soul level, but with many Earth humans it is well-nigh impossible. But then again, a major lesson they need to learn is that Earth human form is not the only humanoid type in the universe, and they really do need to learn to be less afraid of people who look a little different. This lesson is an important part of their soul growth. Anyway, we'll talk more on that later, for now I must leave you, as there is a lot of work to get through tonight."

"But it's morning!" I pointed out to him. "Look, the sun is coming up."

"Ahh, maybe on your side of the planet, but on the other side of the world they are preparing themselves for a good night's sleep, so duty calls. Besides, I have a veritable mountain of work to take care of up on the disc before our northern-hemisphere shift begins, so I'd better get myself on board.

"By the way, Alarca, speaking of work, do you think you could possibly manage a few nights with us on top of your human activities? We really do need all hands on deck, what with the vibrational shift happening, and now that you know who you are, you'll be reasonably aware of what is going on. You won't be able to remember everything because your human brain cannot cope with all the extra input, but you'll recall quite a lot of it. How about it? Want to take up some Guardian duties too?"

"Wow, you mean go on the disc and all?" I replied excitedly. "How will I do that?

Maris smiled at my obvious excitement. "Of course you'll have to come onto the disc, Alarca. We'll place an implant into your chakra system to raise your frequency enough to allow you to come on board. Also, if you need to carry out physical work on our Earth human guests, we'll have to supply you with a gray Zeta container to wear as well. So I take it you agree to help out? It won't be too much for you living a double life?"

"Oh, yes, please let me come on board!" I begged. "And no, I'll be fine. I'm on holidays from school for the next few weeks, so that'll make it easier!"

"Right, then," said Maris, standing up and straightening his long, black cape. "I'll organize getting the implant done very soon. See you tonight, then."

True to his word, that night Maris again appeared in the corner of my room, indicating for me to follow him. Down the hallway and through the kitchen we went, with me having to almost run to keep up with his long strides — after all, being an Elder, he's nearly eight feet tall. When we came to the door of the house, my jaw dropped in amazement as Maris passed straight through it without a backward glance.

Figuring that, as a Guardian, I too would be able to do such a thing, I stepped forward... and walked straight into the unyielding wooden surface, giving myself an awful shock.

"Come on, Alarca, stop dawdling about," said Maris, sticking his head back in through the closed door. "The disc won't wait all night for us. We have only a few minutes to get on board."

"It's not my fault," I grumbled. "I tried to go through after you but I can't. I am in an Earth human body you know!" I added for good measure.

"Oops, sorry!" he apologized. "I forgot. Hang on, I'll give you a hand."

So saying, he touched the knob on the door, which opened with a soft click, and the next moment we were standing side by side in the back garden. Again he touched the knob, and the door closed behind us.

I turned to him with a worried look. "Maris, what if my parents notice I'm gone, or that the door is unlocked?"

His mouth did not move, and his face registered no physical expression, but his huge, black eyes danced with amusement as he replied, "It's all right, Alarca. They will not know you are gone, and be assured that the door is firmly locked behind us."

Feeling confused and a bit scared, I followed along as he strode briskly down the garden path. Then I noticed something else very peculiar — a strong wind was blowing, but I could not feel it! My head was bursting with a million questions, but I didn't know where to even start, so I just kept walking silently after him.

He came to a halt about 50 yards from the house, stopping so suddenly that I almost walked into him.

"We should see it any second now," he said, then, "Ah, here it is!"

I turned to look into the darkness, and there before us appeared a large "blob" of shining white light almost almond shaped, but more rounded. As my eyes adjusted, I could see different colored lights around the perimeter. It was not until we came closer that I could see that the "light" was actually a huge, metallic disc. In fact "huge" wasn't the word for it — it was gigantic, but the weird thing was, it seemed to be parked quite comfortably in our back yard, which was large but certainly not as large as this disc appeared to be.

Then I noticed the outline of two doorways on its side that were in the shape of an archway. One was very high, at least nine feet, and the other was much lower, at about the height of my waist, and this small one fitted inside the large one. As my Teacher stepped forward, both large and small doors slid upward in a smooth and silent movement, and it was as if the front of the disc melted to form a ramp. For a few seconds I was rooted to the spot in shock, and then had to run to catch up with him, feeling trepidation at the thought of following him in, but even deeper concern at being left out on my own.

Passing through the open doorway into the disc, I found myself moving through a gooey substance of about 12 inches in thickness. It sparkled and shimmered with a pinkish-silver light that rippled like water but felt like jelly. It was a color I'd never seen before, and was so beautiful that I wished I could have stayed there looking at it all night. Closing my eyes and holding my breath as I walked through, the sensation was warm and tingly, and quite pleasant. Passing through it felt wet, but as I stepped out on the other side I found myself perfectly dry. And then I was filled with a feeling of incredible upliftment and joy — pure bliss such as I'd never experienced before — and with it came a sense of freshness, healing, renewal, and deep, boundless love.

We then entered what appeared to be an office area in which there were a number of gray beings with the same large, dark eyes as Maris. Some of them were very short, about three feet in height, and some taller ones, up to about five feet. They were either sitting at desks, writing on "paper" that looked like canvas, with strange-looking "pens" that had a yellowish-white light coming out of where the nib should have been, or else interacting with a bank of computers which lined one wall. Still others were simply standing about communicating with each other telepathically, or in a strange form of speech that resembled the clicking sounds of dolphins, and one or two were eating something from what looked like toothpaste tubes. They all turned their heads in astonishment as we passed through, obviously surprised at seeing an Earth human in their midst.

Then something suddenly occurred to me. "Maris!" I called, halting my Teacher in mid-stride. "Will you please explain something to me? Why am I in human form and not in a gray body? I am totally confused. Things are happening too quickly for me. I don't understand, and I'm scared."

The determined, no-nonsense, work-to-be-done expression on my Teacher's face softened. He walked back to where I was standing and placed a large hand on my shoulder. "Come, Alarca. We'll go to my office, where we can communicate more privately."

So saying, he guided me through one of the many doorways leading out of the main office area, all of them being similar to the double doorway we had passed through to enter the disc, and into a quiet and very pleasant but sparsely furnished room.

A large console with a chair in front of it took up one corner, and to the left was a computer, similar to those in the main office. Much to my amazement, this computer seemed to react as Maris entered the room. A distinct feeling of welcome emanated from it, and Maris reciprocated by going over and touching its screen with the palm of his hand. It was as if it were alive with sentient consciousness, greeting him on his return to the disc. I felt something... a thought... or was it an emotion... that reached out towards me also, gently touching the very edge of my mind. As this happened, a light began flickering on the computer screen that seemed somehow connected to this feeling that I was experiencing. Maris looked at the computer and then at me. "You see, Alarca! Your presence has been sorely missed by everyone on board. Here, come and sit down and we'll talk."

At first I looked around in puzzlement because the only chair seemed to be the one behind the desk in which Maris was already sitting, but as soon as I thought of needing a chair, one formed from the wall as if by magic.

"Oh, dear, you really have forgotten what it is to be a member of the Guardian consciousness, haven't you!" he chuckled. "Don't you remember how our computers have sentient consciousness that is linked directly into our minds and how the disc itself is tuned into our essence to provide everything we require? It's all right," he went on, amusement still glinting in his eyes, "sit down, the chair won't disappear from under you. Or at least I hope not," he added. "If it's in a playful mood strange things can happen!

"Now, Alarca, the fact that here in our higher energy frequency your conscious awareness is still expressing itself in Earth Human form tells me you have still not quite integrated the reality of who and what you truly are into the parameters of your mind. This is understandable, because up until this point in your present life you have only been able to consciously access a very limited amount of the full soul memory that is potentially available in your DNA. Now that fully awakened contact has been re-established between us, you will be able to download a greater expanse of soul consciousness which in turn will enable you to express yourself more easily as one of us. However, this does not mean that you cannot carry out certain duties — in fact, your being in Earth Human form is a distinct advantage in the work I have planned for tonight."

"W-why, w-what sort of work do you want me to do?" I asked with some trepidation, not sure whether I felt excited or terrified at the prospect.

"Well," Maris sighed, "I really do need your help. For example, one of the jobs on my schedule is a visit to a young Russian boy who badly needs our healing, but every time I try to approach him, he becomes quite hysterical with fear. I suppose I could shape-shift and appear in Earth human or angelic form to reassure him, but really and truly, it's time people started accepting us as we are. I thought perhaps if you came with me, dressed as you are as an Earthling, and showed him that you weren't afraid of me, then he too will feel better about my presence. I've tried sending some of the little workers to him, but even they frighten him badly, and we must visit him, as he is very ill and in need of our help."

"B-but Russia?" I stammered, totally taken aback. "H-how can I go to Russia? It's on the other side of the world! What will my parents think when they find me gone? Maris, I can't!"

"Alarca, Alarca, you are a Guardian! We're on the disc! We'll be there and back before you know it. Don't you remember? The disc is also a time machine. We can visit the young boy in Russia, get you fitted out with your implant, and have you home safe and sound in bed before your parents even wake up, so don't worry. Please trust me!"

I couldn't help sighing in frustration and bewilderment. I'd forgotten so much! Of course, we Guardians could do this.

"Okay Maris," I agreed, "anything you say. You're the boss."

He reached over and patted me affectionately on the cheek.

"Come on then, Alarca, we have work to do. Russia first, then your implant. Off we go!"

10 ▶ ASSISTANT TO ANGELS

Maris led me out of his office by another door, and down a long, dark passageway with a bright light at the end.

"Oh, no!" I cried in alarm, jumping back. "This is how people describe dying — going down a long, dark tunnel towards a bright light! I don't want to die!"

If he'd been in Earth human form, Maris would have rolled his eyes up to heaven, but being in a gray container he couldn't manage that, so both hands raised in eloquent supplication had to suffice, underlined by a slow shaking of the head from side to side. "Alarca, Alarca, Alarca! You are not dying but simply moving from one dimension to another. Although come to think of it, that is really all that so-called 'dying' is. But no, you are not dying. Don't be so silly."

By this time we'd reached the light at the end of the passage, and again I experienced the jelly-water sensation as we passed through, only this time it was about three feet in thickness. Of course! Now I remembered. That was what it felt like to move through dimensions. My goodness, Maris was right. I *was* silly! Fancy a Guardian forgetting something simple like that.

In no time at all we stepped through the portal and found ourselves in a very small bedroom, containing even less furniture than Maris's office. Directly in front of us was an old, old bed which had definitely seen better days: one corner was now propped up with a wooden crate where a leg had broken off. Another matching wooden crate served as a bedside table, and in the corner stood a shabby-looking chair with a torn and patched cushion, over which a couple of threadbare items of clothing were carelessly thrown. This, I guessed, was the only "wardrobe."

What struck me very forcibly as soon as it registered in my mind was the energy in the room. It was so heavy that without thinking I recoiled, stepping backwards onto poor Maris in the process. He grabbed hold to steady me, and immediately his beautiful, healing energy surrounded both of us like a mantle of protection. Then a huddled form on the bed stirred, and I found myself face to face with a blond-haired boy of about my own age — or perhaps he was older. It was hard to tell because he looked so ill and thin.

His gaze lingered on me for a split second, then widened in horror at the sight of the tall, black-clad being who stood behind me. He began to scream, but the sound died in his throat as I felt something pass through me, directed towards him from Maris, who had paralyzed him to stop him moving or calling out, as he'd done to me on that first occasion of our meeting.

"Alarca, please!" His voice rang in my head with urgency and desperation. "Talk to him. Try to get him to understand that I am only here to help, not to hurt him. I can't get through to him."

Holding my hands out in as reassuring a gesture as I could, I slowly approached the boy. "It's all right," I said, speaking gently and smiling. "Please don't be afraid. I promise he won't hurt you. You are not very well, and we are here to help you. Look at me; I'm not afraid of him. I know he looks scary, but really, he won't hurt you."

"W-who are you?" the boy cried in terror, his voice suddenly restored. "W-what is he? What does he want? He's so horrible! Please make him go away!"

With a shock I realized that I was understanding and speaking fluent Russian — at least that's what I assumed the language to be, because that was where Maris had said we were going. Talk about "speaking in tongues"! Wow! I knew very well that the boy would not relax while Maris was present, so I turned to him and communicated telepathically: "Maris, can you please just go away, or at least make yourself invisible for a while. He is absolutely petrified of the way you look."

A flicker of deep, unspeakable sadness came into my Teacher's eyes, and for a second I really thought he was going to cry. "All right," he agreed, quickly mastering his emotions. "I'll just shift my frequency up a notch or two so I'll be here if you need me, but he won't be able to see me."

The next second he was gone, and I experienced a flutter of fear. What if he left and didn't come back? I'd be stuck here, unable to get home.

"It's all right, Alarca," his voice telepathed in my mind. "I'm still here. I won't leave you stranded. Just get on with the job."

"Look," I said, turning my attention back to the boy. "There really is nothing to be afraid of. His name is Maris, and he belongs to a race of beings who are sort of like caretakers of the human race of Earth. He knows you're sick and that you need help. He truly won't hurt you, I promise. He is a good friend of mine, and if you could just let him help, you'll soon be feeling much better."

"What are you then?" the boy wanted to know. "The way you just appeared in my room — are you a ghost? Or an angel?"

"No," I answered, "not an angel, just an assistant to the Angels, as my friend Maris is."

"But you're different. You look human, he doesn't! How come?"

"Oh, God!" I thought to myself. "I don't know the answer to this question either! Maris, help me!"

The telepathic voice of my Teacher resonated in my mind with words of explanation, which I in turn conveyed to the boy: "We can take any form we want to, but we're trying to get Earth humans used to the idea that they are not the only human beings inhabiting the universe. We are also trying to teach them that they should not be scared of someone just because they don't look like what people down here think of as 'beautiful.'"

I then added my own words, hoping that Maris was listening: "You think that my friend looks horrible and frightening and ugly, but to me he looks fine. It isn't what is on the outside of a person that counts, but rather what is on the *inside*, and inside he is kind and good! Do you understand what I am saying?"

"Yes, I suppose so," he answered, "but he still scares me."

"Please," I said to him, "just let him come back, and try not to be scared. I'll stay right here beside you, and if you can only look past his outer appearance you'll see what I mean."

The next moment Maris appeared beside me. The boy shrank back, but I could see he was trying hard not to panic. Maris again communicated to me telepathically: "Tell him to lie back on the bed and to just relax. I'm going to place my hands on his ankles, so I can channel healing energy into many different parts of his body at once. Ideally I should work on his throat area as well, but that will frighten him too much. Please, Alarca, explain to him what I'm going to do."

I conveyed his message, and the boy reluctantly obeyed, agreeing to cooperate as long as I stayed close by, holding his hand. He flinched in horror as Maris's strange, four-fingered gray hands closed gently around his ankles, but I could both feel and see the healing energy begin to flow, though I was only in contact with it indirectly through his hand in mine. He soon relaxed, and after five minutes his cheeks were glowing with a far healthier color than before, and his breath, which had been rasping with difficulty, was now clearer and easier.

"There now," I said to him as Maris withdrew his hands, "doesn't that feel better?"

"Well, yes, it does," he answered grudgingly, "but if he has to come back again, please will you come with him?"

I squeezed his hand to reassure him, then stood up as Maris reached out to guide me back through the time/space portal which would return us safely to the disc.

"Now do you see and understand what we are up against?" he said, shaking his head in frustration. "The Earth humans are so much in need of our help, caught up as they are in separation and divisiveness, and lagging behind in soul evolution, but approaching them is almost impossible! To their way of thinking outer appearance is everything, and in their eyes we are nothing but ugly monsters. They would much prefer to listen to some of the questionable entities of their own astral realm who often take on an outer appearance of 'angelic beings,' or 'Spiritual Masters,' and then proceed to interfere in areas where they have no business, and cause all sorts of problems! It is so frustrating.

"Well now, Alarca," he said, visibly pulling himself together and putting the unpleasant experience of the boy's negative reaction behind him. "Let's get this implant done so you can come on board the disc without my assistance. It may also make it easier for you to integrate the fact that you are one of us, and restore some of your understanding by raising your vibrational frequency to a higher octave. Come along, let's go to the clinic."

Following along behind, it seemed to me that the disc had literally miles and miles of corridors. They were of a dark color, but as we moved along they automatically lit up. At one point Maris stopped to talk to another Elder, so I took the opportunity to feel the wall. It was soft and pliable, and pulsing slightly under my hand, almost as if it were alive, and in fact, when I tried prodding it with my finger, words telepathed into my mind: "Careful please! Not too hard!" I jumped in alarm, realizing that yes indeed, the whole huge disc was actually a living, sentient organism.

Maris picked up on my thoughts. "Yes, Alarca, surely you remember that! The 'Workshop' is indeed sentient, and intimately linked with the essence of our being. It provides everything we need for our day-to-day living requirements. Try reaching it again."

I did and felt a most amazing sensation pass through my body. It was a feeling of being "mothered" and nurtured at a very deep level. My Teacher saw the look on my face and smiled gently.

"Indeed, Alarca, you have missed that feeling, living in the human world, haven't you?"

"Well, of course my parents love me and care for me deeply, as I love and care for them," I replied, "but this is different again. It is what I suppose living in a giant womb would be like. Yes, Maris, you are right — I have missed it badly, but until now, I have had no way of knowing what it was that I was missing. Oh, God, it's good to be home!"

Placing a gentle hand on my shoulder, Maris guided me into a very sterile-looking room with smooth white surfaces on the floor, walls and domed ceiling.

It was rather strange in that there were no corners or angles anywhere — everything was rounded and molded, and "flowing." In the center were half a dozen metal benches that made me think of operating tables, because they had some sort of apparatus under them that would allow them to be raised or lowered depending upon what was required. Strange equipment lined every wall, and computer screens flickered with weird symbols.

Oh, my goodness, yes! I knew this room all right! How many countless hours had I spent in here, working on the humans we brought on board? Now it was my turn to have a procedure carried out on me.

"Oh, well!" I thought to myself, "Here goes!"

Hopping onto the nearest table, I lay back and closed my eyes, and soon found myself surrounded by a group of six workers.

"Alarca, it's good to see you again! Welcome aboard!"

I immediately recognized the energy frequency of my good friend Entil, who had been with me when our disc crashed. He must have taken the easy way out and reincarnated back with our own people instead of taking Earth human form as I had done.

"Hey, Entil!" I grinned. "What the heck are you doing back with the Realm? You should've been reborn as a human!"

"What's it like being an Earth human?" one of the other workers asked. "Coming up through the first three levels, I've been Pleiadian heaven knows how many times, and I've had several lives in the Sirius System and at least two Arcturian lives, but not a single one on Earth."

"It must be fun getting to eat all those different foods instead of just boring paste in tubes," another piped up. "*And* riding on skateboards!" he added wistfully.

"How do you know about those?" I asked, fascinated.

"Through the TV monitors and implants of course!" he replied, completely amazed that I'd forgotten so much. "You know, the way we can pick up all the TV and radio stations on Planet Earth, and link into exactly what humans are experiencing through the biofeedback implants. Not that we can always understand the data that comes through, mind you. A lot of it is totally puzzling."

"Hey, Alarca," said Entil, "I just had a thought. Maybe you can help us there. For example, what in the name of Oneness is the idea behind all this 'sport stuff' that Earth humans go on and on about endlessly? It seems to be a major part of their lives, but we can make neither head nor tail of it. We watch a puzzling thing called 'football' on the TV, and even more puzzling things called 'cricket,' and 'golf,' then we tune in to the biofeedback implants that some of the humans carry, and we almost get knocked head over heels with all the emotion pouring out of them. They seem to do these things for enjoyment, but their emotions aren't happy ones. We don't understand what or why it is. Do you know?"

"Well, to tell you the honest truth," I chuckled, "I don't really understand all of that either, even though I live there, but I wouldn't dare tell the humans that. The whole idea behind sport is to win, whether as an individual or as a team, depending upon what sport it is. Sport is competition, competing against another person or team to prove you are superior to them."

"But why?" another small worker wanted to know. "Why do you need to prove you are superior to another? If everyone worked together as we do, so much more could be achieved."

"It's just the way Earth humans are," I patiently explained. "Playing sport is what Earth humans call 'fun' and 'relaxation,' as opposed to work."

"But that's not what the data from the biofeedback implants conveys to us," she replied. "Through them we sense huge amounts of tension, aggression, stress and even anger and jealousy to the point of wanting to injure fellow beings. And it is nearly always just to get hold of that silly little ball thing," she continued in total puzzlement.

"I know!" said another worker who up until now had been listening in silence. "Why don't they give every sport player their own ball thing, then they wouldn't have to fight each other over it? Surely ball things are not that expensive and rare. Why don't you suggest that when you go back Alarca? That is a brilliant idea!"

"Please, can you all just get on with giving me my implant?" I sighed, lying back, closing my eyes and giving the whole thing up as a bad job. "And remember," I added, "it's an interdimensional key implant I'm here for, not a biofeedback one. Knowing you lot I've probably been fitted out with half a dozen of those already!"

"A lot of help you are," said Entil, grabbing my head and holding it in a vice-like grip as a taller worker by the name of Zogar approached, wielding a formidable-looking needle of about eight inches in length with a crystal on the end corresponding in color to my Teacher's feather and hatband.

"Ow — ouch! That hurts! Pull it out! Pull it out!" I yelled in pain as the needle was plunged into the chakra point on my forehead, while amazingly strong hands held me down to keep me from moving.

"It's okay, Alarca — all done," said Entil, patting me affectionately on the shoulder. "Just relax. There now, it wasn't that bad, was it?"

"Biological human bodies," I replied, gritting my teeth, "register a hell of a lot more pain than gray containers!"

"There, now, Alarca, see?" said Zogar in a cheerily placating voice. "This is where you are of such immense value to us. I didn't know that! Did you know that, Entil? Or anyone else? No? See, I'll bet even

Maris didn't know that. No, look, he didn't either. Fancy that. See how we're learning new things all the time?"

"Oh, shut up!" I glared at him.

I awoke the next morning safe and sound in bed, but with a clear memory of the night's events. Just to be absolutely certain it hadn't all been a dream I went straight away to check in the mirror. Sure enough, there it was: a small, crescent-shaped mark on my brow chakra, small enough to be unnoticeable unless you were specifically looking for it, but there nevertheless. I also clearly recalled Maris bringing me home and then waiting beside me until I fell asleep.

It was still early, not quite 6:30, so I went back to bed to give myself a chance to think things through. Amazing as it all was, it certainly answered a lot of questions that had haunted me for so long. But now more questions arose in my mind. What was I supposed to do with this new-found awareness of who and what I was? And would I be able to live the rest of my life this way, virtually juggling a double identity, or would it clash too much with my day-to-day human life? Also, and this worried me more than anything, who in the name of heaven could I talk to about this? To keep it totally to myself would be very difficult, in fact almost impossible. It was just too big and would make me crazy in the end.

I thought of how my family would take it if I spoke out about my dual identity. I loved my parents dearly, and I knew perfectly well that my love was fully reciprocated, but the idea of telling them such a thing did not feel right. Even if they could understand — it would cause them worry and concern, which was the last thing I wanted for them. Now I finally understood what Mara had meant when she spoke of my path not being easy, and the burden of responsibility weighing heavily upon me.

Then a light went on in my head — Mara! Of course! She was the one to confide in. The more I thought about it, the more I realized that this was why she'd been brought into my life. The whole thing had been carefully orchestrated, probably by Maris, who, in his greater wisdom knew I would never manage human life on my own, having no one with whom to share my deepest secret. The burden of the knowledge of my dual identity would be far too heavy to carry all on my own. I sent a silent message of thanks to him for bringing Mara into my life, and also for the timing of the revelation. With several weeks of school holidays ahead, I'd have the chance to adjust to my new situation.

I also recalled him saying something about classes on the disc that I would have to attend. This made me think of a Greek boy in my class at school, who was also made to attend Greek School every Saturday morning. We all felt so sorry for him having to do this extracurricular study on top of normal school work. Would I have to attend "Guardian School" on board the disc? Oh, God, no, not more school! Surely not! However, with enough on my mind for now, I put that worry firmly aside and instead turned my attention to Mara, and how to approach the subject of my ET identity with her.

11 ▶ MARA

Mara, can I please talk to you?" I called, as she looked up from the large pot she was stirring over the open fire. I put off my visit until late afternoon, when I knew Paco would not be there. He was busy earning holiday money by looking after some horses on a nearby property while their owners were away. For Paco this was the closest thing to heaven on Earth, as he'd been given permission to ride them as well as seeing to their feed and water. Horse riding was his very favorite pastime, so I knew he'd be well and truly occupied and out of the way.

"Ali, come child, sit over here and make yourself comfortable," she smiled, indicating a convenient log close to where she was working. "I hope you haven't come to see Paco, because he isn't here. He is off with his precious horses. Takes after his father, he does. My son had such a gift with horses. A real true Romany gift. He could work magic with them."

"No, Mara," I reassured her, "it's not Paco I came to see, but you. In fact that is why I've come now, so Paco wouldn't be here. I need to talk to you on your own, in private. You see, it's about Maris, the teacher in spirit that you told me about who would be contacting me soon. Well, he did, and it's just amazing!"

"Oh ho," said Mara with a twinkle in her eye, "And what did he have to tell you, child?"

"Oh, Mara! I hardly know where to begin!" Now that the time had come to share my secret, I really didn't know where to start. It was all too much.

"Just take your time, Ali. Paco won't be back for ages. Tell me, what does your teacher look like?"

"He — he's not human," I stammered, not quite knowing what reaction to expect, but deciding on the spur of the moment to plunge in. "But — I'm not either! Mara, I'm one of them! The Guardians I mean, but I'm here in physical human form to carry out work, and now Maris wants me to work up there too, on the disc!"

Now that the flood-gates were open, the words tumbled out of my mouth as I told her of everything that had taken place over the past two nights — the initial appearance of Maris in my room, the Russian boy, my reunion with old friends on board the disc, and my implant. Mara leaned forward to closely examine the mark on my forehead. "Tell me, Ali," she enquired thoughtfully, "how do you feel about all this?"

I shrugged my shoulders. "Confused I suppose, more than anything, but sad too. Mara, I didn't want to come with Maris when he brought me back! I wanted to stay on the disc with the others, and now I feel so lost and lonely."

As I put into words what was inside, the pent-up emotion of the whole situation suddenly hit me, and I began to cry.

"Oh, Mara, I feel as if I don't belong here anymore! As a Guardian up there on the disc I know where my work lies, but down here I'm only a child! What is the good of me being here as a human? I felt it the most when we were visiting the boy in Russia. He was so frightened of Maris. He could only see him as a terrible 'alien being' who was there to hurt him, whereas I'd felt the love right from the beginning. It was so frustrating!

"I felt bad that we were the ones to cause such fear in a human heart, but I also saw how our healing helped him. It's like I'm being torn in two. I just want to go home to my own people!"

Mara reached out to put her arms around me. "Hush little one. Don't cry. You cannot stay on the disc. Your work is here, on this planet. You must learn from the Romany way. Why do you think we travel endlessly from place to place, never able to settle, always being moved on? We have no home on this planet either, but we have no choice, we must remain, so we adapt. This is the secret behind our continuing existence upon the Earth plane. We adapt easily and are not rigid and set in our ways. We fit in wherever we find ourselves and in this way we are at home, no matter where we are.

"Do you not recall me telling you that you have chosen to carry a heavy burden, and that your way would not be easy? You cannot turn back now, you must go on. Listen and I will explain your role upon this planet in a way that will help you to understand why you have chosen to be here and why you must remain.

"If, as sometimes happens, one of our people becomes lost in the forest, we light a fire to show them the way safely back to camp. Upon it we place fragrant herbs and pine cones so that the familiar scent will reach out to them to guide their footsteps homeward.

"Once you reach a certain stage in your spiritual evolution, you also must light a guiding fire fueled with the wisdom which you have acquired throughout your many incarnations. It begins as a tiny spark of knowing deep within your heart, which over the span of many lives slowly ignites and glows with the warm light of your spirit. It is then fanned by the gentle breeze of trust, and made fragrant by the sweet perfume of love. It shines forth like a beacon-fire to light the way for those lost in the dark and shadowy forest of ignorance, giving them comfort, and helping and guiding their footsteps back onto the path of true knowledge.

"You tell me of the sadness you feel, and the sense of being torn in two when you hear of the terrible fear humans experience in their encounters with the so-called aliens. You have been there, but because of your deeper understanding of the truth of the situation, have felt only the love. Who better than one such as you, to someday bridge the gap, the bottomless chasm of misunderstanding and misplaced fear? That, my child, is where much of your work lies."

"But Mara, how can I do this?" I cried. "How?"

"Ali," she answered gently, "you start right where you are now, by understanding clearly who and what you are, and learning to bridge the gap within yourself by balancing and harmonizing the two sides of your being, Guardian and human. Then one day you will be a healer and a teacher yourself, helping the humans to harmonize and balance their energies so that eventually they too will be able to take back spiritual responsibility for themselves by reconnecting with their own Higher Selves from which they have been separated through the Fall of Man.

"Now you understand! You *are* a Guardian, a Spiritual Warrior, one of those whom the humans in their forgetfulness call 'alien.' That is what I meant when I told you we are old friends from way back, and why I have been prompted to teach you and restore your heritage to you. This is the sacred work our people have carried out upon the Earth Plane in ages past, and it is for this reason that you must conduct your life as a living example of love, harmony and balance. It is the only way the human children can truly learn — by following the example set by their 'parents.' This is our sacred duty.

"The energies of the Earth humans must be raised from the vibration of fear and forgetfulness in which they have been trapped for so long, back to a state of love and deeper understanding, for that is the only path home for them. Like the prodigal son they have strayed far, but now it is time for them to turn their weary footsteps back to Oneness. In order for them to do this they must be re-aligned with the energy frequency of love, or that which they call 'God.' Remember me telling you how long we've waited for our Guardian family to return to the physical plane, and it has taken much patience and perseverance, but at last you are here.

"This *coming* has been foretold by tribal people the world over! Have faith, my dear friend, all will be well! The time has now come to assist the human race of Earth to step from human-hood to Godhood — to restore their lost heritage to them by re-kindling the spark of divine consciousness within their hearts, which will enable them to reunite with the Great Oneness — their true home."

12 ▶ EARTH 101

The following weeks proved to be quite a challenge for me. Each night found me on board the disc with Maris, and the other Elders and workers who were connected to that particular "Workshop," as we affectionately refer to the huge Mothership on which some of our people spend their whole lives. For the first couple of weeks Maris came every night to fetch me, but once I got my confidence back, and a deeper understanding of the process, I was able to board on my own if Maris was busy.

The first time I tried this exercise alone was quite amusing. Still not quite brave enough to walk through the closed door, I made my "escape" through an open window and walked around to the back of the house where I knew the disc would be waiting for me. As I rounded the corner I caught sight of my Teacher, who had thoughtfully come out to meet me. He was obviously expecting me to exit from the back door of the house, and so as I approached, his back was facing towards me as he casually leaned against a corner of the pergola.

Just for a fleeting moment a deep tremor of fear ran through me at the sight of the tall, thin, black-clad being in the darkness of the garden. The disc had just landed, and a strong wind of displaced energy was still blowing, causing Maris's cape to billow around him like some dreaded nightmare figure.

Then, sensing my presence he turned, greeting me. "And how is my 'angel in disguise' tonight? All ready for a bit of work?"

Immediately my Guardian consciousness awakened more fully, enveloping me in a wave of deep peace and love. The bond between a Worker and their Elder/Teacher is very deep, like that between a human child and parent. When we are separated, we feel as if an intrinsic part of our own being is missing — being together is our ultimate joy and completion.

There was so much for me to learn, or rather simply remember, to bring things that I already knew to a more conscious awareness. Entire lifetimes had been forgotten as a result of the amnesia-inducing forcefield of my human birth.

After a while I began to more clearly understand the process which took place each night when it was time for me to go to work on the disc. At first I worried about what would happen if my parents came into my room and found me gone, but then one night I happened to glance backwards as Maris helped me up, and discovered to my amazement that my physical body was still lying peacefully on the bed, sound asleep. I looked at the "body" I was in and it seemed perfectly normal and solid, but I realized then that it was my astral body. So why couldn't I walk straight through the closed door or walls of the house as Maris did?

Then I saw a twinkle in my Teacher's eyes. "Come on then," he said. "Come and have a go. It's just a matter of having faith and trust in yourself, and knowing you can. It will be the same when you're able to fully accept yourself as part of the Guardian Consciousness as opposed to being an Earth human. Oh, don't worry!" he chuckled, highly amused at the panicked thought that sprang immediately into my mind. "Your physical Earth human body will remain the same. After all, you have physically incarnated as a human on Planet Earth, so your human container is not going to suddenly turn into a gray container, but once you step out of that human 'costume' it's a different matter. In the greater reality, of course, you are an immortal spiritual essence — a light body in physical form. Remember, as a Guardian soul, if you do need to carry out physical duties up on the disc or on one of our space stations, we'll provide you with one of the gray 'Zeta-type' containers to put on, which have been specifically developed for such purposes.

"However, Alarca," he added, "we can take full advantage of the situation as we did when we visited the boy in Russia. There are a great number of others we are working with on Planet Earth who are just as afraid of our appearance, but with you accompanying us, dressed as you are in your present human form, you can speak to them and assist in calming and reassuring them."

"Can't you just shape shift and take on such a disguise?"

"Yes, we could, but you're more accustomed to being an Earth human. Come on then, let's get you walking through doors and walls! Don't worry, I'll help you."

Once I got the knack of it, it was great fun. After going backwards and forwards through the locked door of the house several times, Maris stopped me. "Come on Alarca, that's enough. If you keep doing it over and over again you'll wake up tomorrow with a pain in your stomach. Now let's get on board. Duty calls!"

School holidays passed way too quickly, as they always do, and in no time my freshman year in high school began, but with a slight difference — Maris expected me to also attend "Guardian school" every night. I thought Saturday Greek school was bad!

The classroom setting on board the disc wasn't very different from human school, except that the desks were set up in tiered rows more like a university lecture hall than a school classroom, and the other small difference was that everybody was a Guardian. We sat two to a desk, with a total of 30 students to each class.

I soon came to realize that all of us attending these classes were ones who, like me, lived on other worlds in physical forms native to those worlds. In fact during break, we often amused ourselves by changing our form to that of the world on which we lived, and everyone else had to try to guess which planet it was. This was good practice in learning to control our thoughts, because unless we shielded our minds completely, the others could simply tune in telepathically to get the answer.

Our classroom lessons were most necessary, to give us an intimate understanding of universal life-force energy, which we in turn would then be able to pass on to the native humanoid species of these various worlds in which we had taken up residence in order to carry out our work. We also had to learn about the history of our own people, and the important part we've played in the universe, as well as everything that we've forgotten about the many physical planets and their inhabitants, so the curriculum was quite extensive. Because Planet Earth is in the process of a major shift in vibrational frequency, many of us in class were manifesting physical human form on Earth at this time, to lend assistance.

In our day-to-day human lives, most of us were separated by great distances, living out our Earthly existences in many various places, but each night on board the disc we came together in mutual learning and support, helping and encouraging each other as much as we could. Each one of us was well aware of the difficulties we faced in human life on an immature planet like Earth. Some of us were aware of our dual identity in our human minds, some were not, but up on the disc everybody knew exactly who and what they were.

Tonight's lesson was history, and it was to be delivered by Maris, who specializes in this field. Having been a Guardian Elder of the Realm Consciousness for the span of many millennia, Maris has an intimate knowledge of both the first three levels of reality that comprise the physical universe, as well as those higher frequency bands that comprise our Guardian reality. As an Elder and Teacher, he is clearly cognizant of the role our people have played in the scheme of things from many millennia ago to the present day.

Allowing us a few minutes to settle down, he took a sip of yellow-colored vitamin drink from the vial he kept in his pocket. He'd been working hard in the clinic all evening, carrying out genetic work on a number of Earth humans who'd been brought on board, and planned to return to this after the class, so he had not bothered to step out of the biological gray container he donned for that specific purpose. The ones we use for these medical procedures usually have four fingers on each hand to make the handling of delicate instruments easier, and being biological, these containers need to be nourished on a regular basis while we're in them.

"Now class," he began, tucking the vial away safely and leaning back against the desk to regard us through huge, dark eyes. "I will begin tonight's lecture with a quick overview of the universal cycle, or what we call the Human Ladder. I'm aware that many of you who've been assigned duties on Planet Earth and chosen birth into human bodies down there, have been adversely affected by the amnesia screens during the entry process, and so have temporarily forgotten this vital knowledge that is necessary for the type of work you are undertaking.

"Before we start, how many of you don't fully understand this cycle?"

A number of hands went up, including mine.

"Right, then," said Maris, "it's really important for all of you who carry out work on other worlds and in other dimensions to understand it clearly, so that you know what you are dealing with in your contacts with other galactic cultures. To put it simply, the Human Ladder is a term we use for the path of soul evolution that all human species follow through the universal cycle, gradually ascending through ten levels of deepening and expanding conscious awareness which we call 'galactic levels.'

"Those of you who are residing in Human containers on Planet Earth have probably been taught about the emergence of the Earthling species according to the beliefs of the culture into which you have been born. Needless to say, with such a diversity of cultures on Earth, there are many different versions of this Creation story. Why, in Western Society alone there are two vastly different mind-sets at play on this quite controversial subject! On one side there are those who believe without question that the Genesis story in the Bible is correct, while others insist equally strongly on the scientific concept of evolution. Then again, according to much of the Indigenous folklore, mankind emerged from inside the Earth so, as with many concepts on the planet, there is a great deal of divisiveness pertaining to this issue. As you have most likely gathered, Earth humans tend to be rather caught up in duality and separation, and just cannot manage to 'get it together' as it were!"

A ripple of amusement ran through the classroom, especially among those of us who'd been assigned duties on Planet Earth for the span of a human lifetime.

"Yes," said Maris with a knowing look. "I see those of you who are enjoying a 'working holiday' on Earth can really relate to what I am saying." Understanding looks were exchanged between a number of us, and several other heads nodded in sympathy, having "been there and done that" on previous assignments. Still others who were planning to carry out Earth Plane duties in the near future looked decidedly worried.

Maris continued. "The understanding, or lack of it, of human evolution on Planet Earth is a prime example of the dualistic and divided way that human thought processes operate on that planet, and the reason for this is that they are only on the first galactic level of the Human Ladder — on the first 'rung' so to speak. Their conscious awareness is still very underdeveloped, for like all humanoid beings residing on the first universal level, they only have access to one-tenth of their full consciousness potential. Remember that some of them have not long evolved past the animal kingdom out of which their physical containers were developed, and so many of the natural instincts carried over from their predecessors are still deeply rooted within their psyches.

"In fact, it is the territorial instinct of the animal kingdom that gives rise to the war-like nature of Earth Man. Many of them still feel an instinctive need to dominate their own territory and to invade the territory of others, to prove how 'mighty' and how 'powerful' they are. Some will even go so far as to reject, or even kill a fellow human who does not fit within the accepted physical or cultural pattern of a particular society, belief system or nation. It is this instinctive fear of outsiders, of anyone who is different and not part of the 'herd,' that is the root of all problems on Earth, and this is one of the main objectives that we are aiming for in our dealings with this planet. There is a great need for them to learn that just because someone may look different, does not necessarily mean that person is an enemy.

"On the subject of human evolution, there is a grain of truth in all of the various concepts taught on Planet Earth, but all are incomplete. The Indigenous folk come closest to the truth with their acknowledgement of our Star Nations having visited Earth in the distant past. In this way their beliefs encompass the whole universe rather than being limited to just one small planet.

More ripples of amusement spread over the room.

"Now, as I said before," he went on, "Planet Earth is, at the moment, on level one, and therefore the native inhabitants of that planet are able to consciously access only 10% of their total mind capacity. However, Earth is in the process now of moving up to level-two consciousness. The vibrational frequency of the planet has increased quite dramatically over the past few years as part of this evolutionary process, and so those inhabitants who are not able to remain in harmony with their planet's growth are going through all manner of problems, as we are so well aware."

One of the students who wasn't familiar with human life on Earth put her hand up. "Maris, do you know when this process will be completed?"

"Hopefully things will start to improve by 2012," he answered, "providing of course that we can overcome the mind control and brainwashing processes that are still being carried out there on a daily basis. These are blocking Earth humans' progress badly, but at the same time, free will still applies, and many of them simply do not want to progress. They believe that they are the ultimate life form in the whole universe and therefore do not need to improve themselves any further. Some of them even believe that, just because they have the technology to build the biggest bomb, they have reached the peak of 'civilization!' This concept is of course being promoted by the Controllers, with whom we must contend."

A wave of sadness passed through the whole room as we considered the problems facing this young and spiritually blocked race of beings that we, as Guardians and caretakers of energy, had to try to deal with in so short a space of time.

Picking up on our feelings, Maris intervened quickly to get us back on track. "Now remember, all of you, everybody evolves eventually, so there is hope yet for Planet Earth! If we can just help her inhabitants to move up to galactic level two, they will then be able to consciously access *two*-tenths of their mind capacity, and of course their spiritual understanding will then deepen through subsequent lives as they gradually progress upwards. With a minimum of ten lives on each level, by the time Earth humans have even reached the second and third stages, as have our Pleiadian, Arcturian and other friends, they will have manifested lives in many diverse human forms and planetary cultures, and therefore will have much more understanding and appreciation of the oneness of all creation.

"By the time they evolve to the top of the third galactic level, their physical bodies will begin to look more like the containers we use, with a very simple physical form and much larger head to accommodate the greater brain and consciousness capacity. It is of course at this stage that mind focus begins to move beyond limited physical plane reality.

"Now then," he said, looking around the room, "as I'm sure you all know, the next phase of soul evolution — that which has its beginnings at galactic level four, is where we Guardians are in our soul journey. From level four upwards, the need and desire to reincarnate onto worlds of physical matter has virtually disappeared. Those residing on these higher levels have moved beyond that to a point where we are fully cognizant of the fact that 'we' are not the body 'We' — the being, the personality — are pure soul essence, pure light energy. Thus those on levels four and five of the Human Ladder are moving even further away from the need for physicality and deeper into pure mind/spirit.

"Once we evolve to galactic level six, our transmutation and healing work with members of the human kingdom becomes our main focus, as many of you here are now doing, and at level seven we begin training as Teachers, as others of you are involved in at the present time. Those at level eight are the Teachers and Elders like myself, and those at levels nine and ten are, of course, known on Earth as 'Angels.' They are caretakers of energy throughout the universe, and those of us working at the Guardian levels below them are their assistants, carrying out work in places and situations where the energy is too dense for level nines and tens to enter."

"I do realize all this can be rather confusing, because within the Guardian consciousness, or what we call the Realm, we also have our own levels within the galactic levels, so those of us at level four on the Human Ladder are only at level one within the Realm. So to summarize, we begin interacting with humans at level three, teacher training is at four, and at level five of Guardian consciousness we become teachers. The angelic guardians are on ascending levels above that."

One sitting next to me asked, "So if as Guardians we've moved past the need for physical form, is that why, if we do have a physical body at all, it is always very simple, and rather different from a human container?"

"Yes, absolutely!" Maris answered. "Unlike human races dwelling upon those planets on the first three levels of the Human Ladder, we are not permanently part of the physical universe, and therefore we are not focused on the physical plane. Earth humans direct so much of their energy into physicality and judge others on what they perceive as physical beauty. Consequently, when they see us in our very simple gray containers, they become scared. They do not understand that physical form and appearance is of no importance whatsoever. When we appear before them clad only in our light bodies, they believe we are angels or fairy folk, but if we put on our gray containers, as we must in order to carry out physical tasks, then they see us as 'monsters' or 'evil aliens.' That, unfortunately, is just how the Earth human mind works!

"The Angelic Guardians of the ninth and tenth galactic levels are so completely focused in the reality of pure soul/God essence that they very rarely put on any sort of container or carry out physical work at all. When they do enter the world of human perception in order to assist in the dying process, they simply tune in to the mind of the one with whom they wish to interact, and manifest an image of what that person expects an angel to look like. This image often rather resembles the Pleiadians, or one of the other human species from the second galactic level.

"This actually causes some confusion in Earth human minds," Maris explained, "because these second-level humans such as the Pleiadians do visit Earth sometimes as teachers and healers, and they often get mistaken for angels because of their appearance and the fact that they are further up the 'Ladder' than Earth humans. People on Earth tend to feel more comfortable with these beings, because unlike us, they are still mortal, biological humanoids, and therefore closer to Earth folk in their energy frequency. This is why sometimes we call upon them to help us out in our dealings with very fearful Earth folk.

"Now class, I would like to present a brief overview of our own history for those of you who may not be clear on this endlessly fascinating subject. As many of those on Earth with whom you are working are completely unaware, we also have experienced many lives on the physical planets of the first three galactic levels of the Human Ladder. We too have had lives as Earth humans, Pleiadians, Sirians, etc. Of course we have followed this same path of evolution as do all humanoid species in the universe, before they are able to access Guardian Consciousness.

"Our Guardian Consciousness has been present in the universe for billions of years. We developed space travel technology millions of years ago, and it is our task, as Workers of the Angels, to oversee the planets and life forms of the physical universe. In fact, by making use of a very ancient technology that enables us to tap into creative life-force energy, or what Earth Humans call 'God,' we could be thought of as 'agents of creation.'

"Over the span of many millions of years, our expeditionary forces have made periodic visits to the Milky Way galaxy. We were part of a group which was responsible for bringing souls from a number of different planetary cultures to Earth during those times referred to as 'Lemuria.' Back then all of these souls were fully awake and aware of their true state of immortality. They were not anchored in physical form and could move easily between the dimensions, coming and going at will. Some Earth humans still carry soul memories of this beautiful time on their planet, when the finer dimensions and the magical creatures which dwell therein interacted easily and fluidly with those in residence on Earth. The barriers between dimensions were not as solid as they are now, which allowed freer movement back and forth. Human, Animal and Devic Kingdoms could communicate with each other easily.

"But then came a time when some of these interdimensional souls began to crave the pleasures of the physical Earth plane. As a result, their vibrational frequency began to drop down the scale as they indulged themselves more and more in fleshly pursuits. Some of our people too got caught up in this way, and eventually a whole new and different era came about, which Earthling consciousness recalls as 'Atlantis.'"

"Maris," one of the students put up his hand, "why is it that some Earth humans can easily relate to the concepts of 'Lemuria' and 'Atlantis' whereas others totally reject these legends?"

"Because some present-day Earth humans were on the planet back in those times and some were not," he answered. "To put it simply, the ones who came to Earth at the time of Lemuria were all from elsewhere — there were no humans resident on Earth back then who were native to the planet. The Earth-born ones were developed later, so they have no soul memory of those earlier times. Lemuria and even Atlantis have never been part of their reality, so they reject any possibility of such times and places. These are also the ones who find it very hard to accept the possibility of sentient human life on worlds other than Earth."

Another student had a question: "So what happened with Atlantis? This really interests me because I'm resident on Earth at the moment, and there have been a few psychic predictions that Atlantis will rise again. For some reason this makes me feel very nervous and uncomfortable."

"Ah yes, Atlantis!" Maris replied, "That was not a very good time for us. You say it makes you feel nervous and uncomfortable? May I ask you a question? What do you feel about the power of crystals?"

"Funny you ask that," the student replied. "As a matter of fact I don't feel at all comfortable with them. Yes, I admit they're lovely to look at just sitting on a table, and as long as that is all they do that's okay, but someone once tried to do a chakra balancing on my human container using crystals, and I almost passed out, then felt sick and dizzy for several days after. I hate them being used anywhere near my energy field," he added with a noticeable shudder.

Maris looked down for a moment, and we could all clearly discern an energy of deep sadness permeating his entire aura. "Yes," he repeated, "Atlantis! Your difficulties do not surprise me, given the fact that you are here now, as a member of the Guardian Realm. Some of our people have had very nasty experiences with crystal power, going back to Atlantis.

"Up until the time of Atlantis," he went on, "we were all members of one big group — not Controllers and Guardians as we are now. We were caretakers of energy and agents of creation, as we still are, who have always been present in the physical universe as overseers of all planets and life-forms therein, and all of us evolved from those various planets and life-forms.

"At the time of Atlantis certain members of our group, in fact I believe it was the ones who are now referred to on Earth as 'the fallen angels,' allowed their position of power in the universe to 'go to their heads' as the Earthly saying goes. The Realm had been responsible for the development of all biological life-forms throughout the Cosmos, but because of the responsibility involved with such work, very strict ethical guidelines were in place. Experimentation was allowed of course, as in the early stages of developing a suitable physical container for the humanoid species of Earth, but strict guidelines still applied.

"However, some younger members of the Realm Consciousness resident on Earth at the time of Atlantis felt that these rules did not apply to them. They decided to do away with these restrictions and work to their own rules because they felt they knew better and that they were superior to the rest of us. They also experimented with crystal power, firstly to enhance their own abilities, which were beginning to dwindle as a result of their out-of-control ego and pride, but later on for more dangerous applications concerning generating power. As some of you probably know already, crystals do not discriminate — they simply magnify. In fact, they amplify whatever energy comes into contact with them and can therefore be used in either a negative or positive way.

"Crystal power began being used to keep the general populace under control, and it was used against any members of the Realm who attempted to stand up to the break-away group. This was done through secretly developed techniques which had the effect of short-circuiting peoples' energy systems, thus causing them to lose their natural ability to come and go at will from their physical containers. In this way, those whom the 'elite' group considered lower classes or enemies of the state could be kept trapped and under control on Earth, with no way of returning to their original off-planet home worlds, or in our case, back to the Realm Consciousness. As a result of the brainwashing, many of these unfortunate souls had no memory left of their former existences."

"And what about the force fields?" I asked. "I thought all planets had these around them to keep younger souls confined to their own frequency band, to stop them from entering higher-frequency areas until their energy has reached the appropriate level of evolution. Why are they such a problem on Earth?"

"That is a very good question, Alarca!" Maris responded. "On Earth we are up against two problems. Firstly, the Controllers have set up some of their own force fields much closer to the physical plane, which are a real hazard for everybody concerned, as you found out when your disc hit one of them. Secondly, to get past the astral plane force fields after so-called 'death,' a soul must raise its frequency to a higher level through reincarnating a number of lives. In this way they begin to vibrate at higher and higher frequencies and eventually reach a point of conscious awareness where they evolve past being affected by the force fields and are able to move on. This however must be a conscious and free will choice for each individual soul. On Planet Earth, however, this opportunity has been taken away from many people through vital information being withheld and replaced by inaccurate and misleading dogma put out by the Controllers.

"In addition, they keep human energies vibrating on a low frequency through brainwashing campaigns which affect almost every level of society through advertising, big business and the media. A lot of this brainwashing is centered around tempting humans to indulge in negative and harmful habits such as taking drugs, consuming alcohol and putting unhealthy foods into their bodies. These are all ways of causing peoples' consciousness to become trapped on the astral plane after the death experience, and then drawn back, time after time, to the physical, with no hope of ever progressing to higher planes of reality."

"Maris," the young worker beside me raised her hand. "Could the custom of mummification in Egypt possibly be a part of this brainwashing agenda? Was it also a way of stopping souls from moving on to higher realms by directing their focus back into the mortal, physical body, which, they believed, had to be carefully preserved for their return to life on Earth and why their Earthly possessions were buried along with them?"

"Yes," our teacher replied, "that is absolutely correct. And many of those ancient 'gods,' of Egypt, Greece, etc., were simply Controllers pretending to be gods in order to keep the general populace in line. One of their most effective means was the 'divide and conquer' technique — sending various human tribes out to war against each other. This was a way of keeping them weak, divided and therefore vulnerable. Over the millennia some of our Guardian people have put in occasional appearances to try to get the humans back on track, but they always ended up being put to death or else given the amnesia treatment."

"And what about our people back in Atlantis?" somebody asked. "Did we get trapped too, or did we manage to escape back home to the Realm?"

"Well," Maris replied, "the 'amnesia' technology was initially developed by just a small group. At first they worked in secret, but as their power grew they became more confident, and others joined them. There were, of course, many of us who did not agree with what was happening. We objected to the way universal free will was being overridden. No one, and I repeat, *no one*, has the right to alienate any sentient being from their soul heritage. For the conscious soul awareness of an immortal spirit to be removed or inhibited to a point where they believe that they are nothing more than a physical body, is the cruelest and most evil act that can be perpetrated by anyone.

"Those of us who objected did everything in our power to block the efforts of this rebel group, who we now refer to as the Controllers, but their lust for power continued to expand, and eventually imploded upon itself, totally destroying the whole Atlantean civilization. Luckily we foresaw this happening, and removed ourselves, along with some of our human charges, to a place of safety.

"Now class," said our Teacher, taking another sip of yellow liquid from his vial, "if there are no further questions, we shall continue this lecture tomorrow night. Class dismissed."

13 ▶ REVELATIONS ON GENESIS

As promised, the following night Maris continued with his fascinating history lesson. It was obvious that every one of us had been giving this subject a great deal of thought, because no prompting at all was needed from our Teacher to elicit questions.

As soon as we were settled, a student at the back of the hall raised her hand. "Maris, can you please explain a little more about the history of Earth and the Bible story of Genesis. The time frame is very confusing, and there are parts that just don't make sense. For example, Adam and Eve are described as the first two humans on Earth, but what about other civilizations such as Lemuria and Atlantis?

Another hand popped up eagerly. "And why were they punished for committing a sexual act together? Is that *really* what the so-called Original Sin is all about? And also, if they were the first, and the only two created at that time, then whom did their children marry? And why is it that there are so many different interpretations regarding all these ancient writings on Earth? How can people know what is correct?"

"Oh, my! It's good to see you all so excited about tonight's topic. These are very good points," our Teacher added. "As for the time frame, yes, it is confusing because in actual fact there were several 'Genesis' events, which are acknowledged by a number of indigenous cultures on Earth who speak of the first, second, third and fourth worlds, and the fifth world that Planet Earth is in the process of entering now. There is no mention of any of this in the Bible, which deals with Genesis as one single event. In reality, there were vast expanses of time involved.

"What also must be taken into consideration," he went on, "is that all of these ancient scriptures and texts are composed of three levels of understanding, and this is why such writings can cause so much argument and confusion. For example, there is an outer level, or parable, which could be likened to a bedtime story suitable to be read to a young child by their parents. This outer level certainly contains valuable lessons and principles to live by, but these are greatly simplified, and set in a way that younger souls can comprehend.

"Then there is a second level, hidden a little deeper beneath the surface, which can only be understood by studying the text with a more educated mind. However, to get the most out of such study, the mind must be open and clear of preconceived ideas and prejudices, which tend to cloud one's true comprehension of what the original author was trying to express. Unfortunately, some translators have fallen into the trap of introducing some of their own mind-set into their interpretation, thus obscuring the original meaning. The story of Adam and Eve is an example of this.

"The third and deepest level of scripture comes only through prolonged contemplation and meditation. Symbolic language has been used in all these texts, the inner meaning of which can only be revealed through many hours of study and meditation involving an esoteric understanding of what we know as Source, or what humans of Earth call 'God.' This Source is expressed throughout the universe as life-force energy, and it is this energy that permeates every part of creation from the largest galaxy to the smallest atom.

"Now class, on the outer scriptural level, the story of Adam and Eve and the Fall of Man is a vastly condensed story of the development of the human species on Planet Earth over the span of many millennia, and their subsequent misuse of free will.

"The second level of the story reveals the fact that beings from higher realms came to Earth to carry out this work. At this deeper level, Adam being 'created by God out of clay' represents these finer energy beings from higher-dimensional frequencies taking on gross physical form in order to manifest on a physical planet.

"This work involved the development of a race of physical human-type beings on Earth, so those carrying it out needed to take on biological form themselves, just as many of you are doing now. In this sense, Adam represents the off-world visitors that came to Earth to carry out this work, and Eve being taken from Adam's rib is symbolic of this new race being created out of their genetic material.

"There are versions of this story in many cultures on Earth. For example, ancient Babylonian texts tell of an extraterrestrial group coming to Earth to 'mine for gold.' On a deeper level this actually refers to the transmutation of soul energy from the 'base metal' of lower animal/human emotions to the 'pure gold' of the higher self — exactly the same work as we are doing now!"

Our Teacher paused a moment to lean back against the desk, regarding us all through his large black eyes and sensing into our energy fields to make sure we all understood what he'd told us so far. This is the thing with gray Guardian teachers — you can't get away with simply pretending to understand the lesson. With their highly developed telepathic skills any slightest pretense is detected immediately. Unlike humans of Earth, Guardian consciousness is like an ocean of crystal clear water, with no hidden, murky depths of deceit or dishonesty.

"All right then, everybody," he continued, satisfied that we'd understood the lesson up to this point. "At the third and deepest level of the Genesis story, Adam and Eve are symbolic of positive and negative polarity. These opposite polarities are expressed through all aspects of nature, and the genders of male and female are one such expression. A state of complete non-polarity exists only at the Source, and this is why we refer to Source, or God, as Oneness. Source Energy resonates in perfect balance, but once it begins to move outwards and away from center it becomes more and more polarized into the duality of negative and positive.

"This is why, on planets like Earth, which are on the lowest rung of the Human Ladder, so much duality exists as opposed to oneness and the polarities of negative and positive are so widely separated. This polarization within nature, known in one Earth culture as yin and yang, is symbolized in the story by Adam being divided into two — Adam and Eve — yang and yin — positive and negative polarity. As those of you who are living on Earth in human form are no doubt aware, these two genders are so different they sometimes seem almost like two species.

"Unfortunately too," he went on, "negative on Earth is often equated with 'bad' and positive with 'good,' and so poor old Eve has suffered much at the hands of ill-informed and misguided Earthlings. To think in this way is as silly as believing that the negative pole of a battery or magnet is 'bad' and the positive pole 'good.' Certainly good and bad may be one example of opposite polarity, but there are many, many examples throughout nature — hot and cold, day and night, aggression and submission, white and black, sun and moon, outer and inner — to name only a few. Now is that clear? Do you all understand?"

"So," one of the students spoke up, "what you are saying is that on the deepest level of the Genesis story, Adam and Eve are symbolic of the state of duality and extreme polarization of energy that exists in the frequencies of a level-one planet such as Earth?"

"Yes," he said, "exactly! Well done! Now are there any other questions?"

The inquisitive student at the back raised her hand again. "Maris, I'm still not clear about Adam and Eve and the 'original sin.' Did they really get kicked out of the Garden of Eden for having sex with each other? Weren't they *supposed* to? I'd have thought they'd be *encouraged*, you know, to help expand the newly developed human race on the planet!"

Deep amusement rippled through our Teacher's energy field. "Yes, well, that story has caused quite a lot of 'discussion' in religious circles on Earth, and unfortunately, also some unfair discrimination against the female population!"

"But," the student persisted, "what were they *really* punished for? Is that the 'original sin' the Christian Church on Earth talks about? And where do we, as Guardians, fit into the picture?"

"Well," Maris explained, "as I'm sure all of you know, as guardians and caretakers of energy in the physical universe, it is our job to intervene and provide the impetus on all levels that is required to transmute soul energy from the vibrational frequency of the animal kingdom to that of the human kingdom, and also to develop suitable containers through which these evolving souls may experience physical existence. Now, is there anyone here who can tell me why that has to be done?"

The one sitting next to me put his hand up. "Is it because on Planet Earth it is only through the reasoning power of human consciousness that cosmic, or divine consciousness can be attained?"

"Yes, exactly!" Maris replied. "You see, evolution on the soul level does not occur naturally on a level-one planet. Animal species can only evolve to a certain point. After all, as we know, the Earth apes do not naturally evolve into humans, otherwise the so-called 'missing link' would have been found long ago — in fact it would still be in existence today, because both apes and humans are present on Earth, and the process of evolution is ongoing.

"Once an animal species reaches the point where it is ready to evolve to higher frequencies, then higher intervention is required, because both spiritual and physical input is necessary at this crucial time of transition. We spent many millennia checking out the viability of a number of different species on Earth, carrying out a few initial experiments. There were several possibilities, and each one had to be tried and tested, then left to develop naturally for a while to see how things turned out. Finally, one species emerged whose genetic code seemed the most compatible, and so we got down to business.

"Once we had a successful prototype, we then took genetic material from it in order to create a mate to keep it company. We provided a nice, safe place for them to live where we could keep a watchful eye on them and gradually refine their energies to higher and higher frequencies. They had a good mixture of ET genetics within their makeup, and so in a way were our 'children.' Because of this we wanted to protect them and keep them separate from other members of the species from which they had evolved. The area set aside for them is referred to in the Bible as the Garden of Eden."

At this point I just had to ask a question: "So, Maris, are you saying that these ones were the Adam and Eve of the Bible?"

"Indeed they were," he replied.

"But Maris," I persisted, "I know the story of Adam and Eve, and there's no mention of extraterrestrials being present on Earth back then."

"Well actually, Alarca, there is. Don't you recall a group of beings known as the 'Sons of God,' and also the 'Elohim'? These terms refer to various extraterrestrials visiting Earth from elsewhere. The young Earthling race mistook them for gods because of their advanced technology.

"Everything went smoothly enough for a time with the newly developed species as we slowly worked with them. Our main task was to transmute their energy systems to a higher-frequency band, which involved much fine tuning and re-adjustment.

"That's what we're doing now with Earth humans, isn't it?" I inquired.

"Yes, it is," Maris answered, "and this is why so many contactees develop higher-dimensional senses like clairvoyance and ESP. They are beginning to resonate on a higher-frequency band and can therefore tap into intuitive abilities beyond the third-dimensional human ability to reason. This reasoning power, I might add, was bestowed too prematurely on the Earthling race — in fact, much earlier than they were spiritually able to handle wisely at the time!"

"Ah!" I spoke up, "Do you mean the 'serpent' in the Garden of Eden who tempted Adam and Eve? Is that what it was all about?"

"Yes, Alarca, you are absolutely right! You see, the so-called 'serpent' was a member of a band of renegades who were rebelling against the leadership of the group in charge of the work back then. The temptation to interfere and disrupt the work in order to take control of the newly developed Earthlings was too much for them to resist. Their plan was to keep the humans where they were and exploit them as slave labor, rather than helping them to evolve further.

"Despite the fact that the Earthlings had been transmuted to a higher-frequency band, and therefore were on the borderline of the human kingdom, they were still resonating closely with their predecessors. Consequently, there were two vital 'human' factors still missing in their makeup. One of these was the ability to reason, with its accompanying gift of free will as opposed to the purely instinctive drive of the animal kingdom. The other missing factor was the concept of immortality, which can only be grasped by more enlightened and evolved members of the human kingdom. In the animal kingdom, and even in the lower frequency bands of the human kingdom, the process of immortality through reincarnation of the soul is totally automatic, with no conscious control or understanding of the process.

"These two concepts are referred to in Genesis as the Tree of Knowledge and the Tree of Life, of which Adam and Eve were 'forbidden to taste the fruit.' In other words, they had not at that stage evolved far enough past the animal kingdom to be able to properly comprehend the concept of reasoning power, symbolized by the Tree of Knowledge of Good and Evil — or immortality, symbolized by the Tree of Life.

"This is where our trouble-making 'serpent' comes into the picture, tempting them with the 'forbidden fruit' of the Tree of Knowledge, thus instilling within them the ability to reason, which automatically bestows the gift of free will, which they were simply not ready to handle at that early stage in their evolution, being still too immature on the spiritual level.

"These trouble-makers are doing exactly the same thing again, now that we are involved in the next stage of human evolution on Earth. This time they are interfering by bestowing fifth-dimensional abilities on some who are not spiritually mature enough to handle this deeper sensing wisely, or else tempting certain ones with technology that is beyond what Earth humans are ready to access. Needless to say, this is causing major problems on the planet!"

One of the students raised his hand. "Maris, I understand what you're saying about abilities such as clairvoyance and ESP being a problem if they're bestowed upon humans who are too spiritually immature, and I also see the danger of their being given access to technology that is beyond their level of soul evolvement, but what's wrong with reasoning power and free will as occurred back in Eden? What harm could that do?"

"If you want to see what harm free will can do without the spiritual maturity to handle it wisely," he answered, "just look at the horrible mess Planet Earth is in right now. Free will without the self-discipline that only comes with spiritual maturity is as disastrous and dangerous as letting a class of five-year-olds play with gunpowder and matches. It was this gift of free will without proper understanding with which Adam and Eve were tempted that brought about the 'fall of man.' The results have continued to reverberate throughout the human kingdom of Planet Earth ever since, effectively keeping their energy at a very low frequency level. This 'fall' refers to the dropping or lowering of their vibrational frequency.

"You see," he went on, "back in Eden they were given free will before they were evolved enough to be able to choose wisely between the lower-animal self, out of which they were evolving, and the higher cosmic self within, which had only just been awakened. These two aspects of their psyche are symbolized by the two 'sons' born of their union, Cain and Abel. These two represent the life choice they had to make once the responsibility of reasoning power and free will was bestowed upon them.

"Maris," I asked, "if this story of Adam and Eve is actually a parable, then what is the deeper meaning behind Cain killing his brother Abel?"

"Well," he answered, "the fact that it was 'Cain,' the lower self, who overcame and killed 'Abel,' the higher self, shows which path was chosen. It was at this point that humankind chose the way of the lower self, with its associated lower emotions and vices of greed, lust, jealousy, egotism, etc., all of which are expressions of the energy frequency of fear. The higher self always chooses the energy frequency of love, trust and oneness. It is this wrong choice made back then that is partly behind the concept of 'original sin.'

"So what happened to the Earthlings after that?" somebody inquired.

"Well now," Maris replied, "that is rather sad, because once they learned how to exercise free will, they became defiant and intractable, just as undisciplined children tend to do. In the end they began getting into so much trouble that they had to be forcibly ejected from Eden and left to fend for themselves.

"Guards had to be posted in the area to stop them from getting in to attack us, because if they had, then we would have been forced to defend ourselves, and they would not have had a chance against our highly sophisticated weaponry, which we did not want to have to use against them. It certainly became a difficult and trying situation all around!

"After their eviction," Maris continued, "they scattered far and wide, and many of them began mating back to members of the animal kingdom, so they began to devolve as a species. This, by the way, is another side to the concept of 'original sin,' which I will clarify in a moment.

"A very few of them did learn to handle free will and reasoning power wisely — like Noah and his family. They continued to evolve over time, and even back then they were well on the way to becoming cosmic citizens. Special mention is made in the Bible of their unusually long life-spans, and this, of course, can be attributed to the strong infusion of ET genetics in their makeup.

"We were now faced with a major dilemma, because these more evolved humans needed to be protected from the rest, who were rapidly degenerating. This problem, however, was effectively resolved by that event referred to in the Bible as 'Noah's Flood.'

"As the water level began to rise, a rescue mission was mounted to make sure that the more evolved humans were protected, along with genetic material from as many varied plant and animal species as possible. In this way these ones were kept safe and were used to repopulate the area once it became habitable again. Thus humankind survived the 'great flood,' which is recalled in the folklore of many different cultures on Earth."

"Maris," I raised my hand, "about 'original sin' — you were going to tell us more about another aspect." This was something the nuns at 'human' school spoke of on a regular basis, and I was interested to hear more of our ET version of the story.

"Ah yes — thank you, Alarca," he replied. "I very nearly forgot to clarify that point. Once the human species was re-established on Earth after the flood, dire warnings were issued of what would happen to them if they fell back into mating with members of the animal kingdom. It was sincerely hoped that Homo *sapiens,* after having experienced what punishment 'God' was capable of meting out, would behave like civilized human beings.

"The concept of 'original sin' has become extremely confused in the collective consciousness of humanity. They know that it had something to do with the 'temptation' in the Garden of Eden, and also that there were sexual connotations involved, and so poor old 'Eve' has been made the scapegoat ever since. However, the sexual aspect of 'original sin' was actually humankind reverting to bestiality as a result of the misuse of free will. In other words, it was all about giving in to the lower self rather than following the way of the higher self.

"It is the deeply ingrained memory of a great flood 'sent by God to punish' humankind for this 'original sin' — that is, a cleansing of sin by water — that is at the root of the Baptismal rites carried out by many religions on Planet Earth to this very day!"

14 ▶ MICK THE MOUTH

L ife on Planet Earth with my human family went on as usual, with Mara and Paco often joining us in our evenings of music and dance. Seeing each other on an almost daily basis, Paco and I soon became as close as any brother and sister could be. We were similar in age and even in appearance, but our views on life were contrastingly different. This, however, was not a source of contention between us, but rather brought an element of balance and mutual support into our relationship.

One of the greatest differences between us was that he enjoyed school and the study involved, whereas I detested it wholeheartedly. He was quiet and hard-working, always near the top of his class, and underneath his easy-going nature I could detect a core of grim determination to succeed academically.

In total contrast, I disliked the confines of school intensely. It wasn't that I was lacking in brains, and in fact when I applied myself to study I did well, but there was always a streak of rebellion hidden away, not too far below the surface, especially now with the knowledge I was acquiring each night on board the disc. So much of what I was told in human school was either a badly misinterpreted version of the truth, or simply incorrect. The nuns sensed this in me, and so I often ended up in trouble, sometimes for things I had not even done.

Both of us had been brought up in the Catholic faith and dutifully attended church every Sunday with our families. Paco often served on the altar at Mass, but again, we approached the subject of religion from very different angles. He went along quite happily with the traditional teachings we were given by the priests and nuns, whereas I, of course, questioned many of the things we were taught.

One afternoon after school when we were supposed to be doing our homework, we became immersed in a fascinating discussion on the concept of God. "Why," I demanded, "do they always portray God as an old man sitting on a cloud? That is not how I perceive Him."

"How do you perceive Him?" he asked, curious about what I would say.

"It's really hard to put into words," I had to admit, "but I can tell you one thing: God is way, way beyond the male, human form they show in our Bible history book, which is just so ridiculous. And what really makes me annoyed is the way they ascribe to Him petty little human vices such as anger and jealousy. The God force is the driving energy behind all of creation and surely beyond such limitations."

"But Ali," Paco answered reasonably, "it doesn't really matter. If it gives someone comfort to think of God as an old man sitting on a cloud, or if that image causes just one person to choose love instead of fear, then something positive has been achieved.

"I know you get upset when anyone tells you this, but you are different, and you think differently than most. Perhaps the way you perceive God is right, but most people need to picture Him in a way they can personally identify with and relate to. They feel better and safer by seeing God as a protective old father-figure. That is just the way the human mind works."

"Well," I retorted, "it's lucky you're the one planning to be a priest and not me. I'd turn the whole thing upside down!"

"Heaven help the world," he grinned, "with Pope Ali the First in charge at the Vatican!"

Time passed, and by age 15 I was determined to escape the confining demands of the education system of Planet Earth, to follow my heart's desire to become a dancer. Paco, too, whose mother had been born and raised in Triana, the Gypsy Quarter of Seville in Spain, shared this love. During the past two years we'd often danced together at family fiestas at home, so we both felt confident in our ability to perform professionally.

My father was our guitarist, so it wasn't as if I'd be going off alone at such a tender age to work in clubs and restaurants. He and Paco would be with me, so I'd be adequately chaperoned and perfectly safe. My work "upstairs" would continue as usual, but at least by working as a dancer in the evenings I'd have a legitimate excuse to catch up on sleep during the day.

Paco had two more years of school to go before he was to begin his seminary training, but he felt confident of being able to handle a couple of night's work on top of his studies, providing there was no school the following day. So, with full family approval, we embarked upon a career of professional flamenco dancing — a dream come true for both of us.

Life up on the disc also passed, as I slowly but surely regained my lost Guardian identity and again took my rightful place alongside the other workers and Elders on board. My first night spent working in the clinic proved to be quite a challenge, as well as a major learning curve.

"Oh *no, not* 'Mick the Mouth!'" was Zogar's horrified response as he checked through our duty roster for the night's work. "You'd better put earplugs in for that one, Alarca, or at least completely tune out of your Earth human senses until we can paralyze him enough to shut him up and get him on the table."

"Why?" I asked, starting to feel apprehensive.

"He's a huge, red-haired fellow who lives near you in Australia," Zogar explained. "He has a temper to match his hair color, and a — er, shall we say, a lingual repertoire with which he is able to fully express it. For some unknown reason his friends call him 'Blue,' but up here he's known as 'Mick the Mouth' because of how he yells and swears so much."

"That's just typical Australian humor," I chuckled. "Red-haired males are always nick-named Blue by their friends. But surely he can't be *that* bad. I noticed that the information on him mentions he owns a cat, so he must have a gentle streak hidden away under all the outer bluster."

"Oh, my goodness — yes, the cat! One night we brought it on board with him, thinking that having his pet along would keep him a bit calmer, but the rotten thing is worse than its owner. It wrecked a computer monitor and two laparoscopes, got all tangled up in the opulater and nearly took Dagar's left eye out with a highly effective feline appendage armed with scythe-like claws that lashed out in all directions. Oh no, Alarca, never *ever* make the mistake of bringing Bazza the Cat on board!"

The language could be heard three corridors away — loud, profane bellowing that sounded totally alien in the usually quietly clinical atmosphere of the Mothership. Hesitating for only a moment, I bravely poked my head around the door and came face to face with a red-faced and furious human male of gigantic proportions.

"SHIT! Bugger orff yer little creep!" he screamed, letting fly with a hamlike fist which missed Zogar's head by inches. "If any of youse f—kin' little freaks TOUCHES me I'll bloody murder the lotta yers! Don't you damned-well come near me! I'm WARNIN' yers! Bloody bunch o' friggin' pixies! Piss ORFF!"

A hastily aimed ray of blue light hit him between the eyes, paralyzing him from head to foot but at the same time surrounding him with a protective energy field to prevent his falling to the floor. Dagar was then able to levitate him up onto the examination table, as everyone breathed a sigh of relief. Paralyzed as he was, his eyesight was still functioning, and as I moved towards him he managed to shift his horrified gaze in my direction. His expression shocked me to the core of my being. Never had I seen such loathing on a human face.

I tried to smile in a friendly way, to communicate to him not to be scared and that we meant him no harm, but our gray containers simply don't have the capabilities for such physical and verbal communication with an Earth human, and his profound level of fear blocked any attempt on our part to express a telepathic reassurance. All we could do was to get on with the job.

A quarter-hour or so later, Zogar looked up from the work he'd been carrying out on the lower part of the man's body. Having been totally occupied for the past ten minutes in acquiring a decent sperm sample for our genetic program, it was only now, with that part of the procedure completed, that he could turn his attention to Dagar and me, as we inserted an implant into the head.

"Phew, that's a good job done! How's it going for you?"

"Almost finished," we replied in unison. Delving deeply with long and dexterous gray fingers, Dagar activated the implant while I steadied the man's head. Unlike the 'alien' implants that some Earth humans have been fitted with by the clandestine Controller group on Earth, ours are generally not physical objects but rather of a higher vibrational frequency. They provide us with ongoing information on the person's physical and mental health, emotions, etc.

"Is that a biofeedback one or a frequency modulator?" Zogar enquired.

"Frequency modulator, so it should help alleviate the gall bladder problem he's developing," Dagar replied. "Did you manage to get a decent sample down your end?"

"Not too bad. Funny that, the way some of these Earth humans are happy to spread their seed far and wide without much thought at all for the consequences, and yet when we take a tiny sample they get all upset about it, and so angry and embarrassed. For goodness sake, *they* do artificial insemination procedures all the time on other creatures on their planet, so what's the big deal?"

Once the job was done, I placed a hand on the man's head, causing a shift in his vibrational frequency. That way we could return him safely to his bed, and with a bit of luck he wouldn't remember anything the next morning, although he probably would notice the long, straight, sealed cut on his leg down near the ankle, where a second implant had been inserted to implement further adjustments to his energy system.

15 ▶ BLUE

The public bar of the Exchange Hotel was already awash with conversation and beer. The hour was early, only half-past five on a Tuesday afternoon, so the voices were still reasonably subdued, unlike the raucous crescendo that would fill the room later in the evening as customers became increasingly charged with conviviality, good cheer and drunken outbursts brought about by over-indulgence in the amber fluid so enthusiastically consumed by Australian males both young and old.

A large, ginger-haired and bewhiskered man sat alone in a corner, muddy work boots sprawled under the table, calloused elbows slumped dejectedly on top, and unseeing eyes staring into the depths of an over-sized mug of beer, which sat still untouched in front of him. Just then a small, balding, sandy-colored man with a slight paunch overhanging the waistband of his faded and well-worn jeans approached Ginger Top in friendly greeting.

"G'day Blue! How ya goin' mate?"

No response was forthcoming.

"BLUE!" the small man raised his voice for a second attempt. "Wot's wrong with ya? Ya bloody DEAF or somethin'?"

The man called Blue jumped, as if waking from a dream.

"Ah, sorry mate, I was bloody miles away. How are ya? While since I seen ya."

"Yeah, too right! Been up to me arse in work. Yer'd think they'd give a man a break this time've year in this awful bloody weather, but nah, bloody phone never stops ringin'. Jus' f—in' amazin' wot people'll try ter flush down th' dunny, then bloody ring me at two bloody 30 in the damn mornin' ter git me ter come an' unblock the bloody pipes! Ah shit! Still, can't complain I s'pose. Better'n bein' on the dole fer Chrisake! Anyway, 'nuff of me, how about you mate? Still diggin' holes fer the bloody council?"

"Aw shit yeah, mate! An' still on the same bloody job as last time I saw ya. We'll be there fer the next ten bloody years I reckon, wot with 'go slows' an' strikes! Still, gotta keep the bastards honest, Johnno me ol' mate. Gotta keep 'em honest."

"Yeah mate, you're tellin' me. Bloody council! Pack of bastards if ya ask me! By the way, howzit with the missus away? Last time I saw ya she was takin' orf for two months' holiday on the Gold Coast wif 'er sister, wasn't she? Due back soon I s'pose, worse luck! Bet yous've en-joyed ya eight weeks've freedom, ya lucky sod!"

"Well," Blue replied with a deep sigh, "ter tell ya the truth, I'll be bloody glad ter see 'er back! A man gits a bit lonely after a while on 'is own."

"Oh HO! Ya mean when ya *not* gittin' a bit, ya randy ol' bugger! Thought yers was *well* past it by now!"

"Aw, knock orf the dumb jokes, ya silly bastard! Anyway, that's not wot I'm damn-well talkin' about. An' I'm *not* bloody past it if ya really wanna know! Not by a long shot! Jes' ask the missus if ya don't believe me! But hell no mate, that's not the bloody problem."

"Well, wot is it then, Blue? Don't tell me ya scared stayin' in the house all on ya lonesome. Wotcha worried about? Bogey Men or some-thin'?"

"Ah, shaddup, Johnno! Yer an idiot!"

"Nah, seriously mate, all kiddin' aside. I could see when I come in that yers were worried about somethin'. Fair dinkum, yers were right orf with the fairies! Look mate, ya can tell me, after all, we bin mates fer a long bloody time — ol' cobbers through thick an' thin. Wot are mates for, anyway?'

"Shit no. Yer'll jes' laugh!"

"No I won't, Blue. Fair dinkum! Struth mate, we all got some-thin' we're scared of. You'd prob'ly piss yerself laughin' if I told ya I was scared bloody stiff of frogs. All soft an' spongy an' slimey! Yuk! Couldn' touch one o' them nasty little buggers if ya paid me a million dollars! Now come on, mate, out with it! Wot's botherin' ya?"

"Ah shit, Johnno, I dunno! It all started with these funny sorta dreams I bin gittin' for Gawd knows how long."

Blue shuddered at the memory, and took a long swig of beer. The pair of them sat in silence for almost a full minute as he went back to staring unseeing into his mug.

Finally Johnno's curiosity and impatience got the better of him. "Well, go on, mate," he prodded. "Wot about the dreams?"

Blue took another prolonged swallow, his Adam's apple bobbing up and down as he emptied his mug in an attempt to give himself 'dutch courage' before going on.

"Well, let's see. Mostly they start with this really weird sensation of me whole body bein' lifted up orf the bed, an' I'm all sorta paralyzed, like I can't move a bloody muscle. Bloody awful feelin' it is I'm tellin ya. Look, you know me, Johnno mate. I'm a bloke who likes ter be in control of the situation — ya know wot I mean? Me own boss kinda thing, not a bloody puppet controlled by some other bastard. Anyway, after I'm lifted up, I find meself on board some sorta bloody craft, like a flyin' saucer thingo. I'm lyin'on a table, with these really weird little creeps doin' things ter me. Oh, Gawd, it's bloody 'orrible!"

"Jeez mate! Like wot do they *do* ter ya?" Johnno was agog.

"Aw cripes, it's like they take stuff outta me, blood an' such like. An' sometimes the dirty little creeps even put some sorta contraption over me privates an' you know, *do* stuff ter me ter git a *sample*!"

"Wotcha mean — a *sample*, Blue?"

"Aw fer cryin'out bloody loud, Johnno! You know wot I mean! Do I hafta spell it out for yers? SPERM mate! Bloody SPERM! Gawd it's embarrassing, I'm tellin' ya!" Blue shuddered at the very thought, his face turning bright crimson right to the roots of his ginger hair.

"Now jus' *hang on* a minute mate!" Johnno interrupted. "First ya tellin' me it's dreams ya havin', now ya tellin' me ya atcherly getting' stuff *done* ter ya! Who is it wot's doin' all this anyway?"

"Ah jeez mate, that's the worst bloody part! They ain't human! They jus' *ain't bloody human*!"

"How do ya friggin' mean they ain't human?"

"Jus' wot I said! Not bloody human! They're real freaks, like bloody robots, or puppets, or insects or somethin'! All really skinny an' a sorta gray color, with big heads an' *huge* bloody black eyes that sorta wrap around their skulls!"

"Crikey Blue, ya kiddin'! Hey, I've jus' had a thought! Whyn't ya set ol' Baz on 'em next time they come afta yers. Good ol' Baz'd give 'em a run fer their bloody money!"

"Aw come orf it Johnno! Wot'd an ol' ginger tom like Bazza do against little creeps like that? They ain't sparrers or grass'oppers! A man'd be better orf settin' a cattle dog on 'em — or better still, a bloody great pit bull! Yeah, come ter think of it, I might jus' git meself a nice big bully! But hell's bells, I don' reckon even one o' them'd do much good against those little bleeders! It's like I sed before mate — they jus' ain't bloody HUMAN!"

"Bloody hell Blue, you sure ya ain't dreamin'? I mean ter say, maybe yers're goin' balmy an' imaginin' all this! Shit, it can't *really* be happenin'. Maybe ya should go see a shrink or somethin'."

"Johnno, mate, I'm not bloody imaginin' it! I've got friggin' proof! Physical bloody evidence as the coppers'd say!"

"What? Aw come orf it Blue!"

"Struth I have mate! Look here."

So saying, Blue bent down and rolled his thick sock down to the top of his boot, revealing bruises on his lower leg in the exact shape of four-fingered hands. Between them was a long, perfectly straight cut, obviously caused by an extremely sharp surgical instrument. Tiny blisters ran the length of the incision, as if it had been sealed artificially.

"Jesus H. Christ!" Johnno gasped in a voice tinged with fear and disbelief. "I need a drink! A bloody strong one!"

"My shout mate," said Blue in a sick and quavering voice. "Let's make it a double bloody scotch!"

"Aw shit, Blue, I could go a triple. With a beer chaser!"

16 ▶ REALM HISTORY 101

"Your attention, please, everybody!" Maris's strong telepathic command cut through the conversations of the assembled group of 30 as his blue light body floated up to the front of the lecture hall on the big disc. With no clinical work scheduled for the night, he was able to comfortably remain in his true form rather than having to don one of the specially created gray containers which constitute our physical working garb. He was appearing tonight as a blue light, as he was carrying out communication work. A couple of the students were also completely out of body, although most, myself included, still dressed in a container while on the disc. These containers were stored on board, ready for us to step into when required. Our gray containers are totally attuned to our own individual energy signature.

"In tonight's lecture," he began, "I will cover a little more of the fascinating history of our beloved Realm. After the destruction of the Atlantean civilization, which gave rise to the so-called 'great flood' of the Bible, our people were forced to leave Planet Earth in the hands of the Controllers. Over the following millennia we regrouped, expanded and grew in strength, and eventually were ready to return, to try to make things right. Nothing had been heard of the negative group for some time, so we assumed they had self-destructed, along with Atlantis.

"Our people established a base in the northern part of what Earth humans call India, in the Himalaya Mountains. This base housed about 3,000 personnel and was set up inside a mountain which had been hollowed out to create a large enough area to accommodate a number of our discs as well as staff members. Thus our installation was well hidden from the local human population, who, seeing our ships regularly coming and going overhead, came to know them as 'Vimanas.' It was during this period that we introduced the Vedic Teachings to this area on the planet, in a bid to restore some of the lost spiritual heritage to the native inhabitants.

"Not too long after we'd established our presence there, our base came under a surprise attack from a remnant of the Controller Forces. We were completely unaware of the fact that they had their own underground base on Mars, probably since the time of Atlantis, and had been observing us for some time. All of our personnel were captured, subjected to torture, including brainwashing by the Controllers' crystal-energy technique, then forcibly removed from their gray containers and imprisoned inside Earth human containers, from which they could not escape."

It was obvious to all of us present in the room that, even after many millennia, our Teacher was still deeply affected by the memory of this terrible catastrophe that befell our people. Unlike Earth humans, dying does not interfere with our soul memories. With so much more soul consciousness awake and expanded, especially at the Teacher level, Maris is consciously aware of his entire soul history plus that of our whole civilization, so events that occurred long ago are still reasonably fresh in his mind.

To Earth human eyes we may seem lacking in "normal" qualities and emotions, but we, the soul essence and personality motivating the artificial containers we reside in, are every bit as alive, sentient and "feeling" as any Earth human. In fact we share exactly the same God Consciousness as Earth humans, and of every other civilization throughout the universe. The only difference is that our emotions vibrate on a higher frequency, way beyond the very limited perception of energy that Earth humans can detect. And, being in artificial or semi-artificial bodies, we cannot easily express our emotions physically. These containers are designed specifically for travel in deep space.

The problem is, Earth humans tend to measure everything in the universe by their own capabilities and perceptions, but what they can't, or don't want to understand is that their capabilities and perceptions are extremely limited and therefore do not make a reliable yard stick with which to measure what is going on outside of their own immediate area. Even though we may be viewed as robots sometimes, our emotions run very strong, and at that moment it was obvious to us that our beloved Teacher was still affected by these past memories. Quite some time passed before his light body regained its full brightness, but masterfully controlling his emotions, he continued with the lesson.

"Naturally we were extremely upset by the loss of our recently established base and all of our personnel, including disc pilots and crew, as well as communication, medical and administrative staff, so we sent a rescue mission to Earth to look for them. This group was also attacked, captured and treated in the same way as the others, having their memories removed and replaced with false screen images and hypnotic commands, and imprisoned on Earth in biological bodies.

"Some of them are still down there, along with the native inhabitants of the planet, because until recently the energies of Earth have prevented us from reaching them. Trying to approach physically to pick them up is too dangerous, and their minds are still too deeply affected by

Controller-engendered illusions and fear for communication to be established telepathically. These members of our lost patrol are the ones we are especially trying to re-establish contact with, in order to wake them up to their true identity. We have managed to fit them all with implants so we can keep track of them, but they've been so brainwashed by the fear-mongering tactics of the Controllers, our job is not easy. Our goal is to just wake them up to the truth of who and what they really are, then their own free will and self-empowerment will be enough to set them free. This of course applies to all the others down there as well — they just need to know the truth of what is really going on.

"During our investigation into the loss of our base, we discovered that the Controllers had been operating their own secret base for millennia. We sent our ships out to do battle with them, and we finally defeated them in a massive space war. This battle, which had its beginnings in the skies over India, is the so-called War in Heaven so graphically described in the Vedas.

"One of the cleverest tricks used by the Controllers is to block humans from an understanding and acceptance of reincarnation. To acknowledge the birth and subsequent re-birth of the soul over many lives also entails an acknowledgement of the eternal continuation of sentient consciousness after so-called death. When a person can consciously recall past lives, they are able to access the accumulated knowledge, wisdom and experience that they have acquired over those past lives, and they also gain an intrinsic understanding of the oneness of all life through the memories of having lived in many different forms in various times and places. With access to this deeper knowledge, a soul can eventually break free of the Wheel of Karma, but without access, they become eternally trapped in a role of disempowered robotic obedience.

"It is only when humans become consciously aware of the process of reincarnation, and are able to accept it fully, that they can move past the endless cycle of birth and rebirth. *The key to release from the Wheel of Karma is conscious awareness.* Without this awareness, a soul remains trapped, and unable to move beyond the illusions and amnesia of the astral plane.

"The spiritual knowledge that our people brought to Earth is the basis of the Vedic teachings of India, which is why the doctrine of reincarnation is followed in that country, and has now been carried through into the more modern system known as Buddhism. The plan was working well as the knowledge was passed on to other indigenous Earth peoples as well over the millennia, including the Native Americans and Australian Aborigines, who honor and deeply respect the teachings brought to Earth by the Star Nations.

"With the system and its teachings beginning to spread from India to the west via the Middle East through other teachers, we could see Earth humans getting their power back, but then the Controllers stepped in, labeling it as 'an evil heathen belief,' effectively removing it once again from human consciousness by accusing its adherents of 'heresy' and putting them to death. Exactly the same thing has happened in the other indigenous cultures, where ancient lore passed down from the Star Nations has been labeled as 'heathen superstition' and replaced by Controller beliefs."

"Maris," a student asked, "Why are Earth humans still under the influence of these Controllers if we defeated them all those millennia ago?"

"What you need to understand," our Teacher answered, "is that even though we defeated the Controllers, their influence is still strong on Earth and will remain so while human free will allows it free rein. This we cannot stop. We may be able to destroy their bases and drive them away awhile, but if people on the planet do not exercise their God-given rights to soul knowledge and deeper understanding, then they will always return, as they have, and there is nothing we can do to stop them. That is the bottom line! It all hinges on human free will."

"So what do humans need to do to achieve their freedom?" someone asked.

"Souls can potentially escape from the clutches of the Controllers because their influence only reaches as far as the astral plane," Maris explained. "The Controllers cannot impinge on higher dimensions because of their lower-energy frequency. More highly evolved souls can descend to lower frequencies, but lower-evolved entities cannot rise above their own frequency bands, so the key to breaking free of the Controllers' power play is for humans to raise their own energy frequencies to as high a level as they possibly can. This can be achieved, as the Buddha once taught, through following the eight-fold path of right living, right mindfulness, right views, right speech, right action, right endeavor, right thinking and right meditation or spiritual practice, which must include an understanding of reincarnation. Right views, by the way, simply means learning to look at life through the perspective of oneness and love rather than through the duality of separateness and fear.

"If at the point of death humans are caught up in the illusion that they are nothing more than a physical body, with no soul or spiritual aspect, then their minds will be wiped completely clean. If they have any awareness at all it will be of black nothingness, before they are returned with no soul memory whatsoever to yet another life of mortal toil upon the physical plane.

"If, on the other hand, they believe that at the end of one single existence on Earth they will either be rewarded for eternity in 'heaven' or else be punished for eternity in 'hell,' then that is the screen image that will be placed in their mind by the Controllers. This false image is taken directly from their own personal beliefs of how they expect 'heaven' or 'hell' to be. After this image has been imposed upon them, their minds will then gradually fade away into oblivion, and they will be returned, just like the non-believers, to another life in mortal form.

"A major problem on Earth is that too many people insist on giving their power away. They either cannot or do not want to understand that God is within, and that everything they need in the way of power and knowledge is inside self. Instead, they continue to look outside of themselves for answers. In the old days they looked to the church or government to 'save them,' and now ETs and 'Space Brothers' have been added to the list. We are not here as gods, saviors or demons. We cannot 'save' humanity, neither can we provide all the answers. All we can do is to help humans move beyond the manipulation being imposed on their minds by awakening them to a deeper understanding of their *own* empowerment, but we cannot run people's lives or intervene in all the problems that arise on Earth.

"Because Earth Humans give their power away, they don't take responsibility for their own soul journey! And of course the Controllers have cashed in on this over many millennia, brainwashing them into this state of total disempowerment and dependency. But now the time has come for Earth humans to wake up — and we are here to help the process — to push them past the fear and back into a state of love and self-empowerment. Quite often, just by seeing us, they awaken.

"No wonder the negative forces do everything in their power to convince them that we are 'evil gray aliens' come to abduct them and 'take over the planet.' The very last thing the Controllers want is for humans to be free of their influence and mind control, so their tactic is to turn the whole thing around to make us the demons."

"Is that why they have a snake as their emblem?" I asked. "Is that also to deflect blame away from themselves and onto the Reptoid people?"

"Yes," Maris replied, "that is exactly what their aim is, and it has worked well for them since the time of ancient Egypt and before. It was the Controllers themselves who were responsible for setting up many of the secret societies, brotherhoods and 'mystery schools.' They pretended that they were the keepers of some sort of amazing secret knowledge that would provide eternal salvation to the elite few who were members of these societies. There was a group of Controllers known as the Priesthood or Brotherhood of the Serpent, and the snake has been their symbol for as long as I can recall, so it goes back a very long way.

"The truth of the matter is, however, that the Controllers are totally human in appearance. They are neither 'Greys' nor Reptilians. They usually appear as very good-looking humans, because they know how caught up Earth humans are in physical appearance, so that is how they generally show themselves, sometimes even turning up in meditation groups as 'highly evolved spiritual masters.' Although sometimes when they're getting up to mischief they'll try to pass themselves off as one of our people, but they can never get the eye shape quite right, and their energy feels awful. Really and truly, their cunning knows no bounds!

"And so," Maris concluded, "with strong Controller influences still present in the astral plane, our communication at that level is very often interfered with, distorted and unreliable. Earth humans generally cannot access the higher frequencies in which we can communicate more clearly, so what to do?

"Time is running out as 2012 fast approaches on Planet Earth, and those who are not willing to open up their consciousness to higher realities will be trapped in yet another cycle of divisiveness and separation and reborn into another era of war and conflict, for that is their mindset and the only reality they know and accept and therefore create for themselves. As all of you know, we create our own reality according to the way we think. If Earth humans truly wish to progress to the next level of the Human Ladder, they must change their way of thinking, but they cannot do this without access to deeper understanding and knowledge. It is up to ones such as yourselves, who have bravely volunteered to be born into Earth-plane lives as native inhabitants of the planet, to assist in the spreading of this knowledge and deeper understanding. From experience, we have found that the safest and easiest way to reach those trapped on that planet is through our own people working and teaching down there in physical forms that humans can easily see, hear and relate to on their own terms.

"As many of you now realize, by familiarizing humans with your energy signature in this way, when you do contact them at night in your gray, Zeta form, they still recognize you on an energy level and so experience a little less fear. Your attendance at these classes here on the disc will enable you to access the Guardian Group Consciousness more fully, so you in turn can carry out the work of passing on the necessary information to your human contacts. As Guardians, this is our task. Now, speaking of work, I am aware that a number of you have tasks to complete before morning, so class dismissed."

17 ▸ Dual Lives

After finishing high school, Paco stuck to his resolve of wanting to study for the Priesthood, which meant I would have to perform on my own, and this worried me. I enjoyed dancing, but I found the idea of being in the public eye very daunting, especially if I had to do it alone, with no dance partner. For some time now, Maris had been advising me to take up meditation on a more regular basis, but this wasn't so easy for a professional dancer. He then came up with the idea of Tai Chi, which is known as "moving meditation," as a useful bridge between the two.

The Guardians look upon dance as an outer expression of inner balance and harmony, and Tai Chi is the ultimate form, being a meditation technique as well. If Paco and I could no longer perform together, then I would dedicate myself to learning this discipline to the best of my ability, with a view to one day teaching it to others as part of my Guardian work on Planet Earth. After all, a major part of this work is assisting humans to balance and harmonize their *chi* — their life-force energy, to enable them to evolve to the next level of the Human Ladder.

Early in the new year Paco left for the seminary, and we all missed him terribly, especially Mara. I felt a gaping void in my life without my spiritual brother to talk to, dance with, and generally keep me well-grounded in human life, but I had no choice but to get on with life.

It was almost 12 months before he returned home for the following Christmas holidays. Not having seen him face to face for so long, I worried that he'd be different somehow, perhaps more reserved or overly pious, but he was nothing of the sort. Thank goodness he was still the same old Paco, ready and willing as usual to tease me mercilessly at every opportunity.

In fact, when I told him of my fears, he burst out laughing. "Me? Pious and reserved? Ha! You've got to be kidding! Wait till you hear what we get up to at the seminary! Anyway Ali Cat, you're the one who's changed. You're not the scrawny, scruffy little thing you used to be. I think Tai Chi must be doing you good. Come on, show me what you've learned, then we'll see if we can still remember how to dance flamenco. But hang on a minute," he said, leaning forward and peering at me closely, "What's that?"

"What's what?" I squeaked in alarm.

"Oh my God!" he breathed, leaning even closer for a better look, mouth agape and eyes wide with shock.

"Paco, what is it? What's the matter?"

"Oh, it's okay," he grinned, taking a step back. "It's just your face. I didn't recognize it without dirt on it!"

Meanwhile for me, it was work as usual each night on the disc. As my human body and mind matured, so my "upstairs" life changed as well. It was as though one was a reflection, or perhaps a parallel, of the other. The classes continued, so that along with the understanding I was acquiring from the human perspective through my intensive studies in Tai Chi, Qi Gong and Eastern medical philosophy, as a Guardian I was also opening up to a much deeper understanding of life-force energy and learning how to work with it on multidimensional layers related to healing and transmutation.

As caretakers of this energy within a number of galactic levels, virtually everything we do as Guardians is centered around energy work of some sort, and Planet Earth is the main concern for us at this time, with a huge amount of rebalancing and healing needed over the next few years. The work load is enormous, despite the fact that we're getting invaluable help from several other ET races as well, so it's "all hands on deck" at the moment.

"I really don't know who organizes all this," I grumbled to my good friend, Ashka, when we happened to run into each other in one of the endless corridors of the disc at the start of our nightly shift. I'd spent the past five minutes checking through my task list, and it did not make sense at all.

"Will you look at this? How the heck am I supposed to cover all of this in one night? It's just ridiculous!"

"Well," Ashka shrugged, "you can't really blame anybody. It's the computer that makes up the work schedules."

An uncharacteristically emotional response flashed onto the small monitor I was holding in the palm of my hand: "Now, now, don't go blaming me! I only process the data that's been given me!"

"But it's your job to collate and sort it appropriately into a workable timetable!" I telepathed back at the now rapidly fading screen.

Its rejoinder was a loud and rudely eloquent beep.

A rippling wave of intense amusement washed over me from Ashka. "You don't have much luck with computers, do you, Alarca? It's got you bouncing back and forth from one hemisphere of the planet to the other like a tennis ball."

"Hey look," I interrupted her, touching my finger to the screen to bring the schedule up again, then — "ouch!" as I received a mild electric shock in answer to my earlier remark about the computer's questionable efficiency level. "These first two calls are to psychic-development groups. At least that should make things easier, because humans in such groups are usually open to visits from other dimensions. I'll probably need to use a bit of a disguise, because even psychics sometimes freak out if we appear in our gray containers. One day they'll realize that positive messages and teachings can also come from funny-looking little ETs with big eyes. Oh well, at least they are open to other dimensions and realities."

"Let's have a look," said Ashka, leaning over my shoulder. "Oh, dear! Sorry, Alarca, but no. You've got a problem here, my friend. These two groups were on my schedule last week, and the first one is fine. The woman who runs it is a good soul who is genuinely psychic and is carrying out her work in order to assist others to learn to tap into their own latent abilities. In that group you won't even need to disguise yourself, because she is sensitive to energy and will know that you come in the name of Oneness. In fact the energy generated by that group is so warm and loving I didn't want to leave, but the other group — aagh! They are a different matter altogether."

"Why?" I asked in alarm.

"Well," Ashka replied, "the one who runs it has a ... er, how shall I put it, a teensy bit of an over-inflated ego problem, so if you don't get there early enough, the lower astral entities will beat you to it every time. Once they invade the group, the energies become so heavy and black that you'll have a hard time even getting into the room, let alone into the circle to deliver any constructive messages or teaching."

"Yes, well, Ashka," I answered, "I guess these are the types that think they can recite a nice little prayer of protection before they start, and call down the 'white light' or whatever, then they will be automatically protected from negative astral plane entities — but the bottom line is *intention*. It is not who or what they call in with their mouths, but rather who or what they call in *with their hearts* that counts. If they are caught up with an over-inflated ego, or greed, or a need to control and manipulate others, then you can guarantee there'll be problems ahead, no matter what sort of 'protection' they call upon."

"You're telling me," Ashka replied with a shudder. "Last time I went to that particular group to give out some teachings and messages, one of the Controllers had beaten me to it. When I arrived on the scene he was standing directly behind the one in charge of the group, very cleverly disguised as a Great Spiritual Master, shining white robes and all, giving out a rambling channeled message through the medium, who in all sincerity believed she really was channeling a Master.

"As is usual in such cases, some of the things he was saying were quite correct, and it was all very nice and flowery, but there was also a good amount of unprovable garbage as well, all spoken in a very formal and archaic voice using lots of big words, so it sounded good and impressed his audience. Of course, I could not intervene or do anything about it, because the energy of the group had called him in, and I couldn't override free will. Believing him to really be a Great Master, they wanted him there — in fact, they were absolutely thrilled to bits to have him present. Let me tell you, Alarca, it was most frustrating."

"But what I still can't understand," I went on, "is if they are as psychic and clairvoyant as they think they are — and some are — why can't they see past the outer shell that these negative entities hide behind? I mean, for heaven's sake, even if they are disguising themselves as an Angel, or a 'great Spiritual Master,' or a 'Space Brother,' all dressed up in shining white robes, why the heck don't people try to sense behind all the outer dressing to feel the underlying energy? That, after all, is the only true way to tell if an entity is good, bad or indifferent."

"I don't know, Alarca," Ashka answered, sadly shaking her head. "Problem is, even though humans can sense energy, and some are quite good at it, maybe they simply can't sense past the astral level, so they can't perceive deeper energies. Or they tune in clairvoyantly, but then they get taken in by outer appearance, and of course the Controllers know this and take advantage of it. Unfortunately, many of these groups will allow anyone in spirit to approach, providing they look attractive by human standards — preferably tall, blond-haired and dressed in white! This is precisely why we have so many problems approaching people, and why we often need help from our Pleiadian friends, who look more 'human.' It's so frustrating the way some Earth folk project their own prejudices onto the various off-world visitors. They just can't seem to comprehend that we all work together in oneness, no matter what our container looks like."

"I hear you, Ashka, but all we can do is keep trying. Thanks for the timely warning. I'll make sure I get there early tonight to try to block his entrance, and a bit of a disguise will definitely be needed. With egos like that I really don't think a little gray space person would make much of an impression on them. In fact they'd probably think that I'm a negative astral-plane entity, so maybe I'd better take an angelic or at least more human form for this particular job.

"Gee it's great being back with you, Ashka," I said, putting my arm around her shoulders and giving her a friendly hug. "You've experienced many more past lives on Earth then me, so you have a much deeper insight into the Earthling psyche than I ever will. I'm sure that if it had been you rather than me left behind down there after our accident, you wouldn've been able to bring much more information back to the Guardian Consciousness."

"Yes, well, I did feel awful about leaving you behind down there, Alarca," she replied, "and would you believe I also have trouble driving cars when I'm in human form, just like you? The crash of our disc back then must've made a very deep and lasting impression upon both our psyches."

"Oh, come on, Ashka, don't feel bad about it. After all, on one level of reality it was meant to be, to provide one of us with an opportunity to spend time down there among Earth humans. Anyway, I did learn an awful lot while I was there, and gave them a few things to think about as well!" I added with a chuckle.

"And by the way," I continued, "speaking of spending time down there, have the arrangements been made for us to meet up in human form yet? With the work load we have ahead of us on the Earth Plane, we'll really need to do this soon."

"As a matter of fact, Alarca, I asked Oris about it a couple of nights ago, and he said there are still a few things that need to be put into place. Remember we're working within the time frame of a third-dimensional physical planet, so we have to abide by that and be patient.

"And I still haven't allowed my human consciousness access to my Guardian consciousness. My daughter Kira is still only a baby, and I plan to have at least one more child, so I feel I need to focus totally on my human life at the moment. Conscious recall of the work I'm doing up here would be too much of a distraction. After all, I'm supposed to be completely immersed in human life as a wife and mother, so I'd prefer to just concentrate on that for now."

"You are sensible doing it that way, Ashka, and the experience you're getting as a mother on Earth would be of tremendous benefit to your work up here with some of those weak and sickly hybrid babies we have to rescue on such a regular basis. I wish those humans down there would stop trying to play God and just leave the genetic work to us! Besides, we have billions of years of experience, and it's *human life* they're playing around with, for heaven's sake!"

"I know, and *we're* the ones getting the blame for this, just as they blame us for the animal mutilations. It makes me ill just thinking about it! But anyway, on a lighter note — how is it going down there? Are you managing to get through all that study you planned to undertake? You still have a way to go, don't you?"

"Oh, my goodness, yes! I have years of it to look forward to, because Maris wants me to teach people about energy, but no short-cuts are allowed — you know what he's like. I also have a couple of karmic knots to unravel, so I do agree we'll have to postpone meeting up down there for now, but it'll be fun when we do! Look out Planet Earth — here we come!"

Returning home in the early hours of the morning, I entered my bedroom through the closed door. By now I was quite familiar with the pleasant tingling sensation as the finer, higher frequency molecules of my energy body passed in between the coarser, lower-frequency wood molecules. This ability to move solid objects such as bodies through other solid objects such as walls really had the UFO investigators of Planet Earth scratching their heads in perplexity, but with the technology we have at hand it is not so very difficult — just a matter of temporarily adjusting the vibrational frequency of the molecular structure up a notch or two, and creating a corridor through the time/space continuum.

For a few moments I hovered beside my bed, looking down at my inert human container stretched out in sleep. Thank goodness I'd left it in a reasonably comfortable position! It wouldn't be too stiff and cramped to get going once I slipped back in. Moving slowly and carefully, I gently lowered myself down into the exact position in which the physical body was lying, feeling a cold, stiff sensation as Guardian consciousness melded into human consciousness. It was only then that I was able to wake up properly in my body.

In order to carry out my "upstairs" work properly, the human container requires an adequate amount of sleep — up to 10 hours a night if possible, which requires me to sleep alone, so that I am not disturbed in any way during my working hours on board the disc. When the human container is left behind, it must be maintained in a very deep sleep state.

It took a minute or so of reorienting before I could move my body enough to check the bedside clock. Much to my relief, it was only 5:30, which meant I'd have time to relax for a bit longer to meditate on the day ahead, as Maris had instructed me to do first thing each morning.

"You don't need to spend hours in meditation, Alarca. Just put a little time aside at the beginning and end of each day to look quietly within and to ask for direction from your Higher Self."

Lying quietly in bed, I focused on the written exam in Eastern medical philosophy coming up in a few hours. Without this, I wouldn't have the necessary qualifications to become an instructor of Tai Chi and Qi Gong. The practical examination in Chinese massage therapy had gone well, as had the empty-hand and weapon forms of Tai Chi in which I'd had to prove myself, but today's theory examination was the one that worried me the most. There was just so much to remember.

I attempted to collect my human thought processes of what I'd learned during the semester into some kind of order. My mind went back over such fascinating topics as the five ways to recognize the presence of life-force energy, known in Chinese medical philosophy as *chi*, or *qi*, depending upon whether you were speaking Cantonese or Mandarin, and which acupressure points would be used to ease such problems as muscular pain, headache, insomnia and nausea (a handy one to know when taking an examination in Chinese medicine!).

Then there were the definitions of the three aspects of the *san bao* to remember — those manifestations of life-force known as *qi, jing* and *shen*, and their respective polarities of yin and yang. And of course the important functions of the kidneys in Chinese medicine would be sure to be included, and we had to know all seven. My goodness, it was almost harder than what we had to study "upstairs"!

When I'd raised an objection to all of this with Maris, pointing out that I was learning it in class on the disc anyway, so why must I learn it in human class as well, he very deftly squashed my argument.

"Because, Alarca," he said, "knowing it at Guardian level does not necessarily mean you can access it on the conscious human level. These classes you are attending on Earth serve to ground the knowledge in your human brain. And for the same reason, once you pass this exam, I want you to be attuned to Reiki, which will be highly compatible with the Qi Gong and Tai Chi."

"Oh," I replied with a grin, "that'll be easy. Just the other day I saw an ad in a magazine offering all three levels in one weekend. I'll be a Reiki Master before you know it."

Guardian teachers are usually fairly patient, and not prone to raising their voices, but this time I had obviously over-stepped the limits of Maris's self-control.

"Alarca!" The sheer force of his telepathic outburst nearly knocked me off my feet. "You will *not* learn to be a Reiki 'Master' in a weekend! Don't be ridiculous! As a Guardian you should have far more understanding of and respect for universal energy than to make such an assumption. A human body's energy system frequency needs to be turned up *gradually* — it cannot be done in *one* weekend. One weekend indeed! And don't you dare tell me that as a Guardian you don't need to learn such things as Reiki and Qi Gong. You are in a *human* body, which is extremely difficult to maintain in a state of balance and harmony.

"No, Alarca," he continued a little more calmly. "You will take your time to learn Reiki properly, so that one day in the future — not next month, or next year, or even in three years — but one day when you have gained a little more maturity and spiritual understanding, you will be able to teach it to others, with a proper and thorough comprehension of what you are doing.

"Also," he went on, "while we are on the subject, when you are fully qualified to teach, that is what you will refer to yourself as — a

Teacher! Not a Master! In the Japanese tradition where Reiki sprang, they do not call themselves Master but rather Sensei, which translates as Teacher. You are not a Master until you have learned to master self, and believe me, there are very few on Planet Earth able to make such a claim, and those who can have well and truly moved past any need or desire to attach such a title as Master to themselves!"

"But Maris," I objected, "surely after so many years of study I'll eventually be able to make some sort of claim to mastership?"

"No, Alarca, you will not!" he answered emphatically. "Mastership is not about what knowledge you have acquired, achieved or learned during your life, but rather about what you have been able to *let go of*. And that includes letting go of the need for such labels as Master. And I'm sorry, Alarca, but you *do* have some way to go yet."

My mind went back over the past few years of my life, to all that I had learned and accomplished. I thought of the incredibly mind-blowing experience of being able to see everything from two perspectives, as a Guardian soul in human physical form, but then I thought of the loneliness it entailed, and how I could never live a totally normal human life like others around me. Talk about non-attachment — my whole life felt that way — non-attached! With the responsibilities of a young family to take care of, no wonder Ashka preferred to keep the two aspects completely separate for now.

The examination that afternoon went better than I expected. For once, luck was with me and I was able to remember all that was required, even a couple of the more obscure acupressure points that I really didn't think had registered with me. Maybe more was filtering through from my Guardian consciousness than I was humanly aware of. But then again, I had studied hard as well and actually liked what I was studying.

Feeling reasonably confident that I'd done well, I went to bed that evening in a much more relaxed frame of mind. The atmosphere was relaxed on the disc that night too. In fact quite a party mood prevailed as we mingled with our Pleiadian friends who'd come on board, and also with some others of the various Star Nations who had joined us. I couldn't help but observe how different it was here than on Earth — how such vast differences in physical appearance are respected and honored. This was really brought home to me at the sight of one of our tall, thin, large-headed, black-clad Elders comfortably engaged in telepathic conversation with the equally tall, blond-haired, very human-looking Pleiadian, Solarno. It was obvious they were sharing a joke together, and the aura of deep respect and mutual unconditional love passing between them was quite tangible to behold.

18 ▶ A RITE OF PASSAGE

After passing my exams, I spent three years working as an instructor at the Tai Chi school where I'd done my training, then I took on the challenge of establishing my own school. I also completed three levels of Reiki, spending several years as a practitioner before going on to so-called Master Level, which qualified me to teach. These studies were undertaken slowly and thoroughly, as instructed by Maris, and looking back, I could fully appreciate why such time was required.

Maris was right that profound energy work cannot be rushed in a human body — time and patience are the keys to success. After attaining what Western Reiki practitioners call Master Level, my "upstairs family" put further opportunities in place for me to undertake deeper studies in the original Eastern tradition. This was done over a five-year period, involving a number of very profound initiations connected to the Mandala of the Healing Buddha. These initiations dealt with the attainment of self realization, which in turn enabled me to undergo further upgrades of my energy system to bring human and Guardian consciousness into even closer alignment.

At the same time, Paco followed a parallel path in his more traditional studies, and at the end of six years of seminary training, he took up a position as Assistant Priest in a parish some distance from home.

Mara was still with us and I loved visiting with her as much as possible, but felt guilty that my work now kept me away too often. Her health was declining, so it shouldn't have surprised me that one night during a very profound and lucid dream state, I found myself accompanying Mara up a steep and rocky mountainside. The way was rough and difficult, so I placed my arm around her, so she could lean on me for support. I was not occupying my human body, but rather my more comfortable and familiar gray container. Once at the top, we stopped for a moment to rest, and there, laid out before us, sparkling and azure blue in the sunlight, was the most beautiful lake I had ever seen — so beautiful that I felt my heart would burst with joy at the very sight of it.

Turning large, black eyes towards Mara, I placed my hands on her temples, and, as I looked deeply into her eyes, I was aware once again of the beam of white light passing from my brow chakra into hers, then returning to me. For several minutes we stayed there, wrapped warmly in a cocoon of deep, mutual understanding and unconditional love as we communicated telepathically and exchanged energy through our higher chakras. Then slowly Mara's face began to change, as if a veil were being pulled away. Right there before my eyes I saw her lined and aged visage disappear to be replaced by another. It was still Mara, but she now appeared as she had been in the prime of her life, with a strong and supple body, and a youthful face framed with lustrous black hair.

I then became aware of another figure standing nearby — a most beautiful angelic being — tall, dark-haired and Romany-looking — who stood beside the lake, holding his hand out to her. For a moment she held my gray hands in her human ones, then with a smile of pure, radiant joy, she turned and went to him. I stood for a few moments more, watching them move towards the lake, where they gradually merged together as One, becoming a shimmering pillar of pure white light, which slowly disappeared from my sight.

The next morning I was not in the least surprised to be told by my parents that Mara had passed over during the night. Paco was given leave to attend to her funeral, which he insisted on conducting himself, and so the Romany customs were honored as well as the Catholic ones. As we ritually set fire to her *vardo*, containing all her belongings, he spoke the traditional words of the Romany Rite of Passage:

"The mourned should be allowed to continue on her voyage in the new life, as we should resume our lives. I open her way into the new life and release her from the fetters of our sorrow."

This act of burning all the possessions of a deceased person is done not simply as a ritual to mark their passing — it is done more to release the spirit from gross physicality, to allow it move on to where it needs to be. This is a carryover from the original Romany people of Northern India, who, as Guardians, had a much deeper understanding of the process of death than do Earth humans.

Even more important is the complete disposal of the physical remains of the deceased. Either the body must be buried or its ashes must be scattered and disposed of completely. If ashes are kept, the spirit is blocked and imprisoned from moving on to where it is should be by the emotional energy of whoever is preserving the remains. I realize that letting go may be very hard for some people, but in actual fact it allows the spirit to remain closer to loved ones if they wish to do so. When ashes are retained, part of the spirit's energy is trapped, which surely nobody would want for a loved one. The religious act of preserving saints' relics has the same effect of trapping and fragmenting the spirit.

I knew very well that the tears I shed were more for me than for Mara. After all, I had seen with my own eyes the pure joy on her face, as she set out upon her "voyage" on the azure lake, united at last with her higher self.

Before Paco returned to his work I took him quietly aside and told him of my dream, not mentioning the ET aspect of course, but describing how we walked up the mountain side together, and Mara's meeting with the angelic being. I wondered how, as a Catholic Priest, he would react to such a strange revelation, but I felt it was important for him to know. For a while he just sat there, staring at the floor, and I fully expected him to tell me not to be so ridiculous. But instead, after a few moments he looked straight into my eyes, then suddenly threw his arms around me.

"Oh, Ali, thank you! Thank you for helping her over. I know she had far more innate spiritual knowledge and true understanding than I will ever have, but it is good to know that she was not alone and unaided on her final journey."

Paco left the next day to return to his duties, and at first I worried about him, far away at his parish, being called upon to be a comfort and support to others in their times of trouble, when he really needed some comfort and support himself. However, he was a true Rom, with a far deeper understanding of the perfectly natural cycles of birth, death and rebirth than he gave himself credit for. He had cried openly and unashamedly at his grandmother's passing, thus allowing himself to express his grief rather than bottling it up inside as some tend to do, and so it quickly passed, freeing him to get on with his life.

Just as I had been fascinated as a child by the physical workings of my human body, I was now equally awed by the human perspective of emotion, the like of which my people, the Guardians, had not experienced in millennia. It's not that we lack emotion, but rather that we have learned not to allow it to affect or control our lives. But for me, dwelling as I was upon Earth, a planet governed very much by emotion, in a physical, human body, I could not help but be touched by it. I was not sure whether I enjoyed the sensation or not, but it was an interesting and different experience.

19 ▶ MISSING TIME

St. Sara's Day, May 25th, honors our patron saint and is celebrated by Romany people the world over. It provides us with a link back to our roots — to the time when we had a home and an identity, and a clear understanding of who and what we really are. It takes us back over many thousands of years to our very beginnings on this planet, and our reason for being present on Earth. For those few who know the full story, it also explains why we have never really fit in down here, and why the Controllers have taught others of the Earth human race to despise and distrust us.

Unless one looks at the bigger picture, the fact that Controllers attacked this lost Guardian patrol base in Northern India may seem a meaningless and tragic occurrence, but, from the universal perspective, there are no accidents — everything is meant to be, and happens for a reason. In fact, there was a very specific reason and a need for a small group of our people to be resident on Planet Earth, not clothed in our normal gray containers, or even in our true form as non-physical light beings, but rather housed in mortal Earth human bodies.

Numerous stories and legends have persisted over the years, and many misconceptions and untruths have been spread about the so-called "Gypsies," just as there have been misconceptions and untruths about the so-called "Greys." Over many generations, our race has been infiltrated by the Controllers, who set a bad example and portray us as very different from how we really are. The true Romanies are a gentle, more matriarchal society, quite different from all the aggressive, male-dominated societies set up on Planet Earth by the Controllers.

Preparations had been underway for weeks, and many friends from the Romany community were gathering for our own celebration of St. Sara. In the days leading up to May 25, the usually quiet road at the front of our property rather resembled the roads leading to the town of Saintes Maries de la Mer, with a number of brightly painted and some quite intricately carved trailer vans pulled up on the grassy verge. The days of colorful horse-drawn wagons are now well and truly over, particularly in a country such as Australia, where travelling from town to town usually involves very great distances.

Of course the battered old van belonging to Uncle Luis held pride of place in our driveway, providing an endless source of good-natured joking and amusement. A true master of lateral thinking and adaptability, he'd somehow managed to fit it out with a number of improvised "mod cons," including his very own private "home theatre" which consisted of an ancient TV set elaborately hooked up to an aerial on the roof of the van. For some reason this weird, patched up-looking device seemed to attract every bird from far and near to come and perch on it, which didn't do much for Luis's TV reception.

Paco too had come to join our celebrations, managing to take two whole weeks off from his parish duties. I had to wonder what excuse he's used! We spent several hours hard at work practicing a couple of dances as a contribution to the evening's festivities. Of course no Romany gathering would be complete without music and dance, and we knew very well that by nightfall everyone would be comfortably ensconced around the traditional campfire that is the heart of all Romany celebrations. With everyone well fed and relaxed under a night sky ablaze with stars seemingly close enough for us to reach up and touch them, guitars and violins would appear, seemingly from thin air, and we would be called upon to dance our *Alegrias*, *Soleares,* or perhaps a *Seguirya,* a favorite *cante jondo* of the *Gitanos,* the Gypsies of Spain.

Surrounded by friends and family from far and wide, and with the festive mood continuing for a couple of days, at first I didn't notice the subtle change in Paco, but as timed passed, I sensed something was badly amiss. By the end of the week life had returned to normal, providing me with an opportunity to speak to him alone.

"Paco, what's the matter?" I asked one morning, confronting him in the kitchen. "Are you upset about coming home for the first time after your grandmother's death?"

"No, Ali, not really. Of course I still miss her badly, but she was very old, and it was her time, so it would be selfish of me to hold her back with prolonged grief. Surely you know that."

"Well then," I pressed him, "what is wrong?"

"What do you mean wrong? Why do you ask?"

"Come on Paco, I know you well enough to know something is the matter. Is it your work? Aren't you happy being a priest anymore? Is that what's troubling you?"

"Oh, Ali, for heaven's sake, don't be silly. I'm perfectly happy and contented in my work, and couldn't possibly imagine myself doing anything else. I really do feel as if I am making a difference in people's lives — and you know what? Old Father Keating is actually proud of having a Gypsy as his assistant priest. One day he started asking me about my family, so I told him the truth, not really knowing what sort of reaction I would get, but he actually congratulated me for my determination and is now very supportive. Would you believe he even admitted to having some Romany blood himself?"

For the first time since he'd arrived home, I saw the old Paco, happy and enthusiastic as he spoke about his work, and his dream coming true of being accepted as a Romany within the Priesthood. I could clearly see that it was not work problems troubling him, so what was it? Paco could be so stubborn at times, and getting information out of him could be like trying to pry open a clam shell, but I was determined to find out somehow or other.

It was business as usual on board our disc that night, and a busy night it was going to be, with four procedures scheduled before morning. Our first human "guest" lay ready on the examination table. We had quite easily managed to teleport her, physical body included, out through the seemingly solid walls of the house and into our hovering craft.

Once on board we brought her back to a state of normal consciousness, and as usual, we attempted to reach her telepathically, but, just as we always found, the walls of emotion and terror closed around her, cutting her off and closing her mind to our telepathic messages of reassurance.

As part of my training I was taking special classes involving in-depth studies on human emotion, so it fell upon me to do something. Pushing my way with difficulty through the negative force-field of fear surrounding her, I placed my hands on her temples, drawing her face towards me and her eyes into mine. Slowly but surely a calm descended upon her, quietening her screams and struggles. Although we don't like doing such things, it was necessary to secure her to the table, to stop any chance of movement during the delicate procedure we were about to carry out. This was more for her safety than for ours.

Although she was not aware of her soul level agreement, we knew her higher self had given us full permission and, in fact, had requested these procedures to be carried out. We were not over-riding her free will, and I sure wish we could figure out how to get through this fear barrier. All our lives would be easier.

My mind began to wander to how I could teach my classes on Earth that human consciousness is multidimensional, and can be likened to an iceberg floating in the ocean. The small part of the mind that a level-one human is consciously aware of in physical life is like the tip of the iceberg which can be seen above the water. However, as with an iceberg, the greater part of the mind is hidden beneath the surface. This is the 90% which Earth humans do not consciously utilize, but whether they know it or not contains vast amounts of knowledge and awareness on a subconscious or super-conscious level.

If one is able to access even a small part of this hidden area of the mind, then information on such things as past lives, soul purpose, higher self and between-life states can easily be recalled. On occasions I raise this point with my students during class to help them to tap more deeply into this vast storehouse of knowledge and awareness of the soul mind, but the thing is, are they acknowledging it fully into both their hearts and minds? I must keep emphasizing that they are vastly more than just a physical body, but are immortal spiritual beings that have existed before and will continue to exist for eternity.

The other big thing I must help them with is mastering the ability to just detach a little from the myriad distractions of life, work and play which govern their lives and fill the minds of most mortals pulling them back again and again to physical life on…

"Hey, Alarca, pay attention!" My hands must have lost contact with the woman and Entil's command brought me back.

Once again, I took up a position behind the woman with my hands on her temples, directing calming energy into the head chakras and she became completely relaxed. This energy flowed automatically as long as my hands stayed in contact with her energy field, but since it took no conscious effort on my part, once again my mind began to wander. I thought of how many times we had done this, bringing both humans and animals on board our big disc, submitting them to numerous tests and probes, and sometimes even artificial insemination, always working towards the same end, which is the preservation of a world, and the species which dwell thereon.

Then a realization hit me about how some of them already feel a deep sense of love and oneness on the soul level, especially after they move past the fear that is blocking their inner awareness and open themselves more fully to us. Then they remember, feel the love and know this is part of their life choice. Maybe we are making progress with…

"Alarca, please. What is wrong with you tonight?"

"I'm sorry, Entil. My mind is full of thoughts about how we can reach these humans in a better way. I mean really get through to their subconscious."

"Well, that's fine, but keep your hands on this woman please."

"Ok, but Entil, have you ever thought about the incredible double life I lead — by day confined to a fully biological human body, then as my container sleeps safely in bed at night, I slip out of it and take up my work here on the disc? And depending on the duties to be performed, I can use either a semi-artificial and totally physical Zeta gray container, or else create an astral body with my mind, or on other occasions when no form at all is required I manifest simply as a light body, which is my true Guardian self?"

"Yes, Alarca. No wonder you are confused sometimes."

Then I thought about our other discs operating in the same area on the same night. Tomorrow's newspapers would perhaps carry reports of "strange lights" seen in the sky along the east coast of Australia, or else perhaps the sighting of a number of UFOs. If enough witnesses came forward, the story could even extend into the news of the day after, then, as usual, it would be brushed aside and forgotten in favor of more interesting and important news items such as the latest sex scandal of Hollywood, or the football and cricket results. Oh, well, in one way this made things easier for us. The last thing we need is publicity of the negative kind that the media seems to thrive on.

Suddenly a most terrible jarring sensation shook my whole body, rudely shattering my train of thought. A horrific vision hit me, of our disc being bombarded by a giant meteor, or, worse still, another collision and crash. Following procedure I threw myself down on the floor, curling my body up, head down, hands over my eyes, waiting for the impact, as the dreadful shaking continued.

"Ali! Ali! For God's sake will you wake up! What the hell is wrong with you? Wake up!"

As I struggled to pull myself free of clutching five-fingered hands, the shaking stopped. Gasping in shock I opened my eyes and half sat up — only to find myself back in my human body, safe and sound in my own room, with Paco leaning over me. His face was as white as the sheet that he clutched in his hands, and the expression of sheer terror in his eyes was beyond words.

I must have still looked dazed, because he grabbed me again, trying desperately to shake me awake and his voice was trembling, in fact he seemed almost hysterical: "Ali, wake up! They took me again! I'm so scared! Please wake up!"

Such was the depth of his fear that I really thought he was going to pass out right then and there. Still feeling dazed, nauseous, and almost ready to pass out myself from being pulled back so suddenly, I somehow extricated myself from the tangled bed clothes and put my arms around him, pulling him down beside me. I could feel him shaking from head to foot, and he grabbed hold of me so tightly that I could hardly breathe.

I eventually managed to extricate myself enough to place one hand on his head, which then enabled me to apply some Reiki. As this slowly took effect he loosened his stranglehold a little.

"Paco, please calm down and tell me what's wrong." I spoke quietly but firmly, all the while keeping a hold on him to ensure a steady and continual flow of calming energy.

Still trembling, he held his arm out to me, and for the first time I saw the blood soaking into his sleeve, and a clean but apparently quite deep cut in his forearm.

"They took me again, tonight," he gasped in horror, "and look what they did! Why can't they leave me alone! What in the name of God do they want?"

"Paco, try to calm down and tell me — who? Who took you, and where? What are you talking about?"

"The aliens! The aliens, for God's sake!" he cried, burying his face in his hands. I sat there staring at him, completely stunned.

"Paco, are you sure?" I replied lamely, not quite knowing what to say or how to react.

After a moment or two he took a deep breath, trying to settle himself. "Ali, that's what is wrong, and why I've been acting so strange, and there is absolutely no one I can talk to about it except you, and I'm so scared! Sometimes I really think that I'm going crazy! Do you think I've gone crazy?"

"Oh, Paco, no! Don't be silly, of course I don't! Look, please, just try to calm down and tell me exactly what's happening."

He leaned back against the pillows, closing his eyes for a few moments, then took a deep breath before answering: "It all began about a year ago, not long after I came back here for Granny's funeral. One night I was called out to attend to one of our parishioners who was dying. She was in a rural nursing home, so it was a fairly long, lonely drive, and on the way back to the presbytery something really strange happened.

I left the hospital at about one in the morning, and should have been home easily by 2:00, but as I came in the door I happened to glance at the clock and it was almost 3:30. At first I thought the clock was fast or that it had stopped or something, but then I checked my watch, and it said 3:30 too. I checked every clock in the house, and they were all the same.

I thought and thought, trying to remember anything unusual about the drive home, trying to work out what had happened to the missing hour and a half, but the weird thing was, I didn't remember until the next day the strange light I'd seen in the sky. When I did recall it, I couldn't understand how I could possibly have forgotten. It seemed to be hovering over a paddock beside the road, and I stopped the car to get out for a closer look, then the next thing I remembered was driving into the church grounds. It was after that night that the dreams started — or really I should call them nightmares — of being taken on board an alien craft and subjected to the most awful examinations and probes."

"What do the aliens look like?" I asked, already knowing his answer.

"Oh, Ali, they're really strange! Small, sort of gray-colored beings with enormous black eyes. It's those eyes that really get to me. It's
like you're going to fall right in and disappear forever." He shuddered
involuntarily at the memory.

"It happened three times in a row, and it got so that I dreaded answering the phone at night, in case I was called out again. I couldn't
stand the thought of having to drive alone after dark. Then it seemed to
stop for a while, but now it's all happening again! Oh, Ali, what in the
name of God can I do? I can't tell Father Keating. I have his trust and
respect, but that won't last long if I start telling him I'm being abducted
by aliens. He's the last person I can talk to about it, but I can tell he's
noticing that there's something wrong with me. I'm so scared, and I just
don't know what to do!"

"Paco, what happened tonight? Were you taken again?"

"Oh, God, yes! I hoped I'd be safe here, away from the presbytery. I didn't think they'd find me, but not long after I got into bed they
came after me again, and there was nothing I could do. When they're
around it's like I'm paralyzed, and I can only move the way they want
me to."

"And what about your arm? What happened there?"

"They cut me with some sort of sharp instrument, like a scalpel. I
don't know, maybe they took blood samples or something. They've done
that before, and normally it seems to heal almost instantaneously, but
tonight something happened. It was as if they were interrupted in the
middle of the examination, and I was brought back really quickly. Normally I'm aware of being returned, but tonight I just woke suddenly and
found myself back in bed.

"Ali, I'm sorry I came barging into your room like that, but I was
so scared! I couldn't stand the thought of being alone. I was scared
they'd come back to finish the job."

Thank goodness Paco was looking better by now. The normal
color was back in his face and he wasn't shaking any more. We talked
for a while longer before he felt able to go back to his own room. I lay
awake the rest of the night, staring at the ceiling and wondering how in
the name of heaven I was going to tell him the truth.

Of course, I was well aware of the examination procedure that
we carry out, and yes, he was quite correct. We do take numerous blood
and tissue samples, as well as sperm and ova from the bodies of our human "guests." I was also quite sensitive to how terrifying and unpleasant
it could potentially be for them, but it's for their own good. How to explain to him and others that the manmade chemical pollution on Earth is
a major concern to us, and as caretakers of the planet, the only way we

can monitor its effects on living creatures is to take these samples on a regular basis.

For humans, a visit to the doctor or dentist is not always pleasant either, as I was finding out now that I inhabited an Earth body — in fact such visits can be downright painful and quite terrifying. However, they are nonetheless carried out for the ultimate welfare of the patient, and are most necessary for the prevention of more serious problems arising. The work we are carrying out on Earth humans is no different.

I considered telling him about the problems with nuclear weaponry and of the very real possibility that all life on Earth, including all of humanity, could be wiped out, as has happened before. Maybe then he would understand that this is why sperm and ova are taken, both from humans and also from various animal species, so that if life on Earth is destroyed, either through man-made or natural catastrophe, the continuation of these life-forms will be assured elsewhere. Surely he'd understand the importance of this, but I decided not to say anything quite yet.

20 ▶ FACING REALITY

A couple of nights later the unthinkable happened — Paco was taken on board the disc in which I was working, and we came face to face. I deeply hoped that he wouldn't recognize me in my Zeta form, but I should have known better. As our eyes met, recognition dawned, not physically, but on deeper levels of his being, and what I saw in his eyes was disbelief, horror and betrayal.

The following morning he would not look at me. He spent the whole day very carefully avoiding me and by late afternoon it had reached a point of ridiculousness, with his walking out of the room as soon as I came in, so I went after him to get the inevitable confrontation over with.

"Paco!" I called to him. "We have to talk."

"What about?"

"You know very well. You saw me last night, didn't you?"

"Just leave me alone, Ali! Get away from me. I don't know what the hell is going on with you, but I don't want anything to do with it. I've finally got to where I've always wanted to be in life, and now you're going to ruin it all. Why can't you and your damned alien friends just leave me in peace!"

He turned his back on me and stormed out of the room, slamming the door behind him. I had never seen him so angry. I went to my room, locked the door, and cried my eyes out for the next hour. It was as though he had stabbed me with a knife, and it was not only my human heart that was in pain but my Guardian one as well.

He left early the next morning before I was even awake, with the excuse of going to visit a friend, and two days passed with no word from him. Only I knew the real reason for his absence, so my parents could not understand why I was so upset and worried, but the look of fear and loathing in his eyes at the sight of me in gray form haunted me day and night. I had been the only one he felt he could trust, but now, as far as he was concerned, I had betrayed that trust. What could I do? Finally, in an attempt to still my mind and perhaps find a solution to the problem, I went to my favorite corner of the garden, to meditate.

An hour or so later I opened my eyes, to find Paco quietly sitting on the ground opposite me. I started to speak, but he put his finger to his lips, indicating that I should stay silent and not move. This was all very well, but I had a cramp in my leg from sitting still for so long, and I couldn't stand it any longer — I just had to stretch.

"Oh, no, Ali," he begged, "please don't move yet. The light is so beautiful."

I stared at him. "What light? What are you talking about?"

"Your aura!" he answered, his eyes alight with wonder. "Oh, Ali, I'm so sorry for what I said to you the other day! Now I understand who and what you are. You really are one of the ones Granny used to talk about — one of the Old Ones — the Guardians.

"I got back about an hour ago, and your parents said I'd find you out here. You were in very deep meditation and I didn't want to disturb you, so I sat down here to wait for you to come back. Then something really strange happened. As I watched, it was as if a veil lifted from my eyes. Your human appearance completely disappeared, and I could clearly see you in your alien form, just like the other night on board the disc. But the light around you was incredible! I could hardly see your features it was so blinding. Pure, dazzling, silver light — absolutely beautiful! And the feeling of love was beyond words. It reached out and wrapped around me like a warm blanket. I have never felt such love. That's why I didn't want you to move. I wanted to stay there forever, bathed in that incredible light and love!"

"Oh, dear," I answered lamely. "Then I had to get a cramp in my leg, right in the middle of your mystical experience. Sorry."

Paco came over and gave me a hand to help me up, lending an arm for me to lean on until I got the circulation going again in my leg. Watching me hobbling around, trying to shake the feeling back into my foot, he burst out laughing. "Now I know what Granny meant once when she said that the Guardians sometimes have trouble manifesting in gross, physical form on Earth. If I wasn't here right now, you'd fall flat on your face!"

"Yes, well," I answered, accidentally stepping on his toe, "Human bodies are cumbersome things to manage at times."

That night we again met on board the disc, but this time Paco came consciously and voluntarily, as an observer. Now that the fear was gone he radiated only love and peace, and so was free to move about at will. An overwhelming aura of curiosity emanated from him, and I knew very well he had many questions to ask, so as soon as the opportunity presented itself, I took him aside.

"Ali!" he exclaimed in wonder. "This is just amazing! How come I'm free to move around instead of being paralyzed and helpless as I was before?"

"Because," I answered him, "your fear has been released. The paralysis is purely a safety measure, both for us and our frightened human 'guests.' You see, many humans tend to regress to the level of their ancestors when they are confronted by what they fear. The rush of adrenalin through their system enables them to perform feats of incredible strength to protect themselves, and in this state they are likely to become unpredictable and dangerous, as we have found out in the past. To allow a terrified human to run amok on board one of our discs would be an extremely dangerous situation for everyone concerned, so we take the only measures we have to prevent this occurring.

"Back in the olden times when we were carrying out the transmutation and genetic work to assist in the ongoing development of the human species we had to be very careful. Just as human veterinary surgeons must make sure to tranquillize a large animal before carrying out any type of procedure, we had to take the same precautions. Can you even begin to imagine what an artificial insemination upon an enraged or terrified Neanderthal would be like? I don't think many present-day humans would volunteer for such work!

"However," I went on, "Earth humans have progressed since then, and many have now learned how to use the gift of free will with self-discipline and compassion. We are truly amazed at the spiritual progress that has been made upon the physical Earth Plane, for it is not an easy school to attend, as I well know from personal experience!

Unfortunately, though, many have not progressed much at all since those very early times. Outwardly they may appear completely human, but their energies are still focused almost entirely in the lower chakras, and they have not yet come to appreciate the qualities of a more spiritual state of being. Until these ones have learned to respect and honor all living beings in the universe, even starting with the other creatures on their own planet, then our work here is not finished. What we are trying to achieve is a return to oneness and unity, as opposed to the divisiveness that came about after the *fall*, which again can lead only to ultimate chaos."

Paco listened to what I had to say, but then countered with another question. "Well, okay, but the inter-breeding that seems to be going on between your people and ours? I mean the half-human half-alien babies that are seeded in the wombs of human mothers, then removed and placed in those incubator contraptions. I've been doing a lot of reading on the subject, to try to get a handle on it, and this aspect is very upsetting to those who have experienced it. Can you please explain to me why this is going on?"

"Look, Paco," I replied, "what you need to understand is that only the end result, the hybrids themselves, have been seen by humans taken on board our discs. They do not know the reasons behind our so-called breeding program, and why these hybrids are being produced. They cannot know, because until now most human contact with us has been clouded by fear, and the memories retained by the contactees are fragmented and only partly understood. Tell me Paco, do you recall reading in any of these books of the phoenix symbol that has been shown to some of our human guests?"

"Yes, as a matter of fact I do remember that particular symbol being mentioned, and also the fact that it represents rebirth, but what does that have to do with hybrid babies being created?"

"Everything, Paco! As you say, the phoenix is used to symbolize rebirth or reincarnation, rising as it does from its own ashes. It represents rebirth to higher vibrational frequencies, and is symbolic of the role we play in the process of human evolution.

"The thing is," I continued, "the human species of Earth cannot go on forever in its present form. In fact there is a strong possibility, especially since the advent of nuclear weaponry, that this race will eventually destroy itself, as has occurred in times past. This is why there's been such an increase in our surveillance program since the last world war, when the first atom bomb was detonated. In fact, what Earth humans are experiencing at this time is almost an exact repeat of the downfall of earlier civilizations on the planet, and has been of great concern to us, as we observe the parallels that are at present occurring in human society."

"But I still don't understand what this has to do with your people breeding those hybrids," Paco insisted. "It just doesn't seem right! What is your ultimate goal?"

"Surely that is obvious!" I replied, a little more curtly than I'd meant to, after all, how could he, or any other human for that matter, truly understand the seriousness of the situation?

"Please Paco," I sighed, "before you pass judgment, let me explain. As I said before, there is a very real danger that the human race of Earth, as it is in its present form, will destroy itself, and because Earth humans are a small but nonetheless very necessary component in the overall plan of creation and evolution, this must not be allowed to happen. The cosmic reverberations would be catastrophic, so as caretakers of energy it is our responsibility to make sure it doesn't happen.

"We are aware of a growing number of caring people on Earth who are trying their hardest to reverse the negative effects of global warming, degradation of the environment and the dangers posed by diseases such as AIDS, but they may not succeed in time. Added to this is the on going possibility of nuclear, chemical or germ warfare, so as a precaution, we are in the process of developing a more resistant strain of human being, to ensure continued population of the planet if need be. This is the role the hybrids will play, being a stronger and more resilient species. It is exactly the same process Earth scientists are using through the genetic engineering of domestic livestock to produce more resilient and disease resistant strains."

"But Ali, for heaven's sake! We are talking about *human beings* here, not livestock! What do you do with the hybrids? Keep them in laboratories like animals?"

"Oh, Paco, for crying out loud! What sort of monsters do you think we are? They're as much a part of our people as they are humans. We treat them the same as we treat ourselves. They are family. They work on the ships alongside us, they eat and sleep the same as we do, or *almost*, anyway, because they are half-human and fully biological, so their physical needs are a little different from ours. We even bring their human parents on board so they can relate to both cultures, and in this way they grow up understanding clearly who and what they are.

"If Earth humans do wake in time and make the necessary changes to ensure that they don't wipe themselves out, then the hybrids will gradually be introduced to life on Earth, to live openly among the present population, in which they will be able to improve the human gene pool by introducing a more spiritual aspect to the present war-like tendencies that still affect many Earthlings. They will also play an important role during the coming shift, as teachers, comforters and sources of love to support Earth humans through the change of planetary consciousness that lies ahead.

"So your people are not simply using ours for breeding purposes, as some of the testimonies on alien abduction imply?"

"No we are not! And please will you stop calling us aliens! We are no more alien than you are!"

Poor Paco spread his hands in frustration. "Well what the heck do you want us to call you then?"

"We don't really care," I answered, "just as long as you call us for dinner!" I added, making a lame joke out of it in an attempt to lighten an increasingly heavy discussion. "But seriously," I went on, "Guardians, Greys or Zetas will do — or better still, family!"

"Family! What do you mean by family?"

"Well, we are all related on the Human Ladder after all — you are our past, and we are your future, and we have all been created out of the same Source and to that same Source we shall all eventually return, united in Oneness."

"Ali Cat," said Paco, taking a deep breath to regain his composure, "what exactly do you mean by 'us being your past and you being our future'? Does this mean you are human time travelers who come to us from the future? Will you please explain this more clearly? And while you're at it, what is the Human Ladder?"

Just at that moment one of the Elders came past on his way to another part of the ship. I really thought Paco's eyes would pop out of his head at the sight of the extremely tall and very imposing-looking black-clad figure. Thank heavens he wasn't wearing his black cape and hat, which would have added to the strangeness of his appearance.

"Oris!" I called, to get his attention. Huge, dark blue eyes turned in my direction, freaking Paco out even more.

"Yes, Alarca, what is it?"

"May I please be excused from duty tonight? My friend Paco here has been asking a million and one questions about our intergalactic development program, and now I'm going to have to explain about the Human Ladder as well. It'll take ages, because knowing him he'll have a million more questions to ask."

Oris's eyes gleamed with amusement. "Of course, Alarca! Take all the time you need. After all, you are training to be a Teacher, so take every opportunity you can to teach, both here and in your human form on Earth. And remember, be patient! Asking questions is the only way anyone can learn.

"And," he continued, waggling a long, thin finger at me, "just make sure you teach him properly! The Human Ladder can be very confusing to understand, so make sure you get it right yourself. Remember just the basics for now — don't confuse him by bringing the extra Guardian levels in."

Oris left the room, much to my relief, as I turned my attention back to Paco. For a horrible moment I'd thought he was going to stay to supervise the lesson, which would have thrown me completely. Our Elders have an awful, disquieting habit of just standing there, motionless, staring out of those huge eyes. If we do something wrong, they very rarely raise their voices or lose their tempers with us — they simply glare, but that glare is far more articulate than a thousand words of disapproval.

"Who, or what the heck was *that*?" whispered Paco, eyes still wide in horror and fascination.

"Oh, just one of our Elders." I replied. "His name is Oris. As you can see he's pretty old, so he's quite knowledgeable. He can be a bit grumpy at times and an old fusspot, but he's okay."

"W-what do you mean by 'pretty old'? H-how can you tell?"

"Oh, that's easy! Didn't you notice how wrinkled his container is, particularly around the lower part of the face? But you can mainly tell by the eyes — they're dark blue rather than black like mine. He's actually not that old by our standards, otherwise his eyes would be a much paler blue."

"Do you mean to tell me that al…, I mean Greys' eyes fade with age, just like human hair turns white?"

"Yes, of course."

"My goodness," Paco shook his head in wonderment, "when I think of all the speculation that has caused confusion among human observers who've seen some Greys with black eyes and some with blue. All sorts of theories have been put forward."

"Well, as the saying goes," I answered, "the simplest explanation is usually the right one, and the main thing is," I added, "when you get to know us better you'll see we're really not all that different from Earth humans, except that we aren't so focused on physicality."

"And how old is what's-his-name — the Elder you were speaking to?"

"You mean Oris? Ummm, let me see … I think he's about two million, give or take a century or three. Not really old by our standards."

"What! Do you mean two million *years*? You're kidding!"

"I'm not, Paco, honestly, but the thing is, we are completely and consciously aware of the fact that we are immortal beings, and have almost total recall of all the various lives we have lived. Our Guardian consciousness isn't subject to the illusion of death that affects Earth humans and causes them to become caught up in the limitations of mortality. This is a false perception which clouds the awareness of all those who don't have expanded soul consciousness.

"Now, I went on, "this Human Ladder teaching will be a good way for you to understand more clearly what I'm talking about. The Human Ladder is comprised of ten what we call 'galactic' levels, all vibrating at gradually ascending frequencies on the electromagnetic scale. These ten levels form what could be called a multiverse, as opposed to a universe, because the physical universe is only a very small part of the whole. Each galactic level operates on its own unique frequency band, like radio and TV stations, so they don't interfere or impinge upon each other.

The galactic level to which Earth belongs is number one, the bottom rung of the Ladder, so to speak. There are approximately 1,000 different humanoid species inhabiting almost as many planets on this level, and they are all at more or less the same evolutionary stage. Some are a little behind, some a little ahead of Earth humans, depending upon the age of the species."

"And how did humankind evolve on Earth?" Paco asked. "As a priest I'm very interested to know, because there's so much controversy over this subject. Science of course insists that Darwin's theory of evolution is more or less correct — that man evolved naturally from the animal kingdom — but the church insists that humans were created as a separate entity, designed in the image of God. So, who is really right?"

"Well, the truth of the matter is," I answered, "neither is correct. The weakness in Darwin's theory is that it takes physical evolution into account, but completely ignores spiritual evolution, and the problem with the creation belief of the church is that, if taken fundamentally, it goes against nature, and everything must follow natural law. Man is a multi-dimensional being, so both physical and spiritual aspects must be taken into account. Once a species evolves to the point of attaining reasoning power, as opposed to the purely instinctual drive of the animal kingdom, then responsibility and free will come into the picture, for it is through the correct application of the responsibility of free will, in other words, the voluntary choice of right over wrong, that dictates whether one evolves or devolves through the universal cycle.

"Evolution in the human kingdom is really all about making choices! This spark is first ignited at the point where man evolves from animal, so it is at this point that higher intervention is required. Thus humans evolve on two levels — physically from the animal kingdom, as illustrated by Darwin's theory, and spiritually through intervention in the form of energy transmutation by an outside agent under the direction of God/Source."

"Okay," Paco responded, "these 'galactic levels' you're talking about — what are they exactly? Are they galaxies?"

"No they're not." I answered. "What we refer to as galactic levels are actually states of mind or consciousness. They are not physical places as such."

"Huh? Come again Ali Cat, I don't understand."

Oh, God, Paco! This is *so* hard to put into third-dimensional language! Hang on a minute while I think…. Okay, the galactic levels are gradually ascending and expanding levels of conscious awareness through which all human species evolve. As we ascend through these levels, our consciousness becomes deeper and stronger, because we are able to utilize more of our mind."

"What do you mean by that?"

"Well, on galactic level one, we use approximately 10% of our consciousness; on galactic level two we are able to access 20%, etc. As we progress upwards through the Universal Cycle, which is another term for the Human Ladder, our mind, or consciousness, becomes increasingly more expanded as a direct result of moving closer and closer to One-ness."

Again poor Paco shook his head in bewilderment, so I continued with my explanation: "By that I mean all the different one thousand or so human species come closer together. We cease being so separate and gradually return to Oneness — to God in other words, but this is not a physical process — it is about mind/spirit."

"And when you speak of different human species in the universe, are your people included in this?"

"Well, Guardian consciousness has moved beyond that, but yes, we most definitely have been part of the human kingdom for many, many millennia — millions and millions of years actually. On the first three galactic levels there are many human species manifesting in mortal form. On level one and even two they are very diverse and separate, with distinctive physical or biological forms adapted to suit the conditions of the various planets on which they reside. You could think of all these different human species being like small streams flowing into and joining up with a large river, which eventually flows into and becomes part of an eternal Ocean, which is God. This is what evolution on the spiritual level is really all about. It's all about evolving past the need for physical form.

"And the beautiful part of it is every human species has something of value and importance to contribute to the *whole*, so it is only by coming together in this way that total balance and harmony can be attained. This is what we mean when we say 'You are our past and we are your future.' By the time you reach the third galactic level, all human species start evolving past the state of separation and individual physicality, and begin melding together in oneness. This doesn't mean you'll lose your individuality," I hastily reassured him. "It's more about moving into a state of deeper empathy and God Consciousness.

"It's during this process that one begins to focus less upon physical form and more upon mind/consciousness and the higher-energy centers. At level three the physical body becomes very simple and basic, and the head and eyes much larger. At this level, consciousness is centered in mind/spirit and can move freely in and out of the physical shell, with complete awareness that the body is nothing more than a container or vehicle for the immortal spirit and soul.

"Once a soul evolves to this point, such a degree of inner connectedness has been attained that we then begin to lose the need to reincarnate back into forms of gross matter — physical bodies in other words. We then ascend to galactic level number four, where we become part of the Guardian Consciousness, whose job is to assist in the evolutionary process of those on galactic levels one, two and three. From there we continue to evolve upwards through levels five, six, seven and eight, gradually accessing more and more conscious awareness until we reach levels nine and ten, which are the ones known on Planet Earth as 'angels.'

"These highly evolved Guardians on levels nine and ten are operating at 90% to 100% consciousness, which is pure mind /divine consciousness, with no need at all for physical form, although they can appear temporarily as humans if they want to. For example, if an angel wishes to make an appearance on one of the lower galactic levels then they can 'clothe' themselves in a form to suit that level of consciousness. They are known to us as workers of God, or Oneness, and are caretakers of life-force energy on all levels of the universe. We are their assistants."

"Many of the Earth people we take on board the discs are experiencing their last incarnation as level-one humans. These ones are now preparing to step up into level-two consciousness in their next life, in order to stay in tune with their planet."

"What do you mean?" Paco asked.

"Well," I replied, "planets too are living, evolving entities, and Earth Herself is about to take this important step up into galactic level two. Those humans who wish to remain in tune with their planet must also evolve to level-two consciousness. This is part of the reason for our intervention. Many, many children born over the last couple of decades, the next generation of humans in other words, carry a higher percentage of ET genetic material in their makeup.

"These are the ones known as the Star Children, and it is in this way that humanity's vibrational frequency is being slowly tuned to a higher octave, to assist their evolution into level-two consciousness. This program has been going on for over half a century on Planet Earth, so there are also a number of adults who carry extra ET genetic material in their makeup as well. A number of different ET cultures are contributing to the gene pool.

"This is why many who have encounters with us develop deeper psychic and spiritual sensitivity and awareness. It is a spiritual transmutation process, an evolutionary process on the spiritual level that will eventually bring about the expanded state of Divine Consciousness towards which we are all heading."

"Well," Paco answered thoughtfully, "that does explain why I've started seeing auras more clearly since my abduction experiences began. I had wondered about that."

"There you go then," I smiled, placing a long, thin, gray arm around his shoulders and giving him a friendly squeeze. You'll be one of us before you know it!"

"Oh, great," came a most unenthusiastic response. "I can hardly wait. Can't I just leave out that bit and go straight on to being an angel? But seriously," he went on, "how are you actually bringing this transmutation about?"

"We're doing it in three ways," I explained. "First, the long-term processes are adjusting and fine-tuning the physical makeup of Earthlings and upgrading their DNA structure through genetic engineering.

Second, a number of our own people, like me for example, are at present incarnating on Earth in physical human form to work among the Earth human race. We are there to teach them about life-force energy, the concept of oneness and spiritual evolution, and we also try to set an example for them on how to live life as citizens of the Cosmos, by showing respect to all, and by caring for the planetary environment.

"The third, short-term process, which is for the purpose of speeding things up a little, is through the implants we're placing in people's bodies when we bring them onto the discs."

"Ah yes!" Paco responded. "What's that all about? Those implants are causing a lot of conjecture, concern and downright outrage within the field of ET investigation. What are they for?"

"Okay," I replied, "some are monitors which allow us to keep a check on health, effects of pollution on the body, different emotional states, etc. Others allow us to tune in to what a person is experiencing at any given time. For example, I carry one of these in my body so that my feelings and reactions to different things can be automatically monitored on board the disc, which saves me having to be de-briefed at the end of each day's work in human form. Some also are tracking devices so we can keep an eye on a group of our own people who got trapped on Earth in human bodies many millennia ago. We're trying to rescue them to bring them home, but the problem is, they've forgotten who and what they are, so until they can all be contacted and awakened, we need to keep track of them.

"But, to get back to the transmutation process of humans, many implants are placed directly into the chakra system — the energy system of the body. In this way the vibrational frequency of the chakras can be adjusted in order to speed up the transmutation process. This in turn can have the effect of automatically opening the person to psychic and clairvoyant sensing without the need for many years of training.

"The advantages are that communication becomes much easier, because these ones can be used as 'telephone lines' between us and the rest of Earth's population, and it also makes it easier to get them onto the disc. The disadvantage is that, without the years of discipline and training to back it up, the acquisition of these seemingly 'special powers' tends to cause ego problems with a few of the contactees. Still, this is all a part of the testing process that Earthlings are going through at this time, and it distinguishes between those who have learned from past mistakes and those who have not. As I said before, human evolution is all about having the free will to make choices, right choices or wrong choices.

"Okay Paco," I said, bringing us back to the lesson I was supposed to be giving him, "do you have any more questions?"

"Well, you keep going on about 'deepening conscious awareness' as we evolve up the Human Ladder. I still don't quite understand. For example, what can we, as Earthlings, do to assist this process?"

"Evolution on the soul level," I replied, "is simply the deepening and expansion of conscious awareness into other dimensions, but conscious awareness cannot be expanded and deepened unless you are willing to break down and move past the limitations and boundaries imposed upon you by your own mind. These limitations and boundaries are a product of fear — the 'Satan' within. It is this fear that limits the expansion of your conscious mind, but many Earthlings refuse to look at these inner fears, preferring to remain static and stuck in a comfortable little rut, and totally brainwashed and controlled by certain elements within society that are deliberately imposed upon Earth humans to keep them in a state of fear.

"But the thing is," I went on, "evolution cannot be static. There must always be momentum and growth for evolution to take place. Evolution is a perpetual state of becoming and unfolding, which, by the way, is not always pleasant or easy by any means. This is where we, as 'tryers or testers of souls,' come into the picture, drawing to the surface these inner fears that people have, so they must be looked at and faced up to. It has to be done at this time, or Earth humans will begin to *de*volve instead of evolve.

"It is most important to keep yourselves flexible in mind, body and spirit to assist in moving past these boundaries and limitations. This is why practices such as tai chi, yoga and meditation are of such benefit."

"Do Guardians meditate?" Paco asked, fascinated.

"Yes, of course we do, to stay closely in touch with Oneness. All of us need a little time of quiet, inner reflection each day.

"Now, Paco, I don't know about you, but I really need a few minutes' break — all this talking is making my head spin. How about I take you along to our meditation area here on the disc — would you like to see it? And on the way we can get something to eat."

"Oh, wow! Yes, please, can we really?"

"I don't see why not. Come on, I'll show you."

21 ▶ ONENESS

As I led Paco through the computer bay on our way to the meditation room, dozens of pairs of large black eyes, and a few blue ones as well looked up in amazement. Humans were not generally brought into this part of the ship, so everyone did a double take. Even those engrossed in work stopped what they were doing, fingers poised over the touch screens, turning to get a good eyeful as we passed. A couple of small workers taking a meal break stood rooted to the spot, tubes of blue paste halfway to their mouths, gaping in surprise.

"What the heck is that they're eating?" Paco whispered loudly in my ear. "I didn't know Greys ate food!"

"Some of us do," I explained. "It depends upon what sort of container we're occupying, which in turn depends upon the work we're carrying out."

"Huh? Come again? You keep going on about these containers. What did you mean before when you were talking about that Elder, Oris? You kept referring to his 'container' as if it were something separate from him. It was his body you were talking about, wasn't it?"

"Okay Paco, just hold on a bit until we get to the meditation area and I'll explain. Here, do you want to try some of this? It's only a vitamin drink."

He took the vial of yellow-colored liquid and sniffed it suspiciously before taking a tentative sip. For a moment I expected him to spit it out, but he bravely swallowed it and even managed not to pull too much of a face.

"Well," came the diplomatic comment, "it certainly is, umm, different! Rather pleasant actually… in fact quite pleasant. But are you sure it's safe for human consumption?"

"Oh, yes," I assured him, "quite safe." I waited until he'd downed the whole lot before adding: "At least I think it is. We've never given it to an Earth person before."

"Gee, thanks a lot!"

"Oh, come on, Paco, I'm only joking. I'm not going to poison you now, after spending so much time and energy explaining all this to you. Besides, I've got heaps more to show you."

"Hey, wow! What are those pen things they're using?" Paco kept turning around and craning his neck trying to get a better look."

"Oh, they're just standard infrarays," I explained. "Although we have extremely advanced technology, we also take great pride in the arts, especially our script work, and these are a type of lower-intensity laser device that burns the script into the writing surface. That is how we write by hand. Some documents and manuscripts are prepared in this way, as a counter-balance to our technology."

I took Paco over to stand behind one of the scribes as he worked, deftly manipulating the instrument between four long, gray fingers, the yellow-colored laser light burning away the surface of the sheet on which he was writing. This took an awful lot of practice, as it was very easy to burn a hole if the light paused too long in one spot, as I well knew from experience. What makes our scribing even harder is the fact that our script is multidimensional, with strokes overlaying strokes to change the meaning of certain symbols.

After a few minutes observation, I led Paco down past the rest of the computers and through one of the many doors leading out of the work area. As we stepped into the meditation area, a sense of deep tranquility closed around us, wrapping us in an almost tangible blanket of serenity. Paco sighed, closing his eyes and leaning back against the door that had slid shut behind us. The room was round in shape, not overly large, and illuminated by a softly glowing light that emanated from the walls themselves. Sweet-smelling incense permeated the atmosphere, and calming music played quietly in the background. Lifelike effigies of enlightened beings seated in cross-legged meditation lined the outer walls.

Paco stood staring in sheer amazement. This was obviously the very last thing he'd expected to find on an ET ship.

"My God!" he exclaimed, trying to take in every detail at once. "This is just *incredible*! Feel the energy! It's making me tingle all over! And just look at those figures! Who are they?"

"These are the ones we refer to as the Buddhas," I explained. "It's not that we especially follow Buddhism, or any religion for that matter. We use the term Buddha quite literally to mean enlightened be-ing, and that is exactly what these are — representations of various en-lightened beings from throughout the entire universe. If you go around and examine them you will see that they take many forms, not just hu-man as you think of humans."

One in particular caught Paco's attention, and he went over to look more closely. It was obviously the figure of a Grey — one of our past Elders to be precise, who had since moved on to higher realms. It sat, like the others, in the lotus position, large head bowed in silent medi-tation and long, four-fingered hands placed in what we call the Peace

Sign, fingertips together on the lower abdomen. This being was enveloped in an aura of calm serenity.

"Who's that?" Paco enquired in a voice hushed in reverence. "Do you know his name?"

"Oh, yes," I replied quietly. "He was known on Earth as Osiris. And next to him is his female half, Isis."

Paco stared in amazement at the figure of a female Grey sitting beside him, her likeness captured for eternity.

"You're kidding!" he gasped. "Do you really mean to tell me that those two are *the* Isis and Osiris of ancient Egypt?"

"Yes, Paco, and I'm not kidding. They're Guardians, and they were very advanced Elders when they came to Planet Earth as teachers God knows how many millennia ago to try to introduce a bit of civilization to a very primitive planet."

Paco's eyes suddenly lit up in understanding and recognition. "Hey, now I get it! Oris, Osiris, Isis — do all of your Elders' names end with the suffix 'IS'?"

"Yes!" I replied, giving him a congratulatory pat on the back. "Now you're beginning to catch on. Anubis and Serapis are ours too, along with the ones known as Quetzlcoatl and Pan, and a few others besides. If humans only knew, we've played quite a major role in the ongoing development of the human species of Planet Earth.

"The problem is, our teachings have been so badly misinterpreted and manipulated since then. For example, Osiris and Isis never embraced the concept of embalming and preserving peoples' physical containers in elaborate tombs and pyramids. That was introduced by a negative group that came to Earth, posing as 'gods' in order to block the evolutionary path of human consciousness by teaching people to focus on the physical body and its material possessions, rather than on the eternal and immortal soul.

"You've read about the so-called 'Gods of Olympus,' who were totally caught up in all the pleasures of human physicality! They were extremely competitive and warlike, and their high level of technology caused the younger Earth human species to perceive them as gods. All those so-called gods ever seemed to do was wage war on each other and exploit the poor humans as slaves. This has happened over and over again on Earth, and it is still going on today.

"Now Paco," I went on without letting him get a word in, "let's get back to the subject of containers, so sit on one of those cushions over there, and I'll try to explain. It is because of these incorrect teachings that have proliferated on Earth seemingly forever, that many Earth humans have become totally focused almost exclusively upon their physical bodies, to the detriment of true spiritual understanding. Because of this they have lost touch with the immortal spiritual beings that they truly are. Sadly many actually believe they *are* the physical body and nothing more.

"As you evolve to higher levels of the Human Ladder and your consciousness opens up more, you are able to fully grasp the concept that the real 'you' is not your body — neither is it your astral form, which is only your mind/spirit. In fact, you will come to understand that 'you' are nothing less than a soul — a pure expression of immortal God/Source energy, which, during the early stages of spiritual evolution, makes use of a physical body, or container, to undertake physical experiences. This act of experiencing is carried out through your five physical senses of sight, hearing, touch, smell and taste.

"Earth humans have been continually brainwashed over the millennia into believing that physical form and appearance are the 'be all and end all.' This has carried through to the point where, if you think of an angel, or of a highly evolved ET or spiritual teacher, you immediately and automatically visualize a being in 'perfect' human form, but this is simply not correct. In fact, it is a total misconception!

"Physical form only exists on the lowest galactic levels. As a soul evolves into level three, the biological form becomes simpler, and it is eventually left behind altogether, except when one is involved in carrying out physical work on the lower levels, as the Guardians are doing."

"You mean your people?"

"Yes! Remember I said our specific role is to assist in the evolutionary process of those beings inhabiting the lower levels of the Human Ladder. This includes all races inhabiting physical planets such as in the Sirius system, the Pleiadians, the Arcturians, Earth humans, and many others, all of which we ourselves have been part of over many billions of years of evolution. In other words, we have experienced physical lives in all of these many planetary cultures.

"We also play what could be described as a peacekeeping role on level-one planets like Earth. While we do not interfere in the internal affairs of the planet, we do provide as much protection as possible from outside interference.

"Some facets of our work require our physical presence, and some can be carried out in astral form, as when we bring humans up onto the disc in their astral bodies. For those jobs in which physical interaction is involved, we make use of specialized physical containers, just like the special suits that astronauts of Earth put on to travel in space. The difference is that ours have been developed over billions of years using technology way beyond anything presently available on Earth. These containers are more than just 'suits,' and are closer to what you think of as a living body. In fact, they are 'living' in a manner of speaking."

"But how do you get into it? I can't see any zippers or seams, or fasteners of any sort."

"There's no need, because we don't put them on like clothing. Our soul essence simply merges and melds into the container so that it becomes a living part of us."

"You're kidding! Do you mind if I touch yours to see what it feels like?" Paco reached out a tentative hand and placed it on my arm. "Wow, that is *so weird*! But yes, as you say, it's not a suit of clothing — it's your actual body and it does feel 'alive' — sort of! Oh, my God, that's spooky!"

"It *is* alive, while I'm in it. It has a very specialized nervous system and operates via an energy/chakra system, just like a human body. Its nervous system is fully attuned to my energy frequency, and I animate it through my thought processes. This one I'm in is partly biological and needs to be nourished, so I take food in the form of that paste you saw some of the others consuming. When we're out of the container it's kept in a state of suspended animation in special liquid. Some of the containers used by those who are travelling long distances through the physical universe, such as the disc pilots, have no biological components at all. Those ones are specially developed for prolonged space travel and don't need any nourishment or atmosphere to survive."

"But what animates them? How do they stay alive?"

"As I explained, we operate them with our energy, so when we meld our soul essence into them they 'come to life' as it were. We, the Guardian soul, provide the life-force energy, so we can operate in any planetary environment."

"Now I understand why some humans have mistaken your people for robots. What's the difference anyway? You *are* sort of robots, aren't you? But no you're not — I know you're a living person, with emotions and feelings — now I'm totally confused."

"Paco, the difference is, with a robot the intelligence driving it is artificial, whereas we are fully conscious, sentient beings — only the body is artificial. Do you understand what I'm saying?"

"Yes, sort of," came his very doubtful-sounding reply, "but what I want to know is, what the heck do you look like when you're not in your 'container'?"

"Oh, that's easy to show you — just watch."

Going by the way he backed away from me, he'd obviously been watching too many B-grade horror films involving horrible-looking space aliens hiding behind human façades. I'm not sure what he expected, but the look of profound relief on his face when my light body emerged from the gray container as a glowing blue-colored orb was quite amusing to behold.

"Oh — my — God!" was all he could manage.

Floating above my now-vacated container, I continued to communicate telepathically with him. "Now do you see what I meant when I said 'I' am not my body? I *have* a body, in fact I have two of them, this one and my Earth human one, but neither of them is 'me,' just as your body is not 'you.'"

"So what you're saying is that I can move outside of my physical body, too, and when I do, I also look like a ball of light?"

"Yes, absolutely, because all of us, Earth humans, Guardians and all other inter-planetary and interdimensional beings are, in reality, pure life-force energy — God Consciousness in other words. We all share *exactly the same stream of conscious awareness*, and the higher we evolve on the human Ladder, the more of it we are able to tap into and utilize.

"This is why we feel sad when you call us 'aliens,' because we are *not* alien to you. We may be 'dressed' in a different 'set of clothing,' but our soul essence — that which makes us what we are — the real 'us' in other words, is no different from the real 'you.' This is also the reason why, if Earth humans can only get past their fear, they *can* communicate quite easily with us, because soul-to-soul communication can only take place in a state of total trust.

"The other thing is," I went on, "you asked if you also resemble a ball of light when you leave your physical container. Earth humans can potentially look like that, because that is what you are in your purest, truest form, but many still can't move past their astral form — their mind/spirit body, in other words — which is a blueprint of the physical form. Your astral body is created out of your own mind, and most humans are caught up with the deeply entrenched mindset that they are nothing more than a physical body, maybe with a soul or spirit floating around somewhere, although some don't even believe in that, so when they leave the physical body, their consciousness still expresses itself in the form of that body. It is this inability to get past the astral that causes humans to keep reincarnating back into human life."

"But some of your people are in astral form too, aren't they?"

"Yes, but because we've evolved past human mindsets and belief systems, we have complete control over the process, and so make use of whatever energy frequency — physical, astral or pure soul essence — that is appropriate to what we are doing at any given time."

"What do you mean, Ali? I still don't quite understand."

"Well, say, for example, that our job is to operate a disc to carry out a task on a physical planet such as Earth. Perhaps we need to collect some plants or a water sample or something to check pollution levels in the atmosphere. In such cases we don a physical body, one of our 'custom-built' gray containers, to enable us to do whatever work is required.

"This has caused a huge amount of speculation among researchers on Earth, because the containers are quite literally 'custom-built' to carry out many different tasks, and we use one that is most suitable for what we need to do. The result is that researchers have now classified us as 'four-fingered Zetas or Greys' from such-and-such a planet, or 'three-fingered Zetas or Greys' from such-and-such another planet — but we aren't a planetary species — we moved past all that eons ago. The only reason why some of us have four fingers and others three is because the containers have been made that way for different jobs — it's as simple as that.

"In other cases, our work may involve bringing the astral form of a sleeping human up onto the disc to carry out some sort of procedure. Because they are in astral form, we also must operate in astral form so that we're on the same wavelength and can interact with them. When we're off duty we generally just express as a light body, and our discs are the same. They too are living, sentient beings that can also appear simply as a light."

"And what about the Angels?" Paco wanted to know. "You said that they're Guardians too, so how come they don't use gray containers?"

"They don't need to because they don't carry out physical work at all. They've moved beyond that, and vibrate at too high a frequency to be able to operate a physical container. That's where we come into the picture, as their assistants in cases where physicality is needed, and also in some lower-astral plane work where the energy frequencies are too low for angels to enter. They can, and do, appear on the lower levels of the Human Ladder in astral form, to assist humans in the dying process, but to do this they simply tap into the mind of the person they're helping, and then create an astral form for themselves which resembles what that person expects an angel to look like. In reality they are pure light energy, without form.

"Okay now, Paco, it's just about time for both of us to get ourselves back to Earth, so do you have any more questions on the Human Ladder? Do you understand about how evolution is more a spiritual process than physical, and that it's all about moving upwards through higher and higher frequencies of energy? Do you understand that it is this refining and leavening process that enables us to gradually tap into deeper and more expanded states of conscious awareness?"

"Yes, yes, stop testing me. I see that the whole process deals with energy and that we are all energy dressed up in various forms. So really, the belief that Earth humans are on a different evolutionary path than ETs, and that angels are separate again is all an illusion. The truth of the matter is that we are all one, and simply at different levels or energy frequencies on the path of evolution."

"Exactly, Paco! You got it! See how simple it really is? Some are more highly evolved and some are more lowly evolved, some seem to be good, some seem to be not so good, and some seem caught between the two, but we are all a necessary part of the whole, each with our own lessons to learn and tasks to carry out.

"This is why we are working so hard to ensure human life of some sort or other is able to continue inhabiting Planet Earth, for to lose even a small rung of the Human Ladder would bring about a state of imbalance and disharmony to the whole. There will always be souls needing a 'school' planet such as Earth as a place to grow and learn, so it must be preserved at all costs. Even those scientists of Earth who do accept the fact that ET civilizations are visiting their planet still cannot understand the reasons for our coming, simply because they don't understand the concept of Oneness, which is all important. Oneness is the underlying concept, the 'pivot point' of the whole of creation. We are all one, a universal family, and if a single member of that family needs saving from themselves, as Earth humans do at this time, then the rest of the family will step in to intervene, as a family should! We are all an intrinsic part of each other — nothing and no one is separate

22 ▶ FEAR

During the remainder of his holidays Paco and I spent many hours talking, and when the time came for him to return to work, we continued to meet a couple of nights each week on board the big disc, or "Workshop," so-called because of its numerous examination rooms, medical facilities, offices, crew quarters, general work areas and computer equipment, including extensive files. These giant Motherships remain in orbit around whatever planet we are working on at the time, and they operate on a frequency band which is generally kept beyond the range of human perception so that they are not readily visible.

Paco was determined to learn as much as he possibly could about us, and my job was to teach him. His understanding was most important, for someday he would be called upon to act as a bridge between our people and those of Planet Earth, and after all, who could be a better bridge between dimensions than a priest?

Dressed as I was in human form, I was able to reach a good number of people, but I could clearly see, especially by some of the questions and concerns Paco put to me, and his reaction to certain aspects of our work, that my mind was essentially that of a Guardian. Paco, on the other hand, thought more like a human, and was therefore more easily able to relate to and communicate with other humans as I could not.

One of the big questions that came up during our discussions was fear, and Paco tackled me head-on with this issue. Why, he demanded, did we not do more to allay human fears concerning us? And… why was it that at times we seemed to deliberately create scenarios to cause fear in human hearts? He went on to describe some of the so-called alien abduction cases he'd read about over the years, which often carried harrowing descriptions of painful and frightening procedures performed on humans on board our discs.

"Well," I countered, taking a deep breath, "if you really want to know, some of the fear element involved in contact between humans and so-called 'aliens' comes about through a lack of understanding on both sides.

"Yes," I went on, as his face registered genuine surprise, "I freely admit we are equally to blame, because some of our people, particularly the younger workers, sometimes forget what it is to be human, and they can be a bit rough at times. The Elders are forever reminding them to be more careful, but with some of them it goes in one ear and out the other. The main problem we face is work-load — some nights we're flat out covering the territory we're supposed to. All we need is for one procedure to go wrong and it throws our whole schedule out. Then on top of that there's the communication problem. When humans determinedly wrap themselves up in impenetrable cocoons of fear, or ego for that matter, which is a by-product of fear, no one, not even the most experienced Elder, can get through to them. This is really frustrating!"

"But Ali," Paco objected, "I read recently of a case where one of your lot suddenly appeared out of nowhere in the middle of the night in some poor girl's bedroom and went straight for her throat with four long, thin, gray fingers. I mean to say, the girl just freaked out! What the hell do you expect?"

"As a matter of fact, the worker got into trouble over it," I replied, recalling one of the others discussing the incident. "He was supposed to be giving her healing on the throat area, because this is the one place on the body where all the upper-body energy meridians come together, so we often give healing on the throat, and on the ankles for the lower body meridians. But yes, I admit that was our fault entirely and the worker should have known better."

"Mmm, maybe so," Paco said, not looking very convinced, "but it still seems to me that some of you are a bit questionable in your methods. Tell me, are all Guardians highly evolved, or are there some less evolved ones among you?"

"To answer your question," I countered, "let me ask you one: 'Are all humans highly evolved, or are some less evolved?'"

Paco grinned in acknowledgement. "Yes, well, Ali Cat, I asked for that, didn't I! It's just that I thought, maybe because your people are further up the Human Ladder than we are, you'd have overcome such things."

"No, not necessarily. Our people are also at different levels, and are still learning and evolving too. Evolution and spiritual growth occurs on all rungs of the Human Ladder, and a certain degree of negativity has to exist at every level outside of Oneness. Just think about it for a moment — you cannot have positive without negative, just as you cannot have up without down, or day without night. It's all relative. Opposites must exist for energy to be present, but negativity always has a positive aspect to it."

"Huh? How do you mean?"

"Well," I replied, "take, for example, the seemingly negative side of the so-called 'alien abduction experience,' in which humans are exposed to really bizarre and sometimes potentially frightening imagery. This is done to help break down the barriers that humans place on what they perceive as 'reality' and 'truth.' We are simply trying to open human minds to the possibility of other realities.

"Much of the fear aspect of these experiences actually comes from within the human psyche itself, and one only has to look at the number and severity of wars that occur on Earth to realize that the Earth human is a very fearful being, because war is all about fear — fear of lack, wanting what the other person has and fearing they will take what you have.

"On top of this, humans receive their information and experiences filtered through the curtain of their own personal perceptions, which in turn are colored by their mind set as well as by their personal belief system, again often based on fear. This then tends to place limitations and a ceiling upon what they are able to perceive and accept as 'truth' and 'reality.' Breaking through and moving past these barriers is a most important facet of all genuine contact experiences, which are all to do with the transmutation and transformation of energy to higher frequencies.

"In fact, Paco, this is where I told you that we are 'tryers,' or 'testers' of souls, in that our job is to try, test and push humans to their limits so they can break through the fear, on the other side of which is the limitless freedom of pure, unconditional love. In other words, we force humans to come face to face with the Satan within — the vibrational frequency of fear. Once a human breaks through this barrier and reaches a state of pure love and total trust, fear then has no power over them whatsoever. When all of humanity comes to this point in their evolutionary process, there will be no more war on Planet Earth, just as it doesn't exist in our culture."

"Ali, what do you mean by the Satan within being the vibrational frequency of fear? Wasn't it Satan who tempted Adam and Eve in the Garden of Eden?"

"No, Paco, this was just a member of another group on Earth at that time, the ones we call the 'Controllers,' who were trying to interfere with the work we were carrying out. No, Satan is not a person as such, but rather the energy, or vibrational frequency of fear, as opposed to the Christ, or divine energy of love. Christ too is not a person but rather a vibrational frequency, and so 'Christ Consciousness' is actually a state of being which can potentially be achieved by anyone.

"In the Christian tradition, Jesus is the person, and Christ is his energy frequency. In the Buddhist tradition the term Buddha is the equivalent of Christ, and so Buddha Consciousness is the state of being which Buddhists strive to achieve.

"Everyone has the potential to attain this elevated state of divine consciousness by cultivating unconditional love within their being, but to reach this state takes a number of lives, for one must first overcome the Satan consciousness of fear, which is directly opposite to love. As caretakers of energy within this universe, this is where we assist."

"But Ali, surely hate is the opposite of love!"

"No, it's not," I corrected him. The opposite of love is fear, for it is fear that is the root cause of hatred, and also of other vices such as greed, envy, anger, lust, intolerance and bigotry.

"Fear being 'Satan,' our aim is to give humans the opportunity to face that fear — the Satan within, and in so doing, to overcome it. This is the ultimate lesson that must be mastered if one is to aspire to divine consciousness, and it is the meaning behind the Bible story of Jesus being confronted by the 'devil' when he'd been fasting in the desert for 40 days."

"That's interesting what you're saying Ali, because even though the Bible and the teachings of Jesus are taken as a guide for those following the Christian faith, really, they are relevant to everybody, whether Christian or not"

"Indeed, as are the teachings of all those great Avatars, and what's important for people to understand is that the story of Jesus's life as portrayed in the Gospels, is symbolic of the story of every human being. All the major events in his life — his birth, his 40 days in the desert, his temptation by the 'devil,' his suffering, death and subsequent resurrection, are all symbolic of certain 'rites of passage' through which all human souls must pass."

"Well now, that's another very relevant point you're bringing up. I've meditated a lot on the deeper meanings behind the Gospels over the years, and I have reached exactly the same conclusion — that the life of Jesus itself is one big parable that applies to everybody, without exception. And taking what you're saying about Satan being our own inner fear that needs to be conquered, what the story of Jesus' temptation is really saying is that even the most highly evolved soul is still potentially vulnerable to temptation by their 'inner demons' during moments of weakness."

"Hey Paco — you're pretty smart for a human brother! But yes, we all need to be on guard against this, because just when a person feels they've done really well in overcoming fear in their life, up it comes again in the guise of over-inflated ego, which, in reality, is nothing more than another form of fear."

"Boy, it sure isn't easy, is it? No wonder they talk about the spiritual path being like a razor's edge! But anyway, getting back to your lot, what about the really awful things we come across in connection with alien abductions? For example, I've read about women who have recalled being raped by ETs on board the discs during abduction experiences. What do you have to say about that?"

"Look, Paco," I replied with a sigh, "remember a moment or so ago I specified '*genuine*' ET contact. All I can say is, there is a whole lot more going on and around Planet Earth than the majority of ordinary people know about in the way of advanced technology, mind-control techniques and covert cooperation between certain Earth human agents and the renegade Controller group with whom they are aligned. Unfortunately, all ET groups who happen to look a little different, are being made the 'scapegoats' by this renegade group who are deliberately trying to make our people, as well as the Reptoid folk, look bad in the eyes of humans.

"The truth of the matter is, the Controllers are entirely Earth human in appearance, and in fact often portray themselves as 'highly evolved, perfected humans' in the Aryan Ideal sense put forward by the Nazi regime during the last major world war.

"Many of the more negative 'abduction' experiences by 'evil Greys' are actually carried out through the very advanced mind-control techniques that this group has at its disposal. They also spread a huge amount of negative propaganda about us via books, magazine articles, the internet, and through certain ones 'planted' in ET research and investigation groups throughout the world, whose specific role is to spread frightening stories about us.

"Just as has happened before, this group of rebels is again tempting Earth humans with knowledge, technology, and in some cases psychic abilities that they are not mature enough on the soul level to handle wisely, thus causing the human race to be drawn down paths that can only lead to ultimate destruction. The sadness and frustration we feel to see history repeating itself in this way is beyond words! And," I added, "Would you believe they are even using this newly acquired technology to shoot down our discs!"

"Ali," Paco reached out a tentative hand and placed it on my shoulder, "are you okay? I didn't think you lot were supposed to feel emotion," he said, putting his arm around me and peering closely into my eyes, which were moist with tears.

"Believe me Paco," I answered, brushing one from my cheek with the back of my hand, "there's a whole lot that humans don't know about us. Just because we have less muscular structure in our faces, and that we have gotten to a more balanced place with our emotions, doesn't mean we don't still feel. We are living, sentient beings, not robots!"

23 ▶ PURPOSE

Paco!" I called in telepathic greeting, "Welcome aboard! Nice to see you!"

"Well, as a matter of fact, Ali, I'm lucky to be here," he replied, making himself comfortable on one of our seats. "I was called out tonight to help one of our hospitalized parishioners, but I managed to escape just before midnight and got to sleep, so here I am.

"Wow! These seats are just incredible!" he exclaimed in delight, wriggling himself around into various positions to see how quickly the chair would accommodate him. Even though he'd been on the ship many times, our furniture technology still fascinated him, the way these seemingly quite ordinary plastic chairs automatically molded themselves to the shape and size of the body seated on them. With so many different body shapes using them, from small workers to very tall Elders, as well as various other ET types, this was most necessary, especially for those stationed full-time on the ships, needing a few home comforts.

"So what do you want to talk about tonight, Ali Cat? Have you got an interesting lesson lined up for me?"

"Well, as a matter of fact I have, and it's really important. Tell me, Paco, did you watch the TV news last night?"

"Yes, of course; we always watch that if we're in."

"Okay. Did you hear the report on the world-famous celebrity whose highly complex and convoluted love life ended in a tragic death?"

"Oh, God, yes!" he answered, lifting his eyes to heaven, "over and over again, all evening. They kept interrupting the normal programming to go on and on about it."

"Tell me how you felt, listening to it."

"Well, at first of course I was shocked and saddened. I mean you don't expect a thing like that to happen to anyone in such a position, but then it just went on and on, with all the usual lengthy, in-depth interviews, and nosey reporters asking all sorts of silly, tasteless questions and obviously trying to wring every last drop of emotion out of the whole affair. They even tried to interview close family and friends, people who were terribly affected and upset, almost as if the whole aim was to parade their personal tragedy, and all the emotions that went with it, in front of as many people as possible. In the end it was making me feel quite ill, and I was so relieved when the phone rang, calling me out to the hospital. It gave me an excuse to leave the house and get away from it. I would've turned the TV off, but the others, Father Keating and our housekeeper, Mary, wanted to hear all the details. Why are you asking me about it? Surely your people aren't interested in such sordid little human affairs."

"No, we're not, but what does concern us is the way the media on Earth is being used in this way as a channel for the dark forces. This negative force gains tremendous energy and strength by feeding upon the lower emotions of humans, and it's so beneficial to their interests to stir up these emotions as often and as continually as it can, to keep the fire burning as it were, in order to generate maximum energy to feed off."

"Ali, you speak of this negative force as if it's a living being, with a mind and intelligence of its own."

"It is, or at least it expresses itself through the mind and intelligence of living beings. The Christian Church personifies it as Satan, and in fact all religious traditions have personified it in some way, but it's simply a very low-frequency energy of fear that any of us can potentially tap into if we allow ourselves to. The danger is, it can be extremely subtle and cunning, and can easily sneak up on you, and before you know it, you're caught up in it."

"Well," said Paco, "it seems to me that it's fairly open and obvious on Earth at the moment, what with all the wars, greed, selfishness, racism and religious intolerance going on. I wouldn't exactly call that subtle."

"Oh, yes!" I agreed. "You're right enough there, but it's also expressing itself in other more subtle ways as well, for example through music that disharmonizes rather than harmonizes the vibrational frequency of those who listen to it. It's also being expressed through all the violent movies, negative internet sites and electronic games that distort and unbalance the energy frequency of those who regularly watch or link into them. It's present in any form of so-called 'entertainment' that incites feelings of anger, hatred, lust and other negative emotions in those who come into contact with it.

"The problem is," I went on, "negative emotion and drama are highly addictive to the human psyche. There are many who get a real 'high' by allowing their emotions free rein. These uncontrolled emotions tend to blind one to the true picture, and are the cause of many problems faced by Earth humans. They are the greatest block to soul evolvement and must be overcome if one wishes to be a clear and true channel for Divine Consciousness.

"Honestly Paco, we too have walked this path. We have all manifested human lives in various planetary cultures on the physical plane, and so we know and understand the difficulties and pitfalls that you face in living out your lives on Planet Earth. All beings fall at times

— even those who dwell in the angelic realms have all 'been there, done that' during the course of their evolution. It is the falling and getting up again, many times over, that enables a soul to grow in spirit, and to gain understanding and compassion for others.

"What Earth humans need to learn most of all is non-attachment, to learn to turn the other cheek rather than grimly holding on to past grievances and hurts. For heaven's sake, some people hold onto such negative 'baggage' over generations! By determinedly 'maintaining the rage,' your judgment becomes clouded by negative emotion, which is always divisive and destructive. It is only through non-attachment, release and forgiveness that one can practice unconditional love, thereby allowing Oneness to manifest on Earth. This pure love carries you far beyond the blinding and binding limitations of physical, Earthly emotion and into the all-embracing realms of the Great Oneness, which is your ultimate destiny."

"But how do you know all this?" Paco queried. "Honestly, Ali, I know that as a priest I shouldn't think this way, but really and truly, how can we be sure? Sometimes I have to wonder if it isn't all just one big lie — a huge and cruel practical joke that's being played upon all of us, and that the truth of the matter is that we get born, we live out our puny little lives, then we are snuffed out like a candle, and that is all there is to it."

"Oh, Paco, I'm surprised a priest could have such doubts! Not you of all people. Look, I realize how hard it is for Earth humans who don't have the ability to see from our perspective, to recall past lives and the time spent in between, as well as lessons learned during those lives. If only you could, then you would *know* — it wouldn't have to be a matter of faith and trust. One of your greatest lessons is trust, for until you learn to trust, fear will dominate your life. This is one of the hardest tests that humanity faces, for to learn to trust is to overcome fear and doubt in your life, and it is fear and doubt that feeds the negative force, in other words, the 'Satan' within.

"Please Paco, believe me, there truly *is* a purpose behind it all — a goal to be reached and a destiny to be fulfilled, for all of us! And what I've been talking to you about regarding the mastering of the emotions is an extremely important step towards attaining that goal and living out your destiny.

"It's just that we're a much older culture than Earth humans, so we're further along the path, which enables us to see where we have been, and where we are headed. Like it or not, together we are all evolving through the various levels of the Human Ladder. It is only the fact that some of us too have fallen, and made mistakes, that gives us the right, the knowing, and the compassion to reach out and try to help our human children avoid those same mistakes that we have made along the way. We know where the pit-falls are, and the steep and treacherous edges where a foot can easily slip, plunging one right back down into the abyss, because we have walked the same path."

"Oh, shit! What was that?" came a most unpriestly oath as the disc, seemingly right on cue, suddenly dropped like a rapidly descending lift, leaving our stomachs up above our heads somewhere.

"My goodness!" I replied shakily. "Talk about plunging into an abyss! That must have been an enormous atmospheric disturbance to affect a Disc this size to such an extent. Normally you hardly feel them on these really big ones. I hope everyone's all right."

It was then that Paco's eyes widened in panic. "Oh, my God, it's got me! I'm trapped! Help! The chair is going to swallow me alive!"

It took a second or two to register what he was going on about, then I burst out laughing, or at least expressed profound amusement as far as my gray container would allow. "Oh, Paco, for heaven's sake, it's okay. That's just a safety measure! Haven't you ever been on a plane and seen the '*Please Fasten Safety Belts*' sign come on during a patch of turbulence? Ours are automatic! In the same way that the seats mold themselves to accommodate whichever body sits in them, they also immediately close those arm things around us at the first indication of turbulence. The sudden drop activated it. Hang on, it'll release you in a moment. Just talk to it with your mind — assure it that you're okay and that the danger is past. They usually sense into these things themselves, but you got such a fright, the chair is probably still picking up on your nervousness and holding on. Take a deep breath and relax, and it will too."

The look of relief on poor Paco's face was so comical as the arms finally folded themselves neatly back with a click.

"You and your damned alien devices! For a second there I thought the rotten thing was attacking me."

"Now Paco, don't get annoyed with it. It only has your safety and welfare in mind, and you have to admit, it did its little job really well, didn't it? So thank it nicely."

"Huh? Thank it? But it's only a chair, for goodness sake. Why should I thank a darned chair?"

"Paco, just *do it!* It's not *just* a chair. It's part of the Mothership, and therefore linked into the disc's consciousness. If you don't treat it with respect it *might* just decide to hold on and not let go — and don't tell me I haven't warned you!" I added for good measure.

"Oh, great! That would be just my luck — trapped for eternity by a temperamental ET seat belt, doomed to orbit Earth for the next two million years!"

"Don't worry, brother dear," I assured him. "I would keep you alive and well by feeding you yummy blue and pink paste out of tubes, washed down by a choice of blue or yellow liquid, and you'd never need to go to the toilet ever again."

"Oh, goody," came the most unenthusiastic reply.

"Now where were we?" I frowned, trying to remember what I'd been telling him prior to the disturbance. "Ah yes, I know — we were all falling into holes, weren't we? As I said before, our people too have had their share of ups and downs through countless physical-plane lives in mortal form, with plenty of tests and learning experiences along the way, so we know very well where all the difficulties lie."

"This is something I've been meaning to ask you, Ali. What planet do the Guardians come from? Are you from the Zeta Reticuli star system as some Earth researchers claim?"

"We've had lives there, but now we don't actually come from any physical planet as such, having evolved past the need for mortal form, except of course to carry out our work with physical-plane humans. We do have a home base however, which has an energy signature that translates roughly as birthplace, home or realm, and we also maintain a base in the Zeta Reticuli Star System, as well as in other places."

"But what about the planets you were just talking about before, you know, where your people have had so many lives?"

"During the course of our evolution we've experienced lives in all the various planetary cultures. I can most especially recall a number of lives in the Sirius star system as well as several as an Earth human. In fact, I've had heaps of lives in many different ET cultures. Once we evolve to Guardian level, we've moved past all of that, except to go among those cultures to carry out work.

"The Altarians and Pleiadians are right at the top of level two, so they are able to access 20% of their full conscious awareness, which is why they seem so highly evolved in the eyes of Earth humans. They also look more human than we do, at least in the Earth sense of the word, so they often step in to help us with really frightened level-one humans."

"And why do we need to experience life in human form? What's it really all about?"

"Well, the human kingdom on planets such as Earth forms a bridge between the animal kingdom and higher realms of spiritual realization, and as such, it carries certain learning opportunities. As human beings you are creators in the making, so, it is within the human kingdom that you must learn to master emotion. Creation is simply the process of transferring the energy of thought into physical matter, and herein lies great responsibility, for to create in a positive way with thought, it is first necessary to learn to master the negative emotions through self-control and discipline.

"This is the main reason for human existence — to learn to work with emotion and thought in a positive and constructive way so that order and positive creativity are the result rather than the chaos and disorder that results from thought patterns which stem from negative and uncontrolled emotions. And if humans wish to know how well they are learning this lesson, they must look closely at their own lives. You are as you think, so you need to look at whether your life is in order or in chaos.

"It's really important for Earth humans to clearly understand the potency of their thoughts, and the very tangible thought forms that all of you are capable of creating. Most people on Earth do not have the faintest idea of the damage that can be done with uncontrolled emotions and thoughts of anger, jealousy, resentment, hatred, lust and intolerance, which, as I said before, all stem from the Satan within — the vibration of fear. The results of these negative thought patterns and emotions of humanity are expressed most strongly in black and ugly thought forms which inhabit the lower astral planes. These are the devils and demons which plague humankind and are, in their own way, very real, having been created out of the collective consciousness of the human race."

"What do you mean exactly by the astral plane?" Paco wanted to know.

"The astral plane," I replied, "is also known as the plane of emotion, illusion and dreams. It is not very far removed in vibrational frequency from the physical plane, and covers a wide band of frequencies from the very low, which is that region Earth humans think of as 'hell,' to the higher ones that most people think of as 'heaven,' for it is to this level that souls generally go after physical death. It is from this astral plane that spirit communication originates, and because it's composed of such a wide range of frequencies, this communication is not always of the highest order, and can be confusing and misleading at times.

"There are plenty of ego-centered entities of the lower-astral realms who gain huge amounts of energy and amusement by attaching themselves to human mediums and channeling all sorts of messages which are purported to be from 'highly evolved spirit guides and masters.' These are also the ones responsible for such phenomena as spirit possession, the more nasty types of hauntings, and many of the supposed negative ET encounter experiences. Some of these thought forms have been created by minds affected with drugs or alcohol, and can be extremely dangerous, cunning and controlling if they manage to hook their claws into human minds whose psychic centers are open and unprotected through also using drugs or alcohol, or even doing psychic experimentation and development without proper preparation, self-discipline, understanding and intent."

"Ali," Paco interjected, "please excuse me for interrupting, but this is something I've heard about before, in the way of certain dangers that are involved in psychic development and so-called occult practices. Can you explain this more clearly?"

"Yes, Paco, I can. Occult practices which are designed to open oneself to the super-conscious, if not undertaken correctly and with proper control of the emotions, can instead open one's psyche to the realms of the subconscious mind, which is the dwelling place of a person's own hidden fears — fears which may have their origin in distant past lives. This is why dabbling in such pursuits as crystal gazing, fortune telling, seances and ouija boards without proper understanding, control and intent can very easily open the psyche to interference by negative energies and entities, which can be very dangerous indeed and a huge stumbling block to true spiritual awakening.

"Lower-astral-plane entities are trapped in their 'hell' because they will not let go of fear-induced emotions and vices. Cosmic Law states that like attracts like, so if a human being on the physical plane embarks upon any form of psychic development without the very best and purest of intentions, then they will automatically attract these lower entities to themselves like a magnet, thus unwittingly becoming a channel for the dark forces."

"But surely," Paco asked, "If a person is very psychic, then aren't they highly evolved spiritually as well, to have those abilities?"

"No way, Paco, absolutely not, and it is because of this misunderstanding that many people become hurt and disillusioned after visiting a psychic reader for advice and being badly misled or told something that is completely wrong or even quite destructive or dangerous. Just because someone is psychic does *not* mean that they are necessarily highly evolved spiritually. Being 'psychic' and being 'spiritual' is not the same thing, and, in fact, some who display psychic talent have not progressed very far at all, and one must be extremely wary of taking advice or guidance from such individuals. Think about it — many members of the animal kingdom are extremely psychic, but would you want advice from them?

"More and more people on Earth are beginning to manifest psychic and healing abilities now that these perfectly natural talents have become more widely accepted through the New Age movement which has come about as a result of the vibrational shift that Earth is undergoing — the shift from the Piscean to the Aquarian Age.

"It's through these emerging abilities that many are at present being tested to see whether they are truly ready to step up to a level of greater spiritual responsibility, or if they are going to abuse the limited powers they have been given. Learning to work correctly with psychic energy is one of the hardest tests that humans come up against on the path of spiritual awakening, as there are many emotional traps and pitfalls for the unwary. One of the main tests lies in the fact that those who manifest these perfectly natural abilities tend to be regarded on Earth with awe, reverence, and envy, when sometimes the reality of the matter is that they have failed the test of ego, power or greed in past lives, and so now are being tested again to see if they have learned better this time.

"These are often ones of a rather emotional temperament, and it is this facet of their character which attracts like-minded, emotionally charged astral entities to them, like moths to a flame. These entities will, in exchange for energies created by the negative emotions of their 'host,' help them manifest psychic abilities, which eventually result in the host being caught up in an ego trip expressing in manipulative or controlling behavior. This 'wonderful and powerful' psychic then draws a gathering of adoring disciples around them, all eager to give away their personal power to their 'guru,' thus providing even more emotional energy for the entity to tap into and feed off. This can potentially be a very dangerous situation for all concerned, except for the astral entity, who is having a wonderful time basking in the glory of its host's ego-trip and all the while growing stronger and more potent by tapping into the emotional energies thus created. The end result for the humans involved is often sickness, either physical, mental or emotional, and a most disenchanted and disillusioned group of disciples who may be turned off from any form of spiritual development for many lives to come, thus causing a block in their soul journey.

"Wait a minute," Paco interrupted, "are you saying we shouldn't even try to develop psychic abilities?"

"Please don't misunderstand me. There is nothing intrinsically wrong with possessing psychic ability, in fact it is perfectly natural and certainly not evil, but if one wishes to make use of these abilities, it is most important to examine the motives behind the wish. If it is to make heaps of money, or to manipulate and control others, or to show off how sensitive or 'powerful' you are, then stop right there.

"Over the span of millennia, the negative force has manifested on and around Earth through the group we refer to as the Controllers. These beings are the hidden force behind many secret societies, and they have also manipulated and controlled humankind through fear-based dogma and superstition entrenched within traditional religions of Earth. Now that they are losing their stranglehold in this area, various New Age belief systems are being used to manipulate and control minds through the myriad psychics, seers, channelers and prophets of gloom and doom that have been so prolific upon the Earth plane over the last few decades.

"So," Paco sighed, "this is why we need to work on our feelings that bring up fear."

"Yes, as their name implies, the Controllers use mind control and can impinge upon the minds and auric fields of psychics to influence the messages and teachings given out. In this way they have fuelled the fear behind the concept of 'evil aliens' who are conspiring to take control of Planet Earth. This negative propaganda is carefully designed to play upon humankind's intrinsic mistrust of anyone who looks a little different or is not of *your tribe*, and it is proving to be a huge test for those humans who get caught up in it. Overcoming this negative message involves tapping in to your own self-empowerment — the God within, in other words. It also involves placing your trust in the ultimate good and getting past the barrier of fear.

"Believe me, it is not 'evil aliens' of whom the human race needs to be wary, but rather those of your own kind who strive for positions of power and control among your people and then proceed to preach the gospel of intolerance, bigotry, hatred and fear. Surely we do not need to point out to the people of Earth that the Commandment to 'Love Your Neighbor as Yourself' refers to every soul upon the planet, no matter the color of their skin or the particular belief system they may choose to follow. This also includes all other living creatures upon Earth and of other planets and dimensions as well, for we are all One.

"Well," said Paco, "it seems to me that the bottom line in all of this is trust and love — pure unconditional love that has nothing to do with emotion or passion, but rather of tolerance, respect and *com*passion! It's the message I'm trying to teach at church."

"Absolutely!" I replied. "It's that simple. And simplicity is the essence of the whole thing. Don't allow yourself to become caught up in complexity. There's no need for complex dogmas, belief systems or rituals — in fact the negative force uses complexity and 'mystery' as a tool to create confusion in human minds. Just keep everything in your life simple and pure, and remember that God is love. Love is the motivating energy behind all of creation, and is all that truly counts in the end."

"My goodness!" said Paco. "I should get you up in the pulpit delivering a sermon. I can just see that weird, gray face with its huge black eyes peering out from under a monk's cowl. I know! You could start the sermon in your human form then shape-shift in the middle of it!

"Gee! I wish I could do that," he added thoughtfully. "At least it'd be a good way to keep their attention. Although knowing my congregation, they probably wouldn't even notice!*"

24 ▶ AN ET HOUSEKEEPER

Hello, anybody home?" I called, taking the back stairs of the presbytery two at a time. Paco had only recently moved to his new parish closer to home, and this was the first chance I'd had to pay him a visit. I was justifiably proud of my adopted brother, and as I stood there waiting for the door to open, I couldn't help but think of how far he'd come in the years since his ordination, and how well he'd succeeded in what he'd set out to prove: that a Rom could indeed do anything!

Up until the time of his acceptance into the Priesthood he'd taken great care to keep silent about his Gypsy background, however, once he was safely and irrevocably ordained, he quietly but proudly proclaimed his true heritage to anyone who enquired, and was pleasantly surprised to find himself accepted far more readily than he'd anticipated — another example of operating in fear vs. trust. In fact, in the parish where he'd been serving until recently as assistant priest, his superior had proven extremely supportive and had given him every encouragement to remain in close contact with his family and the others of the Romany community. Now here he was, finally appointed to his very own parish, a fully ordained member of the Roman Catholic Priesthood, as self-assured, secure and confident as the best of them.

"Oh, Ali," he greeted me. "Thank God it's only you! But what are you doing here anyway? I wasn't expecting you. Why didn't you call to say you were coming?"

"Paco, for crying out loud! What's the matter with you? It's *me*! Do I have to ring up and make an appointment to visit my own brother? Out of the kindness of my heart I decided to drop by to say hello and to see how you're settling in to your new parish, and *this* is the welcome I get! Look, if you're *that* busy I'll just go away and let you get on with it, no problem!"

"No, no, Ali Cat, it's not that. Course I'm glad to see you. It's just that everything's in a bit of a mess, and..."

"Paco, don't you remember? You're my dearly beloved brother, who's *always* in a perpetual mess! So what's the difference? You can't be any worse than when you were living at home. Now let me *in*!"

So saying, I pushed him aside none too gently and stepped into the house.

"Hell's bells!" I gasped, stopping so suddenly at the door of the living room that Paco walked straight into me. "What's happened?" It looks like there's been a tornado through the place! What have you been *doing*, throwing wild parties or something?"

"Oh, for heaven's sake, it's not *that* bad — you always have to exaggerate! Father Ryan, the priest I took over from, offered the resident housekeeper a position at his new parish. He's getting on in years and had let things go a bit here, so I've been really busy catching up with parish work and haven't had time to organize somebody else to fill the position, let alone time to do much in the way of house cleaning myself. If I'd known you were coming I would have neatened it up a bit. Here, look, I'll just pick up these cushions and put those books back on the shelf — there now, that looks better already."

As he spoke, a brilliantly clever solution to his dilemma began formulating in my mind — a solution that would take care of my ongoing difficulties as well. "Paco," I interrupted his cleaning-up efforts, "why don't you call upon the awesome powers of the Guardian Consciousness to solve your little problem?"

"Huh? What do you mean?"

"*Me,* of course! What other Guardian do you know?"

"Ali, *what* are you going on about?"

"Look, you need a housekeeper, and I'm sick to death of living all on my own way out of town. I absolutely *loathe* having to drive such distances to get to my classes, which are all here in the city anyway, and Maris keeps telling me I need to be closer in to be able to reach more people through my work, so, problem solved — I'll be your housekeeper!"

"Now just hang on, Ali Cat! You're a *hopeless* housekeeper and an even *worse* cook. Remember the time you accidentally put God knows how many tablespoons of cayenne pepper into the stew instead of sweet paprika? And how you almost poisoned the lot of us the other time with that revolting half-cooked chicken? God, I've never felt so sick in my whole life! I still feel ill just thinking about it. You know, I was never quite sure which I dreaded the most — the food they served us at the seminary or your cooking when I was home on holidays."

Oh, Paco, for heaven's sake, that was years ago. You know I've been fending for myself for ages now, ever since Mom and Dad decided to go back to travelling. I am a perfectly competent housekeeper *and* an excellent cook, even though *you* always insist on ordering takeout when you come to see me. Anyway, you've seen how neat and clean I keep the house now, so don't be so rude. It's clean enough to eat off the floor."

"Well, the way you spill everything when you're cooking, that's probably the only way to get a decent feed.

"Anyway," he went on bravely, holding up a hand to defend himself as I picked up the nearest cushion and threatened to throw it at him, "who ever heard of an ET presbytery housekeeper? What if one day you forget which body you're occupying and answer the door in your gray form? Can you imagine what it would be like for one of my poor, unsuspecting parishioners to arrive at the presbytery and be greeted by a small, gray-colored alien with huge, black eyes and four long, thin fingers? What an awful thought! It doesn't even bear thinking about!"

"Stop being so damned racist and prejudiced!" I snapped at him. "There's as much chance of me doing that as there is of you turning up on the altar to say Mass with a scarf tied around your head and gold earrings dangling from your ears. You think you're so smart and so wonderful being an Earth human. You don't know what it's like to be caught between two species, one human and one ET. Whichever one I'm part of at any given time I feel homesick for the other. Sometimes I feel as if I don't fit in properly anywhere and I don't know what I am. Now that you're a high and mighty priest with your own parish even *you* don't want me around in case I embarrass you!"

At this point I managed to squeeze out a couple of tears, knowing that would get him. Sure enough, the next moment he was there beside me, with a protective and brotherly arm around my shoulders. "Oh, come on, Ali Cat, I'm sorry. I was only joking. I didn't mean to hurt you. You know I wouldn't do that for the world."

"Oh, Paco, it's just that it's so lonely at home all on my own." Now sniffling for real. "First you went off to the seminary, then Mara died, then the rest of the family went back on the road. I know I used to grumble about never having any privacy or peace when you were all at home, but now that I'm stuck out there on my own it's awful, and the place is so far out. I seem to spend half the day driving and you know how I still hate it. I've never really gotten over the experience of that awful crash, and the sensation of hurtling forward at high speed is far more tangible in a car than it is in our discs. At least if I lived here I'd be handy to everything. In fact I could even walk to some of my classes."

"Well, I must admit," he grinned, "it would be fun having you around. Lately we never seem to have the opportunity to really talk. I always enjoyed the challenge of our theological discussions, and hearing your people's side of things. I know at some level we're having discussions *upstairs*, because more and more things are just *dawning* on me, but now I can pick your brain down here, too. Believe it or not, our discussions give me many good themes for sermons. The only thing is what are we going to do about the family home if you move in here? It'd be too much for you to look after both places, but we can't just sell it without consulting the family first."

We both considered this problem for several minutes, before Paco snapped his fingers in triumph. "I have it! There's some people I know who are looking for rental accommodation. They're a Romany family who've been living in a couple of old wagons parked on council land, just like Granny and I used to, and the local authorities have been putting pressure on them to move on but they don't have anywhere to go. God, that brings back horrible memories! We could rent the place out to them. It'd be ideal, because there's plenty of room for their wagons, and they are really good people who I know will look after the place properly."

"Paco, that is brilliant! There's just one problem though. What happens when our own family takes a break from their travels? Where can they stay?"

Paco's face lit up with a wicked grin. "Why can't they park their wagons out back here? There's plenty of room. That'd give the neighborhood gossips something to get their teeth into — a couple of genuine Romany *vardos* parked out back of the presbytery! I can just hear them now: "You let *one* into the place, and before you know it the whole *tribe* is there! Damned Gypos, they breed like *rabbits*!"

"Paco," I said, shaking him by the hand, "you are truly a devil!"

"Well," he answered with a pleased grin, "I do try!"

25 ▶ VIBRATIONS

Hey, Ali Cat!" said Paco, blissfully stretching himself out on the couch and almost pushing me off in the process. "How about explaining that electromagnetic thingummy to me — you know, whatever has to do with vibrational frequencies or whatever it is that I was supposed to have studied in physics at school."

"Instead of looking out the window or reading comic books?" I added, giving him a good shove to remove his feet from my lap.

"Well," he blithely replied, "why bother studying these things when you have an ET in the family, that's what I say! After all, isn't that why you're here? To fill me in on it all?"

"I wouldn't have to if you'd listened at school, would I?"

I'd been resident at the presbytery for a couple of weeks now, settled very comfortably into the private housekeeper's quarters, which suited me admirably, providing the peace and quiet I needed to get on with my work. Paco had offered me a bedroom in the main house, but I knew very well that, being a priest, he would sometimes be called out during the night, so there'd be the phone ringing and him moving about, and I really needed to be left completely undisturbed to carry out my work up on the disc. However, when he was home, as he was this evening, I took the opportunity to get on with the job of teaching him what he needed to know.

"Okay, then, if you really want to learn about the electromagnetic 'thingummy' as you so eloquently put it, then please turn off the TV so I can concentrate. Everything around us including our own physical body," I went on once he was seated and paying attention, "is composed of atoms grouped together to form molecules. These molecules are in a continual state of vibration. It is this vibration at the molecular level that the brain, via the sensory organs such as our eyes, ears, nose, fingers and tongue perceives as sight, sound, smell, touch and taste. For example, if the molecules that form my physical body suddenly decided to stop vibrating, or changed their rate of vibration or frequency to a significant extent, then my body would cease to register upon your sense of sight. You would not be able to see me, and as far as you were concerned, I would be invisible. Just think what havoc I could create then at Sunday Mass!"

"Heaven help us all!" he gave a mock shudder. "That doesn't bear thinking about. Go on, this is getting really spooky."

"Each color of the spectrum," I continued, "vibrates at a different rate, as does every musical note. The color violet, for example, vibrates at a much higher frequency than red — a whole octave higher to be precise. Ultraviolet has a higher frequency still, placing it beyond the human range of perception, so it's invisible. However, just because it's invisible doesn't mean it isn't there. Anyone who's had a dose of sunburn should know that! Infrared, at the lower end of the color spectrum, is also below our human range of perception."

"So what you're saying," Paco queried, "is that this 'frequency' you refer to is actually the rate of molecular vibration?"

"Yes, exactly," I answered, "and everything has its own particular frequency. The vibrational frequency of every living creature is unique, and that of course includes humans. The sound of a person's name carries its own unique and individual frequency, hence our Romany tradition of keeping one's true name a secret, so that harm cannot be done through interference with the person's personal frequency on an energy level. One can send healing to another by tapping into their personal frequency, but unfortunately, harm can also be sent."

"And what about the electromagnetic scale?" Paco asked. "That has to do with vibrational frequencies too, doesn't it?"

"Yes," I replied, "it certainly does. Everything that can be perceived by our eyes as sight, by our fingers as touch, by our tongue as taste, by our nose as smell and by our ears as sound has its place upon a scale of measurement, which is referred to in physics as the electromagnetic scale.

"This scale covers a vast range of energy frequencies from very low to very high, and that part of it perceptible by humans is extremely small, even taking into account those normally imperceptible wavelengths such as radio and TV, which need specialized receivers to enable them to be translated into the very limited range of human perception. Other frequencies such as alpha, beta, delta and theta brain waves, microwaves and X-rays also need specialized equipment if they are to be monitored or measured in physical terms.

"Just as there are colors such as infrared and ultraviolet which, although beyond the range of human sight, are there nonetheless, there are also sounds extending below and above the human range of hearing. A good example is the special dog whistles which are readily available in any pet shop. Their sound is of a frequency too high for the human ear to detect, but a dog, whose hearing mechanisms have access to a higher range than humans, can hear the sound very clearly."

"The sonar signals used by bats would be the same, wouldn't they?" Paco queried. "And I believe whales also communicate ultrasonically, don't they?"

"Exactly!" I answered. "And the sound that our discs make is the same. This is why animals become so badly agitated when we're around.

We also have equipment that can alter vibrational frequencies to a marked degree, and this is the secret behind much of our technology. For example, when our discs disappear suddenly, becoming instantaneously invisible, we've simply changed the frequency of the molecular structure up a few degrees on the electromagnetic scale, thus rendering the craft and all on board completely invisible to the eyes of any human observers."

Paco shook his head in amazement. "I wish I could do that," he sighed wistfully. "The possibilities would be endless. And what about ghosts in relationship to all of this?"

"Well," I replied, "now that you hopefully have a better understanding of the electromagnetic scale, and a fuller appreciation of humankind's very limited access to the endless range of energy frequencies potentially available, you can begin to comprehend a little more clearly such phenomena as ghosts, clairvoyance, auras, psychic senses, etc. These all operate on wavelengths or frequencies which, like ultraviolet light and ultrasonic sounds, are beyond the perception of most human senses. Dogs, cats and other animals can sense ghosts much more easily than average humans can because they can perceive vibrational frequencies that are beyond the range of human perception.

Many humans are also born with clairvoyant and psychic abilities, but as they progress through childhood, the conditioning they are subjected to gradually causes these natural perceptions to close down. In societies such as tribal cultures where these abilities are understood and recognized rather than being brushed aside as trivial and time wasting, nothing but 'silly imagination,' or even downright evil, many more individuals carry these perfectly natural senses through to adulthood, often passing down particular gifts like healing through generational family lines. For example, you've inherited psychic abilities from your grandmother."

"Ali, to tell you the truth, this is something I just don't know how to handle at times, and it really confuses me."

"How do you mean?"

"Well, sometimes I'll get a very clear dream or 'flash' about a future event and I know it's an insight on the psychic level, but it doesn't always come to pass. This can be a blessing, because the insights aren't always pleasant, so I'm relieved when they don't happen, but what I can't understand is, why do I get them in the first place if they're not right?"

"That's simple," I replied. "You see, all psychic 'flashes' originate on the astral plane — the plane of emotion — and negative happenings tend to generate stronger emotion than positive happenings. Everything that manifests as a happening or event on the physical plane is born out of infinite possibilities, both negative and positive, but it is the negative possibilities that are the most readily perceived through psychic awareness, because, being negative, they generate stronger emotion."

"Okay, so I'm more likely to pick up on a negative possibility, but this isn't necessarily what is going to manifest into physical reality?"

"Right! Psychic ability works by the seer tapping into the infinite possibilities surrounding any given event or situation. All these possibilities are actually occurring simultaneously, because in the greater reality, time as we know it doesn't exist. In other words, there is no past and future, just an eternal present. The outcome of any given situation depends entirely upon the free will of the person to whom the situation applies, which can change from moment to moment.

At the time you receive the flash, that negative possibility may very well be the correct one, but at the time of the situation itself, circumstances have changed and another more positive possibility has been brought into play through the free will of the person involved.

This is where psychic readings and 'fortune telling' can potentially fall apart at the seams, because by putting a negative idea into a person's mind in the form of a prediction, it is possible to influence the eventual outcome of the event or happening in a negative way, by overriding the person's free will. And no one has that right! Even done with the best intentions, it is still a form of control and manipulation of another, so you are better in the long run to keep such information to yourself, thus allowing the person's free will to choose the correct outcome according to the needs of the higher self."

Paco still looked puzzled. "But what about when a psychic sees some sort of major disaster occurring, like a public figure being assassinated, or an aircraft crashing and everyone on board being killed? Shouldn't they try to give some sort of warning?"

"No, not really, because everyone freely chooses the time and circumstances of their own death, and there is no such thing as 'death' anyway, because we are all immortal spirits. Sure, the physical body may be destroyed by an assassin's bullet or a plane crash, but that is not the end by any means. We simply step out of that container, then, when we're ready, we step back in to a new one. If it's not our time to step out, the 'accident' or 'disaster' won't happen to us — the assassin will be stopped by someone, or we'll be 'miraculously' blocked from getting to the airport or boarding the plane. What I'm trying to say is that if a death is not meant to be then, it won't occur then, but if it is someone's 'time,' then no psychic has the right to interfere.

"Don't get me wrong;" I went on, "psychic ability is fine if it's used to assist others to look within in order to help them find their own hidden potential, which hopefully will enable them to develop self-empowerment — but it must *not* be used in an interfering way. Remember our conversation on the disc about the astral plane — that it is not very much higher than the physical plane? Well there are parts of it that are actually lower in frequency."

"Do those lower parts by any chance relate at all to the Catholic's view of hell and purgatory?"

"Yes, and a spirit can certainly be drawn to these regions after physical death and become trapped in the torments of this plane of existence for as long as they refuse to let go of whatever negative-behavior patterns that drew them there in the first place, especially if that's what they believe. However, for ones trapped in these lower regions, there is no such thing as eternal damnation, for no one is ever eternally lost. Help is always available if and when the trapped spirit truly seeks love and forgiveness and is ready to move on to higher frequencies.

"What is really important to understand in all of this is that *the raising of your vibrational frequency to higher levels is what soul evolvement and spiritual development is all about.* This is the all-important link between science and religion that has been lost to the majority of Earth humans, and is the crux of the transmutation work that the Guardians are carrying out down here. To learn to meditate at this time is so important, because such practices have the effect of speeding up and refining the energy frequency of humans, whereas mind-altering drugs and alcohol have the very opposite effect, and so should be avoided.

"The Source, or 'God,' if you prefer that term, vibrates at an incredibly high frequency, so, by raising your own vibrational frequency, you draw closer to that Source. Once a spirit reaches this very high frequency level, its vibrations synchronize and meld with those of the Source, thus the spirit 'reunites with God.' If, however, a person chooses to indulge in behavior that causes the opposite effect, that is, a lowering of the vibrational frequency rate, then they are effectively distancing themselves from the Source."

"And is meditation the only way to raise your vibrational frequency?" Paco wanted to know.

"Certainly not," I answered, "although if real progress is to be made, then meditation eventually becomes a necessity, for to truly 'find God' one must learn to go within. However, anything that brings you peace and upliftment affects the vibrations in a positive way. For example, listening to beautiful, harmonious and inspiring music has this effect — or looking upon a scene of beauty, or showing kindness and compassion towards others.

"Some people raise their vibrational frequency by praying or attending religious services, which is very effective, providing it is done in love and sincerity, and in fact if you closely examine religious music, you will notice that much of it is set in certain keys. For example, the key of D major evokes a sense of devotion, happiness and joy, while E major is full and serene, and B minor puts one in a meditative mood. The Romany people understand the way music affects the mood of the listener, and certain scales and harmonics are used to bring about various healing effects. This is why sensitive people can detect 'enchantment' in Romany music.

"Oh, yes. I can even detect people's reactions to the different music in church."

"I'm sure you can. Music affects the human psyche very deeply, so much care must be put into the type of music you choose, for the wrong sort can be extremely harmful to your vibrational frequency. In fact, the Controllers are doing exactly that on Earth right now, using a certain type of music to exert mind control and bring disharmony into the energy field of many young people, causing untold damage to sensitive psyches. The only protection humans have against these Controllers is to raise their vibrational frequency through spiritual practice to a level beyond the astral plane, where the Controllers can't access.

"What level do the Guardians operate on? Are you from the astral plane or higher?"

"As caretakers of energy within this galaxy," I replied, "we are able to operate on all levels, wherever we are needed, including higher cosmic levels. However, much of the work we do with Earth humans is carried out on the plane of illusion, the astral plane. It is here that we are able to set up certain scenarios to test the level of spiritual evolvement that various souls have reached, sometimes tempting them with illusions of grandeur, or 'great psychic abilities,' just to see if they have overcome ego — or else we push them to the limits of their fears, to help them overcome this major block to their spiritual progress.

"It's in this way that we are able to gauge the areas in their development needing to be worked on. We act as mirrors to the human psyche, reflecting back what is in the heart and in the subconscious mind of those who look upon us. We can manifest as objective beings, but we can also enter the subjective realms to carry out our work."

"And what about ghosts? Why do they sometimes appear misty and vaporous?"

"This is because they're operating on a slightly higher frequency than physical beings, and the higher you go, the more dissipated your molecular structure becomes and therefore the finer the substance of your makeup. For example, solid ice molecules vibrate at a lower rate than those of water. By applying heat to ice the vibrational rate is sped up, and a liquid substance, water, is the result. If you continue to heat the water, the frequency rate rises still further and you are then left with a vapor — steam.

"Ghosts can pass through solid objects such as closed doors and walls because the higher the vibrational rate of the molecular structure, the more widely dispersed the molecules become, so the molecules that make up the form or substance of a ghost are much more widely dispersed than those that form a seemingly solid wall. The ghost literally passes through, in between the more solid molecular structure of the wall, just like water being poured through a sieve."

Light suddenly dawned on Paco's face. "Aha!" he exclaimed. "That's how you sneaky little Greys come and go as you please through locked doors and windows, and also how you remove your human 'guests' from their bedrooms and take them on board your craft. So, you are you able to change their rate of molecular vibration, as well as your own?"

"Aha!" I mimicked him. "We have our ways and our means! For us, changing vibrational frequency is as easy as changing our underclothes!"

"Good grief!" said Paco, "I never thought about that. Do Guardians wear underclothes?"

"Depends on the weather," I replied, then added, "and also what type of container we're wearing at the time...."

"Yes, well, I don't need that picture in my head."

Now, moving on from the Guardians and our undergarments, or lack thereof — a ghost that is easily perceived by many people is one that is trapped on the etheric plane, which is between the physical and astral levels. These ones are easily seen because their frequency is so close to that of the physical plane. On the other hand, a more evolved spirit guide or guardian from a higher level would vibrate at a much higher rate, making it harder to perceive physically. However, these ones can lower their frequency rate to a certain extent to make it easier for their human charge to perceive them if contact is necessary. To do this they will often make use of past-life personalities to form a grid system between themselves and the one they wish to contact."

"How does that work?"

"Those who meditate on a regular basis may come into contact with spirit guides. The first ones they encounter are usually of a lower vibrational frequency — a frequency that the physical channel can cope with. As the person develops through much training, gradually raising their vibrations to higher and higher frequencies, so the guides will change to higher ones. Sometimes the first spirit guides encountered are actually your own past-life personalities, because they are the ones closest to your physical wavelength. These can be the 'Indian Chiefs' and

'High Priests of Atlantis,' etc., channeled by many spiritualist mediums. This type of channeling can be done easily with minimal training, and, providing the channel controls his ego and doesn't get caught up in manipulative behavior or a power trip, he can receive quite pleasant and positive messages, because he is, in fact, tapping into his own higher self.

"However, if one wishes to access even finer frequencies which are potentially available, then one must eventually move beyond these 'personalities' to realms where the energetic frequencies are even higher and purer — cosmic realms beyond the astral where such things as personality and rank are left far behind. This is why much care must be taken, and why it is most important to be wary of anyone who claims to channel 'high spirit guides,' unless they have undergone many years of training and meditation. It simply *cannot* be done without this preparation and training. Unfortunately many in this field *think* they are tuning in to highly evolved beings, when, in actual fact, they have linked up with one of the Controllers, or perhaps an entity from the lower astral plane out to cause trouble at the expense of the human psychic. Remember, like attracts like, so look to the channel for their degree of purity, love, humility, unselfishness and compassion, for they will reflect accurately the spirit guides who speak through them.

"Yes, I've seen those differences among priests as well. As above, so below..."

"Exactly! Very high levels of spiritual awakening can be attained without any of this astral-plane contact, and unfortunately, more often than not it is more of a block than an aid to your progress, so no one should get too caught up in it. You do not need to be particularly psychic or clairvoyant to make good progress. Sometimes you've already moved through the tests and potential entrapments of the astral plane in a former existence, so you no longer need to experience such things."

"So how do you know when you've reached the higher levels?" Paco asked.

"That's easy," I replied. "True soul evolvement manifests as inner peace, inner contentment and inner knowing that reflect through into your physical life. A truly evolved soul may not seem to have any 'special abilities,' but you can detect them simply by the feeling of ease and peacefulness you experience when you are with them. A gentle, healing, relaxing aura emanates from their very pores, without a word being spoken."

"So, tell me again what is the end result of spiritual awakening?" he wanted to know.

"The goal we are all striving for is to be reunited with our higher self/soul essence on a conscious level." I answered.

Again his eyes lit up with understanding. "And could this so-called higher self be what is referred to in the Biblical decree: 'Man, know thy self'?"

"Absolutely," I assured him, "for that is the God-part of us. You see, Paco, the great truth that every human being must eventually come to is that God is within. This is the key, and it is the forgetting of this basic truth that causes a lowering of the vibrational frequency, which in turn keeps one in a state of separation from the Source.

"Even as a priest I experience a conflict between the concept of God being 'out there,' and my heart that feels Him in here." said Paco as he tapped his chest.

"Yes, this is something many people must deal with, the Source or God is not something exterior to us, and is certainly not a white-bearded old man sitting up on a cloud watching over and judging us. God is within, so the basis of all meditation techniques is to learn to look within, not to become psychic or clairvoyant, although these things may occur along the way, but if we allow ourselves to get caught up too much in such distractions, our progress will be slowed and blocked, and the final goal will take just that much longer to attain."

"And how do we know when we are close to attaining it?" Paco queried.

"Again, that is easy," I replied. "A young, unevolved soul needs an external 'God-figure' as an incentive to do right. Like a child at school who needs the supervision of a strict teacher, it is only the dire threats of punishment or promises of a heavenly reward that keeps a young soul on the straight and narrow. Unfortunately the Controllers have exploited this, inciting Earth humans to use the 'gods' or 'God' as an excuse to maim and kill each other. So much for the commandments of 'Love thy neighbor,' and 'Thou shalt not kill!'! Religion seems to have become one of the most common excuses of all for breaking the commandments as far as I can see!

"However, Paco, to answer your question —a soul that is truly evolved doesn't need any external god or goddess figure as an incentive to do right. Rightness and goodness are so much a part of their nature, they can be no other way. To hurt another either by word or deed is inconceivable to them, not because they fear retribution, or because they believe that by doing what is 'right' they will earn themselves a place in some heavenly paradise. Such a soul does not need these incentives. They do what is right simply because they are so closely aligned to the God within, and the God within is such an intrinsic part of them that they could express nothing other than goodness, kindness and compassion towards their fellow creatures."

Paco shook his head sadly. "You know, Ali, this is something that really gets to me at times. I see some people at Mass every week, coming to confession regularly and praying like good little Christians, absolutely sure that God is pleased with them and that they'll go straight to heaven when they die. But I know that as soon as they leave the church and go home, they're beating their wife, cheating on their husband, giving their kids hell, gossiping maliciously about their neighbors or mistreating their animals. Do you know what I mean?"

"Unfortunately, yes, Paco, I do. If only Earthlings would practice a little less religion and a little more spirituality, this planet would be a much happier place. But so many do not understand the difference — that religion is the outer expression, and spirituality the inner. Still, I suppose they do have to work from the outside in. In fact, I have a brilliant idea! Why don't you compose a sermon along those very lines!"

"My goodness," said Paco, his eyes lighting up, "what a useful little gray space person you are at times! I wish I'd thought of that. And what's more, I have an even *better* idea! You can write it for me so I can have an early bed for a change."

"You lazy wretch!" I said, picking up the nearest cushion and throwing it at him. "Go and write your own darned sermon!"

Deftly ducking out of the way and making a dive for the door, he poked his head back around the corner. "By the way," he added, "I'll need it by 6:00 tomorrow morning — sharp!"

A second cushion missed him by a whisker.

26 ▶ FORGOTTEN AGREEMENT

Ali Cat, what's the matter? You've been acting strange all week, even for you. Is something bothering you?"

Sitting at the kitchen table and staring off into space, I'd not heard my brother enter the room, and I jumped at the sound of his voice. "Paco, for goodness sake, don't sneak up on me like that. You gave me an awful fright. I was *miles* away!"

"Gee, I'm sorry," he apologized, "but you've been so withdrawn and distracted lately. Is something wrong?"

"Oh, I don't know," I sighed, with the effort of trying to externalize what I was feeling. "I think it's more the frustration of having to be down here on Planet Earth in physical form. It's really starting to get to me. I feel so lonely and isolated."

"But Ali, you've got me to talk to. I know who and what you are, and even though I'm an Earth human, I come onto the disc with you sometimes, and I understand the whole situation, so you're not isolated. And after all, you do go 'upstairs' every night, where you can interrelate with your own people, so what's the matter?"

Again I sighed in frustration, still not sure in my mind what the full extent of the problem was. Then it hit me. "Paco, believe me, I really appreciate having you to talk to — in fact if it weren't for you I'd have gone crazy long ago — but what I need is one of my *own* people from 'upstairs' living down here in physical human form whom I can talk to, compare notes and exchange ideas with. Yes, it's great having you, and I could never manage without you, but there's no way you can truly know what it's like to be in my position."

"Well, Ali Cat," he shrugged, "I really don't know what you can do about it. I mean to say, you can't very well place an ad in the personal column of the local newspaper, can you — 'ET person from Guardian Consciousness wishes to meet like-minded ET person also from Guardian Consciousness for friendship and outings. Non-smoker and social drinker preferred — although it might be fun to give it a go. You never know who, or what, might turn up!"

"Gee, thanks a lot, Paco. You come up with some really brilliant ideas. In fact I don't know how you ever manage to fit them all into a normal, human-size head."

"Yes, well," he replied with a wink, "I even amaze myself at times!"

With my human consciousness opened more to my Guardian consciousness, I would have expected that I could recognize that once there is a desire in the human psyche, you can bet there is a manifestation going on behind the scenes. But, no I still viewed it as a strange coincidence that very night up on the disc when my requests were answered. We'd just completed a standard procedure in which a small implant was placed in the nasal cavity of one of our human 'guests,' when Ashka turned to me. "Alarca, I've been thinking. I feel it's time we linked up with each other on the Earth Plane, so I've been busy arranging things to help it happen."

"*Have* you? That is truly amazing! You know what, Ashka, you must be psychic or something!" I chuckled. "I've been feeling a bit down and thinking all week about how good it would be to link up with another Guardian in physical human form, but completely lost the fact that I could manifest it. I think I'm going backwards as a human!"

"No, you're not. Linking up with you has been on my mind for a while now, but remember it had to come from me since I was hesitant because of my children. So, I think I'm ready now to handle 'both worlds.' It's down there that we really need each other to turn to for support and encouragement when things get hard. And believe me, things are going to get very hard if Earth humans don't wake up to themselves soon."

"You're right there, Ashka!" I replied, shaking my head. "Despite all the messages we've relayed through the Crop Circles, and the contact we've tried to establish, so many of them still simply refuse to acknowledge that there could possibly be other intelligent life-forms in the universe apart from themselves."

"Yes, Alarca, but remember, they are only on the very first rung of the Human Ladder, so in a cosmic sense are hardly past kindergarten. Taking this into consideration, it's hardly surprising that some of them still hold on to such immature and self-centered notions, as many youngsters do."

"I know." I answered, "But it's frustrating that we repeatedly fail in our attempts to get them to look at things on a multidimensional level rather than simply taking everything at the shallow, physical level. It really and truly is like trying to teach astrophysics to a five-year-old. As far as I see it they are being exposed to so much disinformation and lies on the physical level by the Controllers that I think we need to approach them on their own terms, in physical Earth human forms that they can feel comfortable with and relate to without fear. To do this more effectively, I really think we need to join forces down there."

"Well, Alarca," Ashka replied, "when you think about it, that is what we set out to do originally, when our disc crashed. We were planning to eventually make physical contact with them. But we now know it just doesn't work — they're too defensive and scared. Why, many of them still don't trust members of their own species who look different, let alone ones like us!"

My shift that night finished earlier than expected, so I put out a telepathic request for a seat in which I could just relax awhile and absorb its therapeutic benefits before returning to my human container. Cradled and comforted by the chair's healing embrace, I suddenly heard someone crying. This was a sound not generally heard in the comforting atmosphere of the Mothership, apart from sometimes in the clinic when our attempts to reassure one of our Earth human "guests" fails, and their fear or anger gives way to tears. But the clinic was on the other side of the ship, so no Earth humans should have been anywhere near. Investigation was called for, so I set off to try to find its source.

As I moved further along the corridor, the sound became more and more distinct, until I found myself standing outside a closed door. Someone was there, clearly unhappy. The door slid open automatically at my approach, and there sitting on a table crying his heart out was Entil. Large, black, tear-filled eyes looked up in shock at my sudden and unexpected entrance. "Alarca!" he gulped, awkwardly attempting to wipe tears away with the back of a long, thin, four-fingered hand. "What are you doing here? You're supposed to be on duty."

"I finished early, and was just wandering around before returning to my other container." I explained to him, "but Entil, whatever is the matter? Why are you so upset?"

"Oh, Alarca — I can't — I just can't do it anymore!"

"Do what Entil? What can't you do?"

He tried to answer, but instead broke down in a fresh torrent of tears, shaking his head and covering his face with his hands. I levitated myself onto the table beside him, put my arm around his small, thin body and drew him close to comfort him, placing my other hand on his head to allow calming, healing energy to flow.

After a minute or so he seemed a little better, his heart-rending sobs having given way to occasional sniffles, so again I tried to draw him out on what was troubling him so deeply. "Please, Entil," I gently coaxed, "tell me what is upsetting you so much. Did one of the Elders yell at you? I know both Oris and Maris can be old grouches at times, but you've just got to learn to ignore them, like I do. I'm always getting into trouble over something, but five minutes later it's all forgiven and forgotten, so don't let them get to you. They really aren't all that bad."

"No, no, Alarca," he sniffled, making a valiant attempt to get a hold of himself, "it's not that. My teacher is Garnibis, and she never yells at me — she's really kind. No, it's — it's these ones on *Earth* that I'm supposed to be working with!" Again his mouth quivered on the verge of tears, necessitating another pause in order to pull himself together before he could go on. "I've been working with one of them since she was a child, and everything seemed to be going well — at least I thought so. Last time I went to her she was about ten years old, and was perfectly happy to see me, as she always had been, but now she's getting older, suddenly she hates me."

"How do you mean Entil? What makes you say that?"

"Well, when I went to fetch her tonight to bring her on board, she started screaming and yelling at me to go away and leave her alone. The thing is, we have been leaving her alone for the past three years, and now the time has come to continue working with her, but she can't seem to remember that she agreed to take part in the program. Now she doesn't want anything to do with me, and in the end we had to paralyze her to get her onto the disc. It was just awful! I *hated* having to do that to her!

"It's — it's like once they begin to mature, they lose connection with their higher self and inner knowing. And because we are linked on the soul level, she has also lost her connection to *me*, and truly, Alarca, this breaks my heart — after all, we had a plan to work *together*!" At this last heartfelt statement poor Entil burst into tears again.

What could I say to him? I knew how he felt, but at the same time, living a life as an Earth human, I also knew how they felt.

"Oh, Entil, you just need to remember that their worldview is so physical. The majority of Earth humans have lost nearly all conscious connection to the higher aspects of themselves that vibrate on our higher, finer frequency range beyond their physical range of perception. You know that any agreements made with spiritual beings is buried deeply within the hidden recesses of the 90% of the human psyche that is not consciously accessible to the average Earthling.

"I know," he sighed. But I really want her to be one of the Star Children, open to 20% of her conscious awareness and therefore able to more easily access her extrasensory perceptions and also to recall past-life and between-life states where she knows me, or, at the very least, to have greater awareness of the higher-dimensional realities in which we operate. However, it seems now that she is getting older, she's becoming trapped like the others who are stuck within the narrow and confining limits of third-dimensional awareness, with no concept of anything that could possibly exist outside of her limited band of 'reality.'"

"You know very well, Entil that when they are confronted by other realities outside of that narrow band of reality, especially in en-countering us or other ETs, it is so foreign to them that they immediately close themselves off in an impenetrable cocoon of fear and denial, thus communication with them becomes almost impossible."

"Thanks, Alarca, you're right. Sometimes we just need to remind each other."

Herein lies a vicious circle, because a large part of the genetic work we carry out concerns the development of another strand in the Earth-human DNA. This will then enable them to access higher-dimensional frequencies. Conscious awareness, as opposed to those parts of the mind that cannot be accessed consciously, such as the subconscious and superconscious mind, is dependent upon DNA, so higher or deeper conscious awareness depends upon the activation of extra DNA, or what Earth scientists refer to as "junk" DNA. DNA contains everything — genetic blueprint, imprint of past lives, karma and soul memory.

Those species able to access higher levels of conscious awareness upon the Human Ladder, which is the evolutionary path followed by all human species in the universe, can have DNA structures of up to 12 strands or more, enabling them to tap into the full potential of mind/consciousness. Those at the top "rung" of the Ladder are what Earth humans think of as "angels," and this is where human evolution is heading. But reaching through to Earth humans to assist them with this process is one of the hardest tasks we have ever undertaken. They truly are one of the most difficult life-forms in the universe to work with! Ashka was right — more focused team work on the physical Earth Plane was most definitely needed.

27 ▶ Linking Up

Making my way through the supermarket aisles the following Monday morning, I was, as usual, off in a world of my own. The human aspect of my mind was fully occupied in the onerous task of controlling a particularly temperamental shopping trolley with a left-hand front wheel that possessed a mind of its own — a wheel whose entire thought processes ran contrary to those of its more sociably inclined fellow wheels — in other words, a born rebel.

The other aspect of my mind, the Guardian part, was busy mulling over the problem that had arisen on the disc several nights before. It was a problem that came up on a painfully regular basis during the course of our work — of getting through the fear barrier that our Earth human "guests" wrap so determinedly around themselves, effectively blocking all attempts at communication between our two species. With my thoughts still on the distress and frustration of Entil, I was suddenly and rudely jolted back to full-conscious alertness by a loud crash behind me.

"Oh, *damn*! Stupid, rotten trolleys never go where you *want* them to. A bloody mind of their own!"

Turning around, I found myself face to face with a slim blonde lady of about my age, but possibly a little taller. It was hard to tell as she was knee-deep in tins of baked beans — the large economy-sized generic ones that give you an extra 30 grams for the same price, some of which were still in the process of coming to rest all around her. Quite a number of them had ended up in her trolley, while others seemed desperately determined to roll as far away from her as possible, probably in a bid to escape further assault by taking refuge under the nearest shelves.

I made a hasty attempt at arranging my face into a suitable expression of concern and sympathy, but the bemused look in the pair of large blue eyes that regarded me over a veritable mountain of collapsed baked-bean tins made this impossible. I burst out laughing instead. "Oh, God, I'm *sorry*!" I apologized. "Here, let me help." Luckily there was no one else around, and between us we were eventually able to get a rather shaky-looking display set up again.

"Hell's bells!" she exclaimed, "I need a fag and a fix after that lot." Then realizing what she'd said, she hastily added, "A *caffeine* fix I mean — not the other sort. I'm not into *that*! Oh, dear, what must you think of me? I'm Kaz, by the way, and thanks heaps for your help. Can I shout you a coffee?"

"Kaz," I replied with a grin, "you are a girl after my own heart. Grocery shopping first thing on a Monday morning calls for at least one caffeine fix, but preferably two, so yes, I would love one. My name is Ali," I added, "and if a good, strong coffee is unavailable, a large chocolate milk shake will suffice."

Some 15 minutes later we were settled comfortably at a corner table in the cafeteria. "Ali," said Kaz, "it's so refreshing to meet up with a fellow health-food addict! I was beginning to think this place was completely uncivilized. Mmm," she turned to peer short-sightedly at the blackboard menu on the wall behind her. "I wouldn't mind a pie or a sausage roll to go with my coffee. Damn it, I left my glasses at home and can't see a blasted thing without them — God, I hope it's not all lettuce and tofu and stuff like that. Ah, what a relief — pies, sausage rolls, and chips, yum, I'm *starving*! Now then, Ali, can I tempt you to join me?"

"'Er, thanks, but no thanks, Kaz. I'm not quite that fanatical about healthy eating, at least not this early in the day. Although, come to think of it, a nice slice of that mud cake wouldn't go astray. And it does look rather sad and lonely sitting there in the cabinet all on its own with no one to love and nurture it. Now will I or won't I?"

"Oh, go on! Do your second good deed for the day. Just *look* at the poor little thing. Say, you're not a vegetarian by any chance, are you? Not that there's anything wrong with that,' she hastily added, "It's just that I wouldn't want to make you feel ill having to watch me stuffing my face with sausage rolls and such like."

"Heavens no!" I reassured her, "I'm not a big meat-eater, but I couldn't go without it completely. I still enjoy a bit of steak or a sausage or two, and after all, human bodies need iron, especially female ones."

"You're right enough there," Kaz laughed. "With two lively kids and a husband to look after, *this* body needs all the energy it can get. So many vegetarians really don't look all that healthy to me, and unless they supplement their diet, they often seem to lack stamina. But then I suppose in the end it's up to the individual, and some seem to thrive on a no-meat diet. I must admit if I had to go out and catch my own, I'd most definitely be a vegetarian."

"Ew, yes — I couldn't agree more. It's got to come wrapped up neatly and tidily in a little plastic packet with all the nasty bits removed in the way of livers, kidneys, brains, hooves, beaks, feathers, the *lot*! That's why I prefer supermarkets, especially for meat — I hate the smell of butcher's shops. Do you come here often for your groceries?"

"Well actually," Kaz replied, "this is my first time. We only moved up here last week. Sam, that's my husband, got a job transfer from down south, so we've had to relocate completely — new house, new city, new schools for the kids, everything. It's been pretty damned horrendous to tell you the truth, with all the packing up, then unpacking, and not knowing a soul here.

"Still, they reckon a change is as good as a holiday, and the weather here is so nice after Melbourne. Down there it can be a real pain — rain one minute, then blowing a bloody gale the next. That's where we're from by the way, *and* we managed to get a house up here with an in-ground pool, so the kids are over the moon. How about you Ali — are you from around here?"

"Just a five-minute drive away. Do you know St. Mary's Catholic Church over near the high school?"

"Umm, yes, only just. We enrolled our eldest, Kira, there last Friday, at the high school, I mean, and yes, I vaguely recall seeing a church close by — one of those nice old stone buildings, isn't it? Why, do you live next door to it?"

"No, there at the church. My brother Paco is the local priest around here."

"Oh, sh…, I mean *sugar!*" Kaz clamped both hands over her mouth. "I am *so* embarrassed! Here I've been, swearing my head off like a bloody outback shearer. Oh, *God,* no — I've done it *again*! Ali, I'm *sorry!*"

"Hey, Kaz," I laughed, "it's okay, truly! You should hear my brother when he gets going. Our family background is Spanish Gypsy, so we're very down-to-earth and not into putting on airs at all, and both of us have fairly fiery temperaments hidden away under a cool, calm exterior. Paco's not a bit like you'd expect a priest to be, especially with me around to stir him up. Would you believe we used to dance flamenco professionally when we were in our teens? We only stopped when he went to seminary. And he's got the wickedest sense of humor, so we used to have great fun dancing together."

"Wow, that's amazing! How *interesting*! What's he like? Does he look like you? Small and dark I mean."

"Yes, very much, but the funny thing is, he's only my adopted brother, so it's weird how much we resemble each other. His parents came here from Spain when he was very young, but they both died in a car accident, and he was raised by his grandmother. They lived in a caravan that was parked on council land close to where my family lived, and when they were eventually ordered to shift, my father invited them to move onto our property — we had five acres, so there was plenty of room. Paco was about 12 when they came to live with us, and we've been together ever since, and as close as any brother and sister could possibly be.

"He's a real sweetie and very handsome in a Gypsy sort of way, you know, dark skin, black eyes, a bit taller than me — but then everybody's taller than me — and his hair's curlier than mine, which is so annoying. You'd love him — in fact all the women in his parish are madly in love with him."

"Hey, I'm looking forward to meeting him!"

"Well, you probably will some time, because the high school where you enrolled your daughter approached him only last week to ask if he'd do some work for them as a school counselor. He's going to take up the offer because he likes kids, and really gets on well with them. I reckon he'll do a great job, but I wouldn't tell him that — in fact I'm teasing him about his 'lack of maturity' being what makes him so well-qualified for the position."

When the waitress arrived with our food, Kaz's eyes lit up at the sight of the sausage roll and chips she'd ordered, along with a generous mug of cappuccino. I watched in fascination as she proceeded to drown the lot with almost half a bottle of tomato sauce, but was soon distracted by the arrival of my slice of mud cake that had lured me remorselessly into its sticky clutches.

Watching Kaz daintily but effectively demolishing her food, I wracked my brain trying to recall where I'd seen her before. She felt so familiar. "Kaz," I finally asked, curiosity getting the better of me, "how long have you lived down south? Have you ever come up here before, on holidays or something?"

"No, Ali, never been here in my life. I was born and raised in Victoria, and have never travelled further north than Sydney. Why?"

"It's really weird;' I shrugged, "I feel like I know you from somewhere. It must just be that you remind me of someone, but I can't think who it could be."

Kaz leaned back in her chair, savoring her coffee and glancing up at a couple of new arrivals settling themselves at the table next to us. "Course you know what they say, don't you? That all of us have a double, a '*doppelganger*' I think the term is, somewhere or other in the world. But the really weird thing is I was thinking exactly the same thing about you. Have you ever been down south, to New South Wales or Victoria?"

"No, never been out of Queensland. But someday I'd love to travel to the four corners of Planet Earth and beyond," I grinned. For just a fleeting second a strange expression passed across Kaz's face. She leaned forward with a slight frown, and seemed to be peering through rather than at me.

"What? What's wrong?" I asked. "Have I got some chocolate on my nose?"

"Umm, no, no!' Kaz answered, looking a bit flustered. "No Ali, it's nothing — just something I suddenly remembered. Hey, about that flamenco dancing you mentioned before, do you still do it? I've never met a flamenco dancer, but I love watching it. Can you play castanets?"

"Oh, yes, I learned when I was very young. But no, I don't dance any more now, at least not in public."

"Gee, that's a shame! But what *do* you do for a living? Do you have kids? I used to work for the government, but I'm a full-time mom now, and proud of it." she added.

"Good for you, Kaz — if more were like you, the world'd be a better place I reckon. No, I don't have children — in fact I've never married. Unofficially I keep house at the presbytery, cleaning up after that messy brother of mine whose whole purpose in life seems to be dropping things from one end of the house to the other, forgetting to pick them up and then swearing when he can't find them. Would you believe he misplaced a whole set of Mass vestments a couple of weeks ago? Officially I teach Reiki and Tai Chi for a living."

Kaz's eyes lit up with interest. "Hey, wow! You teach Tai Chi! I took up Yoga a year or so ago, but needed three days to untangle myself after every class, so in the end gave it up. Would you believe I once managed to get my big toe caught in my own ear? And another time I lost my balance trying to do a shoulder stand and landed on top of the instructor, breaking her left thumb in the process.

"Say, Ali," she went on brightly, "where do you hold your classes? I wouldn't mind coming along and having a go. Hope they're close by because I hate driving, being a bit short-sighted and all. You do things with swords in Tai Chi, don't you? Do you use *real* ones? That'd be great fun!"

"Well, um, actually Kaz, my classes are miles away — over on the other side of town, in fact, involving a *horrendous* drive along an eight-lane freeway."

Suddenly Kaz was leaning forward giving me that same strange look again, but now a quiver of profound amusement played around the corners of her mouth, and large, innocent-looking blue eyes turned momentarily into huge black ones, glinting with mischief: "Bullshit Alarca!" she telepathed at me. "*You* hate driving as much as I do."

My coffee cup clattered back into its saucer as I very nearly dropped it: "*Ashka* — it's *you*! You sneaky devil! No *wonder* I felt I knew you from somewhere! When the hell did you recognize me? Why didn't you say something earlier instead of letting me go on and on?"

"Come on, Alarca;' she chuckled, "that wouldn't have been *fun*! And if a poor, lonely little gray space person can't have their bit of innocent fun down here in human form, life wouldn't be worth living. And oh, dear, the look on your face when I threatened to join your Tai Chi class after telling you how accident-prone I am! Oh ho, what *havoc* I could cause!

"But honestly," she went on, 'I didn't recognize you either until we both commented on how we felt we knew each other from some-where — then you said something about 'Planet Earth,' which is a bit of an unusual turn of phrase down here. That's when it suddenly fell into place and I remembered our discussion the other night up on the disc. And it's just amazing how so-called coincidences work! I'd been think-ing about this for a while, of trying to find your Earth human form, and then seemingly out of the blue we were forced to come up here to relo-cate in Queensland, and then we 'just happened' to find a suitable house in this area, so close to where you live as it turns out. I wonder who had a hand in it — my Teacher, Anarkis, or your Teacher, Maris."

"Ah, both of them for sure! After all," I pointed out, "they are really all one anyway. It's just that you link into one aspect, one facet, and I link in to another. But Ashka, it's so good that we've found each other like this. Now that you mention it, I do recall our discussion the other night on trying to find each other, but my limited human brain wasn't able to retain it. Maybe now with both of us getting together down here it'll be easier. After all, as they say, two heads are better than one. But Ashka," I went on, "are you certain you didn't know all about this and plan it beforehand? Are you sure you didn't knock those tins of baked beans over on purpose to get my attention so we'd connect?"

"Oh, come on, Alarca — you know *me*! *Course* I didn't! I was just walking along quietly, minding my own business, when they sort of jumped out in front of me. *You* know what it's like, the way weird things happen to us down here. It must be something about our energy fields. That's why we really need each other, for protection as well as for sup-port."

"Absolutely, Ashka! I couldn't agree more!"

O
h, no!" came Paco's heartfelt response when I told him of my encounter with the Earthly aspect of my friend Ashka. "You're joking — please tell me you're joking!"

"Why, what do you mean? What's the problem?"

"Look, Ali Cat, you are my favorite, my one and only, my dearly beloved little sister, but 'one and only' is the key here. What I'm trying to say in as polite a way as possible is that one little gray space person around the place is enough! I can't take two of you — it doesn't even bear thinking about! Anyway, which one is Ashka? I know you've told me before, but truly, all you Greys do look exactly alike, and I know the name, but putting a distinctive face to it is beyond me."

"Honestly, Paco." I gave him a withering look. "You are *hopeless*! Ashka was the one piloting the disc with me when it crashed. That's why she hates driving too — the trauma has carried over for both of us from that past life. Mind you, now that she's in a human body, her eyesight's not real good, so that doesn't help the situation."

Paco shook his head in puzzlement. "Now that's really weird! How come we hear all about those so-called Star Children who've been born on Earth since the 1980s — the ones who are supposed to be carrying ET genetics in their makeup? They are said to have unusually high IQ levels and to possess abilities way beyond average humans, but you and Ashka, who are ETs here in human form, both have problems.

"Now don't get me wrong," he put in quickly as I opened my mouth to protest, "I'm not saying you're dumb exactly — in fact you're quite smart when you choose to apply yourself, but you aren't a genius by any means, and I doubt Ashka is either in her Earthling form. You are very intuitive, and certainly possess understanding beyond that of the average human, but at the same time, Ashka has physical problems with eyesight and you with hearing, so neither of you are 'super' humans by any stretch of the imagination. So what is all this about special abilities and genius IQ?"

"You know what, Paco? That's what I really like about you — you are so complimentary at times, but for a start, we aren't quite what are known these days as Star Children. Star Children are a newly developed, upgraded generation born since the 1980s, who will form the basis of a more highly evolved human species which will inhabit this planet in the future. All Earth humans carry ET genetics in their physical makeup, otherwise they'd still be swinging through the trees by their tails, but the

Star Children carry more, hence the special abilities that some of them are able to express on the physical, conscious level."

"But what about you and Ashka? Now I'm really confused. Aren't you ETs? So why can't you do all that stuff?"

"Because we're not in upgraded physical Earth human containers, that's why. We were both born into the older-style Earth bodies. In other words, we simply don't have the memory capacity built into our 'hard-drive.'"

"But surely with the technology your people have at their disposal something could have been worked out to provide you with special abilities, especially since you were coming here to do a job."

"Well, maybe, but we chose not to."

"But why? Surely having miraculous abilities, or being a genius by Earth human standards would be an advantage."

"Come off it, Paco — you've got to be kidding! It was hard enough for ones like us as children. I wouldn't have wanted to be any more 'different.' If you really want to know, we had *three* good reasons for choosing birth into ordinary, two-strand DNA human containers. Firstly, we wanted to experience first-hand what it's like to be limited to such a physical, biological body. In this way we can understand more clearly where assistance is needed in the process of Earth human evolution.

"Secondly, as I said on a purely personal level, both of us decided it would be just too hard to bring advanced ET abilities down into a physical, Earth human form. As Guardians, we have access to a very large amount of knowledge and vastly expanded consciousness, which would not be easy to express through the limited sensory system of an Earth body. The human emotions just wouldn't cope.

"To have to live with that level of conscious awareness 24 hours a day, seven days a week, on a level-one planet such as Earth would be almost impossible Also, as Guardians living down here in human form, we have to protect ourselves from the astral influences permeating such a planet, because they too are almost impossible for us to cope with. When we take up residence here it's rather like a deep-sea diver having to encase themselves in a heavy suit for protection. It may cut them off from direct interaction with the subtleties of the environment, but they cannot survive without it.

"The third and main reason is that we simply don't want to draw attention to ourselves. We don't want electrical appliances and light bulbs blowing around us all the time, or shop-security sensors going off every darned time we walk into the local supermarket. And we *especially* don't want to become famous as 'miracle workers' or 'incredible psychics or healers,' or for people to know who and what we are, because this only causes problems in the end. Such personalities inevitably end up with a cult following and no privacy to get on with the job they're here to do.

"But, that's my point — they have a following."

"Okay, maybe a few such people are necessary down here, because Earthlings always seem to need 'miracles' and 'proof' if they are to ever acknowledge any sort of reality beyond their own limited three-dimensional outlook, but really and truly, the *last* thing this planet needs is more cults, followings and religions, so ETs down here in human form displaying superhuman talents are the exception rather than the rule.

"Most of us just want to live ordinary, everyday lives, doing our little bit here and there quietly behind the scenes. We want to get on with the job we're here to do, part of which involves assisting the new generation, the so-called Star Children, to cope with life in the still-harsh environment that will persist on Earth until such time as the planet herself steps upward to the next evolutionary level.

"This new Earth human species will be better adapted to the level-two frequency band that Earth is now moving in to, because more DNA is in the process of being activated, which means they can easily and consciously tap into fourth- and even fifth-dimensional awareness. In other words, they have an enhanced and expanded level of conscious awareness, hence in some cases extremely high IQ and seemingly special abilities."

"Hang on, what do you mean 'in some cases'? Aren't they all like that? From what I understand, that is what parents of potential Star Kids are advised to look out for — high IQ and special abilities."

"Yes, well, some of them have these qualities, but if that is all parents know to look for, then unfortunately quite a few will fall through the net, so to speak, and not receive the proper assistance, guidance and understanding that these special children need. These attributes are part of the picture, but they are not the main criteria that differentiate a Star Child from other human children.

"The *main* thing that needs to be taken into consideration and looked out for is their nature, which is totally nonviolent. A true Star Child cannot stand violence in any shape or form, whether it is bullying at school or at home, or being exposed to violence through videos, movies, books or whatever. Because of their extreme sensitivity, they may actually have problems in the school environment and seem slow academically. It can also manifest as health issues such as auditory processing problems and difficulties in coping with life in general. Some end up going right into themselves, hiding away, being a 'loner.' Many of them dread the school lunch hour with the screaming, yelling 'rough house' behavior of other children around them.

Paco looked thoughtful. "I think there are some of these ones at the high school. They are really struggling. I could try to make contact with them."

"Maybe you could channel them into some new interests. They're often not into playing sports because of the roughness and competition, but anything to do with rhythm such as dance or music attracts them, as does nature, so they often have an unusual rapport with animals and plants. They have an inner wisdom that expresses itself through incredibly deep and knowing statements that they will sometimes come out with to the amazement of those around them, and they're also into poetry. Star Children will not usually vent their anger and frustration with life by hitting or hurting somebody or by smashing a shop window with a brick — they will write poetry instead.

"This is what Star Children are all about — extreme sensitivity, deep spirituality and total nonviolence. This new generation will put an end to the wars that have plagued this planet for so long, which in turn will allow further evolution to take place."

"So what you're saying is that Earth humans cannot move up to the next evolutionary level until they cease fighting and begin living in peace and harmony with each other."

"Exactly! And until this happens it's unlikely that any ET group will make open contact. It's simply too dangerous. This is why we're coming in the 'back door,' working on the subconscious level to help humans move past the deep-seated fear within their psyche which creates the need for war and conflict."

"Okay, that all makes sense, but what about ones like you and Ashka, who are down here in physical human form? Where do you fit in to all of this?"

"Well, we're a bit different from the Star Children in that we belong to a group of ET and interdimensional helpers known as Star Seeds who've been incarnating here on Earth in human form since the 1950s to help anchor the higher-frequency energy that is initiating the evolutionary process. The Star Children are an intrinsic part of this. Crop Circles also anchor this higher energy, as well as being a means of communication.

"You could think of us as 'Gardeners of the Earth' since we are seeding, tending and nurturing this newly developed species of Earth human to 'take root,' as it were. We are here as guides, mentors, teachers, comforters and in some cases parents to them. Our first task here many, many millennia ago was to develop the species known as *Homo sapiens*; our next assignment resulted in *Homo sapiens sapiens*; now we are here to take Earth humans up to the next evolutionary level.

Paco's eyes widened in shock. "Are you saying you've been playing God?"

"Oh no, Paco — only assisting God!" I hastily reassured him, "we had great plans all those years ago when we received the go-ahead from higher universal realms to start re-connecting once again with the Earth human species in order to assist them up another rung on the evolutionary ladder. We knew we had 70-odd years of Earth time in which to carry out our appointed mission before the planet was due to step up to the next dimensional frequency, so we weren't too worried, but looking in retrospect, I realize now how naïve we were."

"Why, how do you mean?" he frowned.

"Well, we'd run a few reconnaissance missions over the years, especially during that big war that was going on in the 1930s and '40s, just to see what we were up against with the Controllers, and also with the military forces of course. After all, it's the defense forces of a planet that have to be taken into consideration before open, physical contact is ever attempted, and we originally planned for that first contact to be physical.

"Even fewer adult Earthlings had senses that could perceive much beyond the third dimension back then, so we knew we would have to adapt to the situation by presenting ourselves in physical containers if we were to make face-to-face contact with the authorities of this planet. We made a number of reconnaissance flights to check things out, with the intention of trying to make open contact once everything settled down after the war, but then more problems arose."

"Do you mean those foo fighters of World War II?" he was getting excited now seeing history told from the *other* side.

"Yes and various other appearances at that time."

"What else held you back?"

"A major difficulty was the so-called cold war that continued on Earth after the end of the World War II. This served to make those governments and defense forces involved extremely nervous about anything out of the ordinary that happened to appear in the skies above their respective countries, and our discs certainly fell into this category.

"We had originally planned to begin with a friendly cultural exchange, as we have with many other humanoid species throughout the lower galactic levels of the universe. The problem with Earth humans is, although we'd been monitoring them for some time, we hadn't fully realized how fearful and therefore how dangerous they can be to deal with, and how much influence the Controllers still have on this planet.

"We trade freely with many interplanetary cultures, so we just assumed that it would be the same on Earth. With the Earth about to jump to the next evolutionary level, we honestly believed they would be more than ready and willing to accept our help. But we underestimated their fear — we just can't seem to get past it! We're supposed to be acting as midwives to assist their rebirth into the next galactic level on the Human Ladder, but the process is being blocked by fear and ego. The labor pains are happening, but some simply refuse to begin the journey down the 'birth canal.'

"So is this why you and Ashka are down here now in human form — to try to reach them on their own level where they feel safer?"

"Yes, precisely. It's a last, desperate attempt to get through to them while we are also assisting the newer generation, the Star Children."

"And if you fail, then what?"

"Those who still refuse to allow themselves to open up to greater realities will remain stuck where they are, mired in fear and chaos. They will have to wait for another cycle before they can evolve further, and will go through some very unpleasant and difficult times in the process. And as we are all One, if one small part of the *whole* stubbornly refuses to evolve and grow, then everyone else is affected as well.

"It's the same as if you break your ankle, or even your toe. Your whole leg and eventually your whole body ends up affected and aching because of the difficulty you experience in walking. The universe is the whole body, and all the many planets, suns and galaxies are intrinsic parts of that body.

"Earth humans see the *whole* as being fragmented because in their own minds they themselves are fragmented. Everything around you is seen and experienced through the lens of your own subconscious, which is the dwelling place of all your buried fears — your inner demons."

Good God," said Paco after meeting Ashka/Kaz for the first time, face to face in Earthling form, "what a strange little creature! In fact, almost as strange as you!"

"Gee thanks, Paco. Your native Latin charm and chivalry are still honed as sharp as ever I see."

"Well, you must admit she's a bit off. For goodness sake, she smoked at least three cigarettes during the time she was here, and downed a couple of glasses of wine as well. Although I must admit she carries it off with style — an inbuilt aplomb as it were. Don't get me wrong, I *do* like her, but I find her a wee bit weird, that's all. And you say she's married with children? Kept herself in good shape for all that — never know she'd had two kids. Her husband Sam seems a nice, regular sort of guy. Does he know she's an ET?"

"No, I don't think so. Probably freak if he found out."

"Amazing!" Paco shook his head in wonderment. "How the heck does she manage, you know, being married and a mother and all, as well as doing work 'upstairs'?"

"I have no idea. She told me she wanted to really experience what it is to be Earth human. But then that's Ashka all over, tending to grab every opportunity with both hands in order to experience life. Up on the disc she's no different, in fact probably more so, because down here in human form we're more fragmented and 'watered down' as it were — less our true personality. Needless to say, she's finding the experience of marriage and motherhood both interesting and challenging. No wonder she enjoys a cigarette or two and a glass of wine occasionally."

"Now that's another thing. I thought you ETs would know better and that you'd try to keep your physical bodies as pure and healthy as possible. So how come she smokes and drinks?"

"Oh, Paco, for heaven's sake! You carry on as if she's an alcoholic. She probably doesn't drink very often, but just enjoys a glass or two of wine with her dinner or to be sociable, as I do. Yes, we're ETs, but we're also human while we're down here, and can have human needs and desires just like anyone else. And anyway, have you ever seen me drunk?"

"No, of course not." he replied sheepishly.

"Well then," I added, "and besides *you* can't talk! You're not exactly a teetotaller now, are you, and not averse to polishing off a bottle of good red every so often. Stop being so damned judgmental and sanctimonious! Being a Guardian living down here in human form with a husband and two kids to look after, she probably needs a good, stiff drink occasionally to get her through.

"Yeah, I hear you. I need a drink occasionally and I'm not living dual lives!"

"To tell you the truth, I don't know how the heck she does it. Although I do notice she always starts her shift with a few minutes of healing and recuperation time in one of our special chairs. But then again, this is part of why ones like us are down here in physical form. It's to learn about and experience everything we possibly can about being an Earth human, and for some of us that means marrying an Earth human, having a family and holding down a job."

"Ah yes, now I remember! One night up on the disc you told me Ashka worked for the government when she was in her human form."

"Yes, that's right. She worked for the Immigration Department, and her job dealt with tracing the whereabouts of illegal aliens."

Paco gave an ill-suppressed snort of laughter. "Yep, that'd be right! Lucky she didn't accidentally turn *herself* in after a few drinks."

"Oh, knock it off!" I snapped, starting to get fed up with his smart comments. "What's your problem anyway?"

"Well, to tell you the truth," he admitted, "I do feel a bit uncomfortable with the idea of a whole bunch of ETs running around down here disguised as humans, when most of us *real* humans are not even aware of it."

It wasn't often that I lost my temper, but at that moment the temptation to explode got the better of me, and I turned on him. "Oh, you *do*, do you! And why would *that* be? Do you think we're planning to take over your precious planet or something? If you really and truly think that of us, then there's not much point in me going on, is there?"

"Whoa, hang on Ali Cat!"

"No, damn it, *you* hang on! Look, Paco, if I could just up and leave and go back to my own people for good, do you think I wouldn't? Have you any vague idea of what it's like for ones like Ashka and me down here? It's no bloody picnic, that's for sure!

"If we were here for that reason, to sneakily infiltrate your society in order to take over this planet, we'd have done it years ago — in fact centuries or even *millennia* ago, when you were all living in caves or grass huts, with nothing more than sticks and stones to defend yourselves. But no, we waited around for millennia, until you acquired the technology off the Controllers to shoot our discs down and to imprison us in rooms surrounded by electromagnetic fields that effectively stop us from dematerializing and escaping, *then* we make our move to take you over. That says a whole lot for *our* intelligence, doesn't it?"

"But *Ali* ..."

"Be quiet and let me finish! If you only knew it, we would give the world, our world, your world, any world, to just pack up and go home — to go back to the Realm Consciousness with our own people, where there is real unconditional love, caring, compassion and Oneness! Not like this divided, shallow, competitive, materialistic bloody society that you Earthlings guard so defensively and jealously against any change in the status quo, and get so scared of anyone who comes in to try to help you to make this change — to teach you to be one with *all* creatures, no matter what they look like on the outside!"

Here I just had to stop to catch my breath, and Paco took the opportunity to back away, holding his hands up in self-defense. "Okay, okay, I'm *sorry* Ali Cat. Come on now, *please* calm down. Wow, you little Greys sure do display emotion when you really get riled up! Tell me, do tempers ever let fly on the disc?"

"No, of *course* not. At least not often, anyway," I added, trying to crack a smile but not succeeding very well.

"Look, Ali Cat," Paco put his arm around me, giving me a brotherly hug, "I know you get homesick for your own people, and I'm really happy for you that you've connected with your friend Ashka down here in human form, but if you could manage to go home, to go back to your own people permanently, I'd miss you *so* much. We've been together since we were kids, almost like twins; in fact people think we are because we even look alike — same dark eyes, hair color, build and facial structure. It's quite weird when you think about it.

"I know people tend to stereotype cultures, and those who know we're both Romany probably put it down to that. As far as they're concerned, all Gypsies look alike, but we know that's not correct, so it must be as you say — that we belong to the same soul family, and our energies resonate in a similar frequency pattern. If that is the case, then you're the only family I've got, so don't ever go off on the disc and not come back, *please*.

He definitely had me softening now. "Ok, Paco, I..."

"Hold it, let me finish," he went on, "I know this is not an easy planet to live on sometimes, and yes, too, Earthlings can be divisive, competitive, extremely shallow, and materialistic, but the trick is to try not to focus too much on the negative side of humanity. There are plenty of really good, kind, caring people down here too, and as you always say yourself, like attracts like. If you put all your energy into being positive and kind yourself, then that is the sort of person you'll draw to you, whereas if you go through life feeling negative and angry, then that is what you'll attract. It's all in your own hands. You've said that to me enough times."

"There you go, Paco. You really get it! Now you're teaching me." I had to smile. "That's why you're such a good priest, isn't it? With me around giving you advice, you can't go too far wrong. Now come on, you stop being negative too, and tell me what you really think of Ashka in Earth human form. And don't tell me that you don't know her well enough. You're the psychic in the family, and I could see you examining her aura."

"Okay then — looking at the energy field surrounding her, she reminds me of a fairy, or even an angel, but a slightly fallen one — a very 'human' one. I could easily see a halo around her head — a lovely soft, glowing halo in a silvery, sort of mother-of-pearl color, but tilted at a cheeky, jaunty angle on her head.

"Despite those angelic, golden curls and large, innocent-looking blue eyes," he went on, "I can well imagine she keeps everybody *upstairs* on their toes with her wicked sense of fun, but at the same time there's an incredible depth of goodness and kindness there. Yes, Ali Cat, I'm glad you've made contact down here. You'll be good for each other. But my goodness, I hope she isn't Catholic, because with the pair of you let loose during Mass, havoc of some sort would be inevitable."

"No, don't worry," I chuckled, "she isn't … but her husband and children are, so she'll be sure to come along with them on special occasions."

Head shaking slowly from side to side, eyes raised heavenward and hands clasped in fervent supplication was Paco's unspoken but nevertheless eloquent response.

30 ▶ STAR NATIONS CONFERENCE

The very atmosphere itself was weighty with the important issues that were to be discussed during the course of the meeting scheduled for that night in the conference room on the big disc. All of our Guardian Elders were present, as well as representatives from every one of the various planetary cultures that together form what is known on Planet Earth as the Star Nations.

The huge auditorium was abuzz with anticipatory whisperings and twitterings in a myriad of different tongues and dialects, with each individual seat containing a special translation device automatically linked in to the consciousness of whoever was sitting in that seat at any given moment. In this way everybody could easily understand what was being said, either by the speaker up at the podium, or the person sitting next to them.

Potentially, this problem of language could have been overcome through direct telepathic communication, which we generally use, but some planetary species have thought waves that are faster or slower than others, so, for this reason, the translation units attached to the seats make things just a little easier and more efficient.

Our people were to be the main contributors to this evening's program, with discussions centered upon the progress being made in our work with the human species of Planet Earth.

"Alarca!" Ashka greeted me warmly as I moved towards a seat she'd kept beside her. "You're a bit late! I thought you weren't going to get here. And look, here's Solarno and Asara. They also only arrived a couple of minutes ago. Funny that, the way everybody seems to arrive at these meetings at the very last minute."

I gazed past her to acknowledge our two Pleiadian friends who had joined us, and contemplated their appearance — tall, fair, and blue-eyed, with well-proportioned, human-like bodies. I thought it was funny how researchers on Earth who deal with the study of ET races often assume that the same "pecking order" applies with us as on their own planet, presuming that those ETs who are beautiful and normal-looking by Earthling standards are automatically superior and in charge, and ones like us who are not so handsome or attractive in Earth human terms are the "slaves," or at least lesser or sometimes even negative beings. Won't they be surprised to find that the more evolved a civilization is, the stranger it may appear.

"Hey, Alarca," Solarno's telepathic voice rang in my head, "what's in that data pod you've got there?"

"Oh, it's just information for the conference," I answered, holding the tiny silicon wafer out in my palm to show them. "It's a whole file of reports on various Earth folk we've been working with for the past year. That's why I'm late getting here — I had trouble downloading it from the darned computer. Is Maris here yet? I have to give it to him to pass on to the Head of the Council. Ah, speak of the devil — here he comes."

"*Alarca, shhh*!" Ashka hissed. "He'll *hear* you!"

"Honestly, Alarca," Asara shook her head, "I really don't know how you haven't been demoted right back down to level one, the way you carry on with the Elders, especially poor Maris."

My own esteemed Teacher Maris, with his huge black, almond-shaped eyes focused directly upon me, and his black cape billowing behind him, glided rather than walked straight towards us.

Feeling some trepidation that perhaps he'd telepathically picked up on my insolent remark, I remained standing respectfully until he reached our seats, but then I was forced to sit down quickly to let him past. Problem was I hadn't noticed the food tube Ashka had placed on my seat to mark it taken. The top wasn't secure, and the sudden weight of my gray container descending upon it sent a generous spurt of rather messy-looking pink paste all down the front of Maris's black suit. To make matters worse, it wasn't just standard purply-pink paste, but the vitamin-enhanced version, containing sparkly, fluorescent granules sprinkled generously throughout. This paste can be eaten by mouth or rubbed into the skin, and it is nutritionally excellent, but rather difficult to clean up after spills.

My venerable and usually extremely dignified teacher jumped backwards in shock, at the same time letting go a whole string of quite descriptive and colorful words that I'd rather not translate for the sake of propriety. Lucky he wasn't sitting in one of the seats, otherwise they would have been translated automatically for the benefit of all. Not game to look at Ashka, Solarno or Asara, and most especially not at Maris's face, my eyes remained riveted on the large, sparkly, purply-pink stain that now decorated the front of my Teacher's black clothes.

I then felt something shaking, and I turned to see Ashka struggling with every ounce of her small, gray being to stem the laughter that was threatening to explode at any second. With long, fingers clamped over her mouth, her eyes said it all. Solarno and Asara were not much better, with both of them quite red in the face in a massive attempt at control.

Laughter under such circumstances is inevitable and lethally contagious, but just as a giant tidal wave of mirth threatened to engulf me, my Teacher's voice pulled me sharply back from the brink of no return.

"Alarca, look what you've done! *Now* what am I supposed to do? I am first speaker up on the podium. How can I stand up in front of the entire Star Nation Council looking like *this?* Honestly, why can't you be more *careful?*"

"Well," I hedged, mouth aperture trembling and eyes watering, but trying nevertheless to be helpful, "you could always hold your cape closed in front of you. Maybe if you're lucky nobody will notice."

"Well, now, Alarca," came his icy reply, "I'll just *have* to, won't I! You have put me in a position where I have no other choice!"

Gathering all of his considerable dignity about himself, along with his cape, my Teacher stepped up to the podium. I must say he looked extremely impressive as his huge dark eyes regarded the audience from beneath the wide brim of his black hat. With the usually flowing cape held closely around his tall, thin frame, he appeared even more imposing, and dare I say, rather batlike. More waves of barely suppressed amusement from nearby told me that Ashka was tuning in telepathically to my thoughts, so I quickly directed them into safer and more neutral territory to put her off.

"Greetings to all of you," my Teacher began, "as you all know, this conference has been called this evening to discuss the ongoing problems and difficulties we are experiencing in our transmutation work with the human species of Planet Earth. As many of you are aware, they are one of the youngest humanoid life-forms in the universe, and inclined to stubbornness, but at the same time they are also capable of *great* goodness. This is why we have called upon other human species from various galactic levels of the universe for assistance in dealing with them."

Maris paused here for a moment or two to gather his thoughts before going on. "After several unsuccessful attempts at contact immediately following their last major war, and note I say *major* war to distinguish it from the many smaller, regional wars that continually disturb the energy frequencies of their planet, it became obvious that physical, face-to-face contact at that point in time, at least with us, was well-nigh impossible.

"To the Earth human's way of reckoning, the evolution of their species has taken a great span of time, and so they consider themselves to be very mature and advanced, but really and truly, in the eternity of cosmic time this is a humanoid species only very recently evolved, so therefore fear and territorial instinct still control a large part of their makeup and behavior. This fear may be expressed, for example, as a fear of the unknown, which includes an unnatural and exaggerated fear of death.

"Because of a lack of proper teaching, and in some cases deliberate untruths spread by the Controllers, Earth humans are generally terrified by the prospect of death. Because they exist in such a state of duality and separation — duality of the physical and spiritual aspects of their being — separation of lower self and higher self, many of them find it well-nigh impossible to understand and accept death as the natural process of rebirth into higher-dimensional frequencies of reality that it truly is.

"Depending upon which mind set they are trapped in, they perceive death in one of two ways. If they are caught up in the delusion that they are nothing more than a physical, three-dimensional body of flesh and blood, then they see and fear death as total annihilation, and the end of everything they have set out to achieve in life. This in turn often leads to a state of depression, particularly as they grow past their prime. As death approaches they fight it with every part of their being, terrified at the thought of disappearing forever into a black void of nothingness.

"If, on the other hand, they adhere to one of the many belief systems which prevail on Earth, then at their death their mind, which, as we all know, does not die with the physical body and brain, is automatically drawn to the astral plane of emotion, dreams and Controller-inspired illusions, to create for itself and live out whatever belief patterns it has been exposed to and taken in during the course of its past physical-life experience.

"For example, if the mind believes that, providing it has been good, it will go to a heavenly utopia peopled with angels sitting on clouds and playing harps, then that is exactly what it will create for itself. If on the other hand it has taken into itself a belief in a hell full of devils, fire and brimstone, and at the time of death a sense of guilt prevails, then that is precisely what will be experienced, until such time as the mind can wake up and move beyond such limiting illusions, and move on up to the vastly expanded awareness of Divine Consciousness.

"There are still many Earth humans who are trapped one way or another within the different beliefs, superstitions and illusions of reality which govern their lives, and therefore simply cannot conceive of what really occurs in the energy shift they refer to as death. They cannot accept it for the perfectly natural transitional process that it is — a process which enables them to break through all barriers and limitations in order to expand into pure mind, and thus merge back into the blissful ecstasy of the all knowing and omnipotent Oneness that they call 'God.'"

For several moments my Teacher paused, perceptions turned inwards, lost in transcendent memories of his own many passings to and fro between the veils of life, death and rebirth, as the entire auditorium waited patiently for him to continue, moved deeply by the expression of total peace that suffused his features. Then suddenly mindful of the large, intergalactic audience seated in front of him, he pulled himself back with reluctance to continue his talk.

"Fear is often expressed on Planet Earth through over-inflated ego, which is one of the greatest blocks to soul evolution that we, as testers of souls, come up against. So many Earth humans are very afraid of having their ego shattered, either by being made to appear foolish or gullible, or by being proved wrong. They grow up exposed to various beliefs, ideas, concepts and theories through the Controller-influenced education and belief systems on their planet, as well as through their family environment, which itself has been exposed to these same beliefs, concepts, etc. But no matter how well or how badly these concepts and beliefs work, either personally or for society in general, Earthlings tend to stubbornly hold onto them. What *they* believe just *has* to be right, no matter what, and nobody can tell them otherwise. The walls of the mind are up, the doors are firmly closed and locked, and they are safe and secure inside.

"This aspect of fear comes up often within their investigation of ET contact. One of the biggest blocks associated with this on Planet Earth is the possibility that such investigation and contact will ultimately prove that they are *not* after all the greatest, cleverest and most evolved species in the entire universe, alone created in God's image, and with dominion over all 'lesser' creatures.

"With such a deluded mindset firmly entrenched within their psyche, is it any wonder so many of them have trouble coming face to face with ones such as us — or for that matter with anyone else present in this room? The average Earth human believes that either science or religion has all the answers.

"Admittedly, both science and religion are necessary on such a young planet. If it were not for scientific discovery and exploration, they would still be mired in the superstitions of the Dark Ages; and religion, as long as it is based on love, provides a most necessary framework for humanity to function as an ethical, compassionate and caring society.

"But herein lies more fear for many Earth humans — fear of what really exists in the 'beyond' if they are willing to open their eyes and minds to look. Or alternatively and perhaps potentially even more frightening — what they will find within them*selves* if they are willing to open their inner eye and mind to look!

"Another barrier Earth humans need to break through is fear of change. Evolution is never static. It is all about change, movement forward, flexibility of mind and spirit, letting go of the old in the way of outmoded beliefs, traditions and concepts in order to make way for the new. If people refuse to do this, to acknowledge and accept change in the way of new concepts and new ideas, then they will not evolve. And herein lies the problem — they have no *choice* if they wish to remain. The time is ripe for their home world to step up to a higher frequency, and so must they."

Then Maris paused for a moment to sip water from the tubelike receptacle provided. Ashka and I sat with bated breath, waiting to see if he'd forget to keep a grip on his cape, thus revealing our little "mishap" to the entire auditorium, but no, it remained tightly closed, held firmly by all four fingers of his left hand. Whew, what a relief!

Briefly glancing over at us, Maris continued with his talk. "After our initial attempts at contact, we quickly came to realize that this fear factor inherent in the makeup of Earth humans and exploited so cunningly by the Controllers, was going to be a major issue in our dealings with them. There was no way that ones like us, so different in appearance from the human inhabitants of the planet, could possibly make any headway, particularly given the political and cultural climate on Earth at that time, which in their time frame was the late 1940s through to the 1950s. There was just so much fear. And to many people of that era, anyone who looked foreign or different in any way was considered a potential enemy, at the least not to be trusted, and at the worst, destroyed.

"Our work could not be delayed any longer, so our way around this problem was to either obtain assistance from other interplanetary species who are closer to Earth humans in appearance, or else to take on the appearance of Earth humans ourselves, which we can easily do by means of our shape-shifting abilities.

"Both methods worked quite well, and in this way some positive contact was made during the 1950s and '60s. When the inevitable questions were raised by the Earthling contactees as to where the visitors were from, the answer given was generally 'Venus' or 'your own moon' — places within the Earth's own solar system where bases had been established at the time, and which Earthlings could more easily relate to given their very limited knowledge of the universe and space travel.

"This worked for awhile, until the usual problems began to arise, which we have always encountered on Planet Earth. Here I refer to the problem of ego in some of the contactees, which clouds and distorts the information and messages we were trying to convey through them, and ego in some of those who flocked to hear our messages.

"Appearing as we did in 'normal' human form, some began looking upon us as gods, or at least as saviors, which, because of untruths spread earlier on by the Controllers who pretended to be gods, is an inevitable and ongoing problem with ET and interdimensional contact on

Planet Earth. As incredible as it seems, even today there are still some Earth humans who persist in the belief that God is human in form. The reason the Controllers are able to maintain this distorted belief is because they have kept humans in a very physically oriented state of mind, generally lacking any depth of understanding in regard to the finer-energy aspects of their being. Why, some Earth humans even refuse to acknowledge the reality of their soul and spirit, believing themselves to be nothing more than a physical body!"

This last statement caused a murmur of shocked comment to ripple across the auditorium, particularly from those who'd not had much contact with the Earthling species. Those of us who were more familiar with the limitations of Earth human awareness simply shook our heads in resignation.

"This lack of deeper conscious awareness," Maris continued, "is why they misunderstand the energy of Oneness they call 'God.' Very few on Earth comprehend that 'being created in the image of God' simply refers to energy, and that this energy is the driving force behind all of creation. And surprisingly they refuse to believe that no matter what physical form life energy chooses to express itself through, *all* living creatures are in fact 'created in the image of God.'

There was even more murmuring around the room after this disclosure.

"It is this misunderstanding among Earth humans that has caused endless difficulties for us in our dealings with them. If we appear on Earth in human form, we are worshipped as 'gods.' If we appear there in any other form they immediately label us as 'alien monsters' or 'demons,' because in their eyes we are *not* created in 'God's image,' which in actual fact is the Controllers' image — so what are we to do?

"As all of you here this evening are aware, it is our role as caretakers of energy, to assist all humanoid species to awaken to Universal, Cosmic or Divine Consciousness.

"Universal Consciousness is attained by a soul when it reaches a point in its evolution when it can fully and consciously acknowledge, tune into, and empathize totally with all life. On Planet Earth only a few cultures have approached this level. Most are still out to destroy species on their planet that don't serve them or who are ugly or dangerous in their eyes, such as the insect and reptilian species. We are finding that when humans acquire empathy and acknowledgement for all life-forms on their own planet, it more easily extends to those that exist in other dimensions and realities.

"We have been pleased to assist in this awakening process on all levels — physical, mental, emotional and spiritual, for in order to unfold and grow, all limitations and barriers within the psyche must be broken through. This 'breaking through' process could be compared to a chick confined to its shell. If further growth and development is to take place, the chick must break free of the shell. If it is unable to do this it will not reach maturity — in fact it will die of its confinement.

"As tryers and testers of souls, it is our task to assist in the breaking down of the shell of fear and ego which confines a soul from further growth and unfoldment, for it is fear and ego alone that creates this shell, this barrier, that blocks a soul's full potential. We do this by reflecting back to those who look upon us a mirror image of that which lies hidden and buried within the deepest layers of the psyche. It is here too, in these deeper layers, that humans will find the doorway to their higher self, which cannot be perceived accurately and without distortion until the blockages of fear and ego are cleared.

"For many souls, this can be a quite shattering and traumatic experience, to say the least, whereas for others it can be transformational and freeing, for sometimes it is not so much hidden fear that must be drawn to the surface but rather hidden potential! Now, before I proceed further, do any of you have questions?" A pawlike hand went up somewhere down the front, but I couldn't see the body it belonged to.

"Maris," the questioner politely addressed my Teacher, "can you please explain the relationship between the earlier contacts your people had with Earthlings and present-day contact. Why did you change your tactics? Can you clarify that a little more, please?"

"Yes, of course." Maris replied. "Today we are only discussing the most recent, stepped-up contact since the 1940s and beyond, not the contact over the millennia. So these contacts of the 1950s which involved more human-looking entities, were simply a gentle introduction meant only to open them up to the fact that indeed there *are* other sentient, human beings 'out there' on planes and dimensions other than the physical Earth Plane.

"At that stage there was so much fear being spread on Earth through superstitious, Controller-inspired belief systems that we tried to keep the fear aspect to a minimum. Our hope was, that by exposing them to the reality of other more highly evolved civilizations, they would come to see the errors in what they were being taught and cease to be so egotistical. It was most important that they be shown, because until then many of them believed without question that they were the ultimate life-form in all of creation.

"Even the time frame we chose was not by accident. Our plan was to approach them at a point when, after so many years of war and strife on a world-wide scale, they would surely be totally fed up and sick and tired of fighting each other, and they would be craving peace. We hoped that what we were presenting to them at that point in time would give them the incentive to become more civilized, and more united as a planetary culture.

"But no! Ego began to cloud the issue, and the fear persisted. We did not take into account the depth of it. This fear of anyone not part of their own 'herd' had to somehow be drawn out of the Earthling psyche, and the major part of overcoming it lay in making them face up to the fact that *not* all sentient, evolved life-forms in the universe are necessarily created in the image of Earth humans. Thus we began appearing to them as we really are, rather than sending others or disguising ourselves behind an Earth human façade.

"Many of them still do not understand. Although the Controller-inspired concept of a beautiful 'space brother,' or 'angel' may be warm, cozy and very comforting to the psyche, *true spiritual growth only comes from being challenged.* It is only by facing up to and overcoming the highly disturbing and often terrifying experience of having their limiting boundaries of consciousness and their concept of 'reality' broken down, that they will ever be able to move on to the more expansive conscious reality that is their rightful heritage.

"Thus the 'alien encounters' of the 1960s onwards began. These encounters also involved so-called abductions, because physical adjustments and genetic work involving the taking of sperm and ova had to be carried out to assist the evolutionary process on the DNA level, just as it was many, many millennia ago when the shift from animal to human was initiated. In fact quite a significant proportion of the fear they suffer now during encounters with us actually stems from that time so long ago when, as members of a biped primate species that had evolved on Earth, they were taken on board our discs and subjected to the processes that assisted their further evolution into the Adamic Race.

"We began removing the aggressive, territorial instinct from the human psyche back then, teaching them about Oneness, and offering the newly evolved species the protection of what they recall as 'The Garden of Eden,' but then they began mating back with their earlier and less evolved ancestors. In this way they gradually devolved almost back to the level of beasts, which in turn adversely affected their DNA. It is this 'downfall' that now threatens their survival as a species, and the inherent territorial aggression in the nature of the Earth human must be overcome before the next evolutionary step can proceed smoothly. While they retain this trait they can neither be admitted as members of the Star Nations, nor evolve to their rightful place as true citizens of the universe.

"Now," said Maris, stepping back and taking another sip of water, "we will take a short break at this point before continuing. Please feel free to talk among yourselves." My Teacher stepped down from the podium, still mindfully keeping his cape tightly wrapped around his body, and went to join a group of other Elders standing off to the side.

"You know what," Solarno whispered, leaning across to Ashka and me, "you Guardian folk really do deserve full credit. It must be so frustrating doing this sort of work with a stubborn species like the Earthlings. I don't know how you stay so patient with them."

Ashka chuckled. "We don't always. They reckon we lack emotions, but you should've heard some of the colorful language Dagar was using the other night when he came back on board the disc after a particularly difficult 'encounter.' I made the mistake of asking him what had happened, and he almost threw his infraray at me."

"You were *lucky!*" I replied. "He *did* throw it at me, after I innocently suggested that maybe he needed a holiday. Boy, was he riled up, but it made me realize how lucky I am. The Earth humans I'm assigned to at the moment are all quite friendly and easy to get along with, so they're not all hard cases. Would you believe one of them even told me a joke the other night?"

"Really!" the others chorused in unison. "I didn't think Earth humans *had* much of a sense of humor!"

"What was it?" Asara asked. "I love jokes!"

"Well," I began, trying to recall the opening line, "it seems there were these two, umm, Earthlings, Pat and Mick, and ...."

At that point I was rudely interrupted by Ashka's elbow making hard and pointy contact with the side of my body. "Shhh! Tell us later — he's back!"

Sure enough, Maris was up on the podium, effectively silencing the auditorium with a meaningful glare from his huge, black eyes. Funny that, how one Guardian Elder can, with a single, sweeping glance, bring the entire Star Nations Council into line.

"Now," my venerable Teacher began, "we come to the crux of the problem we are facing. As you are all no doubt aware, Planet Earth, as beautiful as she is, is a planet of war, the basis of which is this fear and ego of which I spoke earlier.

"Too many Earth humans still tend to be a fearful and ego-driven species — particularly among their leaders who, after all, are representative of the mass consciousness of whichever country they lead. It is this fear and ego that gives rise to all the contributing factors that result in chaos and divisiveness — microcosmically within family units, and macrocosmically in the many senseless wars that have ravaged this planet over the span of millennia. Fear and ego have caused greed, envy and jealousy, and the need to dominate and control — to impose one's beliefs and culture onto others, whether they want it or not.

"Why, they have even tried to dominate and control Nature herself! And this also causes them to experience fear and a deep sense of guilt when they come face to face with us, the Gardeners of the Earth. As a newly developed human species, Earthlings were entrusted with stewardship of their planet. They were charged with the responsibility of caretaking all other life-forms on their home world, but just *look* what they have *done* to their Mother Earth and her creatures! No *wonder* they dread our coming! This, my friends, is what we are up against.

"This is precisely *why* we must let them see us *as we are.* If they can understand the Oneness of life and appreciate all living creatures as part of the whole, then the next step in their evolution is for them to be able to *accept* other human beings that look so different from themselves. Or vice versa, if they can accept us as part of the universal whole, maybe they will accept all the unique living creatures of Earth.

"No offense to our Pleiadian, Altarian and other such interplanetary representatives, but you do not look 'strange' enough to present the necessary challenge that is needed to push Earth humans past their fear barrier." At this, Maris turned to the representatives of these groups with a small bow of apologetic acknowledgement, as a ripple of amusement passed through the audience.

"Situated as they are on the very first rung of the Human Ladder, Earth humans play the very important role of being a bridge between the animal kingdom out of which they were developed, and the universal consciousness to which they are evolving. As such, it is a transitional phase in the process of evolution in which instinctive, primal fear must be overcome in order to make further progress up the evolutionary ladder. This primal fear may have been necessary in the earlier stages of their development, but unfortunately it has been retained too strongly. It has now been carried through their genetic makeup to become 'cultural fear,' which causes wariness and mistrust of anyone who is not of their own tribe or nation, religion, culture or planet.

"To summarize, as caretakers of energy, we have been responsible for assisting the evolutionary process in Earth humans, which is in three stages. The first stage involved taking a biped mammal of the primate species of Planet Earth, and by advanced genetic engineering procedures the species known as *Homo sapiens* was developed. This first stage resulted in the refinement of the body — the physical aspect of Earth Man.

"The second stage, involving further genetic input and adjustments, this time to refine the mind, the mental/emotional aspect, produced *Homo sapiens sapiens.*

"Our present program, the third and final stage of our ongoing project with the Earthlings, which will result in the refinement of the spiritual aspect, involves still more genetic input and adjustment. Once this stage is completed, body, mind and spirit will unite as One, thus opening the way for cosmic consciousness to emerge.

"Over the past 20 years or more, many of those they call 'contactees' have changed their perspective and after initial fear reactions, have been able to see past our physical shell and feel our energy and love. This is progress. On the other hand, we are flabbergasted that there are still so many who when they find themselves mysteriously transported on board an 'alien spaceship,' and surrounded by strange-looking, obviously non-Earthling humanoid beings such as ourselves, still cling to their limited third-dimensional reality as the only reality. Sadly, despite the effort of many who are in contact with us, the Controllers have kept the truth out of the media where the majority receive their news, and for too many we are labeled as bad, dangerous, wrong, or even demons, which confirms their 'reality.'

"Nonetheless, our people are presenting Earth humans with a very powerful test, or perhaps I should say a 'learning experience.' After all, it is only by learning to open up to, trust, and accept the differences in others that they will ever learn to trust and accept themselves. In learning to trust and accept self in this way, they will eventually attain what all of us here take for granted, that is, *self realization*, which in turn opens the door to cosmic or universal consciousness. But Earth humans must first let go of fear in order to trust — in other words, to become again as little children to enable them to enter the Kingdom of Heaven. This, fellow citizens of the universe," Maris concluded, nodding respectfully towards the Chairman of the Council, "is the project we are at present undertaking, and all constructive suggestions and ideas will be most gratefully accepted.

31 ▸ Spiritual Evolution

The wave of movement and whisperings which arose as Maris finished speaking stopped very smartly when the Chairman of the Council stepped slowly to the podium. Short, rotund and with a head as bald as a billiard ball, he was not a terribly prepossessing figure to behold physically, but the energy of all-encompassing love that emanated from his very presence was beyond words. Buddha-like was the only way to describe him, standing up there dressed in a very ordinary-looking brown robe.

After a respectful acknowledgement towards Maris, his dark eyes turned slowly to take in the entire audience seated before him. As his gaze moved over us, it was as if each and every one present was bathed in a radiance of total love, peace and compassion, such was the strength, beauty and far-reaching energy of his auric field.

No matter the physical appearance of our container, whether tall Earth human-looking Pleiadians or Altarians, large-eyed insectoid-looking Mantis people, our own Guardian species in our artificial or semi-artificial gray containers, or any of the many other varied galactic representatives present in the auditorium under his gaze, each of us felt totally loved, respected and accepted to the very core of our being.

"My dear fellow citizens of the Star Nations," he began, "I thank all of you for your patience in listening to the words of our Guardian brother Maris, who has gone to a great deal of trouble to explain the situation we are all facing in regard to Planet Earth. As Maris has pointed out, time for this planet and her people is running out, and the situation is becoming increasingly desperate. As he has also explained, it is the special work of the Guardians, known on Planet Earth as 'Greys' or 'Zetas,' to carry out this work with the human species of Earth, which is highly appropriate, as the Guardians' appearance alone is a lesson and a challenge for Earth humans to deal with and will pave the way for Earthlings to accept those of you in the room who are even more exotic.

Some chuckling could be heard, especially from some of our more unusual beings.

"As Maris said, time and time again over the millennia we have pandered to Earthling fear, ego and prejudice by sending more human-looking ones to them as teachers and messengers, but every attempt has failed. They have either perceived these teachers as 'gods,' or else put them to death — sometimes both!

"To add to this unhappy situation, in almost every instance the perceived 'gods,' or at least their teachings and messages, have been used by Earth humans to separate, divide and elevate one culture, nation or belief system over all others. This in turn has created excuses for war on Planet Earth, with the adherents of one culture or belief system killing the adherents of another culture or belief system in the name of 'their god.' Such is the perverseness and duality of this Earthling species we are attempting to assist."

The look on Maris's face at that moment said it all. For the first time I saw him as old and tired. Yes, his large eyes were still as black as my own, but there was infinite weariness in them as well, and his face was becoming more wrinkled around the mouth area.

I really did not want him to let his cape fall open, not here in front of the entire Star Nations Council. But what could I do except send up a silent prayer to the Cosmos that he wouldn't forget — that he would mindfully continue holding it around him. Then the Chairman was speaking again, and I quickly snapped to attention because it was our group he was addressing.

"Would all the Guardian folk who are taking part in this project please come down to the front of the auditorium."

Poor Ashka looked aghast. "Oh, gee, do we *have* to? I hate getting up in front of crowds. Why does he want us to do that? You go Alarca; I'll just stay put here."

"I'm not going down there without you." So saying, I grabbed her hand and hauled her out of her seat, much to the amusement of everyone around us, several of whom started clapping as we moved forward, much to our embarrassment.

As it turned out, there was quite a sizeable group of us, and the smaller workers were asked to come to the front, while the much taller Elders stood behind. This was the opportunity I needed — my prayer was answered. Naturally enough, each of us gravitated towards our own particular Teacher, and as it happened Ashka's teacher Anarkis was standing right beside my teacher Maris. Being level sevens, Ashka and I were taller than the little workers, none of whom were more than a meter and a half in height, if that much. We slipped in behind them to stand in the middle, in front of the very tall level-eight Elders, some of whom exceeded two meters in height.

In this way I was able to place myself directly in front of Maris, stepping back close to him and reaching behind to help him hold the edges of his cape closed. He knew what I was doing, for the next moment a wave of beautiful, loving energy wrapped around me like a protective mantle, and I felt his long, four-fingered hand placed gently on my shoulder in an unspoken gesture of gratitude.

Ashka and Anarkis telepathically picked up on what was going on, and lent support by moving closer to us, as did the Elders Oris and Serapis as well as several of the younger workers, thus Maris was safely shielded from any possible embarrassment. With all of our minds thus linked in Oneness, a wave of warm, loving energy flowed over our whole group, causing our normally silver-colored auras to light up even brighter, radiating out across the entire auditorium, bathing everybody present in a soft, silvery glow. Obviously enjoying the sensation, the Buddha-like Chairman of the Council rose reluctantly to his feet. It was clear that he would really have liked to remain in such a peaceful, loving space a little longer, but there was still work to be done.

"Earth humans truly don't know what they are missing out on by distancing themselves through their fear, do they?" he commented with a twinkle in his eyes and a wink in our direction, which set off a ripple of amusement from the audience. "There's nothing in the whole universe quite like a bit of combined energy from the Guardian Soul Group gathered in Oneness. Now," he continued, "the reason I have asked our friends here to come forward is so that all of you know exactly who they are, and what they are doing, because *every* assistance must be given to them. This is a daunting task they have taken on, with full permission and in fact at the *specific request* of the Star Nations Council, so our fullest support and backing is required and must be given. They *cannot* do it on their own.

"Most of you I'm sure are aware of the rebel group that is opposing them. This group is *not* a member of the Star Nations, and is doing its best to stop the Guardians from carrying out their appointed task of transmutation and transformation of the human species of Earth. In fact, this tug-of-war situation has been going on almost from Day One of the project, when the Controllers first interrupted the process for their own purposes. However, strange as it may seem, this 'opposition' is necessary, and is the very reason why Earth humans have been given free will.

"As we all know, evolution up the Human Ladder is all about choice — choosing between right and wrong, no matter which way these opposite polarities manifest within any given culture. Making right choices or wrong choices is what learning to apply free will and reasoning power is all about. Here I am speaking of reasoning power and free will as opposed to the purely instinctual drive of the animal kingdom. It is the greatest test to be faced on level one of the Human Ladder, for it is the very essence of what soul evolution is all about.

"Forcing a soul to make right or wrong choices will not assist them on their evolutionary path, and options must be presented to make the whole thing valid. They must be provided with the opportunity to choose right over wrong, or *vice versa*. If there is no choice and no options, then evolution will not happen. A soul will remain trapped and guided solely by the instinctual behavior of the animal kingdom, which is a behavioral pattern not governed by reasoning power but rather by the law of survival — survival of the fittest. It is this ability to reason that goes beyond the mere survival instinct of animals, which is the essential difference between animal and human. This, my friends, is the role played by the Controllers — to provide *negative* options and choices for evolving Earth humans to take up or to reject.

"However, important and essential as their role is in the evolutionary process, they are nevertheless making the Guardians' job extremely hard to carry out. The problem on Planet Earth is the energy screens that have been set up around the planet and baited with fear and ego-inducing illusions to keep humans trapped in disempowering mindsets. These in turn are reinforced by Controller-inspired belief systems on the planet itself. The Controllers feed off human fear and ego, so it is in their best interests to stir these emotions up to the maximum to keep themselves strong and vital.

"The only solution is for the Guardians to continue to help Earth humans look at and purge their inner fears — to bring them up to the surface in the controlled and therefore safe environment of a contact experience, where they can be more effectively dealt with. Thus, hopefully, the Controllers will eventually be overcome. This must be done, for it is now time for the human species of Earth to begin to awaken to the greater reality, so they may take their rightful place among us as a member culture of the Star Nations.

"Now," said the Chairman of the Council, turning his kindly gaze upon us, "I would really appreciate some comments from the Guardian workers — the ones who are 'in the front lines,' so to speak, dealing with frightened Earthlings on a nightly basis. I am interested to hear some ideas from all of you on how best to carry out your assignments in order to overcome the difficulties you are up against. Now who would like to speak?"

Entil was the first to come forward with the issue of Earth human consciousness, or rather the lack of it. "One of the main accusations that people on Earth direct at us is that we force ourselves upon them and override their free will in the encounter experience, but *no* Earth human is *ever* forced into contact with us. Their higher self knows perfectly well when the next evolutionary step is ready to be made and what is required to initiate it. This higher self also knows what wonderful potential lies within, ready and waiting to emerge once fear and ego are overcome. *They* are *not* chosen, neither are they victims!

"But," he went on, "such is the duality of Earth human nature that all this is forgotten within the hidden recesses of the subconscious mind soon after birth, so they perceive our intervention as 'abduction.' They forget that we simply initiate the necessary evolutionary changes and growth within their consciousness that will bring them to the point of freely choosing the right path. Even if they remember us as children, they tend to be forgetful of our existence as they mature, and this is so frustrating."

Quite a lot of discussion followed Entil's words, but nobody could find much of a solution. As someone in the audience pointed out, with an eloquent shrug of the shoulders: "But this is where Earthlings *are* in their evolution, so we must work with what we have!"

Then Ashka came forward, much to my surprise, since she didn't even want to stand up here, but I guess she was moved to share her experience, as the conference seemed to be getting nowhere very fast. I did have to wonder if her Teacher Anarkis had given her a bit of a shove from behind, which would be quite typical of him.

Displaying the color yellow of the solar plexus chakra on his hat band and feather, the lesson he is passing on to her is self empowerment, and sometimes we *do* need a bit of a push in the right direction to get this aspect of ourselves activated. Students automatically draw from their Teachers the particular color vibrations required for what they need to learn. Working with our Teachers in this way helps us achieve the necessary balance and harmony in our personal energy system, which in turn will enable us to eventually become Teachers ourselves.

Stepping up to the podium, Ashka took a moment's pause to prepare herself before commencing. She began by thanking the Chairman of the Council for giving us the opportunity to speak, then she went on. "As all of you are aware, a number of our people as well as some from other planetary cultures are at present incarnating in human form on Planet Earth.

"This is a two-way exchange, enabling us to learn everything we possibly can about what it is like to actually *be* an Earth human, but also giving us the chance to walk among them in physical, Earthly form so we can give out our teachings and messages in a way they can more easily understand. The majority of them simply cannot pick up on our messages telepathically, and when they are brought onto the discs their fear blocks most of our attempts at communication, so in many cases the only way to get through to them is to mingle with them as one of their own kind.

"The Earth form I have taken is female, living with a male partner in marriage, with two children, aged 7 and 13. Having these children of my own, who in turn have many friends, puts me in an ideal position for communication. It enables me to understand where Earth children are coming from emotionally, mentally and spiritually. It gives me a chance to share our teachings with them and to then observe their reactions. From what Maris has said about the deeply entrenched fear and ego in some Earth humans, and the difficulties Entil spoke of regarding their limited conscious awareness, my feeling is that we need to concentrate on these young ones.

"Having experienced motherhood and the raising of children, I believe that young Earth humans *do* often remember much more of the pre-birth and between-life states than their elders give them credit for, especially now that so many of them carry more ET genetics in their physical makeup. It is the virtual brainwashing they are subjected to as they begin to grow and mature that causes the memory blocks which limit their ability to remain open to their higher consciousness.

"As the mother of two who mix with many others, I have observed a major problem that I believe will have to be addressed before Earth humans can evolve any further on the spiritual level. This problem is the breaking down of the family unit. Far too many children in modern Earth society feel totally lost and without direction because of this.

"The family unit, which is *vitally* important on a level-one planet such as Earth, is breaking down and becoming irrelevant mainly because of ego and selfishness. Surely an important part of spiritual growth and maturity is learning to get along with others in a loving and peaceful way, whether this is on a family, neighborly, national or planetary level. After all, this is what Oneness is about, and it is how our Guardian soul group operates!

"As we all know, in higher and more evolved planetary cultures, every individual's actions and thoughts are aimed first and foremost towards the benefit of the whole. Some Earth humans believe that we have no individuality or free will because we think in terms of Group Soul, but they have this perspective because they can only think in terms of self and individual ego. Many tribal societies live the way we do, but most humans do not.

"Evolution towards peaceful and loving oneness on a planetary, galactic or universal level has to begin somewhere. It has its roots within the family unit, mastering the give and take of family life, which often involves the placing of others before self, and the making of certain sacrifices within one's life.

"Getting this to work takes self-discipline, which is a *vital* ingredient where free will is involved. Free will without self-discipline is a sure way to disaster and chaos, which is exactly what we see happening on Earth right now, especially in modern western society where the family unit is rapidly losing value. How can children ever learn to respect others if they are not first taught the self-discipline which in turn leads to self-respect?

"It is the egotistical and selfish need for more and more in the way of material possessions and self-gratification that brings about a diminishing of spiritual values within any given society — the placing of money, work and possessions before family, ethics, compassion and the cultivation of spiritual values. And it is the children who suffer the most, because they are vulnerable and dependent upon the loving care and good example given to them by their parents. Parenthood is *the* most important vocation anyone can take up on Planet Earth, and like any highly demanding and vitally important vocation, much time, effort and dedication must be devoted to it, for the consequences are far-reaching.

"Because it is so demanding and important, more than any other work an Earth human can carry out, two at least are needed to fill the role. Children need the balanced energy of two parents, mother and father, female and male, yin and yang. This may not always be possible, but at least it should be the rule rather than the exception that it seems to be becoming in modern Western Society.

"Some Earth humans hold what they proudly refer to as 'modern' views, believing the concept of marriage as the basis of family life to be old-fashioned and no longer viable for human society. However, this is because they do not understand energy and the importance of having both negative and positive polarity, female and male, for a balanced and harmonious way.

"Yes, a child *is* better off in an alternative situation than in a family unit where there is violence, either physical or emotional, but violence is the result of lack of self-discipline and respect, so really, this is where we come the full circle! It is only in a family situation that self-discipline and respect can truly be mastered, and so the problem continues and is carried through subsequent generations.

"Children need quality time, and the value of imagination and dreams needs to be respected and acknowledged *much* more, for these are the keys that unlock deeper levels of the psyche beyond the 10% that Earth humans are normally able to access. In tribal societies where such things are understood and encouraged, people have a far more balanced and healthier outlook on life.

"In many of these societies, the recall and open discussion of dreams is a vital and important part of life for everyone. For many Earth humans, dreams are the only link available between lower self and higher self, and they are also an important avenue of contact between our two species, so they should not be so casually dismissed as 'just a silly dream and nothing more.'

"To summarize, I feel that many older Earth humans are too entrenched in the limitations of level-one consciousness, and too caught up in Controller-inspired illusions for us to be able to approach them openly on the conscious level, however, with children and young people it's different. They will be the ones to bring about deeper understanding and to be able to express it physically on Planet Earth, providing there *is* any planet left for them to do this, which is the reason behind the urgency of our work."

Ashka stepped away from the podium to the sound of loud applause. There was not a single one present in the room who did not know about and agree with what she had said. Every one of us had made the slow and sometimes difficult climb up the Human Ladder. Some of us had experienced lives as Earth humans, and others had evolved from different level-one planets, but all had faced the same tests and the same learning experiences in one way or another on the pathway of evolution from human to angel.

Looking back, we knew exactly what she'd meant about the need for love, respect and unselfishness to begin within the family-unit situation on a level-one planet such as Earth. If one cannot master these intrinsic elements of unconditional love in such a small and basic unit as a family, then how can this love be practiced on a planetary, galactic or universal level?

The Chairman of the Council returned to the podium to formally thank Entil and Ashka for their valuable contribution to the evening's program. "And now," he went on, "before we conclude, I would like to introduce the Guardian Elder, Garnibis, to speak briefly on a major issue that arises on a regular basis. I refer, of course, to the question of whether or not we are to make open and public contact on Planet Earth."

Garnibis stepped up to take her place on the podium, calmly regarding us all through the huge, milky-blue eyes of a very ancient Guardian Elder. Her extremely tall, thin body was draped in a long, flowing, black robe with the hood pushed back to reveal the large, bald dome of her head. To Earth human eyes she would have appeared extremely weird, but as she stood before us, I thought she was one of the most beautiful souls I had ever encountered.

"My good friends and fellow citizens of the universe," she began, "the question has often been raised as to whether open contact would be appropriate on Planet Earth at this time. After much toing and froing, as we old ones are wont to do…," here she paused a moment to smile, "…it has been decided that such an approach as landing a disc openly would not be entirely wise, at least for now. For a start it would be too dangerous for us and too traumatic still for many Earth humans.

Until the fear can be healed to a point where war ceases to disturb and disrupt the energetic balance of their planet, the risk is too great. To land a disc openly and to try to approach in this way would almost certainly cause panic and chaos on a massive scale. Shots would be fired and people would be hurt.

Furthermore, our prime concern is not physical now, but rather soul contact, to help Earth humans wake up to a higher level of conscious awareness, which in turn will enable them to access deeper layers of their own psyche. We are not going to achieve this by pandering to their demands for physical proof and physical evidence of our presence. If they truly wish to understand us better, then they will have to break down their inner barriers and learn to tap into these deeper levels. This in fact is an intrinsic part of our *Consciousness Expansion Program* on Planet Earth.

"And besides," she added, casting a kindly look in our direction, "through ones such as these workers, an open physical approach is being made already. As was discussed during the conference this evening, there are now a number of our people incarnating on Earth in human form, quietly working away to assist the awakening of deeper consciousness among the inhabitants of that planet, reaching out to Earth humans in a physical form they can relate to and feel comfortable with.

"So my dear friends, that is our decision — at least for now — to continue as we have been, working most especially with the children as our friend Ashka here has so wisely suggested. What will occur in the future we cannot say, as many possible time lines are present, and we are not God. We may agree to take part in some limited contact with small groups of humans who are willing to welcome us in trust, openness and love, but for now we will just wait and see how things develop.

"There is, however, significant communication taking place on our part through what have come to be known on Earth as 'crop circles, or glyphs,' and many Earth humans are responding to these in a positive way, with two-way exchanges happening in a couple of instances, which is very encouraging.

"As I'm sure all of you here are aware, these designs are being created by encapsulated energy, with the requisite image encoded onto an 'energy stamp,' which appears to human observers as a ball of light. The crop glyphs are being done primarily as a safe means of communication. They serve as messages from us to the people of Earth, to make them aware of the fact that they are not alone. The sometimes quite intricate designs provide an easily observed physical sign to open human minds to other possibilities.

"Earth Scientists have tried to communicate with ETs through radio waves, and the crop circles are our answer. They are meant to assist Earth humans to come to the understanding that there are greater forces out there, and to remind them that they are *not* gods who can freely tamper with Nature. This is why some of the glyphs are created in the form of complex mathematical formulas, so that Earthlings can realize these signs come from an intelligent species rather than simply being the haphazard workings of a mindless but so far undiscovered form of energy.

"The second reason for the crop circles is educational. Many of them are pictograms of other solar systems and galaxies, and some have been symbolic of the Human Ladder. There is so much that Earth humans don't know about time, space, energy and evolution, and we are most happy to share this knowledge with them, if they will use it in a constructive way, and for peaceful purposes, of course. Unfortunately so far their track record is not looking good!

"The third reason for the glyphs is transformational, in that some of them contain special symbols, rather like Reiki symbols. These are designed to activate additional energy points in the etheric field of the planet, to allow for the higher frequency and greater amounts of universal energy that are being drawn in as Planet Earth steps up her frequency to the second level of the Human Ladder.

"The crop circles, like other universal symbols, also affect the energy system of the human body, which is closely linked to the endocrine system. This in turn is the key to activating additional strands of the DNA, which until now have remained dormant. Level-two humans will eventually operate with three strands of DNA. In this way, the crop circles actually affect the energy fields of both the planet and its inhabitants. So, it is through a combination of the crop circle energy work, the genetic work and DNA adjustments we are carrying out, combined with teaching and energy work being done by those of our own people who are manifesting human lives on Earth that there is slow but sure progress being made."

32 ▶ FREE WILL

The morning after the conference I awoke with a very clear recollection of what had gone on, and I told Paco about it over breakfast. He was always fascinated to hear what we were up to, and he never failed to question me on certain points in order to clarify matters in his own mind. He also made constructive suggestions, which in turn helped me to understand the Earth human perspective more clearly. Although he didn't know it, I often took these suggestions to the Elders, or carried them out myself during the course of my work, and I really felt they made a difference in our interspecies relations.

He took a few moments to consider what Maris had said regarding the problem of Earth humans getting caught up in the various belief systems, concepts and mindsets that tend to place a ceiling and limitation upon what they are able to perceive as 'reality.' Then he came out with, "Yes, but hang on a minute, Ali Cat. It's all very well for your people, who are able to consciously access what you call greater realities, but we can't generally do that. Remember you're always telling me that we only have access to 10% of our potential conscious awareness. That is where we are in our soul evolution, and so we have to make the best of it and get by with a bit of faith and trust that there is something bigger and better out there somewhere.

"Now okay," he went on, "I do agree that we tend to get caught up in superstition and in some rigid dogmas. And yes, I can see how this can potentially be very limiting for soul growth, but at the same time, some sort of structured belief system is *most* necessary at this point in our evolution to keep us on the straight and narrow. After all, if Earthlings had no belief systems, some would run completely amok! All you need to do is to look at certain younger ones who've been brought up this way, with no belief in God, no ethical or moral boundaries, and no sense of right and wrong. Maybe we're simply not mature enough as a species to operate this way yet."

"You *are* right, Paco," I answered, "and I agree with what you're saying. What we tend to forget is that Earth humans depend solely on faith and trust when it comes to God. The difference between our two species in this respect is, you *believe*, but we *know*, and therefore we do not have to depend upon faith alone. But as Maris pointed out, there's nothing wrong with belief systems that teach love, compassion and non-judgment, and in fact, yes, on Planet Earth these are most necessary. It's just the ones that preach fear, intolerance and hatred that are a major worry.

"Well, we agree on that." he said enthusiastically.

"I also know exactly what you mean by people needing boundaries in order to keep society functioning in a civilized way. We would never disagree with this either. In fact, as Maris pointed out, humans must first master self-discipline before true freedom can ever be achieved. Free will without self-discipline only leads to chaos."

"Okay now, Ali Cat," Paco put in. "This reminds me of something I've been meaning to bring up with you on the issue of freedom and free will. Much of the fear associated with Earth humans' contact with Greys is centered on free will. Many experiencers of contact with your people see you operating as virtually a 'hive mentality,' with no individuality or free will, and they are terrified that you're planning to impose this lack of freedom and individuality on Planet Earth. What do you have to say on this?"

"Oh, for goodness sake, Paco, absolutely *not*! We wouldn't *dream* of doing such a thing. Do you view your tribal societies as hive mentalities even though they focus on the group?"

"Well, no. But they're familiar, whereas your people aren't."

"Okay, we understand that, but you need to open up to the fact that we've been around you for a long time. We have and are still coming among you and mixing our genetics with yours simply to help you evolve past the self-centered fear and ego that is the root cause behind the divisiveness and wars that have plagued Planet Earth for millennia. We do *not* wish to take your individuality away from you, but we *do* want to help you as a planetary culture to achieve a more unified soul-group consciousness so that you don't end up destroying yourselves and your planet. It's this unified soul consciousness that will eventually lead Earth humans back to oneness with the Source, but individuality and a healthy sense of self must be retained. In fact that is an important part of Self Realization."

"So you would never take away our free will?"

"No, no *way*! But what will happen is that eventually you yourselves will choose to grow past it, for it can actually be quite limiting."

"Hey? Come again? Surely the ability to reason things out and make free will choices is the ultimate freedom any culture can achieve."

"No, actually it's not. You see, free will is all about making choices, including choosing between 'right' and 'wrong,' and at Earth human level, choosing right over wrong usually means having to practice self-discipline. For example, say I'm in a supermarket and I really feel like eating a chocolate, but I don't have the money to buy one. Now do I give in to self-indulgence and make the *wrong* choice by shoplifting one, or do I practice self-discipline and do the *right* thing by resisting the temptation. This same principle applies whether it's a chocolate bar, a partnership, or a multi-million-dollar business deal. It's all about choosing right over wrong — does one pander to oneself and everyone else be damned, or practice a bit of self-discipline to avoid hurting others?

"When you think about it, it's always the self-discipline part of free will that causes all the problems for people. You know, having the necessary self-discipline to make the right choice. It's like you see sometimes in cartoons, with an angel sitting on someone's right shoulder, trying to influence them to do right; and a devil sitting on their left shoulder, trying to tempt them to do the wrong thing. And practicing self-discipline down here isn't always easy. Sometimes it's very tempting to go the wrong way, especially if you know you'll get away with it."

"Okay, so far I follow, but where do we go from here? How do we overcome this?"

"Well, we Guardians and other human species further up the Human Ladder, have moved *past* the free-will 'do I or don't I?' phase and evolved into God's will. You see, as we evolve through the various levels of the Human Ladder, we move further away from duality and closer to Oneness. In other words, we unite more fully with the God Source. It is a 'becoming' and an awakening process really, in that we gradually awaken and thus 'become' Oneness.

"Now the closer we meld back into Oneness, the less we are going to be affected by the polarization of duality, which governs life on Planet Earth; therefore the less we are forced to make choices between right and wrong. In this way, we eventually evolve past the need for free will, because all of our thoughts, actions and choices become God's will. We become so much an intrinsic part of Oneness that there is no desire to act any other way. Our will is automatically God's will, and our actions become God's actions, which are always for the good of all. We are no longer separate from the Source, but rather instinctively and intrinsically attuned to God Consciousness.

"I really have to try that one on," he said, rubbing his forehead. "But then, when you think about it, many Christians already try to live that way, and probably other religions as well. Or at least strive to. So was it God's will or mine to become a Priest?"

"What do you feel?"

"God's will since it was always such a strong calling for me."

"I agree. You see Paco, the problem with free will on Planet Earth is that all too often it's more about *self*-will — what we want rather than what we need, regardless of everyone around us. Have you noticed, however, how we can continually be brought back to doing the right thing, regardless of what we think we want?"

"Yes, it's a funny thing. Like me coming back here to live. I felt it was 'in the cards.'"

"When it is necessary for us to experience something for our soul development, our higher self will nudge us, and possibly push us if it has to. But as we evolve further up the Ladder, we become less and less self-centered and more and more God-centered, thus eventually moving past the need for physical form and becoming pure mind operating in Oneness with God. This is how it is in the angelic realms on levels nine and ten. Angels have moved past the need for physicality — they are simply pure energy, totally attuned to the will of God.

"In fact, the whole universe is energy, and gross physical form is one of the lowest frequencies of this universal energy, so God can*not* be a physical being. However, being omnipresent, God Energy can express itself through physical beings. The spark of God is within *all* of us, becoming brighter and stronger as we open up our inner awareness, which is what evolution on the soul level is all about. Oh boy, this is hard to put into physical, third-dimensional language! Do you understand what I'm saying?"

Paco laughed. "It's okay, Ali Cat. I can see your eyes starting to cross, and I do appreciate the difficulty you're up against, trying to put multidimensional concepts into third-dimensional language, but yes, I understand what you're saying. And as you've said before, it's only by opening up our inner awareness and looking deeply inside ourselves that we can ever face up to and deal with the Satan within, which in reality is our own inner demons and fears.

"And you know what," he went on, "when you really think about it, this is so much like the fires of purgatory spoken of in church doctrine, which are said to have a purging, or cleansing effect upon the soul. Maybe people have misunderstood this whole concept by externalizing purgatory as a place outside of themselves rather than it being a state of inner cleansing that must take place in order to allow the spark of God to shine more brightly from within."

"Ah, yes — that reminds me of something I read once, 'People are like stained glass windows — they sparkle and shine when the sun is out, but when darkness sets in, their true beauty is revealed only if there is a light from within.'"

"Wow; that *is* profound! In fact it sounds like something inspired by one of your Elders. And speaking of Elders, this brings up another question on something that female Elder said... now what was her name again, the blue-eyed one?"

"You mean Garnibis?"

"Yep, that's the one! She was talking about whether or not you're going to land your discs here in physical, third-dimensional reality. What's that all about? Why don't you? Surely it'd be easier to convince people of your presence if you were to do this, maybe not necessarily on the lawn of the White House, but why not somewhere openly and in public?"

"We have, actually, a few times, but we find it too risky, and besides that, it's just not the way we generally operate. We're here to assist humans to access deeper layers of consciousness and get past the limited and physically oriented nuts-and-bolts-must-have-physical-proof mindset that the Earth plane investigators refuse to move past.

"Too many Earth scientists simply refuse to open their minds, and they are totally unable to accept anything as real that they cannot touch, dissect, measure and examine under a microscope. What they cannot comprehend is that our presence is not so much a physical happening but rather a spiritual happening. It's more about evolution of soul than physicality.

"Believe it or not, some Earth humans don't even accept the reality of the soul or spirit because they can't physically prove it by weighing or measuring it. But anything beyond the physical cannot be weighed, and although energy can be measured up to a point, the soul energy that we deal with is of a vibrational frequency way beyond the primitive instrumentation of Planet Earth."

"Sadly, I do believe it and have witnessed it."

"By their willingness to trust enough to open themselves to our presence without the need for physical 'nuts and bolts' evidence, Earth humans are also opening themselves up to greater realities within self, and beyond. This is the main reason why we hesitate to land openly and walk among you — it would make it too easy for people to remain closed on the soul level, and not learn or profit by it spiritually.

"Doesn't it help with people you're already working with?"

"Sure, your curiosity about ETs might be satisfied, but that is as far as it would go — it would not help your evolution as a species. Too often we're seen, not believed and buried with the unconscious again. If it begins to wake someone up, then it was good.

"The impetus behind evolution is always based on the need for change and adaptation, whether it is a need to change and adapt to walking on two legs rather than on four, or a need to expand awareness in order to step up a level on the Human Ladder. To put it simply, our presence here is to provide the impetus for the mind expansion that is necessary if Earth humans are ever going to take the next step in their evolution."

33 ▶ KATE'S DOWNLOAD

ey, Ali Cat, I need some help on something that's come up at the
school. Can we talk?"

"Paco, does it have to be right now? I'm relaxing. Can't it wait?"

"No, not really. I'm going to be busy for the rest of the day and I
need to know by tomorrow."

I reluctantly put the newspaper aside that I'd been reading and
moved my cup off the other seat so he could sit down. A sunny autumn
morning was the perfect time to sit quietly in the dappled shade of a
large, old tree in the back garden, reading the Sunday paper and sipping a
coffee. The sky was a cloudless, cobalt blue, a gentle breeze was wafting
the scent of a neighbor's bacon and egg breakfast through the garden,
and life was *good*.

This little garden behind the presbytery was a totally private oa-
sis where I spent many happy hours. Safely ensconced within the protection of a high stone wall, it was a place where one could indulge in any
chosen activity from nose picking, to navel gazing, or even to a naked
fire-leaping ceremony on the Feast of Beltane, without risk of being
spied upon by curious neighbors.

Not that I would do any of these things — certainly not the last
one anyway, what with the Feast of Beltane falling upon an almost winter's night here in the southern hemisphere. After all, you'd at least need
to wear a pair of sheepskin boots and a nice, warm, woolly cap pulled
down over your ears, which would sort of ruin the effect of the whole
thing. But it was still comforting to know that if such a burning desire
ever came upon me, I could.

"What's the time anyway? Aren't you supposed to be saying
Mass?"

Paco made himself at home in the other chair and helped himself
to a generous mouthful of my coffee, pulling a face because there wasn't
enough sugar in it to suit his taste. "Mass was over half an hour ago —
it's nearly 10:30. I have to go out at eleven, and I won't be back till late,
so that's why I need to talk to you now."

"Oh, come on, Paco," I teased, "don't be such a workaholic.
Everybody else relaxes on a Sunday."

"Ali, I'm a *priest,* for goodness sake! Now are you going to help
me or not?"

"Okay, okay, don't get hot under the dog collar. So what's the matter?"

"Well, it's one of the girls at school — Kate, who's probably about 13. She came to me on Friday all upset because her teacher accused her of cheating. Apparently she's pretty hopeless at math, but she has suddenly developed an uncanny ability with algebra, so of course her teacher is suspicious, but she swears blind that she's not cheating. Trouble is she can't explain how she's acquired this ability, and there are problems at home with her family being haunted by a ghost or something."

"You're kidding! Are you sure she's not pulling your leg?"

"Yes, absolutely sure. I've been a counselor long enough to know when someone's lying to me. And don't forget too, since my contact with your people I can also read auras pretty clearly, and the aura never lies. If you can see a person's aura you can tell whether they're being truthful or not, and she is telling the truth."

"Okay, so where do I come in to all of this?"

"Well, I don't think the family is being haunted by a ghost. I think it's ET contact they're experiencing, and the child is being taken up on one of your discs. That would explain her sudden uncanny ability in math."

"Mmm, that's certainly possible. Have they done anything about it so far, like reading books on the subject or going to the local UFO Association for advice?"

"I'm not sure about those things, but apparently they had a family friend do a Reiki house cleanse for them, but it only made the 'activity' worse. Now I know how much you Greys love Reiki and are drawn to it, which makes me suspect that long, thin, ET fingers are dabbling here, rather than a ghost."

"Yes, I have to agree. It does sound like you're spot on. So what do you want me to do, talk to them or something?"

"I'm not quite sure at this point in time. I've asked Kate to get her mother to call me so we can talk. Maybe it's better for me to handle it first, just to reassure them, so we can get a more accurate idea of what's happening. Perhaps you could do some checking 'upstairs,' to confirm that it is contact by your people and not something else, then we'll take it from there."

"Did the girl describe what's happening in their house?"

"Yes, as well as she could, but the poor little thing is terrified. She said that on a couple of occasions a strong beam of light has descended on the house while they heard a sort of humming and beeping sound that went on for about 10 minutes. Another time, a strange dog suddenly appeared inside the house when all the doors were closed and locked. It wandered through the lounge while they were watching TV one evening, and then disappeared into Kate's bedroom, never to be seen again.

"They were also watched by a large owl for three days in a row a few weeks ago. Every time they went outside they found this weird-looking bird perched on the back fence, staring at them. They tried chasing it but it always came back, then like the dog, it simply vanished as mysteriously as it had come.

"But the worst thing is the black-clad figures they see on occasions around the house. Poor little Kate has had one standing in the corner of her room, all dressed in black and with a hood pulled forward over its head. Needless to say, the first time she saw it she nearly screamed the house down, and when her dad ran in to see what was wrong, he caught a glimpse of it too. It's appeared several times since, so four out of five nights she ends up sleeping on the floor in her parents' room, which is not so good for a 13-year-old."

"I would definitely say it is not ghosts."

"And the big problem is they don't know whom to turn to for help or where to go. Kate is worried her parents will take her to a psychiatrist and she'll be locked up in some mental institution. That's why she came to me for help — she just didn't know where else to go, and she can't handle it any more on her own."

"Oh, dear, the poor little soul! It sounds like we have been busy! But you know what, Paco, this is the whole problem with western society. Unlike tribal people who are brought up with an intrinsic understanding of such things as ET and interdimensional contact and thus possess the tools and knowledge to help themselves through, Western people do not.

"Western society is so left-brained and intellectually oriented and hopelessly trapped within the limited and inaccurate mindset that physical, third-dimensional, waking reality is the *only* reality. The result is that when anything like ET contact occurs, which is much more attuned to alpha and theta brain activity, it is not considered 'real,' and is therefore either dismissed as just a dream or imagination, or else relegated to the 'too hard basket' by counselors and doctors who simply don't have the proper tools or understanding to help. This is where humans like you are of tremendous value — to act as a bridge to assist people through these contact experiences between our two cultures."

"Thanks. I'm trying, but it's not easy."

"If the truth be known, we find it really hard too, because on Planet Earth there's such a broad cross-section of languages, dialects, beliefs, customs, cultures and traditions, and some are more attuned to us than others. It all depends upon the level of consciousness of the culture, and some have a more awakened consciousness than others, like the tribal societies, who are generally more connected to other realities and therefore easier to communicate with. It never occurred to us that Westerners would be so very different, and much more difficult to connect with. That's why we're concentrating more on them now. They're the ones who really need our help. Honestly, dealing with people on this planet is like trying to deal with many different species all at once. We find it terribly confusing!"

"Why? Are other planetary species different from us?"

"Oh, goodness, yes! Earth is actually quite unusual in that there's so much variation and deep division between all the many cultures, nationalities, religions, traditions, etc. We've had to put in a *huge* amount of research and study to even begin getting a handle on it all, so mistakes are bound to occur in our contact with Earth humans. Most planetary cultures we've contacted have only one language and religion, or at the most two or three. This is why we have so much difficulty here — it's so divided and chaotic.

"But anyway, enough of our problems and back to Kate and her family. People going through ET contact experiences really need to understand more about consciousness and energy and try to get through the fear. The big difficulty we're up against is lack of understanding. As they say, 'Knowledge is Power,' or more accurately in the case of ET contact, 'Understanding is Empowerment.' This is *the* most important tool that anyone can have who undertakes a counseling or support role in this field. But what they first need in order to acquire the necessary understanding is a flexible and open mind. If the mind is set and closed, real understanding cannot penetrate."

"Well, Ali Cat, you must admit I certainly have understanding on the subject. You've made sure of that, but it looks like we have a very big job ahead of us."

"Yes," I sighed, "and now maybe you know how we feel. I think we need to bring Kaz in on this one, seeing there's a child involved. Having children of her own, Kaz will have a better understanding, both of where the child is coming from, and also from the mother's point of view. There's bound to be all sorts of family dynamics involved. And, her eldest, Kira, is also 13 and may even know Kate, going to the same school as they do.

"Kaz also has a younger child, her seven-year-old son Ben, who is going through rather similar experiences in the way of 'night terrors,' so she'll really be able to relate to this family. She found it very hard herself, until she regained conscious memory and understanding of who and what she is 'upstairs,' and if Kate's mother is a true Earth human, it'll be even harder for her.

Paco shook his head. "If her mother is a true Earth human? I guess I'm really becoming one of you because I hardly blinked at that statement."

"Oh, God, Paco, this is where I get torn in two, truly! Earth human, Guardian human — life will be so much easier when we're all One. As a Guardian I know we have to carry out this work, but I feel so sorry that we are so divided. Just last night I had to do some work on someone up on the disc, and when I entered the clinic he was lying on a table, able to move only his eyes. Knowing we have to restrain them for protection is one thing, but seeing the look of horror and loathing on his face was beyond words.

"I tried my best to communicate, to tell him not to be afraid and that we weren't going to hurt him, but my thought waves couldn't penetrate the thick cocoon of fear that surrounded him. I still feel upset just thinking about it. Oh, why can't more humans be like you, and there are others, actually, who come up on the disc and are free to roam around and ask questions. It's really quite pleasant then for all of us. Well, at least ones like Kaz and me can hopefully help sort things out down here, with assistance from people like you."

As he got up to go, Paco put a comforting hand on my shoulder. "As you said a while back, Ali Cat, you and Kaz are ambassadors for your people, so I guess this is just a part of your diplomatic role, helping Earth humans understand and hopefully eventually feel better about the ET contact experience. And you're right — I have come around to much clearer understanding. Now, I've got to *run*! I'll be back late this evening if anyone calls."

"Okay, see you later."

Two days after Paco had spoken on the phone to Kate's mother, Maddie, Paco, Kaz and I came together to discuss the situation. After doing a quick check of the computer files on the disc, I'd managed to confirm that this family was being contacted and were beginning to consciously recall significant parts of that contact. Many Earth humans are now being contacted, but most have not opened up enough consciously to remember and perceive the contact experience. Young Kate, like so many of the so-called Star Children, was regularly attending classes up on the disc, which was where she'd picked up her newly acquired abilities in mathematics.

As Paco had gathered from his telephone conversation with her, Maddie was a very friendly, open person who, much to his amazement and relief, reacted quite well to his suggestion that the activity in her home could well be ET initiated. Her reaction was actually one of relief, that here at last was somebody who was willing to believe her, and not immediately assume that she was either imagining things or, to put it in her own words, "completely off her rocker."

At the same time she expressed amazement that a Catholic Priest, of all people, would be open enough to suggest such a thing. This prompted Paco to reassure her that he had in fact had personal contact experiences himself, as well as having a close relative and also another friend who'd had ongoing encounters with ETs. He then went on to tell her about Kaz, also a mother in a similar situation with a child.

"So," said Paco, looking from me to Kaz and back again, "what now? Do you want me to arrange a meeting between the three of you?"

"Well," I shrugged, "that would be the next step I guess. How about you Kaz? Do you feel okay with that?"

"I don't see why not, but Paco, are you sure she's ready to talk so openly? I mean to say, what are we going to do? Just jump straight in? I suppose it'll be fine as long as we don't let on we're ETs ourselves. That would freak her out for sure. God I hope she doesn't pick up on it or ask too many awkward questions."

"Don't you worry about that Kaz," Paco grinned. "Just be your loveable, natural self and light up a cigarette or two in front of her. You could even blow a few smoke rings to introduce a bit of comedy to lighten up the atmosphere. And you, Ali Cat," he added, turning to me with a wink, "tell her one or two of your favorite jokes and wear that awful t-shirt you got at the parish yard sale — the one with the questionable message printed across the front in large, red capital letters. She'll *never* pick up on you two being ETs in a *million* years, believe me!"

"God, Ali," said Kaz, turning her back on Paco and directing her remark exclusively to me, "that brother of yours is just brimming over with charm and compliments this morning, isn't he!" With that she turned back, feigning total oblivion to Paco's presence, and blew a long, pungent stream of smoke straight at him. His response was to madly flap one hand about in front of his face and clutch his throat with the other, all the while making disgustingly eloquent gagging noises.

"Oh, for heaven's sake, will you two knock it off!" I glared at the pair of them, trying hard not to laugh. "This is *serious*!"

With decorum finally restored and Kaz's cigarette disposed of, Paco turned to her. "Kaz, what about you? Ali tells me you have children who are also involved in all of this. But I suppose as a Guardian yourself, it's been easier for you to deal with the situation. At least you know what's going on."

"Actually, I didn't at first. Unlike our Ali Cat here, I only came to conscious realization of who and what I am quite recently. I've always been vaguely aware through dream experiences of having contact with the ones known down here as the Greys, but this never worried or frightened me, it was just part of life, and the encounters were always positive. I tried to do my own investigations by reading up on the subject, but found many books to be quite off-putting, because ET contact seems to be generally viewed from either the ego perspective or the fear perspective."

"How do you mean?" Paco asked.

"Well," Kaz explained, "in ego-centered cases, the contactees see themselves as being specially chosen, usually by very perfect, totally human-looking Space Brothers, to spread 'the message' to the rest of humankind in order to 'save the planet.' They often seem to end up with a cult-like following, and it's all too airy-fairy for my liking, not being into that sort of thing. Even the Space Brother image has never appealed to me. I always felt much more comfortable with the Greys, and now I know why — I *am* one!

"The fear-oriented contacts, on the other hand, always seemed to involve negative encounters with the so-called Greys, which also never felt right and in fact upset me a lot. These were, after all, the very ones I was having contact with, and during those contact experiences there was always so much love, and a deep sense of family connection between us. I clearly recall one such 'dream' encounter in which my Teacher enfolded me in his arms, wrapping his big, black cloak around me and giving me a hug. The feeling of love, total understanding and complete acceptance that passed between us was beyond words, and waking up to find myself alone and back here on Earth caused a deep sadness to remain with me for days after.

"Reading these books only made me doubt and question myself and to feel disempowered and uncomfortable. What used to go through my mind was that, if these beings were really demons, and as bad and negative as all these books were saying, and I felt so good and comfortable with them, then I too must be bad and negative on some deeper layer of my psyche. I knew very well that I *wasn't*, but it was still disempowering and damaging to my self-esteem."

Paco turned to me and said, "Ali, you've been through this sort of thing too, haven't you?"

"I sure have! And it is very disempowering until you manage to bring the two parts of yourself — the Guardian part and the Earth human part — together. Once you're able to do this consciously, you come to realize that what the so-called 'abductees' are going through in their seemingly negative and frightening contacts with 'Greys' is virtually a shamanic experience. It's really all about what they need to clear internally in order to allow themselves to move forward — to expand and awaken spiritually. But there are far too many so-called 'experts' on the encounter experience out there who simply refuse to acknowledge this, and that is where the crux of the problem lies."

"Okay, so what you're saying is that despite how seemingly frightening their experience seems at the time, the ones they think of as 'Greys' are really helping them. In fact, it's a bit like a mother smacking her child to stop them reaching out to put their hand on a hot stove. Although the smack may cause hurt, both physically and also to their ego, it's still a heck of a lot better than the potential serious injury that could result if the child weren't given that correction by the mother."

"Yes," I answered, "that's actually a really good way of putting it. Seemingly frightening contact with our people will be of benefit to Earth humans in the long run. Our job is to help people break free of the limitations of fear and disempowerment imposed on them by the Controllers. This breaking free is often not an easy or pleasant experience, but it is most necessary to awaken human consciousness to a state of more expanded awareness. It's similar to a tribal rite of passage where the youth are exposed to realities beyond this one and they are forever changed."

"Now," Kaz put in, "what are we going to do about Maddie and Kate? I think you should call Maddie back, Paco, and arrange for the three of us to visit her. You need to be there, at least this first time, in your official capacity as a priest and also as the one they first approached for help. And I think she'll feel better if we meet in her home. That way too we can get a feel of the place, you know, check out the energies of the family."

"No problem, Kaz," Paco grinned, giving her a mock salute, "you're the boss on this one!"

34 ▶ Maddie

The following Monday afternoon found Kaz, Paco and me seated around Maddie's kitchen table as she busied herself trying to make coffee. The poor lady's nervousness was almost tangible, and it was obvious from the dark circles under her eyes that she hadn't slept very well the night before. In fact I got a distinct impression that she'd missed an awful lot of sleep for quite some time.

Paco had called her a day or two before to organize our visit, which was arranged for a time when her husband and daughter would be at work and school. We'd all agreed that it would be better to talk to her on her own, at least for this first time. Maddie worked part-time, but this was one of her days off. A broken cup, two dropped teaspoons and a spilt carton of milk later, Kaz the eternal mother could stand it no longer. Stepping quietly to Maddie's side, she put a comforting arm around her. "Come on, darl'," she coaxed gently, "sit down, I'll make the coffee."

"I….I'm *so* sorry." Maddie stammered, almost on the verge of tears. "I really don't know what's wrong with me. Despite all that's happened here over the past six months I've managed to stay reasonably calm. A couple of times in the middle of the night with Kate I thought I was going to lose it — but I didn't — I got through it; *both* of us got through it. But now, now I've finally found someone to talk to who'll *believe* me — now I lose it!" With that she burst into a torrent of tears.

I've never been all that good with emotional humans, but Kaz's hands were full with coffee-making, and it wasn't really appropriate for Paco to give her a hug, so I put my arms around her to provide a shoulder to cry on. She took full advantage of it, sobbing her heart out while I desperately tried to remember if I had a tissue or handkerchief on me. Sensing my dilemma, Paco came to my rescue with a paper towel. We eventually managed to calm her down and get her seated at the table, and Kaz put a strong cup of coffee in front of her, encouraging her to take a sip, assuring her it would make her feel better. Paco meanwhile, ever practical, left the kitchen only to reappear moments later with a half-bottle of brandy he'd found somewhere.

"Here you go, Maddie." he patted her on the shoulder and poured a generous dollop into her coffee. "This'll make you feel better!"

"Just watch him, love," said Kaz with a cheeky wink, "he'll have you up dancing on the table yet." Unable to resist Kaz's warmth and humor, a smile spread across Maddie's face and she visibly relaxed, probably for the first time in ages. After a few sips of brandy-laced coffee, she looked a whole lot better, but taking our cue from Paco we didn't press her. She needed to feel comfortable and relaxed with us, so the three of us just made small talk for a while, letting her settle and allowing her the space to get her thoughts in order. It was only then that Paco began, very gently, "So Maddie, has anything else happened here since we spoke the other day?"

Watching her closely I noticed her hands begin to tremble slightly as she answered, "Yes, as a matter of fact, there was some 'activity' last night. As you can probably see, I didn't get much sleep."

Paco gave her an encouraging look. "Do you want to tell us about it?"

"Well, really," she shrugged, "there's not much *to* tell — just a strange, bright light coming in through the skylight in the lounge, then the TV started going funny again, as is always happening lately. Lucky it seems to right itself by the next day or we'd be paying out a fortune in repair bills. Then about midnight Kate came in crying to Geoff and me with the usual story of a black-clad figure in her room. She was absolutely terrified, so it took a while to calm her down, then she insisted that she couldn't sleep on her own, so Geoff went into her room, as usual, and she settled down with me."

"And did your husband get a good night's sleep in Kate's room?" Paco enquired.

"Actually, no," Maddie replied, on the verge of tears again. "He could feel a presence there, and he couldn't sleep. Then at some point he awoke with a fright thinking someone, or some*thing* was touching him on the foot."

"So he's open to all of this and aware that something is really going on? He doesn't dismiss it as an over-active imagination on Kate's part?"

"Oh, no, Father Lopez! Geoff has no problem believing us. He's seen the figures and the lights himself, but he just doesn't know how to deal with it, and often won't even discuss it. This makes it really hard for me. It's as if he's in some kind of denial, and so usually leaves me to deal with the situation on my own, but now I'm totally worn out. I can't take it any more and neither can Kate." Tears welled in her eyes and I reached out and took her hand, assuring her that now we were here and she was not alone anymore with her problem.

Then I sensed a wave of emotion from Kaz, and I was surprised to see her eyes bright with tears that she was obviously struggling hard to control. I was aware of the fact that she'd been through some similar dramas with her young son Ben, but thought that now, with full understanding of who and what she was, this would have been resolved — but obviously not. Maddie's dilemma was stirring things up again for her.

Then the moment passed as Maddie turned to Paco with a question. 'Father, what I still don't understand is how you can be so sure the activity here isn't being caused by poltergeists, or evil spirits of some sort. After all, the figures we see are all dressed in black, and with hats or hoods pulled down so we can't see their faces. What makes you think they're aliens, and how do you know that they're not evil?"

I inwardly winced at the word "alien." How I hated this term that conjured up such feelings of 'them and us,' when in truth we are all One. Luckily Paco was there to step in calmly and answer her question, because at that moment I was struggling with my own unresolved issues.

"Well, Maddie," he replied, "I began to suspect it was ET activity by a couple of things you told me. Admittedly there are very close parallels between what people call poltergeists, and ET contact. For example the electrical interference, and the strange noises and lights; but the fact that it actually got worse after your friend cleansed the house with Reiki was mainly what made me think of ETs. Ali here has been doing Reiki for many years. In fact, she teaches it and has used it successfully on several occasions to clear negative energy in the form of ghosts out of houses, haven't you, Ali?"

"Yes!" I answered, turning to Maddie to explain. "Reiki is a very potent high-frequency energy that clears negativity and brings good vibes back into a house or wherever there's a problem with disharmonized energy. It doesn't hurt the ghost, but rather heals and rebalances its energy, which in turn releases it so it can move on to where it's supposed to be. If it were a ghost or some sort of negative poltergeist energy causing your problems, Reiki would definitely have eliminated it. The ET visitors, however, love it, because they're also of a higher-vibrational frequency and, in fact, they're attracted by it, recognizing it for what it is."

"So," Paco continued, "that's one of the reasons why I think it's ET contact that we're dealing with here, and the way you describe the figures as being dressed all in black with a hat or hood pulled down over their faces. All of us, myself included, have had close encounters with the ETs known on Earth as the Greys, or 'Zetas.' They're the ones with the sometimes small, but also sometimes very tall, thin bodies, long, triangular-shaped faces and very large, dark, almond-shaped eyes.

"The reason they cloak themselves in black and cover their faces is for disguise. They know how scared people, and particularly children, could be to see them as they are, so they cover themselves to lessen the shock of their appearance. Once you become more accustomed to their presence, they gradually lift the hat or hood back to let you see them properly. I don't think they even realize how potentially scary they look, dressed like that, but they do know humans would be afraid of their strange physical appearance. They're very aware of how much difficulty some humans have with anyone who looks different."

"But for heaven's sake," Maddie protested, "why do they dress in black? Why not in white? People associate black with evil, death and misfortune, whereas white is associated with goodness and purity. Don't they know that?"

"Well, actually, Maddie," Paco replied, "that doesn't even apply with all cultures on Earth. In some traditions it's the other way around. And anyway, look at us priests and nuns — we traditionally wear black, but we aren't associated with evil, death and misfortune — at least hopefully not!" he added with a grin, and turning to me. "Ali, you know more about the Grey teachers than I do. Is there any special significance in their choice of black clothes?"

"The work of the Grey teachers involves healing and balancing human life-force energy, which can be done through the vibrational frequencies of the color spectrum. Each of the seven primary colors of the spectrum synchronizes with one of the seven main chakras, or energy points in our body, and black contains all these colors. The black clothing worn by the teachers signifies that they have balanced all their 'colors,' in other words their whole energy or chakra system, which, in turn, lets them help us heal and balance this important aspect of our being. As part of our energy balancing, harmonizing and healing, we draw to ourselves whichever color is required for this process to take place, and so the Grey teacher working with you represents this aspect and displays the appropriate color corresponding to whichever chakra you most need to work on. The idea is to ask what color you need for clarity and balance, to best enable you to carry out the task at hand or to learn the required lesson.

"Now say, for example, that you need to learn to communicate or express yourself more clearly, or to speak out more, as I have. The color for this intention is blue, which is associated with the throat chakra, so that is the aspect of your Teacher you'd link into."

"And how do you know which color you need?" Maddie asked, quite obviously fascinated by what I had to say.

"Oh, that's easy. Next time you see the black-clad figure, examine the clothing. You'll notice something like a colored feather stuck in his hat band, or maybe a colored trim somewhere on his clothing, on a pocket, or tie, or on the border of his cape."

Maddie shook her head. "Wow, that is so weird! And are you absolutely sure they're not evil?"

"Oh, goodness no, definitely not."

"This is what I couldn't understand." Maddie frowned in puzzlement. "We're just a normal, average family. We try to be good Christians and decent people, always 'doing unto others' as the saying goes, and every time these disturbances happen in the house I wrack my brains trying to work out *why*. We're not into drugs or alcohol. We're not even into all this latest New Age stuff with crystals, tarot, etc. — in fact, none of us are interested in it in the slightest, not even Kate.

"And that's the other thing that doesn't add up," she went on, "Kate's sudden uncanny ability in math. I know my daughter well enough to know she isn't cheating. She takes after me in that she's not good with figures and calculating, but she is also honest. It's not like we're pressuring her to do well at school or anything like that; we know she does her best, but she's more right brain-oriented, and into music and dance in a big way. But this sudden ability! Can any of you explain that?"

Kaz spoke up for the first time. "That sounds a lot like my children, but with Ben it's not so much a sudden and inexplicable brilliance in anything academic, but rather the amazingly profound things that come out of his mouth. For example, just the other day he said to me, 'Mom, I can't actually *talk* to the flowers, but I *know* they understand me.' *That* came from a *seven*-year-old!"

"My goodness," Maddie shook her head in wonderment, "he's so *young*! And you say you've been through this with both of them? Please tell me. You don't know how much it means to me to have another mother to speak to. That is the hardest part. If it were just happening to me, I'd cope, but when your child is involved, and you don't know what's going on, all sorts of things go through your mind. Will she be hurt? How can I as her mother protect her? What's doing this to us? Is it my fault? Where've I gone wrong? What could I have done differently to prevent it? It just goes on and on and on. *Please* tell me what happened with you. Then maybe I'll know what to do. Is it ever going to end?"

Maddie's voice wavered on the verge of tears again, and Kaz sat beside her, taking her hand and brushing a tear from her own eye. "With my son Ben," she explained, "it started with his waking in the middle of the night thinking there was someone in his room. He wouldn't sleep unless I left a light on in the hallway near his bedroom. We weren't too worried because he was only five at the time, and it's normal for children to feel scared of the dark. I put it down to being just a phase he was going through. Then one night I awoke to his screaming in terror, and when I ran into his room, he seemed to be in some sort of trance. He was jumping around the bed, screaming and shaking in fear, and his poor little heart was pounding. I tried to wake him, but I couldn't bring him out of it.

"I turned on the light and tried to get him to take a sip of water. I even recited the Lord's Prayer because I really thought he was possessed, but nothing worked. His eyes were glassy, and he looked at me as if I were someone else, somebody frightening, whom he didn't recognize. I tried to take him in my arms, but he wouldn't let me near him, and normally he loves cuddles."

Maddie looked quite horrified. "Whatever did you *do*?"

"Well," Kaz answered, "in the end all I could do was talk to him. I just kept reassuring him that I was there, that he was safe, and that it was only a bad dream. Eventually he calmed down and came out of it. He put his arms around me and told me he loved me, then he rolled over and went back to sleep. The next morning he was his normal, happy self, not remembering a thing. This has been going on periodically for the past two years, with some trances worse than others. A few times he's started running around the house as if trying to get away from someone, and he often complains of seeing shadows in his room and of hearing noises, usually a beeping sound.

"Like you, I was exhausted and worried, not knowing what to do. Apart from the trances, Ben is a happy, healthy child, having no problems with school or friends. Also like you, we are a close, happy family and not into anything paranormal. In fact I loathe science-fiction movies, but there was something happening to my son that I couldn't control, and this scared me. I've always had strong feelings about love, happiness and security that I've tried to instill into my home and children, so why would something bad or evil be drawn to us? It made no sense, and I knew that something strange was really going on, and that it was more than bad dreams or overactive imagination."

"Yes," Maddie agreed, "we definitely know there's more than imagination or dreams involved, what with the lights, and the electrical disturbances, and the mysterious figures that both Geoff and I have seen as well. I too am a loving, caring, protective mother who adores her family and would do anything in my power to keep them safe and happy, but I don't know what to do, or where to turn for help. How the hell can I protect my child when I don't know what it is I'm trying to protect her against? What have you done Kaz?"

"Well, as I think Father Lopez mentioned to you on the phone, I've had half-remembered contact with the ET visitors all my life, so I had a bit of a suspicion there may have been a connection, because it does seem to run in families, from one generation to the next. But what I couldn't understand was why the extreme terror with Ben. This is what puzzled and confused me. I can recall feeling some fear as a child, but not to that extent.

"Anyway, I decided to go to the library for books on the subject, but most of the ones I read were so fear-oriented and negative that they were of no help whatsoever — in fact, all they did was to make me feel worse. The impression I got was that the authors felt it was their duty to convince readers that these 'terrible, evil aliens' were coming here and doing awful, cruel things to us poor, innocent Earthlings. I could actually sense a huge amount of unresolved fear and anger in them, and in their whole attitude to the contact experience, and most especially in those contacts that involve the so-called Zeta Reticulans, in which there seemed to be an element of racism as well. Thank goodness now there are a few more positive books available, but back then there wasn't much at all.

"And this is what made it so hard for me," Kaz went on, "because the Zetas, or 'Greys' as they're sometimes referred to, are the very ones I'd always had contact with, and I'd never ever sensed evil or negativity with them. In fact my life has been greatly enriched by the experience. But here these people were, setting themselves up as 'authorities' on the subject and almost making the ETs out to be devils or demons of some sort, which left me feeling just awful and even more scared."

"But Kaz," Maddie looked totally confused, "you say these 'Greys' have enriched your life, and yet you've gone through so much with your son. How come there's all this terrible fear with him? And what have you done to help him? The whole thing is so damned weird, and sometimes I have to wonder if maybe we're all going crazy, you know, having a sort of mass delusion. Who or what the hell are these Greys anyway? What do they want with us, and *why us*?"

Kaz took a deep breath, "Okay Maddie, let's start with the basics of who they are and why they're here. By answering this, other questions you've raised will also be answered in the process." She then turned to me. "Ali, do you want to explain this? You know more about the history of this whole contact thing than I do. If you'll talk about that part, I'll go into the fear aspect, and why some are more affected than others."

Now it was my turn to take a deep breath. This was a very wide and complex subject to explain to someone who had no knowledge whatsoever. I knew I'd have to be fairly brief and concise as we only had a few hours, and I also knew I'd have to be very careful of what I said, because I couldn't let on to Maddie our true Guardian identity.

"Okay Maddie," I began, "like Kaz, I've had ongoing contact with the Greys since I was very young, but my first conscious experiences started when I was 13, like Kate, when I awoke early in the morning to find one of the tall ones standing in the corner of my room. He was dressed all in black, as you describe your 'visitors,' and at first I was terrified. Unlike Kate who is able to get out of bed and run into your room, I couldn't move. I found myself paralyzed from head to foot."

Maddie was wide-eyed with horror. "Oh, my God, you poor thing! What did you do?"

"Not much," I replied with a wry grin. "Being paralyzed there wasn't much I could do except lie there. I couldn't even scream because my throat wouldn't work either, but my having to stay there like that enabled the being to communicate with me. I'd always been quite telepathic, and able to communicate with animals right from early childhood, and the Greys' way of communication is by telepathy.

"In fact this is the only way they can communicate with us down here. Problem is, to pick up on telepathic communication, you have to be very relaxed and in alpha mode, otherwise it just doesn't get through clearly. Our normal waking beta consciousness simply cannot pick up on it. It's the equivalent of trying to pick up one TV or radio station while your set is tuned in to a different one. This is why many people who undergo a so-called alien abduction experience complain that their ET 'abductors' won't communicate with them. It's not that they *won't* but rather that they *can't*, because they're operating on a different brainwave frequency.

"Once this being placed his hand on me, I immediately relaxed. It was as if something switched on in my energy system that changed my brain wave pattern from beta to alpha, and his energy felt good, and very familiar. It was as if I suddenly recognized him as a friend from somewhere, and after that it was okay. I was never scared of him again.

"This communication has kept up continually from that time, and I've learned so much — about the ETs, humans, God, life, and, most especially, my*self*. The Bible tells us to get to know our*selves*, and truly, this is the key to the whole thing, and one of the main areas in which the Greys are here to help. And believe me, Maddie, this getting to know, and in the process heal self, is one of the hardest things anyone can face! We really do sometimes need help with this, because it's so hard to do it honestly on our own."

"But Ali, who *are* these Greys, or Zetas, or whatever they're called? Where do they come from?"

"Well, they've actually evolved from many planetary cultures within the universe and have now moved past the need or desire for physical form. But if they have a physical task to carry out as part of their work, they 'dress' themselves in an appropriate body, or as they refer to it, a 'container.' They've come to be known here as Greys because that is the color of the containers they use most often. They're also known as 'Zetas,' but that's not necessarily the star system they come from, although many of them have had lives there. They do however maintain a major base in the Zeta system. I've come to understand that the name they use for themselves is 'Guardians.' They could be described as 'spiritual warriors' in that they're some kind of peace-keeping force in the physical universe.

"The Guardians aren't limited by time or space, so they're very much 'citizens of the universe,' and their culture is very ancient. They could be described as cosmic Gypsies in that many of them no longer reside on any particular planet but rather live permanently on the discs, continually travelling to wherever they happen to be working. The big discs are like mobile cities.

"The most important thing you need to know about them to help you to understand is that they are *not* simply an ET species visiting Earth — they are much more than that! They're interdimensional beings who play a very specific role within the evolutionary cycle, and therefore they are closely linked to the whole future of the human species of Earth."

"Really? What do you mean, Ali?" asked Maddie. "How are they linked to our future?"

"Well," I answered, "many predictions and prophecies have been made about the future of humanity, and also of the planet itself, and most of these prophecies focus particularly on the time period we are going through right now, which is referred to by many diverse cultures as the 'End Times.' Even Revelations in the Bible deals with this, but in a very esoteric way that is impossible to interpret. In fact, it is not so much an ending but rather a new beginning — a rebirth if you like.

"Everything in creation is composed of energy vibrating at different frequencies. It is these continually vibrating bands of energy that our five senses are attuned to pick up as sight, sound, smell, touch and taste, which are relayed to our brain via our nervous system. It is through these five senses that we're able to perceive everything around us.

"Now, energy is created out of movement — in fact, you could say that energy *is* movement, as it continually plays between the polarities of positive and negative. Energy is never static but is always in a state of flux, because, like water, it always moves towards its own level. Once that is achieved, we have perfect balance — a state of non-polarity, which is what we think of as 'God.' This is happening continually throughout all of creation, with the energy of the universe always moving towards this state of perfect balance, or oneness, which is where the process we call evolution is ultimately taking us.

"But," I went on, "it's not just plants, animals and people that evolve in this way. Believe it or not, planets, solar systems, galaxies and even universes evolve, and this is really what the Earth's predicted End Times are all about. Our whole planet is actually evolving to a higher frequency band of energy, and so are we. In fact this is what many of the tribal cultures refer to when they speak of this being the end of the fourth world and the beginning of the fifth. Their ancient lore tells them that Earth has been through such shifts four times previously, and now we're approaching a fifth shift. Although their prophecies may not say it in so many words, this is about changes in the energetic frequency of the planet. Do you follow what I'm saying Maddie?"

"Yes, more or less," she replied. "I did physics at high school, so I do know what you mean about energy and vibrational frequencies, but I still don't quite understand the connection between this and the so-called End Times. What about the biblical 'Battle of Armageddon'? That's also about the End Times, isn't it? How does that fit in with Earth evolving to a higher-frequency level?"

"Well, all these events in the Scriptures are actually multidimensional, that is, they're happening on several different levels of reality all at once. On the cosmic level, the War of Armageddon refers to the opposite polarities of positive and negative, and the continual 'battle' or pull between them, which really is a bit like a game of tug-o'-war. However, in physical terms Earth, a fairly young planet in terms of human evolution, is still very polarized, so this concept translates into physical and emotional warfare, between individuals, families, tribes, nations, religions and cultures. Other older, more evolved planetary cultures don't have this extreme state of polarity, or duality, which results in warfare, because they're more closely aligned to oneness and balance, without the deep cultural, national or religious differences that exist here. Planet Earth will evolve to this state eventually, but it all takes time.

"On deeper levels of the human psyche, this state of duality, described in biblical terms as Armageddon, is actually a battle within the human subconscious. As with so many other issues that affect humans subconsciously, it's being externalized as cultural, national or religious divisions that sometimes result in warfare or other negative behaviors, but in actual fact, its roots lie within. This is where the idea originates that in order to heal the planet, we must first heal self, and this is *so* true. It all begins within our *own* minds!"

"What about the so-called 'anti-Christ' that is spoken of in connection with all of this?" Maddie enquired. "Where does that come into it?"

"Okay," I replied, "This Battle of Armageddon that is being waged within the human psyche is really a battle between love and fear, and therefore it could be described in Christian terms as a battle between God and Satan, or the Christ and the anti-Christ. Love is the God/Christ-part that dwells within all of us, and fear is our inner Satan or anti-Christ — our inner devils and demons that cause us to become caught up in all the lower emotions of hatred, anger, ego, envy, greed, etc. In our own personal inner Battle of Armageddon, we must strive with every ounce of our being to ensure that God (love) overcomes Satan (fear). This in turn will begin to restore balance on the planetary level.

"The problem we come up against is that 'Satan' is very cunning, often hiding deep within the subconscious recesses of our psyche, playing upon our latent insecurities, and outwardly expressing itself in disguises such as egotism, self-centeredness, self-aggrandizement, low self-esteem, needing to control or manipulate others around us, self-righteous behavior, or being judgmental or bigoted towards others who do not follow *our* way. All of these problems stem from fear, insecurity and lack of trust within ourselves. Once we overcome this sense of fear and learn to express only love, then we automatically let go of the need for such negative behavior patterns."

"This is all very well," Maddie replied. "I can understand that people's inner fears and insecurities manifest as ego, greed, bigotry, etc., and that these negative behavior patterns within people's minds cause wars and other awful things, but I still don't understand where the Greys, Zetas or whatever you call them, fit in to all of this."

Now Kaz stepped in. "Ali, do you want me to explain this part? I said I'd talk about the fear aspect, so, if you like, I'll take over here."

"Oh, thanks, Kaz, that'd be great. I'm just about all talked out, and besides, you've gone through more of that with Ben than I have personally, so you're the expert here. It's all yours."

"Okay, Maddie," Kaz began. "The Greys are what are known as testers or tryers of souls. This is part of their job as angelic 'assistants,' which involves helping people to tap into this fear — the 'Satan element' that Ali spoke about — and to bring it out into the open where it can be faced up to and healed more easily. Many people just can't or won't do this on their own, and until they do, they become stuck and unable to move further on their path of evolution.

"As Ali said, looking at and getting to know oneself is one of the hardest things a person can do, because this always involves bringing things like fear and insecurity up to the surface of the conscious mind and examining them honestly in the light of day. Many people deny this inner stuff and absolutely refuse to look at it, so the last thing they're going to be willing to do is externalize it, because that would mean having to acknowledge it consciously. As testers of souls it's the Greys' job to assist with this process, so it's no wonder they tend to be rather unpopular with many people. Being forced to face up to your own inner demons is not the most pleasant experience you can go through.

"This too is why a lot of researchers on the subject of ET contact never really get anywhere. They insist on looking at the Greys as nothing more than a race of physical beings from another planet. In trying to be so 'scientific' about it all, they won't even consider the soul or spiritual aspect, and therefore miss a whole lot because they only look for physical evidence of the ET presence, refusing to acknowledge that they are much more than that. Sure, the 'Greys' can and do manifest physically, but they're also interdimensional beings who are linked to the evolution of human consciousness, so the real evidence of their presence is much more subtle."

"And how do they work as testers of souls?" Maddie asked.

"By acting as mirrors, reflecting back to those who look upon them what lies in the deepest levels of the psyche, and most especially those issues that we haven't managed to resolve and integrate into our nature. This is why for many people contact with the Greys is so traumatic. They go through the experience of having their deepest, darkest fears and insecurities — all their hidden inner demons — reflected back at them, so they have no choice but to look and see. All the fear, ego and insecurity that has been buried and tamped down, not only from the present life but from past lives as well, is suddenly there, right in front of them, staring back at them through those big, black, shiny eyes.

"During the contact experience we go through what is known in shamanism as the 'dark night of the soul.' It's a real test of courage to get through this because it requires having a deep enough trust in self and the God within to enable us to face up to and overcome these inner fears and insecurities that are being brought to the surface."

"But I still don't understand why the ETs must put us through this experience!" Maddie argued. "Surely we can do it ourselves! What right do they have to come in here uninvited and put us through all this fear and trauma, and make us feel so disempowered? Surely the evolution of our species is *our* responsibility and ours alone."

"Well, Maddie," Paco put in, "the truth of the matter is, humans do need outside assistance with this process, which is why we refer to Jesus as our Redeemer and Savior, sent to Earth to help us release the bonds of fear and negativity."

"Exactly!" I added, "and this is also where all the confusion and argument arises between the scientific community, with their theory of totally natural and unaided evolution, and the religious belief in intervention by a higher outside Force. Both are partly correct, because evolution takes place not only on the physical level, but also on the soul level. The reality is, we really are more than just physical beings — we're multidimensional — body, mind and spirit. Once we evolve past the physically oriented animal stage of evolution and begin moving into the more mind-oriented human stage, outside assistance is needed to help open us up to the deeper spiritual aspect of self that is now being awakened — the 'God aspect' in other words.

"For this to take place, certain barriers and limitations which were necessary for survival in the animal kingdom now have to be broken down. These barriers and limitations are based on instinctual fears and needs, for example, the 'fight and flight' instinct, and distrust and fear of anyone who is different and not part of the 'herd.' The need for 'survival of the fittest' is part of this as well, which is in direct opposition to the 'compassion and care of the weak' instinct that is really what being an evolved member of the human kingdom is all about.

"The Greys are coming here and helping this process of breaking down the barriers of fear in our minds because too many humans are lagging behind. There are just so many who are stuck and trapped within their own stubborn and egotistical belief that Earthlings 'know it all' and are the 'greatest, most evolved species in the whole universe.' Then there are lots of others who simply *can't* move past their own inner fears, and who often just refuse to acknowledge that they *have* any inner fears. In fact, I don't think there are too many human species in the lower levels of the universe who haven't needed help in some way. Everybody has problems of one sort or another — not only Earth humans — and, as tryers and testers of souls, the Guardians' special job is to provide this service.

"The amount of fear we go through in the contact experience depends upon how many barriers we've built up within our psyche, and how difficult they are to break down. And the other thing is, these fear barriers aren't always based in the present life. They often have their source in past lives and so are buried very deeply within the subconscious layers of the mind."

"So what you're saying," Maddie interjected, "is that there really is such a thing as reincarnation?"

"Oh, yes, for sure! And if people refuse to be open to this basic concept, then there's no way they'll *ever* get a handle on the contact experience. Why, there are even references to reincarnation in the Bible if you know where to look. For example, that passage about 'the sins of the father being visited upon the son'; and 'he who lives by the sword will die by the sword.' These refer to karma, which is the Law of Cause and Effect. In other words, every action, either good or bad, sets off repercussions, either in the present life or else in subsequent lives."

Unexpectedly, the phone rang loudly, startling everyone. Excusing herself, Maddie went to answer it, which provided some breathing space for us and a most welcome break. Paco leaned back in his chair, stretching luxuriously and absentmindedly trying to get his knuckles to crack, but instead only managed to accidentally kick my leg under the table. "Whoops, sorry, Ali Cat," he apologized, "I didn't mean to do that."

"Quick, quick!" Kaz pushed her empty cup towards him, at the same time craning her neck to make sure Maddie was still occupied on the phone in the next room. "Give me a small nip of that brandy, and *hurry up* for heaven's sake — I need it after all that!"

"Okay, okay, hang on! Let me get the top off." Leaning back himself to check that the coast was still clear, he sloshed a little into Kaz's cup — then helped himself to a a little nip as well.

"Oh, for goodness sake, you two!" I glared at the pair of them. "We come here to help the poor woman and all you do is drink her expensive alcohol. Honestly!"

"Well," Paco hedged, "it's heavy stuff we're dealing with here, and Kaz *is* looking a bit upset, what with having to go back over her traumas with Ben, aren't you Kaz?"

"Darned right I am! It's not easy bringing all that emotion to the surface again; and it's also very difficult to explain this stuff without letting on who and what we really are. The poor lady would freak out completely if we accidentally let drop that we're humans by day but Zetas by night. And besides, we didn't take much.

"Ahhh, *that's* better!" she sighed, taking a good swallow of the fiery liquid — then followed a quite lady-like but obviously still satisfying burp, which in turn resulted in a fit of the giggles.

"You can't do that, can you, Alarca?" she teased, still giggling and now looking a wee bit cross-eyed. "That must be really awkward at times, being resident in an Earthling container that can't belch. How the hell do you manage? There's nothing quite like a good burp, I always say, to clear the air, as it were. What do you reckon, Paco?"

"Oh, God!" he rolled his eyes heavenward. "That's all we need right now — a half-drunken bloody ET in our midst. I forgot how sensitive you darned Greys can be to even a little alcohol, especially distilled spirits. Now Kaz, *remember*," he enunciated slowly and carefully as if addressing a three year old, "you're *human*, you're *not* an ET — and so is Ali. She's *not* Alarca down here — she's *Ali*, and we're *all humans* — perfectly normal Earthling *h-u-m-a-n-s*."

"Absolutely!" Kaz giggled, raising her cup on high. "I'll drink to that!"

35 ▶ HELL ON EARTH

T en minutes or so passed before Maddie returned to resume her seat at the table, and I quickly but firmly stepped in to give Kaz some extra time to hopefully get herself together again. "Now, Maddie," I began, "just to go back to your point about the ETs intervening in our process of soul evolution, and whether or not it's really the responsibility of humans themselves.

"The big problem here is, so many of us have great difficulty in taking responsibility for our own spiritual growth. People have been disempowered for so long, and told so often that they're 'sinners,' and 'unworthy,' and in the process have become accustomed to always looking outside of themselves for their spiritual needs.

"Even now that many are moving away from traditional religion, they still continue to externalize the process by shifting the focus to spirit guides, masters, and even to ETs, again perceiving them as either saviors or demons, and always totally separate from themselves. They just cannot seem to get away from the disempowered, 'needy victim' mentality. What we really have to do is learn is to look at *self,* where all our answers lie. People must learn to take back responsibility for their own soul growth, but most have no idea how."

"Well," Maddie replied, shaking her head, "I must admit I don't. Maybe I'm being stupid asking such a question, but how the heck do we do this?"

Kaz just had to come in on this one, now determined to prove her humanness beyond a doubt: "*Of course* you're not being stupid, darl'! *Everybody* has to ask questions; otherwise how'll you ever understand? Now me, I drive everyone *mad* with questions. I've got a million of 'em and I give the teachers 'upstairs' hell. Maddie, I refer to my teachers or ETs that we talk to as 'upstairs.'"

"Oh, I see. I guess that makes sense."

" Lucky they've got those big baldy heads," Kaz continued, "or they'd be tearing their hair out by the roots with me around nagging them for answers at every opportunity.

"But no, love," she continued doggedly, "don't you *ever* be embarrassed about asking questions, here or 'upstairs.' If you want to get a handle on all this, then it's the only way. That fear stuff we were going on about before is sometimes more about ego, which often stops us from asking questions, 'cause we don't want to appear stupid, or ignorant, or whatever in front of others.

"And believe it or not," she persisted, "it's all ego too with those so-called 'experts' and 'intellectuals' who'll use great long bloody words to answer your questions, each one trying to be more 'scientific' than all the rest, using such complex damned language nobody knows properly what they're saying. All they do in the end is turn people off. The simpler the language, the stronger the message, I always say."

Paco was busily kicking me under the table in an effort to get me to intervene before Kaz got carried away further. Finally, she paused to take a breath, giving me a chance to politely but firmly interrupt. "Maddie, to answer your question, taking responsibility for your own spiritual growth simply involves having the courage to look within, the honesty to admit where your problems lie, and then making the necessary changes.

"The contact experience helps you to do this because the emotions and images that come up during the process mirror whatever it is that's blocking your soul growth. Too many experiencers, however, remain stuck and get caught up in the emotions of ET contact, and especially in the fear, but the only way past that fear is to try to reach a point of understanding. This can only be done by asking questions, and looking deeply within self, seeking the source of your fear, but, because it's really your own unresolved issues being reflected back at you, it's not easy. It takes a lot of courage, time and patience.

"It's important to try to open lines of communication with the ETs," I continued. "Kaz and I have become so familiar with them through our contact experiences, and we have felt such depth of wisdom and unconditional love surrounding them that we've come to look upon them as teachers and to ask questions of them. Sometimes we feel we aren't being answered satisfactorily. Often a Grey teacher will answer one question with another question, or will give different answers to the same question, or even provide an answer that you feel is wrong and just doesn't make sense. And certainly every answer you do receive will only lead to more questions on your part. It seems to be a never-ending process.

"The thing is, when the ETs do this, it isn't that they're being dishonest or sneaky. What they are doing is pushing you to look within to find your *own* answers. The last thing they want is for you to become dependent upon them for answers — to again look outside of self. In our search for answers we must eventually learn to look within. In fact this is the only place left for us to go in the end. This is the whole point of the exercise!

"The really important thing to remember through the encounter experience is that *love conquers all! The key to spiritual transformation is overcoming the fear barrier to get to the love on the other side!* This is what we spoke of before in connection with the shamanic experience — the 'dark night of the soul,' which is exactly what ET contact is all about. We *all* have to go through this in one way or another, because this is the only path to higher levels of evolution. The first thing is to acknowledge love and the God within, which then enables us to reach a point of openness, trust and faith, which in turn endows us with self-empowerment and inner strength. Getting angry about the contact experience is only self-defeating, and won't get us anywhere."

"But what I'm having difficulty with," Maddie persisted, "is that my child is being affected. Kaz, how did you come to terms with this aspect? It's all very well adults being put through terrifying experiences, but I can't accept that a child should suffer!"

"Well, Maddie," Kaz replied, much more soberly this time, thank goodness. "I understand where you're coming from, because I went through exactly the same thing with Ben. There were nights when I prayed, and cried in frustration and anger, and asked God these same questions — Why us? We're not bad people! We don't deserve this! Why Ben? But then I came to realize that I was actually being tested more than him. He would wake up the next morning his normal bright and happy self, often with no memory of and certainly no damage or ill effects from his trance experiences. And in fact it was always after these 'night terrors' that he would come out with incredibly wise statements and deeply profound understandings.

"In comparison, I was the one left angry, upset, and totally frustrated, because I felt powerless as a mother to do anything. This was what eventually brought me to the point of looking at myself. It was as if, I were being forced to face up to my own inner demons through my own flesh and blood.

"Even though it's happening to your child," Kaz continued, "you are also being tested and taught. Do you *really and truly* think God would let evil happen to you, or to an innocent child? As long as you have the love, faith and trust with which to connect to the Spark of God that lies within *yourself*, nothing bad can happen. The key is to acknowledge fully that you *do* have the power and the strength — and *everyone* has this, because we are *all* part of God, and therefore capable of incredible depths of strength and love. God is right there within each and every one of us, and love is our link, our lifeline. Once I began to look at this as a gift, or another opportunity for growth, it changed.

"Once I came to this realization, other forms of assistance seemed to unexpectedly materialize. For example, I'd be guided to read the right book, or to speak to the right person, as if a mysterious force outside of myself was stepping in. But this only happened once I reached a point of being willing to look *within* for answers and strength."

"And were you given any specific advice to help him deal with his terrors?" Maddie wanted to know.

"Yes, as a matter of fact, I was. One morning I woke with the idea of getting him to try to draw his dreams, or at least what he could remember of them, to enable him to more easily bring things up to the surface where I could help him deal with them. I also started encouraging him to talk to me about the dreams, and I made it clear that I considered what he was going through to be valid and important. I stopped trying to make him brush his experiences away as 'nothing but silly dreams.' When he was in the trance-state I would just keep talking quietly, reassuring him that I was there to help him through and that he was not alone. And always I reminded him to *remember the love* — and that the love would keep him safe.

"One thing that I can't stress enough, Maddie, is to always take your child's word seriously. Whether what they're experiencing really is ET contact or just a dream doesn't matter. There are deeper messages there for *both* of you, and you must listen. By working quietly and calmly with Ben in this way, more and more often he was able to describe to me what was happening during the trance, and what aspect was frightening him. I would then suggest things for him to do to allay the fear and to make the situation less scary. I explained to him that when he's in the dream state he has special, magical abilities and can easily change something scary into something funny or nice.

"For example, if he sees a monster that frightens him, he can use his imagination to dress it up in a frilly pink party frock and wobbly high-heeled shoes. Or if he's on the edge of a high cliff and feels he's going to fall, he can magically grow wings and fly to safety. Also I keep reminding him to trust in himself, that love is his special, magical power, and love will conquer all.

"Over time it's become very clear to me that these 'dreams' are meant to give Ben a deeper understanding of himself, and it's my role as his mother to help him do this, which in turn has empowered and connected me even more with *my*self. In fact I've come to realize that in many ways Ben is my teacher, here to make me look at my inner self.

"And you know what, Maddie?" she went on, "This is precisely what ET contact and soul evolution is all about—self-empowerment through connecting back to the God within. When you fight against the contact experience, you are really fighting against your own connectedness. Just learning to let go and trust in the face of a force of such magnitude, mystery and power as ET contact is the key — it's an ultimate act of surrender, faith and trust in the love of God and the intrinsic goodness of your own self. In return you receive so much in the way of personal growth."

"Well," Maddie answered, "I must admit that Kate, and in fact none of us, has ever been actually hurt or threatened by these visitors, and all of you seem none the worst for your experiences. Actually, I sense an enormous strength in you. So what advice would you give to Kate when that being appears in her room? Should she just stay there, or what? What if she feels something touching her on the foot, as happened to my husband? Are you absolutely *sure* it won't hurt her?"

"What Kate needs to do," I replied, "is try to stay calm and talk to the being, but not using physical speech, because he may not be able to hear that. She needs to talk to him with her mind, to ask him his name and why he's there — in other words, to *communicate*. As for the visitors touching her on the foot, what they're really doing is giving her healing, and to do this, they need to work on the energy system of the body, for which the feet are focal points. After all, this is how reflexology works, through the feet.

"If Kate is just too scared to do this on her own, when her visitor returns next time and she runs to you for help, the pair of you should go back into her room. Maybe with you there beside her she'll feel a little more confident to try to meet him halfway.

"The other thing is, once all of you start relaxing and not fighting the contact, other things will calm down as well, such as the noises and electrical disturbances. These are often caused by the combination of your fears and emotions being externalized, plus the frustration of the visitors who are trying their hardest to get through to you and to get you to acknowledge them. Once you establish communication, things should settle down. This is why some people go through quite dramatic experiences during ET contact, while for others it all flows fairly smoothly and calmly. The key to the whole thing is communication. Kate must try to establish communication."

"Okay, then," Maddie agreed, "it's certainly worth a try, but I still don't understand, why us? What makes us different? Why are we going through this and others are not?"

"In actual fact," I answered, "lots of people on Earth are going through this process at the moment, so you're not alone by any means. The thing is," I went on, "many aren't consciously aware that it's happening. Some are able to remember, others cannot. Everyone is a unique individual, so each contact experience is 'tailored' to the very personal soul needs of the individual involved.

"As the psychologists tell us, we only use about 10% of our full brain capacity, so much is going on at deeper levels of our psyche of which we aren't consciously aware, which is generally the case for many experiencers of ET contact. But those who are going through it are generally older souls who are preparing to move up to the next evolutionary level."

"But, Ali," Maddie persisted, "this is what I still don't understand: You talk about 'older souls,' but my daughter and Kaz's son are only children. Why are *they* being frightened out of their wits by these experiences?"

"Maddie," I answered, "this is why it's so important to understand reincarnation. Every person who's undergoing ET contact, whether they're in the physical body of a child or an adult, is, on the spiritual level, an older and more mature soul preparing to step up to a higher vibrational frequency. Of course, when we're reborn into another physical life, we must come in as a newborn and grow through childhood, but this is only on the physical level. On the soul level, we may be very old and mature, and this is the level of our being that chooses contact.

"The contact experience is a preparation we're going through voluntarily because our soul is ready and eager to evolve to higher levels," I went on to explain. "Soul growth and evolution is not an easy process, because it involves cleansing, purging and refining self at very deep levels. It could be compared to the rough and harsh process an uncut diamond or other gem stone must be subjected to in order to polish and refine it to a state of brilliant and sparkling beauty. The Greys are the 'professional gem-cutters and polishers' of the universe, whose special job is to do this.

"We simply *cannot* evolve to a higher vibrational frequency until we've managed to cleanse away all the dross, fear and excess baggage we've taken on board from the past. This all has to be purged from our psyche before we can step up to a higher frequency band. Once we've passed through the 'cleansing fires of purgatory' — our own fear barrier — we will then find heaven/love waiting for us on the other side.

"A very large part of this cleansing process involves letting go of the fear and suspicion of anyone who is 'different,' and not a member of our own 'herd,' or 'clan.' We simply cannot evolve to higher levels until we can learn to accept unconditionally *all* other beings as part of Oneness — of God. This total acceptance and respect of others is what returning to Oneness is all about — in other words, being 'at one' with all life. And for goodness sake, so many people on Earth can't even accept others of their *own* species who are different from themselves!

"The healing process begins as soon as we can feel comfortable with the idea of reincarnation, because the key here is total acceptance of the fact that we've lived many different lives in other countries, born into many different nationalities, religions and cultures other than the one we are presently a part of. We have even lived on other worlds. It's only then that we're truly able to experience empathy, and to look at others who are different from ourselves through eyes of love, understanding and acceptance rather than through eyes of prejudice, or at least separateness. *To acknowledge the concept of reincarnation really is an acknowledgement of Oneness."*

Poor Maddie sat for a few moments looking rather stunned, trying hard to take all this in. Then she turned to Paco, almost as if she were reaching for a lifeline. "Father Lopez, what do you have to say about all this? I've always accepted the Church's teachings without question, but what about this reincarnation? I've never really thought about it, but I do know it's not part of Church doctrine. So what am I to believe? What do *you* believe? Is the Church right or wrong? Give me some guidance on all of this, *please!*"

"Well, Maddie," Paco replied thoughtfully, "as a priest I have to uphold Church doctrine, so, of course, I believe in all the traditional teachings, but at the same time, having had contact with the ET visitors over many years, I've learned many other things, and I have been given different sorts of teachings on subjects that never even came up during my seminary training. As to whether I believe in reincarnation or not, all I can say is, although the modern Church doesn't acknowledge it as doctrine, I do believe it was accepted by early Christians, so Jesus himself may very well have taught it. Also, there are many millions of perfectly good, decent, spiritual people the world over who accept it as an intrinsic part of their belief system, so in actual fact there are more who do believe in it than there are ones who don't.

"However, to my way of thinking, and this is just my own personal opinion, what we choose to believe or not believe really isn't the main issue here. What is important is how well we are living our present life, right now. For example, are we treating others as we would like to be treated ourselves? Are we honest enough with ourselves to look within and acknowledge the faults, then do our very best to correct them? Are we showing compassion, kindness, respect and tolerance towards all others regardless of their race, religion and culture or current predicament? Whether we come to these understandings through what we perceive as 'past lives,' or through some other way of thinking doesn't really matter. The main thing is that we conduct our life in as spiritual and loving a way as we possibly can, and put this unconditional love into practice on a daily basis.

"And really, Maddie," he continued, "when you think about it, this is exactly what Kaz and Ali have been saying about the ET contact experience and how it's designed to make us look deeply within self in order to bring our fears and insecurities to the surface so they can be dealt with. If you take those spiritual qualities like compassion, kindness, respect and acceptance, and look at the opposite side of the picture, you get coldness, cruelty, disrespect and rejection. Now these negative thought patterns all stem from fear and insecurity, so therefore, if that can be addressed, as the ET visitors are trying to help us do, then surely only good can come of it.

"I've received some absolutely fascinating teachings from these visitors," he went on to explain, "and it's truly amazing how much they parallel many of the traditional teachings of Christianity. In fact I believe that my understanding of Christ's teachings has only been enhanced and confirmed more deeply through my association with the ETs. Sure, our interpretation from the human point of view may be a little different, because we do tend to externalize things rather than looking within our own selves, but the basic concepts are the same."

"What do you mean, Father? This is something I need to know, because that's the thing that really frightens me with this 'contact.' I'm absolutely terrified that they're demons or devils or something horrible like that, and that they're trying to possess my daughter. I mean to say, they have to either be sent from God or from the Devil, and I want to know which. I really need some guidance and reassurance on this point!"

"Well, Maddie," Paco answered, "I can assure you that the ET visitors are not devils or demons, and they're not trying to possess anybody. Your view is typical of the polarity of our human concepts — we look at things as either good or bad, black or white. In all the associations I've had with them I've never seen any evidence of anything of that nature. Yes, they can be very frightening, and the experience of contact can seem unpleasant, but their underlying motives are totally positive, and what they're doing is for our own good. After all, visiting a doctor or dentist can be downright unpleasant or sometimes terrifying, but we understand it. Once we understand something, it's not as scary — no matter what it is.

"A good example of the parallels between ET concepts and Church doctrine is what Ali was saying before in regard to the ET-encounter experience being like the Church's teaching on purgatory. As I'm sure you know, to purge simply means to cleanse, and that is exactly what the seemingly negative aspect of ET contact is all about. And as the Church says, once our soul has passed through the cleansing fires of purgatory, which in ET contact is the experience of being brought up against and pushed through the fear barrier, we will find heaven — in other words love and oneness — on the other side. I know that we as humans do tend to think of heaven, hell and purgatory as being somewhere 'out there' that we'll go to at the time of death, whereas the ETs tell us that they are actually states of being within our own self right now. I personally find no great contradictions here, and, in fact, I feel that the two viewpoints balance out quite well.

"Ali," he said, turning to me, "what did you say just the other day about the ETs' interpretation of hell? That fits in here too, doesn't it?"

"Oh, yes, for sure! Taking the explanation of purgatory a bit further, as you know Maddie, according to Church doctrine purgatory is only a transient state of suffering that the soul passes through after death, which has the effect of cleansing or clearing away all sin so that the soul is purified enough to be able to enter heaven. Hell on the other hand is a more permanent state of suffering which, according to human interpretation, goes on for eternity.

"Now I personally do not believe that any soul could be condemned to suffer for eternity. That just doesn't make sense, because soul evolution is not a static process. But on the other hand, looking from the perspective of higher beings such as many of the ET cultures, life on a low-frequency planet like Earth is considered to be 'hell,' and yet many people here would give anything to stay alive forever, and take every available means to avoid death. So really, there are some who are happy to remain in 'hell' for eternity.

"And to expand on that in the context of deeper interpretations, my feeling is that by choosing *not* to take part in the contact experience or refusing to look within to evolve, and as a result being stuck down here in the low-frequency energy of Earth for the duration of yet *another* evolutionary cycle of God knows how many millennia, would certainly be the equivalent to condemnation in hell for eternity.

"Don't get me wrong — I'm not saying that life here is all suffering, because for many of us it's not. What I am saying is that having spent so much time with the Guardians, I've been able to experience an older and more evolved culture in operation. With them there's total oneness, acceptance, understanding and unconditional love, whereas here there's so much separation and divisiveness, and people can be so judgmental and focused on differences rather than on similarities.

"All I know is that when my time comes I'll be more than happy to move onwards and upwards to something better. I definitely would *not* want to spend eternity down here on Earth with all the ongoing wars and other negative, fear-oriented happenings. That just doesn't bear thinking about!"

"Here, here!" Kaz agreed. "You are not wrong there! But you know what the trick is down here to maintain your sanity? You have to always keep things simple and learn to appreciate the 'magic moments,' like taking time to look at a beautiful sunset, or sharing a nice meal with your family at the end of the day, or feeling a little child's arms around your neck, giving you a big hug. And then there's the comfort of a warm, soft, cuddly cat asleep on your lap, or the look of pure and total unconditional love in the eyes of your pet dog! I could go on and on — like being curled up in a comfortable chair with a good book and a *whole* block of chocolate all to yourself, or the aroma of freshly brewed coffee — ahhh! Speaking of which, would you like me to brew up another pot Maddie?"

36 ▶ KIDS ON BOARD

Concentrating hard, I probed the interior of the disc with my mind, knowing my charge couldn't be too far away. Being an interdimensional portal, the Mothership contains endless places into which a small boy bent on adventure can potentially disappear. However, in Ben's case he couldn't get into too much trouble as he's not yet been fitted with the necessary implants to allow him much scope in the way of interdimensional travel.

Kaz's young son is my student, and has been right from the time he was old enough to be brought on board. Like Kaz and me, he's a Guardian who has chosen birth into an Earth human container to provide assistance in the future for the new generation of Earth humans that our people are currently in the process of developing.

Between major pollution, overpopulation, diseases such as AIDS and deadly new strains of influenza, as well as the continuing possibility of nuclear war, this species is now teetering on the very brink of destroying itself. Another stronger and more resilient upgrade has had to be developed, and quickly, if Earth humans are to remain viable. Kaz's son Ben, like his mother and me, are ones who've chosen lives here in order to pave the way for this new generation on Earth. As a member of our own soul group, the Guardian Consciousness, he has volunteered to take on Earth human form to help out in the project. Many varied interplanetary and interdimensional groups are taking part in this, and, in fact, it's a joint effort on a truly universal scale.

Ben has chosen to be born into a standard but genetically upgraded Earth human container, to a mother who is also one of our own, incarnating for the span of a lifetime in human form. This being the case, there was no need for him to be removed from the womb at an early stage of the pregnancy in order to continue his development *in vitro* on the ship. His new body is human enough physically for him to be born naturally as an Earthling, but at the same time he needs to be brought on board regularly to master certain skills and learn to relate comfortably to both cultures.

Ben is a bright and lively lad, both 'upstairs' and 'downstairs,' and I love him dearly. As teacher and student we have a very close rapport, but it will take time for Ben to become fully aware of this link on the human level. Guardian and human consciousnesses will need to become closely integrated, which means all fear and insecurities that have been carried through the physical/emotional Earthling side of his being will have to be addressed and eventually cleared away. Once up on the ship and linked fully into the Guardian Consciousness, he's fine with me, as he is 'downstairs' when we're both in Earth human form, but trying to integrate the two is still posing a few difficulties.

The physical/emotional Earthling part of his psyche still reacts with fear whenever I put in an appearance in his bedroom at night in my ET form to take him on board the disc. Sometimes, even after his astral form has been safely collected, the physical container left behind continues to react emotionally. With his higher-conscious mind thus removed, Ben's body's reaction is involuntary, as if operating on automatic pilot. This results in the strange trancelike state that Kaz had described to Maddie.

To explain the situation very crudely, the vacated physical shell is rather like a chicken running around with its head chopped off. Luckily, Kaz herself is now well integrated as both a Guardian and an Earth human, and so she is able to handle the situation wisely and calmly, to make sure Ben's physical container remains safe while the 'driver,' is away on the disc. However, in Ben's case, he cannot yet fully step out of his vehicle — or at least it's as if he steps out but forgets to apply the 'hand brake.'

Again I sent out a mind probe. Where in the name of Oneness had the little devil got to? There are endless possibilities for mischief on the Mothership, such as taking up a position on one of the elevated walkways for the express purpose of dropping small objects onto the large, bald craniums of passing Elders. Or creating a skate-board for oneself out of the ethers then hurtling along the endless corridors at break-neck speed, trying not to collect pedestrians in the process. Then there's the fun of suddenly poking a head, or else a long, thin, three- or four-fingered gray hand through one of the interdimensional portals to cause a stir with some poor unsuspecting person.

I chuckled to myself, remembering just such an escapade of my own that resulted in a large, balding and very overweight Earthling male running naked and screaming from the bathroom in which he'd been relaxing contentedly in a steaming tub while enjoying a glass of wine and a good book. The last thing he'd expected was a large-eyed ET face peering at him through the scented steam and bubbles. To tell the truth, I'm not sure which of us got the bigger fright.

A frantic call of distress from Ben suddenly telepathed into my mind, accompanied by waves of annoyance on a stronger, deeper level, which told me an Elder was involved as well. Oh, dear! What was Ben getting up to? That is the advantage, or in some cases the *dis*advantage of being linked into the Guardian Consciousness. Operating totally as One, we are intrinsically linked to each other on a telepathic level, so there are no secrets, no lies and no hidden thoughts. The group mind is like a deep but crystal-clear ocean in which all is open, visible and transparent, so we can see what is happening on all levels. And at that moment two of the levels connected to me were at odds with each other on the disc.

Scanning the ship again, what flashed into my consciousness was the 'engine room,' which is as close as it can be described in Earthly terms. Our discs are not powered by engines but rather by cosmic energy, and there is a power center like a main chakra point at the very heart of the disc. In fact, because the disc is actually a living organism, 'heart' is probably the most appropriate term to use — and that was where Ben had got to. No wonder he wasn't feeling very comfortable, because the energy forces there are immense.

"Alarca, *help!*" the call came again, as I responded.

"It's all right Ben, I'm coming — just stay calm."

"I *can't* — I'm being *squashed! Help!*"

Then a stronger, deeper voice commanded, "Alarca — get down here this minute and collect your student!"

Almost instantaneously I arrived on the scene to find a very annoyed Elder, in fact the very formidable black-clad 'Captain' of the disc, whose job is to ensure the smooth running of the ship and the safety of all who travel in her — or else! He was standing at the entrance to the power center waiting for me, dark eyes glaring, arms folded and foot tapping impatiently. Even though I'd managed to send myself backwards in time by ducking through a portal so as to arrive on the spot almost before he'd called me, I was still greeted with an irate "What took you so long? Get that boy out of here!"

Looking past him I could just make out a diminutive, scared and rather guilt-ridden figure hiding in the shadows. Sure enough it was Ben, in his gray container. Overcome in the middle of his escapade by the sheer pressure of the energy, he couldn't move an inch, so great was the intensity of the atmosphere here in the heart center of the disc. Pushing through it with great difficulty myself I managed to reach him, intensely aware the whole time of the disapproving eyes of the 'Captain,' known to us as the Keeper, boring into me. "Come on, Ben," I urged, reaching out to him, "take my hand — it'll help you to move."

Summoning every ounce of willpower and strength, Ben slowly did as he was told, inching the four long, thin fingers of his right hand towards mine as I in turn struggled to connect with him. It was like trying to move through a thick, viscous fluid — but once our fingers touched and our energies connected he was able to move, enabling me to pull him out of the area.

A fleeting wave of annoyance passed through my mind. Why hadn't the Keeper done anything to help? Fair enough he was angry with Ben for going into places where he had no business being, but why hadn't he come to the poor lad's rescue?

"*Because*," a powerful telepathic voice boomed in my head, "*If I had, he really would have been hurt. He could not have coped with my energy on top of that of the Mothership.* Now get *out* of here *both* of you — and do *not* come *back*!" The Keeper's words reverberated through both our heads, sending us scuttling back along the corridor towards the slightly less daunting atmosphere of the classroom from which Ben had made his escape not long before.

"*Why* Ben?" I questioned him. "Why ever did you go into the power center in the first place? Nobody goes in there except the Keepers — not even the other Elders. Everybody knows how uncomfortable that much energy is, and how formidable the Keepers are. Whatever possessed you to go exploring there?"

"I dunno," Ben shrugged absentmindedly, scuffing his foot on the floor, "just wanted to know how it works I guess, that's all. Sorry if I got you into trouble, Alarca, but I was getting bored playing with the stupid energy balls. Keeping them up in the air and floating them around the room with my mind is *nothing!* I just wanted a bit of a *challenge!*"

"Yes, well, I'll give you a *real* challenge if I find you down there again! Come on. Let's get you back into your Earth human container before your poor mother runs herself ragged chasing it around the house trying to bring it out of trance. And speaking of wanting challenges, when the heck are you going to learn to incapacitate your container properly before stepping out of it?"

Again he shrugged. "I dunno — one of these days I s'pose. But you know what," he added with a wicked grin, "chasing my body around the house gives Mom a bit of good, healthy exercise. Hey, Alarca, can we please stick our heads through a portal on the way home?

"*Ben!*"

"Well, it was just an idea."

37 ▶ BOXES

A li, what the heck was Ben getting up to last night on the disc? He had one of his trances, and it started off with him running around the house like a mad thing, cowering under the bathroom basin and complaining that he was being squashed. He was absolutely terrified of something he saw in the doorway. What was going on? Who scared him? He was acting like all the demons in hell were after him."

I couldn't help chuckling at the image Kaz was describing so vividly as we sat over coffee the morning after Ben's little adventure 'upstairs.' The two streams of reality were so similar and yet so different, both flowing along at exactly the same time. "He was running away from class and looking for mischief, if you really want to know," I informed her. "Problem was, he found his way into the power center, and when I got to him he was being squashed almost flat by the strong energy field that's present there. You know how it feels — really, *really* heavy, like a ton weight coming down on you."

"But what was frightening him so? It wasn't just that he felt he was being squashed — someone else was there too — someone he was really scared of."

"Oh, it was just old Tammis, you know, the Keeper. He was the one who found him in the center and called me to come and get him."

"Ah yes, he is a formidable old sod. No wonder poor Ben was scared. I mean to say, even when he's in that trance state and sees *me* in my Grey form, he gets scared, so I can imagine how old Tammis would affect him."

"Well, you'd better put a pillow case over your head for the next session, because we'll be starting to open the door of his consciousness so he can go deeper within, which will bring him face to face with all sorts of things that can be quite unsettling."

"But Ali, he's so young still in human years! Can't we wait 'til he's a bit older? We never used to go into that process with them until much later."

"Yes, I know Kaz, but the whole problem is time is running out, and our young ones need to be brought on line much more quickly now. We just can't delay things any longer. It needs to be 'all hands on deck' as it were."

"Okay, fair enough. I do know what you mean, but please let me know beforehand so I'll be prepared. I'm lucky to have a couple of others assisting me 'upstairs' with the hybrid babies, because when Ben goes off in these trances, I have to get back down here and into my container to help him. There's no way I can just leave him to cope on his own. I trust you to take care of him up there, but down here he needs his mom at those times. By the way Ali, speaking of moms, have you heard any more from Maddie?"

"Ah, that's right; I knew there was something I had to tell you. Don't know what's happening with my memory lately, I can't seem to retain anything. Must be trying to work between two different streams of consciousness — it gets me in an awful tangle at times. But yes, she's coming to the presbytery on Thursday morning to talk about something else that's happened. Is that okay for you? Can you come?"

"Umm, hang on, I'll check." Kaz got up to look at the calendar on the wall that served as her "appointment book."

"Let's see now — Kira's sports day is Wednesday, and parents are invited, so I'd better be there or I'll never be forgiven, and café duty is on Friday — Oh, God, what a week! But yes, Thursday morning is fine. Lucky it's not in the afternoon, because Ben has a dental appointment."

Thursday morning began in a rush because right after early Mass, Paco was called to the local hospital to attend to one of his parishioners. He got back just before Kaz and Maddie were due.

"Now remember," I told him, "don't bring the brandy bottle out no matter how upset Maddie is. Kaz is really sensitive to it, and more than a mouthful or two will have her swinging off the chandelier. You know how we are — our energies just can't take much alcohol, especially spirits."

"Oh, God yes, thanks for reminding me, and *you're* not much better by the way. You totally embarrassed me having dinner at the Kelly's the other night with your hand-farting demonstration after one too many rum and cokes. Where the hell did you learn to do that? Up on the disc I'll bet!"

"No, brother dear — *you* taught me, many moons ago. Surely you remember, but no, perhaps not because I do believe you were drunk at the time!"

"Well," came his reply as quick as a flash, "I *am* only *human* after all — but what's *your* excuse?"

Maddie arrived at the Presbytery right on time and at first glance, we were all stunned at the change in her appearance. She was certainly still stressed about her family's involvement with the ETs, but as she filled us in on the latest happenings in her home we were amazed at the confidence that she'd acquired since our last visit. We all felt we must be on the right track with her.

"Kaz," she began, "you know those funny trancelike dreams that Ben gets? — Kate had one too the other night — I feel there's an important message of some sort in it. It started with her calling out to me, and when I went in to her, she told me she could see these really small boxes all around the bedroom, and she had to count the gaps between them, but this was upsetting her, and she complained of feeling scared and dizzy.

"I sat awhile with her, wracking my brains trying to work out what these boxes were all about, and how best to help her move through it. Then the thought came to mind to ask her what she was supposed to do with them, and she said, 'Make them bigger, but I *can't* — I'm *scared*!' I asked her why she was scared and she answered that their energies felt awful and that they were still making her feel giddy.

"I remembered your advice, Kaz, to tell her how in a dream she has all the power to be whomever she needs to be, or to do whatever she needs to do, so if she must make the boxes bigger, then she can."

"Good for you!" Kaz congratulated her. "So what happened? Did it help?"

"Yes, for sure! I reminded her that she had the power to do what was required — and I assured her that she was not alone, that I was right there with her. I told her to just give it a go, to really concentrate, and to know in her heart that she had the power to do it. As I pointed out to her — who knows what will happen? It might even be fun!

"Then she opened her eyes a bit and moved her arm up to point to them. Her hand dropped, and I could see her really concentrating hard. I asked her what was going on and could she still see them. She answered, 'Yes, they look like little TV sets, and now they're getting bigger — they're all around my room.'

"I asked her what she was supposed to do with them now, and I suggested that maybe she could turn them into something nice, like flowers or butterflies, but she said that she couldn't do that. Next I suggested she try to go inside one of them. I reassured her that I was right there with her and that she'd be safe, so again she concentrated hard, with her eyes closed, and she found herself in a dark room, feeling scared because she could sense something negative around her — what she called a bad spirit.

"I then reminded her of what we'd talked about before when she was scared — of how love conquers all. I told her that love is her power, and that she's much stronger than any bad spirit and that it can't hurt her. I explained how bad spirits feed off fear and are strengthened by it, and when they see you're not afraid of them and instead you are full of love and have trust in yourself and God, then they go away because they know you're stronger than they are. And you know it was really weird the way the words were flowing so easily. I'm sure I was getting help from 'upstairs' as you say."

"Good on you Maddie!" Kaz reached out to pat her hand, "That is *exactly* how it is! So what happened next?"

"Well, I suggested to Kate that perhaps the bad spirit needed a hug. That maybe it was more a sad spirit than a bad spirit. I told her to just give it a try and to remember that love is her power and to have faith and trust in herself. At first she said the spirit was trying to run away from her in a funny way with its arms bent and held close to its body and its wrists sort of loose and flapping, rather like how a penguin runs, but then it turned around and came towards her. Again I reminded her of love being her power, and urged her to hug it — to direct love towards it, which she did.

"Then the bad spirit hugged her back and disappeared completely, and she found herself back safe and sound in her bedroom. Coming out of the trance, she threw her arms around me for a cuddle, and I told her how very proud I was of her, and how I knew she could do it because she's strong and good. And that's it — five minutes later she was sound asleep. So what do you reckon it was all about?"

"Wow, what a dream!" Paco shook his head in amazement. "Makes mine seem tame and boring in comparison. But there's obviously heaps of symbolism in there. Anyone got any ideas? Kaz? Has Ben ever had anything like that?"

"No, not quite," she answered, "but my daughter Kira did once. Not exactly the same, because in her case the 'bad spirit' had a purple ball it was threatening to throw at her, and she was told that if it hit her, it would steal her soul and she'd die. Luckily by then I was in touch with 'upstairs,' and understood enough to know that it was a test of love and courage for her, and that she was not to run away but rather to catch the ball and throw it back. She managed to do this, with a bit of reassurance and encouragement, and as in Kate's experience, the whole thing just dissipated once she overcame her fear. After it was all over, her Grey teacher appeared on the scene to congratulate her and to tell her how pleased he was with her. She felt very good after that, and it's served to boost her self-confidence no end.

"I get the feeling," Kaz went on, "that in Kate's dream the little boxes symbolize the way our human minds are so limited and compartmentalized, you know, everything separate and divided and closed off in its own little box. We often find it very hard to see the whole bigger picture in many situations, particularly if it involves looking at something from another person's point of view. In fact many people find this quite confronting. The ETs, on the other hand, tend to take more of an overview, so they are able to tap in to a truer perception of reality and what is really going on around them."

"And what about the fear factor she experienced, and feeling giddy when told to count the spaces between the boxes?"

"Okay," Kaz replied, looking thoughtful, "it's fear that causes us to tie everything up in neat little boxes, because in order to see the bigger picture of any given situation, we need to look more deeply within our own self, which requires a giant leap of faith and trust. Many people simply cannot do this. It's too confronting and results in their feeling as if they're spinning out of control. Remember it was the act of focusing on the spaces between the boxes that caused Kate to feel scared and dizzy. She was being made to focus upon this hidden aspect of her being, because it is this very thing, these 'spaces between the boxes,' that represent the almost unconscious state of mind in which we as humans operate. Having to look at this brought about a sense of unease and off-centerdness.

"The thing is," Kaz continued, "having to look at the bigger picture in a more unified, less fragmented way, and being made to confront any issues connected to it is a big part of Kate's accepting and melding into the greater aspect of her psyche. For some Earth humans this can be almost impossible, but it's something the Star Children must learn. Some find it easier than others, but it's all about starting to tap into another tenth of their conscious awareness. A lot of the Star Kids go through these difficulties. I know Ben and Kira certainly do.

"And don't forget Maddie, it's not just Kate's journey, but yours, too, as her mother. Think how far you've come since we first met — how well you've handled your daughter's experience, and how you knew what questions to ask."

Now it was Maddie's turn to look thoughtful. "Well, yes, I suppose so. And the bad spirit? What is that?"

"Definitely her own inner fear, which she's externalizing as Kira did. The way it ran from her when she went to heal it with love is clearly symbolic of how the fear is 'tying her up' in her progress and blocking her freedom of movement on the soul level. But it also symbolizes a desire to be healed, so it only made a token attempt to escape. The love is beginning to override the fear, and as with Kira, that's what it's all about — the triumph of love and trust over fear, which in the end will bring about a state of connectedness and wholeness. All the Guardian-inspired tests are directed towards this."

"Wow, thanks Kaz!" Poor Maddie looked so relieved. "That does make a lot of sense. Do you agree, Father Lopez?"

"Oh, yes, Maddie, for sure. People are beginning to realize that the 'Kingdom of God' truly is within. I do tend to believe that a lot of what once would've been looked upon superstitiously as 'demons' and 'bad spirits' attacking us are really our own inner fears being externalized as thought forms. This doesn't mean that they don't pose any danger to us, but the way to overcome them is definitely to acknowledge your own God-given power of love. This is obviously a very important lesson being given to the Star Children, as well as to many others down here on Earth."

As Paco was speaking, Kaz leaned back in her chair, seemingly deep in thought. "You know what?" she put in when he'd finished. "We've talked a lot about love and fear being the opposites of each other, and we've discussed how love is the God within, and fear an expression of the inner 'Satan.' We've gone into a lot of detail about what the different types of fear are, for example fear of death, fear of change, fear of appearing gullible or stupid, and fear of losing control over a person or situation. We've also talked about how these various fears are expressed through the lower emotions of greed, envy, lust, over-inflated ego, bigotry etc., but what about love?

"Remember there are different aspects of love, too, for example, family love, romantic love and love between close friends. And there are many different ways people express love — through touch, words, kindness and compassion. Often what we think of as love really isn't — it's more possession, or neediness, or exploitation. In fact it seems to me that there's much more conditional love rather than *un*conditional love around, and really, it's unconditional love we should be striving for."

"I agree, and it seems that we really need to work hard to develop that quality." Maddie added.

"Yes, as humans, we do." Kaz replied thoughtfully, "My feeling is that real love grows out of a deep, inner connection with self, and an acknowledgement of the God within. This in turn helps us to love ourselves first and foremost, but at the same time this self-love is not about being selfish and egotistical — that grows out of fear. It's really all about connecting with and acknowledging your own inner God spark.

"And when you truly love your*self* in this way," she went on, "you don't become self-centered but rather God-centered, which in turn makes you more patient, more compassionate, and more able to empathize, listen to and tune in to others. Recognizing and acknowledging your God within enables you to recognize and acknowledge this same God Spark in all those around you, which in turn helps you to practice unconditional love, in which there's no room for jealousy, envy and hurt feelings. Just think about what a wonderful world it would be if everyone could do this! No more jealousy, no more cruelty, no more exploitation of the weak and vulnerable by the powerful, no more judgment, bigotry, wars and racism — a real Heaven on Earth in fact."

"The thing is," Paco shook his head, "knowing some humans, it sounds like asking a lot — but then again, as you've just said, Kaz, it all starts with ourselves."

As the four of us sat for a few moments in silence thinking about this, my mind went back to how I'd *not* practiced this concept to the best of my ability over the last few days, and how very easy it is to slip. Sneaking a quick glance at the others it was obvious from their expressions they'd not fared much better.

"Oh, all *right,* then!" Kaz was the first to shatter the guilt-ridden silence. "*Yes* — I *did* swear at that silly woman in the supermarket the other day. And I also expressed *very* deep envy and jealousy towards that lucky sod who won five bloody million on the lotto last Saturday night. Now let's just *move on,* shall we?"

"I agree," said Paco, "and on the strength of that, I reckon this would be a really good time for somebody to come up with another question to, you know, shift the spotlight a little and release us all from under the microscope."

Maddie of course was quick to oblige. "I know what I've been meaning to ask. We were talking before about what's been written on ET contact, but it's all so confusing. One says one thing, then somebody else says the total opposite, so what should we believe? How can you tell who's right and who's wrong, and who's being honest and who is bending the truth or outright lying, and who is motivated by greed or ego? And this doesn't just apply to books on ETs, but also to other spiritual books on subjects such as reincarnation, spirit contact, channeling, ascended masters, angels or whatever."

"Funny you should ask that, Maddie," Paco chimed in, turning to me. "We were just talking about that the other day, weren't we, Ali? How there's so much in the way of confused and very mixed messages coming through in some books on ET contact and other related subjects. I consider myself to be fairly well educated, but I still find a lot of this confusing, and it's very hard to sort out fact from fiction.

"I suppose because ET contact deals mainly with peoples' minds, this confusion on the part of experiencers is quite understandable," he went on, "but what I find very off-putting is the way some researchers and authors are so adamant about who are the 'goodies' and who are the 'baddies' among the ET visitors. They often contradict each other. It seems to me that the negative force of fear that we were talking about before is having a field day in all of this. What do you reckon, Ali? You've been involved with this nearly all your life."

"Well," I answered, "it seems to me that discernment is very important here. You need to recognize and tune into the energy underlying the information and again ask yourself the key question — is the motivating energy love, or is it fear/ego?

"It's really important to remember that a true spiritual teacher *never* criticizes or belittles others — they are always totally non-judgmental. Passing judgment on others indicates a weakness within self. A true spiritual teacher never ever does or says anything to make you give your power away, or to make you feel unworthy, or less than they are. Instead they'll do their best to show you how to tap into your *own* inner God Spark, and encourage you to seek out and find your own inner truth.

"After all, remember what Jesus said about his own seemingly miraculous abilities: 'All of this and more you yourselves can do.' A true teacher emphasizes the equality of all, and that *all* have the Spark of God within. They never put themselves up on a pedestal as being 'special,' 'chosen,' or above ordinary folk, because if they do it shows that they are motivated by fear and ego rather than by love."

Multi-colored balls whizzed crazily around the room, and the sound of happy children at play ricocheted off the walls. Treading carefully to avoid stepping on the little ones crawling about on the floor, I almost missed seeing the bright orange ball flying straight at me seemingly out of nowhere. A swiftly raised hand and a short, sharp burst of energy out of my palm sent it spinning upwards, bouncing off the ceiling to land plop in the lap of the one who'd aimed it. The look of sheer incredulity on his face was quite hilarious. "Matthew, I should have known it'd be you!" I glared at him in mock reproach which quickly turned to a fond smile as two enormous black eyes met mine with a look of bland innocence.

"Sorry, Alarca, but I didn't do it on *purpose.* It sort of just jumped up by itself and flew at you."

"Yes, yes, I know, Matthew. Just like all those frogs that 'accidentally' came in through an interdimensional portal during Maris's lecture on the history of the Guardian culture last week."

"But, Alarca, his lessons are so *boring.* Somebody has to liven them up."

The teeming host of hopping, croaking frogs that had suddenly materialized in the lecture room on the big disc had certainly enlivened Maris's delivery, much to everybody else's amusement, especially when one of them landed on his hat and puffed itself up to enormous proportions, before deflating moments later in a tremendous and obviously deeply satisfying croak. Needless to say, it all went down-hill from there.

My amused train of thought was interrupted by the appearance of Elder Garnibis, not through the doorway I'd used, but rather through another portal, which delighted the children no end. They all ran to her, crowding around, wanting to be touched, to be as close as possible to her beautiful energy.

Up here on the disc things are so different from down on Earth. Everybody, even the youngest child, has a much deeper way of seeing, looking past the outer physical façade to the soul within. Many weird and amazing beings can potentially manifest on our discs because the discs are both time and interdimensional portals, so this deeper way of seeing is most necessary for all of us to acquire.

These children too were all very different from each other. There was a good mixture of Star Children, whose home world is Planet Earth, and the less human-looking hybrids, both our own and ones we've rescued from Earth laboratories. Most of the Star Children have the outer appearance of perfectly normal Earth humans, whereas some of the hybrids look almost pure ET, and there are many variations in between, including bloodlines of many Star Nations throughout the universe. Despite these outer differences, they all play happily together, learning and mastering skills in our classrooms that no school on Earth could ever teach them.

These lessons are mostly about working with energy — molding and shaping it to form physical and semiphysical matter, and levitating and moving objects around using only mind power. They start with light things such as balls and plastic blocks, then, as their skills develop, they move on to more difficult projects such as levitating themselves and each other. Another lesson is to create energy balls — multi-colored balls of light that can be moved about solely by their creator's willpower.

As the children grow older, they move past these games and into deeper learning experiences such as math and science, but of a far more advanced form than is taught on Earth. There are other lessons as well, and many of the Star Children find that the skills they acquire up on the disc often reflect and parallel what they are studying and learning in their daily lives on Earth.

"Come children!" Garnibis called. "For tonight's lesson we will travel through one of the portals to a special place — a magical place where you will get to meet some of the very interesting creatures who live there. As you know, our universe has many different layers and levels, far, far beyond what Earth humans perceive as 'reality.' Because of who and what you are, you are not limited by this narrow perception of what reality is. You must allow your minds to expand and grow — to see and experience fully the true magic of our universe and to understand properly just what it means to be a citizen of the Cosmos. Now come along all of you, and make sure you stay close to either Ashka or myself."

As Garnibis stepped out through yet another portal, the little ones followed, with Ashka taking up the rear to keep an eye on them all. For a moment I had to just stand back and watch. It looked so beautiful seeing Ashka, clad in her gray container with its large head, great black, almond-shaped eyes and thin, quite fragile-looking limbs, holding a pretty, blonde, blue-eyed Earth child by one hand and a half-and-half hybrid child with the other.

The little hybrid boy clung to her with both hands, looking decidedly nervous and not sure if he really wanted this new experience or not, whereas the Earth girl's eyes shone with excitement and expectation. "Don't be scared, Theo," I heard her telepath to him. "It'll be fun, you'll see!"

Ashka looked over to me with a fond smile in her eyes. "Come on, Alarca, it *will* be fun! Come and join us."

Passing through these interdimensional portals always reminds me of stepping through a small waterfall, except that the "water" feels more jelly-like and closely resembles pinkish-silver light. Whether we are simply coming on board the disc or moving from one galactic level to another, our journey always includes moving through these openings. If we are only travelling a short distance, the "waterfall" is only about a foot in thickness, whereas if it involves a longer trip through time and space, it can be anything from about a yard thick to a quite long tunnel.

I thought back to the first time I'd consciously come on board as a Earth human child, almost totally unaware of my forgotten Guardian connection, and how scared I'd been when Maris led me through a portal for the first few times. I really thought that I'd died and gone over to the other side. Closing my eyes and holding my breath as we passed through, I'd fully expected to feel the same wetly suffocating sensation as one experiences standing directly under a shower or waterfall, but it wasn't like that at all. It was actually quite beyond description in Earthly, physical terms, because while it felt like thick, slightly sticky water, it wasn't — it was light, and it had the most wonderful, regenerating effect on the body, which also became light as it passed through.

Keeping a close eye on the little ones to make sure none of them became frightened, I was amazed at how they all took it in their stride. Even the Earth children were fully aware of who and what they were, and they seemed quite accustomed to moving easily through the dimensional veils, having been consciously brought onto the disc from a very early age. Awareness of such things is spreading rapidly on Earth now, far different from when Ashka and I had taken human form down there all those years ago. Time was certainly speeding up.

The next moment we stepped out of the pink-silver light veil and found ourselves moving through an opalescent mist that swirled around us in rainbow-colored clouds of vapor. We stayed close together to make sure nobody got lost, and very soon we emerged on the grassy bank of a stream. Wending its way over smooth pebbles, around large moss-covered boulders and under overhanging branches, the stream emptied itself into the basin of a large, deep rock pool. The falling droplets of cascading water acted like prisms, refracting the filtered sunlight into a myriad of tiny glinting rainbows, which played across the surface of the tumbling water, lending a touch of mystical magic to the scene.

Blending subtly into the tinkling and gurgling of the stream and waterfall came sounds of laughter and much splashing from the pool, where a small troupe of water nymphs, known on Earth as Naiads, enjoyed themselves hugely in the shallows and under the cascade. Delicate green-tinged faces, framed by long, wet tendrils of hair resembling some sort of tangled, grassy vegetation that might be found at the bottom of a pond, turned as one towards us, and large darkly slanted eyes similar to our own regarded us with curiosity.

Here in this magical dimension fear was unknown, and no matter what language or mode of speaking, lines of friendly communication could always be opened up telepathically. These beings knew that a group such as ours, of young hybrid children under the care of a Guardian Elder, posed no danger whatsoever, and so several of them came over to us, offering prettily colored pebbles from the bottom of the pool as tokens of welcome. We passed these among us, delighting in the smooth, soft feel of them in our hands.

The Naiads invited us to join them, knowing that being related to the Dolphin folk of Planet Earth, we also feel deep kinship with the element of water. The more daring ones of our group plunged fearlessly to the very bottom of the pool, moving with dolphin-like grace through the cool, green depths. Here there were small underwater caves to explore, tangled tree roots to poke about in, and tiny silvery fish to be observed darting to and fro among the rocks and weeds on the floor of the pool. Those of us with a less adventurous disposition were happy to splash about in the shallows or else immerse ourselves under the cascading waterfall to watch and enjoy the lively antics of the others.

Finally a telepathic call from Garnibis brought us all back to the grassy bank where, along with a couple of the Naiads who'd decided to join us, we made ourselves comfortable to await her words of wisdom. Naiads are well known for their irrepressible sense of fun and penchant for restlessness and devilry, but such was the respect that everyone felt for Garnibis, even they sat quietly, waiting patiently for her to begin.

"Now children, gather close to me and settle yourselves for a teaching on Soul. This is important for all to understand, because in the greater reality every single one of us is a soul — an intrinsic part of Oneness. It matters not what form we happen to be taking in any one lifespan — it may be Zeta, or it may be Earth human, Pleiadian, Sirian, or else it may be that of a Naiad," here she paused to acknowledge the two water nymphs in our midst, "or any of the other sentient beings who inhabit the infinite planes and dimensions that are part of our universe. Remember, we are *all one*, and the unifying energy of Oneness is soul.

"Sitting here on the bank of this little stream, watching it wending its way around the many various obstacles in its path like rocks and fallen branches, reminds me of a teaching I received when I was a little one just like yourselves. The progress made by a soul through its many incarnations is like the course of a mighty river in the journey from its source high in the mountains to its final merging with the waters of the ocean.

"Sometimes its way is easy, through pleasant fields and cool forests, while at other times it is made difficult by rocks and boulders that interrupt the smoothness of its flow. In some places a dam may be built to block its progress, but eventually it will overflow or else break down the barrier and continue upon its journey unimpeded. Both soul and river must be adaptable, allowing their course to change sometimes — to make their way around obstacles and hindrances barring their path.

"Just as a river contributes part of itself to the area through which it passes by watering and irrigating the otherwise barren fields along its banks, so a soul must also give of itself, not draining itself completely, but contributing its share of refreshment and nourishment to those around it. Like the river that travels for many miles through different towns and cities along its course from source to sea, a soul must travel through many different lives in various lands and cultures in its journey back to Oneness.

"By looking at the river one can begin to understand the physical illusion of time — of past, present and future. A single drop of water in the river must be at a certain point at a specific time, just as part of the soul's awareness places itself in a certain portion of time and space. But remember, that tiny drop of water is not the *whole* river — it is just a very small part of it. If you observe the river or the soul as a whole, which you must if you are to gain a full perception of reality, then you will see that it is in all places at once, always in the present, concerned with neither past nor future.

"Like a river which can be polluted and made unclean by the area through which it passes, so a soul may be adversely affected and brought down by the environment surrounding it. On the other hand, as with the streams of clean, fresh water which continually feed and purify the river, a soul must open itself to receive the fresh and purifying streams of knowledge and wisdom which are all around, ready to be taken in, stored, and used for its growth and evolution.

"At its first emerging from the Source, which is God, a soul may be likened to the tiny trickle of a pure mountain spring in its innocence and simplicity. As it progresses through lifetimes and cycles of learning upon many diverse levels of universal existence, it takes on more and more strength and substance, with layers of knowledge, experience and conscious awareness building up around and within it until it is strong and certain in its course, like a mighty river.

"Through all these varying life experiences and learnings, it is moving ever onward — sometimes slowly, sometimes quickly, sometimes encountering obstacles in its path — which, by slowing its progress, only serves to make it stronger. Other times it moves easily along with its way clear. On occasions, just like the changing course of a meandering river, it will seem to be going backwards, but in reality it is still progressing in its own way, in its own time, to eventually merge back into and become an intrinsic part of the Oneness of Divine Consciousness, just as a river merges into and becomes part of the great ocean."

As Garnibis finished speaking, the Naiads began wriggling around a bit, anxious to return to their own watery environment. In fact it was quite surprising that they'd managed to stay well behaved and quiet in one place for so long. I thought of the time several of them found their way through an interdimensional portal and onto the disc. After they'd left, Maris found pond weed strewn all around his office and a large puddle of water in the middle of the floor — at least he'd hoped it was water — with Naiads you never can tell.

Once they realized that the session was over, they jumped to their feet in a wild and joyous burst of energy, spraying everyone around them with droplets of moisture from their flying manes of seaweed-like hair. With a respectful bow of acknowledgement to Garnibis, they raced each other back to the rock pool, plunging in headfirst, webbed feet propelling them swiftly to the far side, where they disappeared in a froth of bubbles and foam.

"Wow!" said young Matthew, who was sitting next to me, "I wish I had green skin like that — and webbed feet."

"Go on then," said another, "see if you can shape-shift."

And so the next half hour or so was spent with everybody trying their hardest to assume different shapes, with varying degrees of success. Most of them actually did quite well considering the subject of shape-shifting hadn't as yet been covered in class. Among all the deer, wolves, cats and even a fluffy bunny rabbit, Matthew of course had to have his bit of fun. After managing to turn himself into a reasonably convincing frog, complete with green skin and webbed feet, he then proceeded to change himself into a large and tawny owl which, perched precariously above where we were sitting, threatened to deposit little "offerings" onto the tops of our unprotected heads — sweet boy!

Just then we became aware of a figure emerging from within a misty, glowing white light which had gathered between the trees on the far side of the clearing. Everybody looked up simultaneously to behold the in-

credible sight of a unicorn. I for one had never had the privilege of seeing one of these wondrous creatures, and so I marveled at the sight of it.
The pure white body with its lustrous mane and tail seemed to glow in
the rays of sunlight filtering through the tree branches above, almost as if
the creature were illuminated from within, and the silvery-colored horn
protruding from the very center of its forehead gleamed with points of
bright luminescence, as if encrusted with tiny crystals. Large, doelike
eyes regarded us calmly, then with a toss of its elegant head it galloped
back into the shadowy and mysterious depths of the forest, leaving a
shimmer of sparkling mist in its wake.

My eyes as wide as saucers, I turned to Ashka. "Wow! That was
amazing! I didn't know there were such creatures. What's it doing here?
In fact, where are we exactly? I'm sure I've never been here before."

Ashka put a sisterly arm around my shoulders. "Haven't you
ever been here?"

"No, and I'm wondering why?"

"Well, could be that you didn't need to come here because you
never lost your connection to nature, and your Romany background kept
you connected to 'magic.'"

"That's true. I guess 'upstairs' knows what we need."

"Come on, Alarca, let's go for a little walk along the bank of the
stream and I'll explain. Working with the children as I do, I come here
quite often with them. Garnibis won't mind keeping them amused for a
while on her own. She's got all sorts of magic hidden away up her sleeve
to keep them occupied and out of mischief, and, as you can see, they all
adore her.

"As you've probably guessed," she went on, "this is just another
of the many dimensions that we're able to enter through the portals on
the big disc. It's about as close to Fairyland as you'll find in the universe,
and it is a very special world of magic and enchantment created especially for children. The ones we bring here, both the Star Children and
the hybrid children, have a special and important role to play in the future, and this place provides the necessary preparation for them in that it
helps to nurture the spark of fantasy and imagination which we have
carefully preserved in the Star Children, and which must be reintroduced
and ignited in some of the others.

"As you know, Alarca, many, many Earth humans are centered
mainly in the sacral chakra, unable to evolve further because they cannot
heal and balance the deeper issues related to this chakra. These issues
deal with the 'inner child' and creativity in the sense of imagination and
fantasy, which are such an important part of being a happy, balanced and
well-evolved human. It is imbalance in this chakra that causes a person
to become pompous, cynical, and egotistical, and to lose the purity and

childlike innocence that enables one to 'become again as a little child in order to enter the kingdom of heaven.'

"It is this inner-child aspect of their being that is the key to their connectedness back to self and Oneness. This aspect allows them to believe in and accept the possibility of miracles and magic, and it is as important for balance and harmony in a human as the need for nurturing and love. Unfortunately, it is fast disappearing from Planet Earth as they have come to revere scientific facts over intuition, and so distrust, cynicism, and fear have spread.

"If the Star Children are to restore balance and healing to Mother Earth, which is the purpose for which they are being developed, then this inner child part must be protected, nurtured and encouraged. The problem is that it is rapidly deteriorating in other Earth children, who are losing more and more of their childhood innocence and sense of wonder through the terrible things they are being exposed to at such an early age. Some of them are barely allowed to *be* children any more, which is a great tragedy."

"So this is like a Fairyland dimension where you bring them to encourage and nurture this aspect of their being?" I queried, eyes widening in wonder as more of the magical unicorns made a fleeting appearance among the trees, only to dissipate moments later into a swirling cloud of rainbow-colored mist.

"Yes," Ashka replied, "and you know, it's unbelievable, but to some Earth humans such things as fantasy and imagination are considered a complete waste of time, to be stamped out as soon as possible and definitely not to be encouraged. This is *so* sad and is why many Earthlings are stressed, troubled and disconnected from themselves and the greater reality."

She reached out to take my hand. "Come on then, Sis — we'd better be getting back to get the munchkins home safely. I do worry a wee bit that Garnibis will lose one or two along the way. Some of the poor little things really don't want to go back, and sometimes they try to hide from her, hoping to be left behind. The hybrid ones that live with us on the disc are okay — it's the poor kids who must return to Earth who aren't always happy about leaving here. We feel so sorry for them having to return to all that heaviness and negativity down there."

On our way back to join the others we tried to hurry, but with so many wonders to distract us in this magical place, it was almost impossible. Another unicorn, a little bolder, came right up to our path. Ashka plucked a handful of sweet, juicy grass to entice it over, and soon it was snuffling boldly into her hand with its velvet muzzle, flicking its tail, and stamping a back hoof in excitement. "Come on, Alarca, pick some grass and see if it'll take it from you."

"Are you sure they don't bite?" I tentatively inquired, well aware of the difficulties I'd had with Earth horses. Unlike my brother Paco, who had an almost magical way with them, they seemed to sense my off-planet energy and either ran off or greeted me with laid-back ears, bared teeth and viciously stamping hooves.

"Nah, it'll be all right. Unicorns and Guardians get on really well together. Look, bless him, he likes you! The unicorn had in fact come right up to me, but then proceeded to use my body as a convenient scratching post for its head, which would've been fine if it hadn't been for the quite formidable-looking horn that on each up and down stroke was just missing my eyes. I tried to back away, but I found myself effectively trapped between an overly friendly unicorn and a large tree. "Ashka," I cried, "don't just stand there! *Do* something! *Help!*"

Mouth quivering in a valiant attempt not to laugh, Ashka tried grabbing its tail to distract it, causing it to break wind in fright and take off at a full gallop through the trees. "Goodness me," she said, looking quite bemused, "I didn't think unicorns did such things — not in Fairyland anyway. Just goes to show, doesn't it! Now if it'd blown some fairy dust out in the process, it'd be more in keeping with the surroundings — but then again, they do eat grass and other various herbaceous substances, so I guess…."

"Ashka, are you going to stand there all night discussing the ins and outs of unicorns' digestive systems, or are we going back to work?"

"Oh, I don't know," she mused, "I think unicorns are far more interesting and entertaining than taking tissue samples from humans."

"Well it might be fine for you, but I snuck off duty to come here, and I still have five procedures to perform before morning, so I really need to get back."

"Oh, all right, if you insist. Come on, we can take a short-cut through that big old hollow tree over there. It'll be a bit cobwebby and not half as nice as teleporting ourselves through the mist, but it will do the job. Off we go then! All aboard! Anchors aweigh! Or whatever it is you say when you're boarding a ship — or a disc."

"Ashka, you're acting even madder than usual. Are you sure you're not a wee bit tipsy? Have you been sampling nectar or whatever it is they're supposed to drink here in Fairyland?"

"No no, truly I haven't. It's just the atmosphere up here. It can have an effect on you. It tends to make us Guardians act a bit tipsy and it causes uniforms to cart — whoops, I mean uni*corns* to…"

"Yes, Ashka, I *know* what you mean — now let's *go!*"

39 ▶ THE SCHEME OF THINGS

Well, Maddie," Paco began, as we settled ourselves for another session, "what's been going on? Have things eased down at all since the other night when you called?"

"Oh, God, Father Lopez, I'm really sorry I phoned you so late. I thought things were settling down, but that night I was *so scared* — it was just awful!"

"It's okay," Paco reassured her. "That's what I'm here for, but what happened exactly? You said something about them trying to take Kate's soul. What makes you think that?"

Maddie took a deep breath before answering, "Geoff and I were awakened around midnight by Katie screaming. She was nearly hysterical, and it took ages just to calm her down enough to get her to tell us what happened. I'm sorry, Ali, but there is no way I could've convinced her to try to communicate with them. She was absolutely petrified."

"But why?" I queried. "What did they do to cause so much terror?"

Maddie looked around at the three of us before whispering in a tone of sheer horror, as if she were too scared to speak the words out loud, "They tried to *take her soul*! She woke up to see the usual one standing over her, then she felt a sort of sucking sensation in the area of her chest, but at the same time she felt pressure there as well, as if an *essence* was being drawn out of her body. She was shaking all over uncontrollably, and she could hear an awful roaring sound in her head while it was happening. At first she tried to scream, but she couldn't, because her body was totally paralyzed, like what happened to you, Ali, but then, with much effort, she finally managed to pull herself back and scream. That's when we ran in to her."

Paco looked to Kaz and me, obviously not quite sure how to reply, so I stepped in. "Maddie, honestly, nobody can steal anyone's soul, really and truly. I do know what was going on with Kate, and I can assure you that it wasn't that." Poor Maddie didn't look convinced, so I continued, "Most ET encounter experiences take place in a realm known as the astral plane, which acts as a common meeting ground between the physical plane and other higher dimensions. All of these 'planes' that I talk about, physical, astral, etc, are simply bands of energy vibrating at different frequencies. Everything in the universe is energy — cosmic energy to be precise. Even the universe itself is energy — countless bands of energy vibrating at an infinite number of frequency levels that scientists of Earth call the electromagnetic scale.

"This is what I meant last time we spoke, when I said that we are all multidimensional beings, because we too, as an intrinsic part of the universe, also vibrate on a number of different frequency bands. What we on Earth perceive as physical reality is really only a very small, extremely limited band of frequencies. The energy at Earth's physical level actually vibrates quite slowly, so it manifests as physical matter, which includes our physical body, which could be compared to a block of solid ice.

"Surrounding and permeating this physical reality band of slowely vibrating energy," I went on, "is another band of frequencies vibrating at a slightly higher level. You could think of this as being our ice block that has now melted into water and is thus a liquid rather than solid. It's the same substance but its nature has changed slightly because of its altered frequency level.

"This band of frequencies is what is known as the astral plane, and as multidimensional beings, we each have an aspect of us called the astral body, or spirit. This is not our solid physical body, but rather our mind and emotions. Mind and emotion is the vehicle of the astral realms, and if we wish to fully access this finer aspect of our being, we must step away from the physical body and experience life solely through thought, feeling and imagination.

"Surrounding and permeating both the physical and astral/spiritual aspects of our being is our soul, which vibrates at an even higher and finer frequency. It is like the steam that is created when our melted ice block is made to vibrate at a higher rate through being heated past the boiling point.

"This soul," I went on to explain, "is our higher, or true self, and is the cosmic, universal, God-part of our being. Although we do tend to use the terms 'spirit' and 'soul' fairly loosely, they don't quite mean the same thing. The spirit is actually just a small part of the soul and is, as I said before, comprised of our mind and emotions — the astral aspect of our being.

"As I mentioned, it's within this astral part, our mental/emotional body, that most ET contact takes place. The reason for this is that Earth human consciousness is focused more strongly in the physical, whereas ET consciousness is focused more strongly in soul, that's why the astral plane is a good common meeting ground between the two which is reasonably compatible to both parties.

"This also explains the fear factor inherent in many ET contact experiences. Because the astral plane is created out of mind and emotion, Earth human perception of it is nearly always clouded by belief and superstition. A person's memory and understanding of ET contact is always filtered, blurred and distorted through the lens of their own mind stuff, which has been created out of beliefs, fears and superstitions that have built up in the psyche over many lifetimes. In this way, the contact is made to fit their particular belief system, which may involve any number of fearsome or ego-centered scenarios."

"But Ali," Maddie persisted, "what has all this got to do with Kate's *soul* being taken? Can this really happen? Whatever can we *do*? I'm so scared!"

"Hang on, Maddie," I replied, "I'm getting to that. Sorry if I seem to be going off the track, but I had to go into these details so I can explain to you what Kate's visitor was really doing. I especially needed to clarify the difference between soul and spirit.

"The belief that the soul can be stolen from a person's body stems from superstition and misunderstood concepts of what soul and spirit really are. Nobody can *take* your soul, for you *are* a soul, manifesting a lifespan in a physical body. What really happened was that Kate's ET visitor was simply trying to assist her spirit, her astral form, out of the physical body so that they could communicate more easily without her being weighed down by the slow and gross vibrational frequency of the physical plane.

Everybody does this every night during sleep, when the mind/spirit is more easily able to step free of the physical shell in order to experience the lighter, finer reality of the astral realms. In these astral realms beyond the physical plane, time as we know it does not exist. Time is not the fourth dimension as some believe, for it does not reach beyond the third dimension. This is why in the dream world of the astral plane we can travel back into the past or forward into a possible future in the blink of an eye. We may also encounter friends and relatives who've died to physical life on Earth, because, in reality, only their physical containers have ceased to function. The mind/spirit that is much more the real person is eternal and continues to exist in the astral realm or higher after what humans call 'death,' so when we step free of the confines of the physical body during sleep, we can contact those who've passed over more permanently through death."

"But what about the sensation Kate had of an essence being sucked out of her body and a weight on her chest? If our astral form really leaves our physical body each night when we go to sleep, how come we don't feel things like this then?"

"Because," I answered, "Kate's experience wasn't entirely natural and self-induced as it is when we fall asleep. Her ET visitor was assisting the process and Kate became conscious as it was happening. Some people are able to do this consciously themselves during meditation, and it is indeed a very strange feeling if you aren't in a deep sleep when it happens.

"I must admit to getting an awful fright when the first ET came for me and assisted me out of my physical body — I really thought I was dying. And because our astral essence vibrates at a higher frequency than our physical body, it can cause the body to shake uncontrollably and the heart rate to rise dramatically. Also, the roaring sound Kate experienced was simply her senses opening up to the sounds of the astral plane as she hovered between the two states."

"But why couldn't she move? She was completely paralyzed and had to fight to bring herself back."

"The paralysis is just a safety measure to keep the physical body still and quiet while the mind/spirit is absent. Some investigators on Earth dismiss claims of ET visitation or astral travel in which people describe this paralysis. They scoff at any paranormal explanation and insist that what the medical profession calls 'sleep paralysis' is a perfectly normal and natural condition that happens to everyone.

"In one way they're quite correct in that yes, it is a perfectly normal and natural condition that happens to everyone, but they need to take it further to know *why* it happens. If a clairvoyant could be present at the time, they would see the spirit vacating the body, leaving behind only a very low level of consciousness to maintain the inner workings of the body to keep it alive and breathing.

"It's like parking a car outside a shop and running in to do errands, leaving the motor running and the handbrake on. We, the spirit, are the driver, and the physical body is our 'vehicle.' We don't want our vehicle shifting about and potentially getting damaged by falling off the bed, so we apply the 'handbrake' in the form of physical paralysis to prevent it from moving."

Now Paco spoke up. "That is interesting, Ali. In some books I've read on ET contact, a few instances have been mentioned in which experiencers fully believed that their souls were being taken, but they just blacked out at that point, only to wake up the next morning feeling fine, with nothing 'missing.'"

"So," Maddie asked, "you've never heard of it actually happening? You know, somebody dying after an ET encounter because their soul has been stolen?"

"Oh, good heavens, no! And it's like what Ali and Kaz said last time. When they manage to get past the fear factor, then their lives become incredibly enriched by the contact experience. After all, Maddie," he added with a grin, "the three of us are living proof."

"Were you really scared at first, too, Father? I wondered if your being a priest would've made a difference, you know, whether your having so much faith in God would protect you."

"Maddie, believe me, I was absolutely terrified! Yes, I do have faith in God's protection, but when you're faced with something like that, waking up on an ET disc, totally paralyzed and surrounded by weird-looking, obviously non-human-looking beings doing strange and seemingly horrific things to you, the fear is a visceral, gut reaction that you don't have much control over, despite your faith in a higher Force. Luckily for me, I had Ali to help me through and reassure me that they meant no harm. Once I realized that and got past the fear, it was fine.

"The key is to have the understanding — knowledge is power as they say, because that's the only way you can move past the emotion of the situation, whether that emotion is fear or anger. Understanding is the only answer, plus enough faith and trust in yourself to know you can do it. If you can't, then you remain stuck within a horrible, disempowered state of victim mentality that doesn't get you anywhere. In fact, even in your everyday life, being a victim doesn't get you anywhere, does it?"

"You're right there, Father." Maddie sighed. "I guess this will help in many aspects of life".

"It has for us. There's quite enough victim mentality on Planet Earth as it is, and as far as I see it, the ETs are doing their best to push us through and past this. We certainly won't be ready to take our place as citizens of the universe until we stop being helpless 'victims' and learn to stand up and take responsibility for our own selves and actions, thereby becoming self-empowered."

"Here, here!" Kaz put in, "I couldn't agree more, and that holds true both for yourself and for your child, because in helping her to break through the fear you'll also help yourself. What you need to understand, Maddie, is that the encounter experience is not about 'evil' or 'good' ETs trying to take over your soul, or your child, or your planet, for that matter. It's designed purely as a transformative experience, like what trainee shamans must go through. And the mind, power, or energy, if you like, behind it is neutral, not 'good' or 'bad' — that is only our polarized Earthling perception of it. It's neutral, and whether you sink or swim is entirely up to you.

"That's why many people think of the ET Visitors as 'Greys.' Sure, they do generally occupy greyish-colored containers, but on a deeper level it's about their neutrality. The Greys are a tangible, sometimes even physical channel for the non-polarized energy of the universe. They're agents of creation, in other words.

"Transformation on the soul level means overcoming fear. It's not seeing lights in the sky, or having the ability to see auras and spirits

— it's not about being able to perform miracles, or to recall past lives or see into the future. It's not even about having ecstatic meditation experiences. Sure, you might experience some of these things along the way, but the bottom line of the whole transformation process is *overcoming fear on the soul level of your psyche.* Transformation happens when we face up to and move through the fear; otherwise we become stuck, both emotionally and spiritually. It's entirely up to *us.* It is a personal choice — our own inner Battle of Armageddon.

"The Greys are like actors in a theatre company, with our own higher self as director, advising these 'actors' how best to play out the 'drama.' This drama is the core fear in our life that is blocking our spiritual growth, and which needs to be played out on the stage of our conscious and subconscious mind in order to be understood and cleared."

"So what you're saying, Kaz, is that for Kate, and probably for me too, our core fear is having our soul taken? But that's really weird — I mean to say, we're living in the twenty-first century, for heaven's sake!"

"Believe it or not, Maddie," Paco interjected, "that's a very basic, core fear with many people, often buried on deep levels of the psyche. I can't say if it's a carry-over from past lives, or simply something that's passed down through the genes from medieval times, but although modern humans may outwardly scoff at such a concept, it still holds true with many people. Fear of death is similar, and both probably reflect a core fear of loss of control. In my readings, the fear of losing one's soul is quite common, particularly among those who hold strong religious convictions or who have done a lot of Bible study.

"Quite often the authors of these books refer back to earlier times when certain members of the population, usually ones in religious orders, underwent what were perceived as 'attacks' by demons known as incubi and succubi. The succubi were said to be female demons who preyed upon religious men such as monks and priests, entering their monastery cells in the middle of the night and indulging in sexual intercourse with them for the purpose of 'stealing their soul.' Incubi were the male equivalent of succubi, who 'stole the souls' of females, usually nuns, in the same way.

"Now," Paco continued, "the theory put forward in these books is that perhaps those visitations by succubi and incubi were really ET-encounter experiences dressed up by the superstitious mindset of medieval times as 'attacks by demons,' because the basic scenario is so similar. They suggest that back then, these contactees had their minds so steeped in superstition and religious dogma that they perceived ETs as being demons, whereas now that humankind has become more sophisticated and technologically minded, we can see the encounter experience for what it really is, that is, visitation by ETs.

"This theory is fine, and probably quite correct, except that they then go on to surmise that perhaps modern ET visitation really does involve an attempt to steal peoples' souls, and that the medieval monks and nuns had it right after all and weren't just imagining things. However," he went on, "all this says to me is that in reality, humankind has *not* progressed very much since then — not on a spiritual level anyway. Sure, we may have all our wonderful technology, and science may have replaced religion as the leading light in modern society, but deep down on the subconscious level humans are still like frightened and immature children, scared stiff of anything that goes bump in the night, and trapped within this state of fear and disempowerment. Perhaps the Greys are right when they say that Earth humans are only on the very first rung of the Human Ladder, and that in order to reach the next level in our evolution we must overcome fear and learn to trust."

Maddie frowned in puzzlement. "The Human Ladder? What the heck is that?"

"Paco looked at the two of us rolling his eyes and Kaz said, "Oh, boy. We better get some more coffee for this."

After we settled down again, Paco toasted me with his coffee cup and said, "This is your area, Ali. Go ahead."

"Okay," I said, settling in. "It's a term used by the Greys for the path of evolution taken by all human species through ascending energy frequencies of the universe. As we explained last time, our journey does begin in the animal kingdom, so Darwin's theory of evolution is partly correct, but there's much more to it than that, because, as we said, the soul is involved as well.

"When the time comes for us to evolve from the animal kingdom into the human kingdom, outside help is required, because at this point we move past the 'animal instinct' level and into the 'mind' level of developing reasoning power. It's here that the creation story of Genesis comes into the picture, because this is the stage of our evolution where outside assistance is needed to awaken us to a conscious awareness of the fact that we are a soul — a spiritual being inhabiting a physical form of flesh and blood rather than just a physical body and nothing more.

"In fact," I continued, "recent genetic research has actually proven that some sort of outside intervention occurred in the evolution of Man — that Earth humans have not simply evolved straight out of the animal kingdom. It's been discovered that 223 human genes lack the required forerunners in our supposed evolutionary background. These extra genes are completely missing in the invertebrate stage and have not been acquired through gradual evolution along a straight line, but rather have been added as a 'sideways insertion' of genetic material. Also, these 223 genes make up two-thirds of the difference between chimpanzees and Man, and they include important psychological functions. In other words, science has now proven that we did not simply evolve naturally from the apes.

"As members of the human kingdom," I explained, "our lesson is to learn to use our mind's reasoning power with wisdom, compassion, and most especially free will, which is an intrinsic part of our ability to reason. This is an important learning experience that eventually enables us to make use of more and more of our mind. As we evolve up the Ladder, we gradually focus less on physical aspects of our being and more on mind aspects.

"Once we've mastered all the lessons of the mind, which mainly involve using our gift of free will wisely and compassionately at all times, we are then able to link consciously and mindfully with our inner God Spark. This in turn gives us the inner strength, trust and love to overcome all fear, and we are then ready to move onwards and upwards to the next stages of evolution. These are the levels some people think of as the devic and angelic kingdoms, where the ones known as Greys and Angels are situated in the scheme of things. The Angels are known as the workers of God, or Oneness, and the Greys are their assistants. All of them are 'Guardians.'

"The Guardians have evolved from the human species of many different planets and have mastered a much greater part of their mind than we have. This is why they can do such seemingly magical and mystical things as appearing and disappearing at will, and walking or floating through closed doors, windows and walls. These are not physical abilities but rather mind abilities, which we will all master eventually as we evolve further up the Human Ladder. Why, there are even humans here on Earth who can do some of these seemingly magical things. Like those really advanced Eastern adepts who have dedicated many lives to mastering their mind, which is what is meant by the expression 'mind over matter.'

"The ones we know as Angels," I continued, "are on the very highest rungs of the Human Ladder. They have mastered and expanded their minds to such a high level that they neither need nor desire physical bodies any more. They are just pure mind/spirit. If they do require a physical form to carry out certain aspects of their work, as, for example, to appear to someone on Earth, they can create an appropriate container for themselves, but their natural state of being is not physical.

"As we evolve upwards through the Human Ladder, we progress from level one, to level two, and so on, up to level ten. The Greys refer to these steps as 'galactic levels,' but they are not galaxies or any 'places' as such — they are simply states of mind, or states of conscious awareness. Remember what I was saying before about humans having three aspects — physical body, spiritual mind and universal soul? Well, mind/spirit is the bridge between body and soul.

"As our mind evolves through the ascending 'galactic levels' of the universe, our consciousness gradually becomes more and more unlimited, expansive and omniscient as it synchronizes more closely in resonance with the soul essence — the God-part of us. This is the whole point of the need to break down the barrier of fear, because only fear limits the mind's potential. Human evolution is expansion of mind/conscious awareness — nothing more and nothing less."

"But Ali," Maddie interjected, "you speak of mind expansion being what human evolution is all about, but surely brainpower has nothing to do with how spiritual you are. I've met people without much education at all, and they're really good people, and then there are others who seem to know everything and are very clever, but to put it politely, they're real creeps, nasty, cruel, cynical and sarcastic, so I don't see how developing our mind necessarily makes us better or more evolved people."

"Okay, Maddie," I replied, glad she'd brought this point up, "I'm not talking here about brain but rather about mind and intuition. It's not about knowing facts and figures, but all about inner knowing and opening up on a conscious level to other finer dimensions, states of being and higher levels of awareness. Sometimes having lots of brainpower can actually be a blockage to deep inner knowing, because a person can potentially get too caught up in how knowledgeable he or she is, which in turn can lead to an egotistical outlook, and a belief that they 'know everything already' and so do not need to look deeper within self."

"Yes," she replied thoughtfully, "I know what you mean. I have met people like that. Okay then, another question: What galactic level is Earth on?"

"Planet Earth has been at level one," I answered, "which simply means most people here can consciously access about 10% of their potential mind power. Earth is now in the process of stepping up to galactic level two, so future generations will be able to tap into *20%* of their potential mind power, which involves extra DNA being activated. The process is both physical *and* spiritual, hence the genetic work being carried out by the ETs on the physical aspect of our being, and the cleansing and healing work being done on the mind/spirit level to help Earth humans pass through the 'fires of purgatory' in order to grow and evolve spiritually. This is, as we said before, not an easy process for any planetary culture to go through, and that's why we aren't just abandoned and left to do it all on our own. Higher help is provided.

"What is really important to understand here, Maddie," I continued, "is that we are all One. The whole universe is like one big family that is all part of God, or what ETs call The One, or Source. We are not separate — humans, Greys, Angels, etc. — we are all One. We don't all follow separate evolutionary paths. Greys have been human, Angels have been Greys. We all follow the same path back home to Oneness."

"Well, Ali," Maddie replied thoughtfully, "everything you say certainly does make a lot of sense, especially about evolution being just as much to do with soul as with the physical part of us, but there's something else that I still don't quite understand. Why is Kate suddenly brilliant at math? And why are the ETs targeting children so much? I mean to say, nearly all children are scared of the dark, or of being left alone at night, so why don't the ETs wait until they're older and more able to handle such intrusions?"

"Okay, Maddie," I answered, "that's a really good question, but the answer is quite simple. Children are already more open to the unseen worlds, so often it's easier to reach them. Since Planet Earth is stepping up to galactic level two, the children who've been born since the 1980s are the future generation, which is why they in particular are being exposed to greater learning opportunities that expand consciousness. These special classes... Kaz," I said, turning to her, "do you want to talk about this side of things?"

"Yes, well, I've certainly come to a deeper understanding of this aspect of contact. My daughter Kira has less fear and more conscious recall than Ben, and she quite often wakes in the morning with memories of having taken part in classes up on the disc that she refers to as 'children's circles.' As she's explained to me, these classes are conducted by the gray Guardian Teachers to open children up to deeper layers of their psyche, which includes teaching them to work with life-force energy. A lot of what they do in these classes revolves around learning to use their mind to influence energy, and so they're taught things like how to levitate small objects such as brightly colored balls and blocks with nothing but the power of their mind.

"These lessons prepare them for this level-two stage that Earth is now moving in to, and also to help them begin thinking of themselves as citizens of the universe. If we're going to survive in the future as a planetary culture, then it's vital that children learn now, about themselves and about their true relationship to the rest of creation, as well as learning to honor and respect our Mother Earth. After all, they *are* our future, and the health and wellbeing of our planet will be in their hands — that is, if there's anything left of it for them.

"The special ability Kate has acquired in math is simply because she's gaining access to more of her brain power as more of her conscious awareness opens up, which is what the Star Children are all about. Most don't go on board the disc in physical form to attend these classes. It's the mind/spirit part of their being that is taken while the physical body remains behind in its bed. That's why Kate felt a sensation of something being sucked, or drawn out of her body. Her ET visitor was simply helping her out of her body so he could take her to class. Once the class is finished she's then returned to her body safe and sound."

"So what should she do the next time this happens?"

"What she really needs is to have all this explained to her so she understands on the conscious level." Kaz replied. "I can do that if you like, because having a similar child of my own I am an *expert* by now with handling such things. I've sure had enough practice helping mine over the last couple of years! Ben is still a bit too young to understand everything, so at this stage all I can do is reassure him that I'm there for him, and help him deal with the fear aspect, but Kate, like my Kira, is old enough to handle more fully conscious understanding of the situation, so lines of communication can be opened up. Once she knows on a conscious level what's going on and that there's nothing to be scared of, then she can do as Ali suggested and try to communicate with her visitor. Is the one who comes for her tall or short by the way?"

"Short I think. Sometimes there's a tall one too, but it's mostly a little one she sees."

"That would be a worker, or helper, whereas the tall one would be an Elder. Some of the workers have more difficulty communicating with Earth humans because they're younger and not as experienced in interdimensional communication as the Elder Teachers. She needs to try to stay as calm as she can otherwise he'll have an awful time both hearing and communicating with her. Because of the level of communication that Ali and I have managed to access with 'upstairs' over the years, we might even be able to get some more details on what's going on."

"Oh, wow, *really*? Can you do that?"

"Maddie, believe me," I chuckled, "if you want details, you can depend upon Kaz! She's a Virgo, and as she said, she's an absolute *expert* on extracting answers. Even eight-foot-tall Guardian Teachers run and hide when they see her coming towards them, fully armed with questions, and please, don't worry — I can assure you Kate is quite safe and in good hands up there. My Teacher used to do exactly the same thing with me when I was a child of Kate's age going on the disc. He always came to help me out of my body, then he made sure I got back in safely afterwards, and he even waited with me until I managed to fall asleep again. The Guardians love and value the children they're working with, and care for them as much as any human parent."

I was pleased to see that Maddie now looked a lot happier and more relaxed. I knew very well that there would be many more questions for us to answer in the weeks and months ahead, but I also felt that the worst was over. Next time I was on the disc I would make a point of checking things out for Kate and Maddie. I had a suspicion of who the 'visitor' was, but only time would tell.

40 ▶ SYMBOLS

"All right, what have you done with it?"

"Done with what? What are you talking about?"

"The parish newsletter. I had it in a text file, and now it's completely disappeared, off into the cosmos, all 10 pages of it."

"Oh, is that what it was? Whoops — sorry!"

"Ali, for heaven's sake, how the hell did you manage that? What did you do? Try to defrag the computer or something?"

"Well, there was so much stuff in there, I mean to say, the poor thing. It's a wonder it doesn't just up and leave, or at least go out on strike as ours do sometimes on the disc. I thought I'd clean it out and give it a bit of breathing space."

"But it's a *computer* for goodness sake!"

"Now, now, Paco, mechanical things have feelings too, you know. Look at our discs. If you connect with something like that all the time, it becomes imbued with some of your own energy. After all, that's how our discs operate, and our computers too. Why, one of them even swore at me the other night. Our computers have minds of their own — not like these primitive ones down here that keep asking confusing questions and presenting you with silly options. No wonder I get in a muddle with that one of yours. It just will not think for itself. But even so, can't you feel a connection with it each time you use it? I certainly can."

"Ali…"

"What?"

"You are seriously weird."

"You know what, Paco?"

"What?"

"I really don't care — I just wanted to clean it up, but sorry about deleting your newsletter. I'll be happy to type it back in for you if you tell me what to put in. Hey, I could even add some bits and pieces of my own to liven it up, because it does tend to be rather boring. Ah, I know what it needs — a few jokes. How about the one about the man who drops his caramel candy in the cinema, and spends ages scrabbling around on the floor trying to find it, much to the annoyance of everybody sitting near him?"

"I know I'll regret asking, but *why* does he spend ages scrabbling about on the floor for his caramel? Why doesn't he just leave it and get another one out of the packet?"

"Because his *teeth* are in it!"

"Oh, God," Paco raised his eyes to heaven, "please spare us from all ET humor. And never mind, I'll do the newsletter *myself*. But I'll tell you what you can do for me to make up for losing the file. I get two hours from you to answer any of my questions."

"Well, I guess that's the least I can do. So, now or later?"

"Now, or you may not pay your debt."

"Okay, okay — shoot."

Paco settled in and I knew he would fill his two hours. "You mentioned something a while back about the significance of the seven colors of the spectrum. You said once that your lesson in this life has been about the throat chakra, and that you had to learn to communicate clearly and in a creative and positive way in your diplomatic and ambassadorial role here on Earth on behalf of the Guardians, hence you work with blue. I also understand that Kaz needed to clear and balance her solar plexus, to build her self-empowerment to carry out this work as well, so her color is yellow. What about the other chakras and their associated colors? What do they mean?"

"Okay, then, let's start at the lowest frequency, the base chakra, whose color is red, the slowest color vibration still visible to humans on the electromagnetic scale. The base chakra deals with maintaining a healthy physical connection as a human being to your Mother Earth. It's also about keeping your emotions grounded and under control so you don't 'fly off the handle' over the slightest thing. Metaphysically it's about keeping your energy well grounded, particularly if you're involved in spiritual work of any sort — in other words, not being too much of an 'airhead.'

"The next one up is the sacral chakra, color orange. On the physical level this one is about sexuality and reproduction, but on the metaphysical level it's all about creativity and maintaining your inner child. This is the one that many down here have problems with. When you lose touch with your inner child, you lose your spiritual connection, and sense of wonder and 'magic.' This then manifests in cynical, egotistical and pompous behavior. This imbalance is affecting many Earth children at younger and younger ages, which is a great pity and a major block to soul growth.

"The color for the solar plexus is yellow, and this chakra balances your sense of status in relationship to others, your freedom and your authority. On the metaphysical level it's the seat of self-worth and self-empowerment and so is connected with spiritual protection, which must always come from within to be truly effective.

"The green of the heart chakra is about maintaining a healthy balance between the chakras below it, which deal more with physicality and lower self, and the higher chakras, which relate to mind, spirit and higher self. Physically, it governs the circulation of blood and anchors life-force energy. Metaphysically, it's about unconditional love, and the ability to freely express that love towards self and others. Spiritual transformation is dependent upon healing and balancing the heart chakra.

"This is closely linked to the blue of the throat chakra, which is about having the inner ability to feel and acknowledge your truth, and the courage to physically express it in a positive, healing and loving way.

"The brow chakra is indigo, and represents clear thinking and intuition, inner sensitivity and clairvoyance — inner sight and insight. The crown chakra color is violet, and connects you to your higher self and Oneness. Your cosmic telephone line, in other words. The violet color should be bright, clear and sparkling. A dull purple indicates confusion."

"Okay, then, Ali Cat, what about numbers? You've also spoken of certain numbers that are important in ET contact, for example, the three knocks often heard by experiencers of contact with the Guardians. Can you please explain a bit more about that? I know the numbers nine and 13 are also significant, so what's that all about?"

"Yes, you're right! Just as colors are symbolic and very powerful, so are numbers. The number three, and also the triangle symbol we often display, represents creation, rebirth and balance, as well as completion — body, mind and spirit in perfect balance. The number nine is symbolic of evolution, and 13 represents transformation. This is the symbolism behind Jesus and the twelve apostles, as well as the Medicine Buddha and the 12 Yaksha Generals, who are sort of nature spirits who act as assistants to the Buddha. In both these instances, it's the thirteenth one, Jesus and Buddha, who's the transformative aspect of the group as a whole, taking it to a higher energy frequency."

"Oh, I like that. So what does six mean?"

"Six represents reflection, meditation and connectedness in order to gain clarity on self and one's life path."

"And seven?"

"Yes, that's a big one! Seven is all about healing and balancing the seven main chakras of the energy system, thus we have the seven colors of the spectrum and the seven notes in a musical scale, each corresponding to one of the seven chakras. The seven sacraments of the church are also based on this concept, but the 'energy' meaning behind them has been lost to a certain extent."

"What do you mean?"

"Well, the seven sacraments were originally based on seven 'keys' which were introduced on Planet Earth to assist humans in their quest for self realization. These were special processes for people to pass through, which were specifically designed to initiate changes in the energy patterns of the chakras. They were sort of 'keys' to tune and turn up the vibrational frequency and to introduce a higher and more balanced energy flow through the seven main chakra points. In this way, the journey of a human back to the unconditional love of Source was made a little easier and quicker to negotiate. In fact, it is very much like the Reiki attunement process.

"This is why Reiki should really be taught in four rather than three stages. There are four attunements at Level One, and one attunement at each of the next two traditional Levels, which makes a total of six altogether. To make up seven attunements, another Level is required to complete the process up to so-called 'Master,' or Teacher Level, which completes the whole process.

"The seven sacraments retained by the church are an echo — a soul memory — of more ancient 'rites of passage' brought to Planet Earth from elsewhere eons ago. Because of the rift that now exists between religion and science, the understanding of the energy component behind them has largely been lost. People are aware of something significant in them, but they don't quite know why. Paco, tell me, just out of curiosity, how does the Church define a Sacrament?"

"The sacraments are defined as being outward and visible signs of an inward and invisible grace."

"Ah, okay — so how is 'grace' defined?"

"Grace," he explained, "is God's gratuitous love bestowed upon humankind. It's a process which allows us to commune more closely with God."

"Oh, wow! There you go! *Exactly* what I said only in slightly different words! The parallels never cease to amaze me. The seven sacraments are an outer sign of an inner process — an inner process that serves to raise the vibrational frequency of a soul to a higher octave, bringing it closer to the frequency of Source. In other words, it's a process that enables a soul to commune, or resonate energetically, more closely with God. Whatever terminology we use, it all comes back to the same thing — transmutation and transformation of energy to higher frequencies!

"Okay, now, let me see if I can remember my catechism from school — the seven sacraments of the Catholic Church are: baptism, confirmation, holy communion, matrimony, holy orders and extreme unction, or anointing of the sick and dying, right?"

"Almost, but that's only six."

"Oh — hang on — let me think — ah, yes, absolution! Although these days it's known as reconciliation, isn't it? Am I right?"

"Yes, and your lapse of memory goes to show how often you partake of them, doesn't it, Ali Cat? And most especially that one! It's been years and years, hasn't it? In fact, *decades*!"

"Yes, well, I have other ways and means. Now where was I?"

"The energy behind them."

"Ah, yes! Okay then, first up is baptism. The concept of what the Church calls 'original sin' has actually been rather misinterpreted. This concept first came into being after the event recalled in the planetary consciousness as 'Noah's Flood.' Those who survived this major inundation perceived it as being God's punishment on humankind for the 'original sin' of falling back into mating with members of the animal kingdom from which the human race had evolved. I believe this return to bestiality is even spoken of in the Bible."

"Yes, it is."

"Well, the soul memory of humanity recalls the flood as a mass cleansing of 'sin' by water, thus the rite of baptism was adopted, as a re-enactment of this event. Unfortunately, the idea of the 'original sin' of humankind has been exploited to the hilt by the Controllers as a way of promoting a serious guilt complex and disempowering process in Earth humans.

"Also, laying the blame on poor old 'Eve' has been their cunning way of promoting and maintaining a domineering and often aggressive patriarchal system on Earth. Adam and Eve's 'knowing' had nothing whatsoever to do with a forbidden sexual liaison between them, but rather was about reasoning power and free will being bestowed on a newly developed humanoid species before they were spiritually mature enough to handle it. This fact has been conveniently forgotten or quietly swept 'under the carpet,' so to speak.

"However, despite all of this misunderstanding surrounding it, the rite of baptism is still very relevant in that it can be regarded as a symbolic cleansing and clearing of karma from the past life — a 'washing away' of the past by giving the newly incarnated spirit a boost in its vibrational frequency. In each life we hopefully attain a higher level of vibrational frequency until eventually we are able to fully synchronize and meld back into that highest energy frequency we know as Source, or God.

"The very act of raising our frequency rates assists in the clearing and dissipation of negative karma. It burns and purges away the negativity, and so a baptismal ceremony of some sort achieves this aim. Even though the soul is manifesting physically in the body of a newborn, in the greater reality it's ageless and fully cognizant of where it is, where it's been, and where it's going, and it is therefore perfectly able to take advantage of any boost to its energy frequency."

"You know, Ali. I really do appreciate this deeper understanding that you've opened me up to in all of this."

"Well, it certainly has given you a wider perspective, that's for sure!" I grinned. "Now, the next one, the sacrament of confirmation, has the effect of giving the frequency rate a further boost as the reincarnated soul begins its journey into adulthood. This sacrament is usually administered around the age of puberty, and has its counterpart in many cultures, all being equally beneficial in initiating the movement of energy to higher octaves. These rites of passage signify the energy shift from childhood to adulthood, and are an important and integral part of the maturing process. It's a great pity that this rite has been mostly neglected in modern society, because it plays a major psychological role in spiritual growth. It's the intrinsic sense of 'sacredness' within the rite that provides the impetus to get the energy moving in the right direction, to higher levels. It also signifies that the recipient has now reached a mature enough age to begin consciously choosing love over fear."

"What do you mean by that?" Paco asked. "Are you referring to the conscious free-will choices between right and wrong on which evolution depends?"

"Yes, the correct or incorrect application of free will and reasoning power in other words."

"Right, okay. Now what about the sacrament of holy communion? What is your Guardian interpretation of that?"

"The sacrament of holy communion, in which the recipient partakes of the 'body and blood' of Christ — the essence of Christ — is symbolic of the transmutation of energy to the level of Christ, or Divine Consciousness within. In reuniting with our 'inner Christ,' or higher self, we become an intrinsic part of Divine Consciousness, which is the ultimate goal of all sentient beings throughout the universe. Here I'm using Christian terminology, but it's equally applicable to all, and could just as correctly be referred to as our 'inner Buddha,' 'Krishna,' or whatever belief system you follow.

"The sacrament of penance, absolution or reconciliation also assists a soul to dissipate negative karma through the raising of one's energy frequency, which automatically comes about when one sincerely seeks forgiveness and atonement. If true repentance is in the heart, the very act of speaking out, confiding and confessing to another is part and parcel of the atonement process. It's a way of easing and releasing the guilt that could potentially continue to hold the soul back, and can be of enormous benefit in providing impersonal but caring and hopefully non-judgmental support and advice to ensure the mistake will not occur again. The absolution and reconciliation process is an important step in releasing and healing guilt and karma.

"The next one, matrimony, is one of the most beneficial sacraments for spiritual growth. There's a Buddhist saying that marriage provides the best temple training of all for a monk! In the greater reality of the soul there is no polarization of genders, male and female. This is why we may reincarnate into either gender, and in fact this is most important, to provide a sense of empathy and balance.

"A well-known figure in the field of psychoanalysis once put forward the concept of the anima and animus. These were terms he used to designate the female and male polarities contained within every soul. They're the yin and yang of Eastern philosophy and every human being is made up of both. In a life where the soul happens to be manifesting into physical form through a male body, the animus — the male half of the psyche — is dominant and the female half — the anima — is recessive. In the case of a soul expressing through a female body it's the other way around.

"Now every human being manifesting in physical form is instinctively seeking a return to the wholeness of soul, but in order to find that state of wholeness within self, one must integrate the two halves of the psyche, thus a male seeks to unite with his female half, his anima, and a female with her male animus. This inner part of our being is manifested into physicality through the life partner we choose. We tend to attract to ourselves partners who express most clearly certain aspects of our anima or animus, thus the sacrament of matrimony between male and female symbolizes the uniting of the anima and animus — the two halves of the soul — back into integrated wholeness and oneness.

"The word 'wholing' is the origin of the word 'healing,' so the energies generated by the Sacrament of Matrimony assist in the wholing, or healing of the soul. This is why much conscious work and dedication needs to be applied to a marriage. In marriage you do not complete each other — you complete *yourself!* By extending understanding, love and compassion to your partner in marriage, you are, in turn, extending that same understanding, love and compassion to a part of yourself. The same applies if you hurt or betray your partner. The end result is hurt and betrayal to yourself.

"This is why some marriages prove to be so difficult, when two people come together to heal on deep levels of the psyche. Healing is not always an easy or pleasant process, and it requires deep commitment, love, respect, compassion, and self-discipline from both partners. If one or both refuse to cooperate, then the healing cannot take place.

"The transmutation of energy to higher frequencies, which is an intrinsic part of the sacrament of matrimony, is why, no matter how undisciplined and 'free' society becomes, there will always be souls who will wish to commit to some form of marriage through a sacred ceremony of some sort. This is not to say that healing doesn't take place within all human relationships, but it's through the sacred commitment of the Sacrament that true integration on the soul level occurs more readily.

"Even the sexual act between male and female is symbolic of two coming together in Oneness on all levels. The essential difference between human and animal is symbolized in sexual union. Unlike animals, humans generally mate face to face, with bodies touching at sacral, heart and brow chakra points, thus the union becomes a spiritual melding as well as physical.

"Those who indulge in multiple relationships are ones who are either trying to heal multiple facets of their own psyche, or else are dodging the issue. In the latter case the relationships are usually fleeting, with as little commitment as possible, for these souls are running away from self. Marriage is the ultimate commitment to facing up to and healing self."

"But what about folks like me? Are we missing out?"

"Yes and no, let's take a look at Holy Orders — priests, nuns and monks."

"Whoa! This is where I come under the microscope, isn't it? A little respect here please, Ali Cat!"

"Of course, Paco, as always! Now then, in all belief systems there are certain individuals who've undergone further initiatory processes in order to raise their own energy frequency to a level where they in turn can help others do the same. It's very similar to Teacher level in Reiki and also in other Eastern practices, which require initiations from a Master, or Teacher, for aspirants to reach certain levels within the system. In ancient times, those who took on a priestly role were very highly evolved souls, self-realized and totally integrated, not needing to link with their 'other half' outside of themselves. This is actually where the root of priestly celibacy lies.

"As you know, Paco, this Sacrament, or initiation, carries a deep responsibility to live your own life in a state of unconditional love, both as an example to others, and also to ensure that your own energy frequency is held in as high a state as possible, untainted by fear in all its various forms."

"Yes, that does make a lot of sense," said Paco, "but unfortunately I have to admit that there are some serving in the Priesthood who *haven't* yet reached these more spiritually integrated levels, and who really should still be working their way through the healing and wholing process involved in matrimony."

"Well of course you know what the problem is here, don't you? In olden times only those who were highly evolved and totally integrated could be chosen for a priestly role, whereas now such things are not so clearly understood, so you get people who are not necessarily spiritually ready. These are ones who are running away from certain aspects of their own inner self, and refusing to look at or heal these unresolved issues, and so they reject the wholing process of linking with another soul through the Sacrament of Marriage.

"The vow of celibacy in the Priesthood legitimizes this fear of looking within, thus providing a perfect excuse to avoid the whole issue of healing this inner self. It also places them in a position of power and authority over others, which in turn further feeds their fear-based ego."

"And that's a sad state of affairs. I wish the Pope would do something about this."

"Me, too, but let's not hold our breaths. The last of the seven sacraments, extreme unction, or anointing of the sick," I continued, "is administered to a person who's very ill or else preparing for the final rite of passage — death. Its function is to raise the energy frequency to the highest, most balanced and harmonized level possible in order to assist in the healing process, or else to ensure that the spirit gets maximum assistance in stepping out of its physical container to move on to where it's supposed to be.

"The root of all illness is disharmony and imbalance within the energy system, and so, because of its harmonizing and leavening effect on the energy body, this Sacrament can sometimes bring about a spontaneous healing of the condition that was causing the illness. In this way, sometimes a dying person can fully recover after receiving this Sacrament."

"Funny you should say that!" Paco commented. "I've actually had that happen in a couple of instances when I've administered the Last Rites to a dying person. They've suddenly and inexplicably recovered. I didn't really think it was me, but it didn't seem like just a sheer coincidence either.

"But Ali," he went on, "it's all very well the sacraments being a tool to raise a person's vibrational frequency, but what about for those who aren't Catholic and don't have access to the sacraments?"

"It really doesn't matter what belief system or path you follow. Any type of spiritual practice will lead you back to Source, as long as it helps you make the right choice of love over fear in order to integrate and heal your inner self. As I've said before, evolution in the human kingdom is all about making free-will choices, and these choices make the difference in your life between balance, harmony and inner connection, or imbalance, disharmony and disconnection, which ultimately leads to chaos.

"The whole agenda of the Controllers is to disconnect humans from their higher selves in order to keep them disempowered. In this way the Controllers remain firmly in charge on Earth. Peoples' only hope is to 'wake up,' but this in itself is a free-will choice — humans must consciously choose, on a personal and individual basis. This is why most of our contact is carried out this way — personally and individually rather than through mass contact and sightings of discs.

"We're trying to help, but you must meet us half way. Earth humans desperately need to reconnect with their higher consciousness, and until they do, they'll remain trapped in a disempowered state of illusion. This is why there seems to be two or more different realities operating on Earth. You create your own reality with your mind, and there are those whose minds are so closed in and limited that they just can't see past the ends of their noses. Then there are others who can see to far horizons. But the bottom line is, humans must 'wake up' consciously. If you die in an unconscious state, as most do, then you are reborn in an unconscious state."

"But Ali, it's all very well for you Guardians who already have expanded consciousness! How do Earth humans regain their conscious empowerment?"

"Quite simply, as a matter of fact, by being willing and able to see through the insidious control exercised over your minds through such avenues as the media, advertising, materialism and consumerism, 'fashion,' the internet, movies, magazines, sports, etc. I could go on and on! On Planet Earth it seems never-ending! If people can't, or won't do this, then chaos will reign in the end. In fact you can see it happening right now, with stress levels rising dramatically and many people spinning out of control in their lives."

"You're right enough there, Ali Cat! So how do we overcome this?"

"What's really important, particularly at this time of major energy shifts going on down here on Earth, which are affecting people far more than is generally realized, balance must be maintained. As a human species moves to higher evolutionary levels, the spiritual part of each being begins to vibrate at a higher, finer frequency. When this happens, the physical aspect must slow down to maintain balance between the two, otherwise your life-span will shorten. Everything will get faster and faster, as human speech is now doing, if you haven't noticed, until everything just spins wildly out of control.

"What's happening on Earth is that peoples' spiritual frequency is speeding up in synchronization with the planet, but they haven't learned how to balance and deepen their frequency rate on the physical level. This is why spiritual practices such as meditation and quiet, inner reflection are so important for humanity at this time."

"Ah, yes, that makes *so* much sense when looked at in that light!" said Paco. "That's why it's so calming to be in the presence of your people and most especially the Elders. On the other hand, it's also why it's so calming to be in a quiet church, or out in Nature."

"Oh, my yes, Nature is very calming. Earth humans need to spend much more time in it."

"However," Paco continued, "there's a very tangible feeling of depth and calmness about all of you compared to many Earth humans, who always seem to be in a state of chaos, noise and chatter, although there are some here who have this calm depth to them as well."

"Absolutely!" I agreed, "But you'll find that they're the ones who meditate regularly and who put time aside for inner reflection."

"That is *so* interesting!" said Paco. "And it does make a lot of sense that it's up to each individual as to whether they're prepared to put time into cultivating the deeper, spiritual aspects of their being or whether they spend their time running themselves ragged trying to accumulate material wealth and possessions. This solely materialistic approach to life brings about a state of imbalance, because the fear-engendered, perceived need for more and more in the way of acquisitions becomes their whole reason for existence, rather than the pursuit of deeper spiritual awakening and unfoldment. I see this all the time."

"Precisely! Because the more connected you become to things outside of yourself in the way of material possessions, the more *dis*connected you become from self! If humans could only open up to the multidimensional nature of their being, and stop identifying solely with the demands of the physical body, they would see that this is the key to transformation into higher levels of reality."

"That's all fine and good, Ali Cat, but remember how you're always carrying on about the need to stay well-grounded. Now, from what I've observed, there are some who disconnect from physicality too much, wanting to spend their whole lives in meditation, getting annoyed by the normal everyday demands of their body and taking things to extremes with fasting, self-denial and basically copping out of life.

"After all, our physical body is an amazing and miraculous creation given to us by God, and it is a valuable vehicle which provides us with all the many learning opportunities of physical form. And really, the bottom line is, if we didn't have physical lessons to learn, then we wouldn't be here, would we?"

"Yes, Paco, you're absolutely right! And that's why I love having you around — you keep *me* so well grounded! What people tend to forget is that the physical container is a 'temple' for the soul, which should be loved, respected, cared for and honored as such. "Tuning in to your inner self in order to attain self realization includes tuning in with sensitivity to the needs of the physical body, and maintaining it at optimum level. This really is what 'oneness' is all about on Planet Earth — nurturing body, mind and spirit equally, and integrating all three aspects of your being. Neglecting or trying to disown your physical aspect will eventually bring about a state of imbalance in the other two areas.

"Now then...," I took a deep breath, at the same time stretching my arms above my head and managing to produce a satisfying crack in my knuckles, "...is that enough information to keep you happy and to balance the karmic debt incurred for the loss of your parish newsletter?"

"Well, it would've been, but you still have 10 more minutes. Besides, you know that knuckle cracks give me the shivers, so you aren't getting off."

"Boy, you're tough."

"It's a karmic lesson, dear sister. Maybe next time you'll remember not to mess with people's files. Okay, you said something earlier about how your discs operate, and also the computers on your discs — that they're able to think for themselves. I've seen your on-board computers, and they don't look all that different from ours, and I can't see that your technology is all that far ahead of ours, so what do you mean? I remember you mentioning before about the discs being living, sentient organisms."

"Hey, Paco, that is a good question. Maybe I should crack my knuckles more often to inspire you. This is actually a really important point that researchers down here need to look at if they are to properly understand interplanetary technology. Technologically speaking, we're really not that far ahead of Planet Earth, and in fact your present-day computer technology was back-engineered from our crashed discs. The main difference, and Earth technology is beginning to touch on this now, is that our technology and consciousness work together, hand in hand as it were, with consciousness-enhanced technology and technologically enhanced consciousness. Some computer technology on Earth is moving into this area, with direct brain inter-action between machine and operator, but what needs to be clearly understood is that *all* matter is imbued with consciousness at the molecular level. We have learned how to tap into that consciousness and to enhance it with our own.

"This is where we're way ahead of Earth humans, but it's more a matter of spiritual evolution rather than technological evolution. This is part of what I'm talking about in connection with those on higher levels of the Human Ladder having access to broader and deeper layers of conscious awareness. It's all about expansion of consciousness, which in turn enables us to tap into other areas of consciousness that Earth humans can only dream of at this stage in their development. But given the potentials that open up at this level, and the responsibilities involved, one cannot reach it without first attaining a high degree of spiritual maturity."

"What do you mean?"

"All of our technology, right from the tiniest implants up to the giant Motherships," I explained, "has a degree of consciousness that links us together in Oneness. Because of this energy connection, we possess technology that assists us with seemingly miraculous abilities such as telepathy, levitation, bi-location, etc. Some of our more evolved Elders are able to do these things unassisted, but our technology enables everyone to carry out such tasks with ease and efficiency. Needless to say, this carries with it a very deep level of moral and ethical responsibility.

"On a level-one planet like Earth, you tend to rely totally on technology, with consciousness being a bit of a hit-or-miss affair. At our level of evolution on the Human Ladder, we successfully combine technology with consciousness. When you get right up into the angelic realms of levels nine and 10, it is pure consciousness. They don't need technology at all."

"So Ali, what do you mean by consciousness being present at the molecular level of matter? I can understand that concept in a living organism, for example at the cellular level of our bodies, but what about with an inanimate object like a stone or a piece of wood. That really doesn't make sense."

"The problem is that Earth humans generally don't acknowledge the presence of consciousness in anything except what they think of as 'living creatures.' In actual fact, consciousness starts right down as far as the mineral kingdom. Everything on your planet, animal, vegetable and mineral, possesses consciousness, and it is this consciousness at the molecular level that gives form to matter. This is why the molecules forming a stone appear as a stone and not as a lump of wood. The trick is, learning how to tap into that consciousness, and this can only be done by expanding your own consciousness. In other words, *it is your mind that holds the magic key.*"

"Wow, that's so deep my brain is starting to feel water-logged, which is a bit of a worry."

"Bet you don't know the definition of a *real* worry."

"Oh, no — not another Guardian joke coming up I hope! Well, what is it — what *is* the definition of a real worry?"

"Being abducted on board an alien spaceship and finding a copy of *An Idiot's Guide to the Universe* sitting on the control console."

41 ▶ Surveillance Failure

It was turning out to be a very long and extremely difficult night. Zogar, Entil and I had been trying to deal with angry and fearful humans since the beginning of our shift, and this, our sixth 'client,' lay paralyzed on the table in the clinic, absolutely terrified. Again and again we tried to communicate, to penetrate the heavy and all-encompassing cocoon of fear that cut her off from all our efforts. It's even more frustrating for me when I can't bring in my human capability of speech, but up on the disc I simply don't have the necessary anatomical equipment required for it.

Alexander, one of our hybrids, then poked his head around the door. Normally easy-going, happy-go-lucky and always ready for a bit of fun, his expression of intense concern shocked me. "Alarca, Maris wants you in the surveillance room right now! The computers have gone down!"

"*What?* How many?"

"*All* of them! Joseph is there already, and Zogar and Entil had better come too, once our Earthling friend here has been sent home safely. We need all the help we can get, because the situation is critical."

Alexander's brother Joseph was our computer 'whiz kid.' Half Zeta Reticulan and half Earth human, he exhibited the very best of both species, with an extremely sharp mind for technology and five long, slender and very dexterous fingers on each hand that could tackle anything mechanical.

Although he and Alex were full brothers, they were very different from each other. Joseph was physically much more human-looking, except for his eyes, which were abnormally large by Earth human standards. By nature he was intense, quiet, studious and rather introverted. Alex, on the other hand, looked nearly pure Zeta except for a bit more definition in the nose and mouth. Unlike Joseph, he was a happy extrovert, always into mischief and fun, usually at somebody else's expense, particularly Elders, but at the same time he was full of love and good humor. Alex could be counted on to bring a ray of light and hope to the darkest situation, so I knew with a sinking feeling that the problem must be major to throw even him so badly.

"Go on, Alarca, get moving — we won't be long." Zogar was already activating a blue beam of light energy to levitate our human guest off the table so she could be returned home quickly and safely. Then, turning to Alex, he said, "You'd better call Asara and Solarno from their quarters, and Oris, too, if he's on board. And don't forget Ashka and your sister, Angelique — they're both down in the nursery. Oh, my goodness," he added, shaking his head and walking away, "the surveillance computers all down at once! How the heck could *that* happen? Now what do we do?"

These surveillance computers are vital to us because they monitor all the planets in our care, including Earth. Our computers keep a watchful eye on such things as wayward asteroids that could devastate an inhabited planet. And we also watch internal threats to planetary civilizations, such as weapons of mass destruction, particularly when they fall into the hands of unstable individuals or governments. We are not allowed to interfere on every occasion, because we have to abide by the Laws of Karma, but even then we're sometimes able to bend the rules a little to prevent outright disasters.

In my human form on Earth I could recall occasionally reading in the news of a potential tragedy such as a bomb being planted in a busy part of a city, timed to explode at peak hour, but something going wrong so that it detonated half an hour earlier, with few lives lost. That is how we work, along with our angelic friends. We cannot stop all disastrous events, but we often intervene to lessen the impact.

Frequently our discs have also been seen near nuclear installations, and some of Earth's more dangerous weaponry has been neutralized in this way, which is why some down there see us as "evil aliens intent on attacking Earth." We have intervened too in potentially devastating accidents at nuclear sites. The average humans going about their day-to-day business on Planet Earth have no idea of the myriad dangers that threaten their existence on a regular basis, prevented only by Guardian intervention, and we rely on these vital surveillance computers to alert us to the danger.

The seriousness of the situation hit me even harder when I entered the room. My Teacher, Maris, was sitting at the main console looking more worried than I'd ever seen him. Joseph had pulled up a seat beside him, and several others including the two Pleiadians, Asara and Solarno, were leaning over their shoulders looking equally upset and helpless. A number of workers, hybrids, and Elders were busy at other consoles, working feverishly to find the problem.

Many millions of years of evolution have endowed us with almost complete control over our emotions, but that night nearly everyone lost it at one point or another. Even the ancient and usually extremely serene Garnibis, paced up and down looking decidedly shaken, directing huge, pale blue eyes towards the blank screens every so often as if her stare alone could restore them to life.

Finally it was decided that there was no point in everyone being there. We were just getting under each other's feet, which was causing nerves to become even more frayed. Joseph was fairly confident that he'd managed to trace the problem to its source, so now it was time to leave him in peace so he could concentrate on getting the system up and running again as soon as possible; and there was still much work for us all to complete before morning. "Alarca," my Teacher Maris called to me, "please come into my office. There's something I need to discuss with you — a special job that needs to be carried out."

"Damn!" I thought to myself. "Surely with all the computers down, we'd be able to finish work early!"

Picking up telepathically on my rebelliousness, Solarno grinned broadly and winked at me. "Now, now, Alarca, Guardian Workers are supposed to *work* — not fantasize about knocking off early. Only humans are allowed to do that!"

"Right," said my venerable Teacher, seating himself behind the large console that took up a goodly portion of his office space: "I have a project for you, Alarca — a project that requires your special expertise as a Guardian manifesting in human form on Planet Earth in a diplomatic role."

"Oh, dear," I thought to myself, "that sounds ominous." The look he cast in my direction told me he'd picked up on me telepathically, but of course he would've. Sometimes I must think I'm in my human form with a closed off mind.

Ignoring my questionable train of thought, Maris went on, "Alarca, the young worker, Entil, is having a lot of problems with a human child named Kate with whom he is supposed to be working. She is being brought on board for classes in one of our children's circles, but every time he approaches her she still becomes quite hysterical with fear. It's time she began to understand things on a more conscious level, but fear is blocking her so badly that extra help is required.

"Ashka has made contact with her in human form, trying to explain things a little more clearly, and I know you have also met her briefly on a visit to her mother's house, but I feel that if you were to accompany Entil into her room at night, dressed in your Earthling container so she can see the pair of you interacting in a friendly and non-threatening way, she may lose some of her terror. Surely seeing a human being alongside her ET visitor will help to allay her fear."

"But Maris, wouldn't it be better for Ashka to do this? After all, she is a mother in her human form on Earth and therefore much more experienced in relating to and communicating with children than I am. Why can't she do it?"

"Because it is not her job! Her work is to look after the hybrid children here on the disc, and right now we have over a dozen poor little mites that we confiscated from that Earth laboratory last week. Ashka has spent much time matching up DNA samples trying to locate their human mothers so we can bring them here to provide the maternal love they so desperately need. No wonder the poor little things are so listless and lethargic! I do wish these human scientists would stop trying to play God, dabbling and experimenting in areas where they totally lack proper spiritual understanding. Surely they realize human life is more than just physical genetics! I'm sorry, I'm off on a tangent. But no, Ashka has her hands full at the moment. It is up to you."

"Maris, on the subject of trying to get through to these children, what happened with the Russian boy we visited a while back? He was so sick and so scared. Is he any better now?"

"Yes, he is, as a matter of fact, but we only just intervened in time. The Controllers were starting to infiltrate his mind, causing him to fall into trance states during which he would recite all these very complex mathematical and scientific formulas, which of course had everyone around him firmly convinced that he was some sort of miraculous and very advanced 'Star Child.' However, cunningly mixed in with this information some very negative things were also being conveyed through him, including dire warnings of 'evil gray aliens' coming to Earth to interfere with people, which was part of why he was so scared of us.

"After the night you came with me, he started becoming more aware of the difference between the Controller-inspired contact and our genuine contact, and once he began to wake up consciously, we could reach him more easily to heal him on all levels. We placed an implant into his body to help alleviate the lung problem he'd developed, and he's now moved past his fear and is living a normal and much happier life.

"Now, Alarca, back to our difficulties with Kate — it's really just a matter of your helping her to overcome her fear enough to allow Entil to place the palms of his hands on hers, so their heart chakra channels that run down the arms into the hands will reconnect and instantaneously she should feel the love energy between the two of them. It will only take seconds."

And so it was — no refusing an Elder.

Utilizing the blue beam of light energy, Entil and I transported ourselves from the hovering disc down into Kate's bedroom. Using our eyes we paralyzed her as she began to wake up. It took a bit of focused concentration on my part to maintain a human appearance while in this altered astral state, and I hoped that I wasn't looking too wavy around the edges, because the last thing needed was to make her even more scared than she already was.

As her terrified gaze fell upon us, I greeted her in as friendly and non-threatening a way as possible, "Hi Kate! Don't you recognize me? I'm your mom's friend Ali. Please don't be scared — we're not going to hurt you, I promise."

Kate said something, but because Entil and I were in the astral state, we couldn't quite make out her physical speech. Once again, here I was faced with this damned communication issue between the energy fields. I held my hand up. "Hang on, Kate, I can't hear you. You need to think your words clearly to me with your mind. Just concentrate hard on what you want to say and I'll understand. Our communication needs to be telepathic."

The next moment a torrent of jumbled words flooded my mind, almost knocking me backwards with the force of emotional energy behind them. In fact, poor Entil, who was standing slightly behind me, did get knocked backwards, and would have disappeared into the energy portal if I hadn't grabbed his hand and held on. "Kate," I telepathed, "please try to calm down — *please*. I'll lift the paralysis off if you'll just calm down, and no, I won't let him touch you — it's okay, neither of us will come any closer — we'll stay right where we are, but you must try to calm down so we can talk. And by the way, this is Entil, whom you've known for a very long time."

Kate's thoughts took on a semblance of order at the sound of my perfectly normal human speech resounding inside her head. "Ali, is that *really* you? What's going on? How can you be here in my room at night with *him*? What does he want? What do you mean I've *known* him for a very long time? Why won't he leave me alone?"

"Hold on, Kate, hold on! One question at a time! So you do remember me as a friend of your mom's?"

"Oh, yes, Ali, and you're also Kaz's friend, aren't you? Her daughter Kira and I go to the same school, and Kaz told me Kira and Ben both have ET visitors coming to them at night too, and not to be scared, but I can't *help* it — they look so weird." She cast a quick sideways glance at Entil and shuddered.

"Look, Kate, I know he does seem a bit strange, but truly, he won't hurt you. Why don't you try just reaching out and letting him touch your hand — come on, please. I promise nothing bad will happen."

"Wh…what did you say his name is?"

"It's Entil, spelt E-n-t-i-l, and maybe you can't remember, but he used to visit you when you were a very young child."

"And what about the really scary tall one dressed all in black who comes as well? That one is even *worse*!"

"That is Entil's Teacher, Garnibis, who accompanies him sometimes. She's very old and wise, and you have absolutely nothing to fear from her."

"And are you *sure* he won't do anything to me if he touches me? He won't paralyze me again?"

"Kate, I promise, you have my word. Just hold your hands out with palms facing upwards, and try to relax so he can touch you. Believe it or not, he's really sad that you're scared of him. You used to play together when you were little. Go on, just reach out to him."

Trembling slightly, Kate held her hands out towards Entil, and as she did so I instructed him to come forward slowly so as not to frighten her, but he hesitated. "Are you *sure*, Alarca? I don't want to upset her and make things worse." A look of trepidation filled his eyes, and for a moment I thought he was going to cry.

"Go on, Entil," I encouraged him, "it'll be okay." There I was between these two scared beings — talk about an intergalactic ambassador!

With eyes closed tightly, Kate tried to hold her hands steady as Entil reached out towards her and very gently gripped her hands so as to bring the center of his palms against hers.

"That's it, Kate! Try to relax — he won't hurt you. Just see if you can feel the energy passing between his hands and yours."

Frowning in deep concentration, she stayed still and unresponsive for a moment, then her fingers began to close on Entil's hands, as an incredibly strong energy current passed between them. Kate's eyes suddenly opened, and her face lit up with a look of total amazement as recognition dawned, along with an expression of profound joy, and the next moment they were hugging each other like old friends.

"Entil," Kate cried, "of *course* I remember you! You were the one who used to lift me up out of my cot when I was tiny, and take me to play with the other children. We used to have so much fun floating those pretty-colored blocks around the room and making lights turn on and off with our minds. How could I ever have forgotten! And that's what you've been doing again, isn't it? Taking me to classes on the big disc? Now I finally understand why I'm suddenly so smart at math." The look of sheer relief in Entil's eyes said it all, and the next moment they were chatting away telepathically, almost unaware of my presence.

But then Kate turned to me with a frown of puzzlement. "Ali, there are still lots of things I don't understand. Do you mind if I ask you some more questions?"

"Course not, Kate. That's why I'm here tonight, to help sort things out for you, but by the time you wake up tomorrow morning you're not going to remember that I've been here. You'll remember Entil coming, but not me. All that you'll be aware of is that you had a dream about me, but it won't be very clear."

"But why, Ali? Why won't I remember you coming?"

"It's just the way things are Kate. Maybe someday you will, but not quite yet. Now what do you want to ask me?"

"Umm, okay, for a start, how do I get onto the ship from here? One minute I'm in my bed, and the next minute I'm up on the disc. I'm sort of aware of being floated out through the closed windows of my room on this beam of light coming down that both mom and dad have seen. What is that all about? Is it the light that lifts me up?"

"Well, Kate, let me start by asking you a question. Do you study physics at school?"

"Oh, yes, you mean learning all about electricity, atoms, magnetism and stuff like that?"

"Yes, exactly. So do you understand about the composition of seemingly solid physical matter — that it's not really as solid as it appears to be but rather is made up of billions of atoms grouped together to form molecules which are all vibrating at a certain rate?"

"Yes, Ali, I know that. And also that atoms are made up of electrons orbiting around a central nucleus, just like planets orbiting around a sun."

"Correct, and if you think about a solar system, with the vast distances between each of the planets and the sun, you realize that it's really composed of more empty space than solid matter. And believe it or not, the atoms that make up our bodies and everything else around us are exactly the same, so therefore, we ourselves are really composed more of empty space than solid matter."

"Hey, wow, you're *right*! I hadn't thought of that."

"So therefore," I continued, "moving a physical, human body composed of mostly empty space through a seemingly solid closed door or window which in reality is also mostly empty space is not all that difficult providing you can just align the empty spaces with the solid bits, as the ET visitors are able to do when they transport you. Especially if they take you in astral form, because your finer astral or spirit body is a lot more 'widely spaced' than your more solid physical body. To get your astral body through the closed window is like pouring water through a sieve, and it is simply a matter of energy passing through energy. Do you understand what I mean?'

"Mmm, yes, I think so. What you're saying is that because everything is composed of atoms, everything is energy, even though it looks solid. Like, my body is really just all energy, and so is the window."

"Yes, Kate, and the higher energy vibrates, which is simply the continual movement of the electrons around the central nucleus, the finer the substance becomes. This is the difference between your physical body and your astral or spirit body. The astral body vibrates at a higher frequency that the physical body."

Kate's eyes suddenly lit up in understanding: "Ahhh, now I remember being told something about that in class. Our teacher used ice, water and steam as an example of increasing vibrational frequencies in relationship to matter. That's what you're talking about, isn't it?"

"Absolutely! And that's an extremely good example we can relate to in everyday life. This too explains the light beam you asked about. Very high frequency energy manifests as light — in fact it *is* light, and it's the beam of light energy that causes your vibrational frequency to go higher. Your energy frequency synchronizes with the light frequency, so for a little while you become light, and that's how you're transported onto the waiting disc."

All the time I'd been talking to Kate, Entil sat quietly on the side of the bed, allowing her to become re-accustomed to his energy, but now it was his turn to speak up. "So, Kate, perhaps after this you will appreciate the need for the classes you attend on the disc, and will now consciously retain more of what you are taught. Most of the lessons concern energy, because the human species of Earth needs a deeper understanding of this aspect of your reality, and most especially the intrinsic link between science and religion, which of course is learning how to work with energy frequencies at a higher rate in order to meld with the light."

"And," I added, "it is knowledge such as this that ones like you are to bring to Earth, which is why you are being taught so much about how to work consciously with energy, for the evolution of the entire human race depends upon this understanding. This too is why it is vitally important for you to move beyond the fear barrier, so that your mind is no longer blocked and limited but rather open and flexible enough to absorb and retain this sacred knowledge in order to pass it on to others. This high-frequency energy is not only light — it manifests also as love, and to meld with it fully all fear must be purged from your inner being."

Then Entil continued, "A big part of our job is to help you with this process, and now that you have faced your greatest fear in opening up to me, you can see that in reality there's nothing to fear. You now understand that I am not here to 'steal your soul' but to help you unfold and expand into your full potential on a higher level of awareness."

"Well, Katie," I put in, "I think you've had enough lessons for one night, and I can see you're now feeling a lot more comfortable with Entil. As I said before, when you wake up you won't recall my presence here, but you will remember him, and not be afraid any more." With that I leaned forward and touched her lightly on the forehead. She settled herself back under the bedclothes and within seconds was sound asleep.

42 ▶ ONLY THING TO FEAR IS FEAR

"You're looking a bit wiped out this morning Ali Cat," said Paco. "Have you put in a heavy night 'upstairs'?"

"Don't even ask!" I yawned, rubbing my eyes and stretching to try to ease the knots of tension in my neck and shoulders. "The Controllers were having a real picnic last night and managed to sabotage our computer system, which put our Earth surveillance out of action."

Paco put the newspaper aside that he was reading and looked up in amazement. "You're kidding — your computer system? I mean, you're really kidding, right?"

Looking at my face, he knew I wasn't.

"How the heck could that happen? How could anything negative even get on board the disc to do such a thing? I'd have thought you Guardians, of all people, would have some sort of sophisticated protection device installed. How could the Controllers infiltrate and interfere with your computer system?"

"They do have a high level of technology," I shrugged, at the same time trying unsuccessfully to stifle another huge yawn. "Nothing is completely foolproof, I guess, and they are incredibly cunning. It was our Earth surveillance system that went down first, so it had to be somebody down here up to no good, directing the interference to put us out of action."

"Hang on, hang on, now you've really lost me. What do you mean 'somebody down here'? On Earth you mean? But who would have the technology to disable computers on an ET disc?"

"I just said, Paco, the Controllers do, and they're even using our own technology against us; technology that was back-engineered from our crashed discs. We really hoped that it would be utilized for the benefit of humankind, but we hadn't taken into consideration the incredibly deep level of brainwashing and mind control that is being exerted over a vast majority of the population. The cunning, greed, over-inflated egos and hypocrisy that motivates some people down here is truly beyond words."

"Oh, come on, Ali Cat! I know you're feeling a bit off at the moment, but surely we aren't that bad."

"I'm sorry, Paco, but yes, this planet is a real worry. I'm not saying there aren't any good people here, because there are — in fact there's plenty of kind, decent folk, and the majority of them wouldn't have the foggiest idea of what is really going on behind the scenes. If they did, I can guarantee they'd be just as horrified as we are. The situation is so sad, because Earth is a lovely planet — a real jewel in the cosmos, and life could be wonderful for everybody if only greed and the tendency to exploit the weak and vulnerable could be purged from the consciousness of humankind, particularly of those who are in authority."

"But, Ali, I still don't understand how somebody on Earth could possibly interfere with anything up on an ET disc? Okay, I can believe certain ones here have acquired the technology to shoot down discs that venture too close, but to actually sabotage your computers — how can they do that?"

"Just as they can interfere with and intercept communication equipment down here. Billions of Earth dollars have been spent to send hardware out into space for such purposes. And then there are the mind-control techniques and psychic-spying practices that have been perfected over many years. Most people have no idea of how much this is being used and how successful it is, not only in the field of espionage, but also in connection with ET and interdimensional contact.

"So why is this happening? It doesn't make sense?"

"Okay," I replied, settling myself down for what was going to be a long session, "it all began millennia ago in Atlantis, so let's look at the re-emergence of the Atlantean civilization in recent times here on Earth, just as some psychics predicted."

"Wow! Yes, I have read about this, that Atlantis is predicted to rise again. But what do you mean? What's the connection?"

"Well, Atlantis has already emerged, but not quite in the way the predictions have been interpreted. The problem is that you're all so physically oriented down here, so people have mistakenly looked for a physical event in the way of land rising up from the sea. Atlantis has already risen again, but it's more a rebirth of part of the Atlantean consciousness rather than a physical reincarnation of the actual landmass.

"It's like when people reincarnate. It's not their physical bodies that rise up to live again, but rather their minds or spirits that return in new physical containers to learn new lessons and to balance karma. Atlantis is flourishing right under your noses, growing more powerful with each passing decade, and most of you are not even aware of it.

"A part of the Atlantean culture, and most particularly the group referred to as the 'Sons of Belial,' continue to reincarnate here on Earth because they need to face certain karmic choices involving technology, ego and power, all of which were abused before, and which eventually led to the demise of the whole civilization. This karma must be allowed to play out again in order to hopefully be balanced and resolved, hence our technology 'accidentally' falling into their hands."

"Are these the ones you refer to as the Controllers?"

"Yes! These souls, the 'Sons of Belial,' who abused technology and power in Atlantis, have become trapped down here, unable to move on to higher levels. They've had to wait for similar conditions to be present on Earth again so they could 'repeat a grade and re-take their exams' — those tests they failed so miserably before. The problem is, many of them don't want to move on. Their goal is physical perfection and eternal life on the physical plane on Earth, with slave labor to do all the work for them."

"Ali, before you go any further," said Paco, "I've got a question. Do souls always have to return to Earth to work through karma, or can it be balanced on higher levels as well?"

"The Law of Karma applies on all levels, but it's on the first galactic level in which Planet Earth is situated at the present time, that there is more opportunity to balance it."

"And why is that?"

"It's because of the extreme polarization here. This is one of the main reasons that we've tried to stop Earth humans from destroying themselves and their planet. Earth is a very important and necessary part of the cosmic plan in that it's a major 'school' planet and an ideal environment in which to work through karmic lessons and tests. There are other level-one planets where this can be done as well, but Earth is one of the best. It's sort of like a cosmic Oxford or Harvard, if you know what I mean, and it is a major learning center offering a wide range of choices and opportunities because of that polarization. This provides its inhabitants with plenty of scope to exercise their free will so they can make the choices which dictate whether they're ready to evolve to higher planes of reality or not. As I've said before — evolution is all about making choices.

"This too is why there's so much diversity among Earth humans. People from many different planetary cultures have chosen birth here over the millennia. Because of the astral energy screens that effectively keep younger souls trapped here for many lives, Earth has also become something of a 'prison' planet. Until these souls begin to mend their ways by making right rather than wrong choices, they remain imprisoned here, unable to go elsewhere to cause trouble."

"Ah, okay," said Paco, "that makes sense, I guess, but let's get back to this Atlantean thing. What's it got to do with all the negative stuff that's going on in connection with ETs visiting Earth?"

"Well, just as happened before, this Atlantean group has become very power-oriented. This group is comprised solely of the 'Sons of Belial,' because they are the aspect of the culture that is still held by bonds of karma. The positive aspect of Atlantis has been able to move on to higher realms. The Controller group has again got itself into a position of power from which it is able to exert maximum control over planetary affairs. This suits it very nicely, and naturally it doesn't want to lose this. In fact one of the group's main purposes is to safeguard the *status quo* on Planet Earth, from which it is benefiting in a big way, but which it also believes is threatened by our presence here.

"Unlike legitimately elected governments, lack of funds is not an issue with this Controller group. Endless funds are available to them for research — funds which are the result of nefarious activities such as drug trafficking. Why do you think this is such a seemingly unsolvable problem on this planet? Wouldn't you think that something as devastatingly evil and as potentially threatening to the whole fabric of society as illegal drugs would be determinedly stamped out by any government worth its salt? But no, the problem only grows bigger, the reason being that there are others more powerful behind the scenes pulling the strings, as it were, and there isn't a lot that legitimate governments can do about it."

"But where do your people come into the equation?" asked Paco.

"Well, our presence on Earth is posing a big threat to this be-hind-the-scenes shadow group who run the show here. They've been top dogs for many centuries, in fact millennia, often operating through clandestine secret societies, placing certain ones of their own into positions of power where they're able to exert total control over world economy, politics, religion, etc., and therefore total control over the entire planetary population. The very last thing they want is their age-old enemies, the Guardians, stepping in to offer self-empowerment to people. It's in their best interests to keep the people of Earth imprisoned, disempowered and dependent, both on physical and spiritual levels, and fear is, and always has been, their most powerful weapon.

"With endless funds at their disposal, massive amounts of research have been devoted not only to physical technology, but also to psychic technology in the way of mind control, psychic spying, and manipulation of astral-plane energies for their own ends. Also, experiments have been repeated which were first carried out in Atlantis, experiments dealing with the creation and hybridization of human life.

"These ones still, as before, get a huge ego trip out of playing God, experimenting with and making use of advanced technology they developed back in the time of Atlantis or before. They also dabble in occult practices such as creating thought forms by tapping into lower-astral energies, and they have even created some in our image so as to introduce as much fear as possible in connection with the ET presence.

"The Controllers were originally from elsewhere, but settled on Earth millennia ago and claimed it as their own. Over many thousands of years they've adapted themselves genetically so that they are now completely human in appearance — in fact they are 99% Earth human. Because of their 1% off-planet bloodline, they consider themselves to be above everyone else down here, and exploit other humans shamelessly. They look upon the whole planet and all who dwell thereon as their property. They were the driving force behind the 'Aryan ideal' of Nazism, which gives you some idea of their mind-set!"

"So what you're saying is that all negative interference is coming from right here on Earth?"

"Yes! We can protect you from outside influences, but we cannot act upon anything coming from within your own society or planet. All the problems occurring on Earth are coming from within rather than from outside. And what people need to understand clearly is that the Controllers have two powerful weapons at their disposal — fear and confusion. They confuse people by taking a basic truth, for example the fact that there is a God or Source Energy present throughout the universe, and then bend, twist and manipulate this truth for their own ends as a means of controlling others. And this control and manipulation is always fueled by fear or ego. Another basic truth they use to spread confusion and fear is the fact that there are other sentient life-forms 'out there' on other planets and in other dimensions. This too is exploited and twisted for their own ends in the form of 'evil aliens' who are going to come here and take over the world."

"But Ali, what in the name of heaven can people do to protect themselves against this type of mind manipulation?"

"The main thing to understand is that lower astral and other negative entities actually feed off fear and confusion, so once people come to realize this and refuse to be hooked in to their mind games, then they cease to hold sway. That is the key to protecting yourself against them.

"What Earth people need to understand clearly is that you create your own reality. If you wish to change your world then you must first begin by changing the way you think. Positive creation through thought patterns can be a slow process in the heavy and dense vibrations of third-dimensional reality on Planet Earth. It often takes much patience and determination, but it will happen, just as long as people don't allow themselves to become trapped in negative emotions of anger, hatred, envy and fear. Try to stand back a little from all the emotional manipulation being dished up to you on a daily basis, and live your own life in the most ethical and honest way you possibly can. An example, Paco, how do neighborhoods have success against the drug problem?"

"How?"

"From within the community, by joining together and making the decision that they are going to take their community back. That's the only way."

"Okay," interjected Paco, "so we need to be real careful about getting caught up in all the fear and confused emotions that are running riot on Earth right now."

"Exactly! Look to the God Essence within yourself. Seek it out with every ounce of energy at your disposal. This is where you will find peace and self-empowerment. Every single person on this planet and throughout the entire Cosmos is an immortal, all-powerful spiritual being and an intrinsic part of God, of Oneness. Nobody is separate, or cut off, or alone, but you must come to this understanding consciously and with all your heart. And bear in mind that the negative force will do everything in its power to distract, dis-empower and confuse you in order to block this deeper understanding. After all, life on Planet Earth can be full of distractions and negativity — if you allow it to be."

"Well, Ali Cat, what you say certainly does make a lot of sense, but now I've got another question for you. What about those hybrids some people have seen on board your ships? Some of them seem to be okay, and working alongside your people quite happily, but then there are these others, usually babies, who look very sick and listless, so what's going on there?"

"Okay, a hybrid program was initiated by us not long after the Second World War, and it was prompted by the invention of nuclear weaponry down here. A planetary species that carries out warfare with swords, arrows and guns is bad enough, but when a weapon such as an atom bomb is invented, then higher forces must intervene.

"Many Earth humans are still programmed in the 'survival of the fittest' mind-set, along with an in-built fear and distrust of outsiders. This genetically encoded fear has led to countless deaths on Planet Earth, and once authorities here had nuclear weapons at their disposal, we knew that this fear would eventually lead to your extinction as a species, unless it could be removed from Earthlings' makeup, hence our ongoing genetic upgrading program since the war. But don't forget we're not the only ones doing a hybrid program, and these others are the ones who aren't faring so well. We are however intervening where we can to remove the hybrids created by this group so they can be given protection and healing."

"Fair enough," said Paco.

"You know that love energy is what drives the human heart chakra and keeps a person healthy and functioning normally. This is why we bring female humans, particularly mothers, onto the discs, to provide maternal warmth and nurturing to these poor little mites to try to heal them and bring them back to a state of healthy balance. It's the act of hugging and touching that ignites the Spark of God within, and teaches a human to love. Because these hybrids have been created on Earth and are part Earthling, it is an Earth mother's touch that they need, which we cannot provide. At the same time, ones of our own, like Ashka, are in charge of this program. Such ones are also operating through human containers on Earth, and are mothers down there as well, so they fully understand and can relate deeply to the needs of Earth human children.

"Our own genetic program is multidimensional and not only aimed at physical, mental and emotional improvement, but is also intended to sow the seeds of spirituality among the human species of Earth. Without this intervention you will simply not survive as a species, for in order to evolve further, body, mind and spirit must be brought into balance. Anyway, you've met some of our hybrids on board the disc — Alex, Joseph and Angelique. You know what nice people they are."

"Oh yes, absolutely — a bit strange-looking maybe, but good and loving people. And what about the Star Children? What's the difference between them and the hybrids?"

"The difference is that our hybrids up on the disc are essentially ETs with an infusion of some Earth human genetics in their make-up, whereas the Star Children are essentially Earth humans infused with just a little more ET genetic material than other Earth humans.

"With our hybrids we aim to retain the higher emotions, which includes such attributes as compassion, ethics, morals and in fact everything that makes an entity 'human.' In other words, ours is a humanizing program."

"But Ali, surely your people could stop others from creating hybrids down here!"

"No, we cannot. They have free will to choose right from wrong, and as I said before, they're facing the same tests and choices they came up against in Atlantis. Some are making the right choice this time, not to participate in such projects, but others are still caught up in ego and power and so are making wrong choices, for which they will pay as they have done before."

"But Ali, what I still can't get my head around is why your people, or the Star Nation Council or whoever, allowed all of this to happen in the first place. Surely with the level of spiritual knowing that the Guardians have at their disposal you could have anticipated all of this before it occurred and taken steps to prevent it happening. I mean to say, the way you can all operate across time as well as space, wouldn't you have known that your discs were going to crash, and that these former negative Atlanteans who were manifesting on Earth were going to get hold of your knowledge and technology and use it again, as they did before?"

"Yes," I replied, "on a higher level of our being we were aware of what was potentially going to happen, along with all the implications. But the cosmic Law of Karma which governs such processes cannot be over-ridden. It must be played out in full and given the chance to re-balance, which must always happen eventually. Everything returns to perfect balance and oneness in the end. That is just the way universal consciousness operates!"

43 ▶ THE HUMAN LADDER

It was a cool Friday morning in August, and Kaz, Paco and I were again sitting around Maddie's kitchen table. We'd all been busy over the past couple of weeks, and this was our first chance to get together again.

A large and friendly tabby cat purred loudly as it coiled itself around our legs, paying particular attention to Kaz and me, obviously enjoying our energy fields. After all, we Guardians do have a special affinity with cats. Soon it was up on my lap, arching its back and generously offering a silken ear to be scratched.

"Oh, Tiger, for heaven's sake!" Maddie shook her head and rattled a packet of dry cat food to entice him away, but he ignored her completely, as only a cat can, determined to stay right where he was.

"It's okay, Maddie," I assured her, "I love cats. Let him stay if he wants to."

Obviously understanding every word, Tiger immediately curled himself into a furry ball, digging his claws in a couple of times before dropping a stripey head onto my hand and closing his eyes in blissful relaxation.

"Well, Maddie," Paco began, "what's been going on? You said over the phone that new developments were taking place."

"Oh, my goodness, yes!" she replied, looking slightly frazzled but certainly not as scared as before. "The biggest thing is that Kate has finally managed to communicate with the little one that comes into her room, and believe it or not, she now knows his name."

"Hey, that's great Maddie!" I responded, keeping my voice as casually neutral as I could. "So what is it?"

"Umm, it's a funny name, and Kate's not sure if she heard it right because her memory of the visit is a bit clouded, but she thinks the name is Entil — E-n-t-i-l. She's certainly feeling better about the whole thing now and is much less scared."

I frowned slightly, as if trying to remember something. "Mmm, Entil, did you say? Yes, that name does seem familiar…" Then, as if a light were suddenly switched on in my mind, "Ah, yes, of course, Entil! There *is* one with that name up there."

"Really!" For a moment I thought Maddie's eyes were going to pop right out of her head, then the inevitable flood of questions came pouring out. "*Tell* me, please Ali, who *is* he? What does he want? Is he a Teacher, or an Elder, or what?"

"He's not an Elder," I replied, "or he'd be taller. Maybe he's had a taller one with him on occasions when he's come to visit, but Entil himself is what is known as a worker, or a helper, and he's really sweet — very gentle and kind, so you can assure Kate there's nothing to fear from him."

"So you do know him?"

"Yes, as a matter of fact I do, and another thing I know is that he's been really upset about Kate's fear, and of not being able to connect with her. In fact I remember him being in tears over it one night."

Maddie's eyes grew even rounder. "You're kidding! Can Greys cry? In the book I'm reading about alien abductions, it says Greys have no emotions — that they're nothing but bio-robots, with no feelings."

Paco cast a worried look in my direction, obviously recalling the Earthling-created robots in the form of Greys that I'd once spoken of, and how they were being used to intimidate and frighten people, but there was no way I'd go into such things with Maddie at this point in time. I knew very well it would only cause her more fear, and I also knew that in this instance the contact was genuine, and certainly not human-initiated.

"I'm sorry, Maddie, but that's not true. Some books on the subject of human/ET contact are okay, with quite a bit of accurate information, but there are also an awful lot of misconceptions out there, along with heaps of downright rubbish and outright lies written on the Greys. Remember what we said about most ET/human contact taking place on the astral plane — the plane of dreams, emotion and illusion?"

"But what about when people go through hypnotic regression to access hidden contact experiences? Isn't that accurate?"

"Only up to a point," I replied, "because again they're filtering their awareness of the experience through the clouded and blurry lens of their own subconscious mind. Maybe with a properly qualified therapist this can be overcome to a certain extent, but unfortunately in the field of ET contact research there are some people doing this work who are not properly qualified, or do not possess the necessary experience in this particular field. They're often enthusiastic researchers, with their heart in the right place. They genuinely want to help those experiencing contact, but when one is dealing with the human mind, expertise in psychology is most essential. The other problem is, this is a highly emotional field of study, and some therapists subconsciously impose their own perceptions and beliefs onto clients.

"Greys *do* have emotions, and they can potentially get stressed, tired and frustrated just as we can, but the difference is they practice nonattachment, just as students of Eastern spiritual practices are taught on Earth.

"Also, the Grey containers don't possess the same facial musculature as humans do, so human facial expressions are almost impossible for them. Their physical bodies are perfectly adapted for travel in deep space, where there is no atmosphere to breathe and incredible extremes in temperature, so they are very different from humans in this respect. They express their feelings more through their eyes and hands. Emotion is simply a form of energy, and the Greys operate on a higher-frequency band of energy that Earth humans cannot readily perceive; however they're certainly capable of both joy and sadness, and, believe it or not, they have a great sense of humor as well."

"Do they really? That's amazing!"

Then Paco stepped in to lend me his support. "What Ali says is right, Maddie. I have quite clear conscious recall at times of being on board the disc, and when you really get to know the Greys, and your perceptions aren't clouded with fear, you come to realize that in this way they aren't all that different from us. If someone makes a joke, everyone laughs; if someone is unhappy, you can feel it in them; and yes, they can cry. And the love that emanates from them is just amazing. The only difference between them and us is that they're less judgmental and generally much calmer and kinder. There's no competitiveness among them and therefore no jealousy or envy. Each one just gets on with the job at hand, and they work together in total peace and unity."

"Wouldn't that be a nice way to live," she sighed.

"Hopefully we'll get there some day. In many ways they are like us," he went on, "some seem wiser and more mature than others, and as Ali has explained to me, this depends upon their level of soul evolution because some are younger souls and some are older. Some of the younger ones have a lot of trouble handling the lower vibrational frequencies of human emotion, and the older ones seem more able to express emotion than the little workers."

"But," Maddie responded, "if that's the case, then why don't the older ones interact more with humans? Why do they even allow the younger, less evolved ones near us, when they can't properly relate to humans?"

"The whole thing is," Kaz put in, "the little workers are a counter balance. The excess of lower emotional energy is threatening the continued existence of the whole human species and the planet as well.

"When you get an imbalance of energy like this, the opposite is automatically drawn in to counter-balance it. Energy is exactly like water in that it always finds its own level. Earthlings are automatically drawing in whatever they need to restore balance within the energy system. You draw to yourself what's required, even in ET-contact experiences."

"Ali or Kaz," Paco looked across at both of us, "why don't you explain to Maddie about who and what the Guardians actually are, so she'll understand the whole process a bit more clearly."

"Oh, yes, please!" Maddie put in. "You said something before about their bodies being specially adapted to travel in deep space. What do you mean? In one book they also mention autopsies being done on the alien bodies that were retrieved from these crashed discs, and how they seem to be sort of artificial. This is the book I mentioned before, where they talk about the Greys as being sort of manufactured robots, and they surmise that they've been specifically designed by some very advanced ET culture, but you say they're *not* robots, so what are they?"

"Okay, Maddie," I answered. "The problem with a lot of these conclusions that researchers come to is that they can't seem to grasp the fact that elsewhere in the universe things can be vastly different, especially with a culture as ancient and advanced as the 'Greys,' or Guardians, to give them their proper name.

"They seem to be having trouble with the fact that the physical universe is only a very small part of the greater reality. They see the whole universe as being comprised of physical matter — physical planets, physical asteroids, physical galaxies, etc., but it isn't. Physical 'reality,' or what can be observed through Earth-bound telescopes, is quite small compared to the greater reality, which is why most attempts made by Earth scientists to contact what they call 'alien life-forms' is just about doomed to failure. The signals they send out are in such a tiny, narrow band of the electromagnetic scale. It's like trying to find one particular single grain of sand on all the beaches in the world. Earth human minds simply cannot grasp the magnitude that is involved!"

"Ali," Paco cut in, "how far up the Human Ladder does the physical universe actually extend? I know you said there are ten levels, but how many of them are physical?"

"Only the first three," I answered, "and even by the time you evolve up to the third level, things start getting very fluid, with people able to move in and out of physicality very easily and consciously."

"So what are the inhabitants of these first three levels like?" he asked.

"First-level folk," I replied, "are like Earth people. In fact, there's been a lot of coming and going over the millennia between the level-one planets. Because Earth is a really good 'school' planet, people from many other level-one planets have come here to master certain lessons, which has caused such a diversity of races, religious beliefs and customs on Earth — a lot have been 'imported' from elsewhere.

"Level twos are more 'perfected' humans, like the Pleiadians, Sirians, Arcturians and many others, who have been through the 'rough and tumble' of many lives on level-one planets like Earth — planets on which they've had all their 'rough edges' rounded off, so to speak. They've learned the value and importance of keeping their energies well balanced and harmonized, and they're able to access 20% of their potential conscious awareness, which makes them geniuses, compared to Earth humans. With more of their DNA activated, and therefore operating through a more expanded state of conscious awareness, they're able to tap into fourth- and fifth-dimensional reality.

"They're still centered in mortal bodies, but their deeper conscious awareness gives them greater control over the physical aspect of their being. A hint of this can be seen in some of the Eastern adepts on Earth, who have mastered the ability to control body temperature, blood pressure, etc. In level-two reality, illness and physical degeneration as occurs on Earth is less of an issue to contend with, hence their much longer life-spans and more attractive physical appearance.

"Level twos have also moved beyond the Earth human state of disharmony and fear and are much more peaceful, lacking any warlike tendencies. They have a much deeper respect for other life-forms and the environment, and they understand how to access clean, natural energy, so their technology is more efficient and far less destructive than here on Earth. Everyone's needs are met, and there is no poverty, hunger or misery. Life may not be perfect, but it's certainly an improvement to down here!

"It's no wonder that level-two civilizations like the Pleiadians appear to Earth human eyes as 'angel-like,' because they truly are very beautiful souls on every level of their being. That is where Earth humans are heading on the next stage of their evolution, if only they can move beyond their fears, which in turn create their need for war and aggression."

"And what about the level threes?" Maddie inquired. "What are they like?"

"By the time a soul evolves to galactic level three of the Human Ladder, they are beginning to move beyond the need or desire for physical expression. They have mastered almost all there is to learn with life in physical form, and the focus starts shifting entirely into the 'mind' stage of evolution, hence the small, frail bodies without much physical detail or substance and the larger heads and eyes that Earth researchers label 'Zetas.' But these ones come from a number of home worlds, some of which are beyond the Earth human range of perception. Level threes can access 30% of conscious awareness, so the advanced technologies and mind abilities of level two are taken a step further.

"Here one fully grasps that the body is really nothing more than a temporary vehicle, or container, for the pure soul essence that can move easily, freely and consciously in and out of its physical body. This is why level-three bodies are very basic and simple — convenient 'tools' to be used by the soul only when needed.

"Once a soul evolves past this point and into level-four reality, mortal form is discarded completely. This is the first step into what is known as the Guardian realm, which is beyond and above the physical universe in vibrational frequency. From this point on, the soul essence vibrates at higher and higher frequencies through what Earth humans call the devic and angelic realms, to eventually meld back into the Oneness of Source. These are the levels to which the spiritual warriors and care-takers belong, whose job is to help beings of the first, second and third galactic levels evolve up the Ladder. The Guardians are caretakers of the life-force energy of these first three levels."

"So what about those like Entil, who are coming here and con-tacting people?" Maddie asked. "What level are they from? And how are their bodies specially adapted for space travel?"

"Okay," I answered, "Entil, and the other so-called 'Zetas,' or 'Greys' that are involved in ET/human contact actually come from levels six, seven and eight. Smaller ones like Entil are from level six, slightly taller ones are level sevens, and the really tall teachers like the one who sometimes accompanies Entil are from level eight. Beyond that, at levels nine and ten, are the Angels.

"People from level-two and level-three planets also visit Earth. Some physical, human species breathe an atmosphere like Earth's, but if they don't, then they need some breathing apparatus to enable them to visit, whereas the Guardians don't, because of their specially adapted, semi-artificial, bodies.

"What most researchers on Earth still don't understand is that the Guardians have actually evolved beyond all these planetary cultures. Some may have been Earth humans long, long ago, as well as inhabitants of other planetary cultures of our universe, but now they are no longer physical beings from any physical planet. They don't think of themselves as 'having a soul' — they know that they *are* soul. However, much of the work they carry out in the physical universe requires a physical body, or what they call a container, just as Earth human astronauts who travel in space need to don special, protective suits to enable them to operate and carry out tasks in the totally alien environment.

"Those Guardians whose work takes them to the far reaches of the universe to carry out physical duties on planets with various atmos-pheric conditions and temperatures use semi-artificial bodies to enable them to carry out this work. The soul, being pure energy, doesn't need atmosphere to breathe or food to eat, but unlike biological human bodies, neither do these containers. This is how the so-called 'Zetas' who appear in physical form are able to operate without any breathing equipment."

"But then," said Maddie, "that means they *are* robots!"

"No, they're not," I explained. "The physical body may be artificial, but the soul operating it, which in the greater reality is what we *all* are, is totally sentient consciousness. In this way they can and do experience emotion just as we do. In fact, because their emotions aren't filtered or dulled by the gross physical matter, they can feel more intensely, which is why they have some trouble with the lower human emotions. The older Guardians are so balanced with their energy so they have learned to protect themselves, but the younger ones feel very intensely the emotions being put out by humans because they are still working to balance their energy.

"These artificial containers used by the Guardians are why many people down here who've had contact experiences with them since childhood, often have a deep-seated fear of artificial humanoid representations such as puppets, clowns and dolls. These stir up memories of the Guardians who visit them during their sleep-state, and until their consciousness opens up, remembers and recognizes the soul inside the artificial container, they experience these deep fears on the subconscious level."

I could see that Maddie still wasn't quite convinced and didn't fully understand, but at that point Kaz stepped in, coming to my rescue.

"Maddie, I've just thought of a good way to explain what Ali's trying to say. You could think of a Guardian like the lead character in a fantasy movie featuring a 'hero' who has been involved in some terrible accident in which nearly his whole body has been damaged beyond repair. Through really advanced medical intervention, most of his body parts are subsequently replaced with artificial components which enable him to carry out 'super-human' feats. He's still a perfectly normal human being, but with an extra strong, extra resilient part-artificial body. Why, medical science on Earth is moving in this direction with artificial limbs that can be controlled by thought alone; and remember, the Guardians are way ahead of Earth scientists in their technology!"

"Ah, okay, I sort of understand that," she replied, looking a little more relieved, "but I'm still a bit confused about all these levels. Ali, you described the level-three people as having small, frail bodies with large heads and eyes, just like the Guardians' containers, but if the Guardians have moved beyond the need for physical bodies, how come they resemble the level-three folks?"

"Level three is the last level of the Human Ladder on which souls express through physical form," I explained, "so that particular level-three form is very simple anatomically and thus easier and more efficient to reproduce artificially. That's why the more highly evolved Guardians still use that body type as a blueprint for their containers."

"And do the Angels of levels nine and ten use these containers as well?"

"No, because they don't carry out physical work on the lower levels of the universe. When they do put in an appearance down here, to assist human souls at the time of death, for example, they just tap in to the mind of the one they're assisting and create an astral body to fit whatever form that person expects an angel to take. If physical intervention is required, then they call on the 'Greys,' the lower-level Guardians who are sort of 'assistant angels,' to carry out the task for them. The different levels of Guardians have quite specific jobs to do within the general framework of working with life-force energy to assist the human evolutionary process.

"Universal energy expresses as life-force, and so the creation and evolution of life is all about working mindfully with the creative energy of the universe on all levels — physical body, spiritual mind and universal soul. The Guardians are transmuters and transformers of life-force energy, and in this way are closely linked to human evolution, which goes hand in hand with reincarnation where a soul gradually evolves back to Source, or Oneness. *Evolution is not physical — it's a soul process.*"

Just then Tiger Cat decided it was time for a good stretch. His back arched, his tail almost went in my mouth, and his claws dug into my lap. Loud purring filled the small room as puss did everything possible to focus my attention wholly and completely upon his little head, which badly wanted a good scratch around the ears.

"Ow, ouch, settle down, Tiger!" I pleaded, running a soothing hand through his sleek, thick coat and receiving a head butt under the chin in reply.

Maddie couldn't help smiling at his antics. "He's really taken a liking to you, Ali. Trouble is he can be a bit pushy. Have these Guardian folk always looked like they do now, or were they once more human-looking?"

"Well, Maddie, they've 'been there, done that many times over, just as we are doing now. They've slowly evolved up through the Human Ladder from many different planetary cultures and star systems, and like all humans, they've fallen down at times, and picked themselves up again, so they do understand intimately just what we're going through.

"This is why some of them seem fascinated by and drawn to human emotion. It's a bit like the fascination we have in studying ancient cultures of Earth. It's like — 'Wow, is *that* how we used to do things way back then? Isn't that *amazing*!' And for the genetic work they're carrying out to create the hybrids and Star Children, they're really only borrowing back a bit of what they gave to Earthlings originally. After all, it was their own genetic input that made us human in the first place. If it weren't for the Guardians and other higher ET cultures, many of us would still be swinging through branches by our tails."

Maddie looked a bit doubtful. "Well yes, I suppose so, if you look at it that way. So how are ones like Entil connected to ones like Kate? Is that some sort of genetic thing too?"

"Yes!" I replied. "Star children like Kate have an upgraded genetic blueprint. When these children are conceived, the mother is taken up onto the disc, and the newly conceived embryo is upgraded through advanced genetic engineering procedures. In other words, extra ET genetic material is spliced into the Earth human genetics already present from both parents. This material comes from a number of different ET cultures that are contributing to the gene pool, so Star Children can be part Pleiadian, Altarian, Zeta, Sirian, or whatever, depending upon who's been the donor.

"In Kate's case it would be Entil, and so he's kept in close contact with her since her conception, and will continue to do so throughout the rest of her life. The concept of family and Oneness is important to the Guardians, which is why Entil was so sad about her fear and rejection of him. He feels a very deep, close 'family' connection to her because part of him is in her genetic makeup."

"But if his physical body is artificial, how can he donate genetic material?" Maddie asked, looking totally perplexed.

"The Guardians who are involved in this program," I explained, "often make use of a couple of containers — a wholly artificial one for physical space travel and a biological or at least part-biological one for other aspects of their work. Guardians can have a fully biological body if they so wish, but it's entirely voluntary, unlike Earth humans who have no choice in the matter."

Poor Maddie shook her head, obviously not comfortable at all. "I just don't know how I feel about all this genetics thing! Do you mean that Kate's not totally our own daughter? But she's taken after both of us so strongly, particularly Geoff's side of the family. You've only got to look at them together to see that!"

"No Maddie," I quickly stepped in with words of reassurance, "that's not what I'm saying. Of course she's your daughter, wholly and completely, but she just has a wee bit more added, as you and probably your husband have too, because these genetic upgrades tend to run in families. Perhaps you have no conscious recall, but it's likely that you were both taken up as well when you were children. It's a very gradual process carried out over several generations."

"Maddie," said Paco, stepping in to back me up, "what you have to realize is that no child is created only from their parents' genetics. Remember that both parents come from family lines themselves, and every child is a product of generations of genetic input in the way of aunts, uncles, grandparents, great-grandparents, etc. There are some children who don't even look like their immediate parents, but rather throw back to a grandparent or some other distant relative. And anyway, who knows, if the Guardians are as ancient a culture as Ali says, and they were partly responsible for developing the human race of Earth, then maybe Entil is a distant relative of your family. As I've found out through my own dealings with the Guardians, anything is possible! And actually, it's our human way of seeing ourselves as separate from everything. When we view it all as One, it changes the picture, doesn't it?"

A look of profound relief came into Maddie's eyes. "Oh, wow, yes, you are right, Father Lopez. Maybe that's why the Guardians and other ETs seem to work with certain families down here, because they're distantly related from way back. This Oneness concept still feels strange, but how could it be anything different when we believe in one God?"

"When you look at it in that light," Kaz put in, "going up on the disc is nothing more than visiting the rellies, because after all, everyone down here has ET genetics in their bloodlines, otherwise, as Ali said, we'd be swinging through the trees and throwing banana skins at each other. Mutual grooming practices to rid ourselves of fleas and other parasites would also be part and parcel of our species, as would screeching loudly at the approach of strangers. Hey, come to think of it, I used to date a fellow like that before I got married — hmm, I wonder!"

Out of the corner of my eye I could see Paco having an awful struggle to keep a straight face. I knew very well that if our eyes met we'd both lose it. Damn Kaz! Mouth trembling ever so slightly, Paco quickly lowered his gaze to meditate deeply upon a stray fleck of lint on the sleeve of his shirt, while my mind busied itself elsewhere by focusing intently upon the cat's left ear, which had somehow turned itself inside out.

"Funny thing though!" Kaz plowed on with true Guardian determination — "He was really hairy all over as well. I always had a worry in the back of my mind that if we ever married and had kids, they'd be born with tails — and cute little bottoms that'd flush bright red when they got excited."

Several seconds of dead silence followed, then an ill-suppressed snort of laughter from Paco set both Maddie and me off simultaneously. Then just as things began to settle down again, an all-too-familiar glint illuminated Kaz's eyes, and I knew more was to follow. Having had plenty of experience with her unique sense of humor both 'upstairs' and 'downstairs' — in fact in her Grey form she was even worse — it was time to intervene. "Kaz — will you *please* knock it *off*!" I begged, wiping tears from my eyes and burying my face in my hands. "We concede defeat!"

In a massive and determined effort to bring the conversation back to where it was supposed to be going, I turned to Maddie. "The important thing that needs to be understood if people down here really want to get a handle on the whole ET contact thing is, that what most people on Earth think of as 'reality' is, in fact, only a very limited part of the whole. As we evolve, with help from the Guardians, a wider and deeper spectrum of conscious awareness will gradually unfold for us. As human beings this is our birthright, and it is only a matter of expanding our senses to a broader band of frequencies that are already right here and now. Once we're able to open up more in this way, our perception of 'reality' will be vastly different."

44 ▶ 9/11

"Wat's the matter with *you*? You look bloody *awful*!"

"Gee thanks, Paco. You really know how to make a person feel good about themselves," I replied, making a valiant attempt to focus my thoughts through a bleary-eyed fog of nausea. Resisting the urge to throw up all over him, I made it to the bathroom — just. Emerging five minutes later feeling a little better, I found him waiting in the hallway for me.

"Ali, seriously, what *is* wrong? I've never seen you looking so sick. Come on, go back to bed and lie down. Here, I'll help you. Do you want me to call the doctor?"

"No, no, I'll be fine once I take some aspirin. My God, I don't know what the heck happened last night, but when I got back from 'upstairs,' this terrible headache came on. It's making me feel so sick. Sometimes I get a slight headache after a heavy night's work, but never this bad. Lucky I don't have classes today and I can stay in bed. What I really need is sleep. Please, Paco, just get me some aspirin and a glass of water — that's all I want."

"Okay, but are you *sure* you'll be all right? I don't like leaving you on your own, but I have to go out for a while."

"Honestly, I'll be fine. I just need to sleep."

By the time Paco arrived home later that morning, I was up and about and feeling a little better, but now he was the one looking pale. "Ali, something terrible has happened. Look, it's all over the front page of the paper. There's been a really serious terrorist attack in America."

One glance at the headlines brought another stabbing pain to my head, causing me to stagger slightly. Luckily a chair was handy. Graphic images of horror, mayhem and broken bodies exploded into my conscious mind, bringing with them the clear and sickening recall of the past night's work. Accompanying these images was an overlay of the events of a night exactly three weeks ago, of the failure of our surveillance system up on the big disc, and of our frantic attempt to repair the damage — to get the system back up and running as quickly as possible.

"Ali, what is it? What's wrong? Is this what made you sick this morning? Were your people helping out over there?"

For a few moments I couldn't manage to answer him. The whole thing was just so overwhelming. Surely in the time our system was out of action such a massive tragedy could not have been set in motion. But all it takes sometimes is a very small cause to result in a catastrophic effect. And it was *exactly* three weeks to the very day — the very hour in fact. It could not be coincidental. I didn't want to acknowledge this, even to myself, but I knew deep down — I just *knew* it.

"Oh, my God!" I finally managed to respond. "So *this* is why our surveillance system was sabotaged up on the disc."

For the next week or so I really came to appreciate how lucky I was to have my brother Paco on hand as a professional counselor, because recall of each night's healing work and the awful things witnessed at the scene were clearly etched into my human consciousness every morning. It was my duty as a gray Guardian to be there helping out. I had no choice in the matter, for this is what part of our work entails.

That Kaz's daughter Kira was involved as well made it even harder. Even though she was very young, it was a facet of her Guardian training to be there, under my care, but this made things twice as hard for me. Apart from doing my own work, I had to worry about her too, making sure she was safe, trying to keep her away from the worst of it, and trying to mitigate its effect on the Earth-human level of her psyche.

The attack had involved hijacked airliners being flown directly into New York's high-rise World Trade Center to cause maximum damage and loss of life, so the number of dead and injured was very high. With the Elder Oris's help, I managed to keep Kira away from the worst scenes by assigning her the equally important task of giving healing energy to the many human rescue workers on the site. She did this by placing her hands on their shoulders at every opportunity as they took even just a few minutes break from the massive and heart-rending task of search and rescue that lay ahead. We of course were in our astral forms, invisible to normal human sight, but it was clear that they were still benefiting hugely from the healing and strengthening energy that we channeled to them to assist them in their work.

With thousands of tons of debris to dig through, many of the victims could not be reached by human hands, but Grey and Angel hands are a different matter entirely in such a situation. With our ability to move easily through seemingly solid objects, even the most deeply buried victim could be reached and given comfort, healing and hope.

Nobody was left to die alone. We did everything in our power to keep alive those people that had a chance of being rescued, and to telepathically touch the minds of the rescuers to try to lead them to places where buried survivors needed help. Those who could not be reached were not forgotten either. We stayed close beside them, placing comforting hands on them to ease their pain and fear, and helping to assist their passing so the suffering would not be prolonged.

One morning I awoke with the clear memory of moving through tons of rubble. Generally we floated a little off the ground because of all the dust, mud and debris, but this time I was so distracted by everything around me that I'd forgotten to do this. Suddenly I pulled up short, realizing with a shudder that I'd been about to step on a dismembered human trunk — no head, no arms, no legs — just a decomposing trunk.

Through it all we worked side by side with the Angels. This actually provided a little humor at times among all the horror. Some of these highly evolved members of the Guardian consciousness can be a wee bit formidable, but most have a great sense of fun, and just like humans who work in the various emergency services, we also joked among ourselves to keep stress and tension at bay.

The way the two Guardian groups, Angels and Greys, work together would undoubtedly have caused some confusion for any human survivors caught up in it. I can guarantee that at least one survivor would have awakened in the hospital with an unnerving memory of seemingly being fought over by two very different-looking entities. One they would recall as being obviously angelic, dressed in a flowing white robe and looking like a perfected human being, whereas the other would have been clad in a long black cape, with two huge dark eyes set in a thin, skull-like face peering from beneath a hood or broad-brimmed black hat.

The human would, of course, assume that the Angel must have "won the battle," wrenching them from the icy clutches of the black-clad "Grim Reaper," thus saving their life. In fact, it would have been the other way around, because in such instances the Angels only take those who are meant to die, whereas the black-clad gray Guardians are there to give healing. If the human caught between the two survived to wake up in hospital, then the victor must have been the Grey.

On one occasion I was involved in such a tug-o-war situation with an angelic being. By this stage there were very few survivors left, and, moving through the rubble, I came upon two men trapped in a small pocket under great slabs of fallen concrete. One was dead and the other only just alive. I knelt beside him, placing my hands on his body to allow healing energy to flow. There was a team of human rescue workers close by, so there was still hope — if only he could be kept alive long enough for them to reach him. Just then one of the Angels appeared on the scene. "Come on, Alarca," she said, "move back and give me room. I have to do an aura cleanse before I lift him out."

"But the rescuers are so close!" I protested, feeling tears of tiredness and frustration welling in my eyes. "Can't you let me work on him just a little longer. If only *one more* could be saved it would give people a little bit of hope, you know, it'd be like a miracle!"

"No, Alarca — it is his time!" The Angel's voice was firm and final, but her hand gentle with understanding as she reached over and touched my arm, directing a flow of comfort and healing into my energy field. Shifting her attention back to the human, she took both of his hands in hers. "Come on now," she encouraged, "let me lift you up and out. It's time for you to wake up!" The man's inner sight opened at her touch, and I watched as his astral form rose up into a sitting position, leaving the discarded physical shell behind, lying broken and battered on the ground.

At first his face expressed shock and disbelief that such a thing could really be happening. His eyes shifted over to me then back to the Angel as a look of sheer, unadulterated bliss suffused his features with the dawning of full realization. His badly injured body was forgotten in the excitement of the moment as he rose easily into the Angel's waiting embrace. She looked at me over his shoulder, and I was left basking in the warmth of a cheeky wink as they both disappeared into the light.

"Hey, Alarca!" came another angelic voice behind me. "Here's one you can help. You start giving her healing while I fetch Maris. The rescuers aren't far away so maybe you'll get your wish for a miracle."

Once I'd completed the aura cleanse that both Greys and Angels carry out as standard procedure before either healing or lifting the person free of the container, Maris came over to kneel beside me. This cleansing prepares the person for whatever is to follow by balancing, harmonizing and clearing any blockages from their energy system so that the healing penetrates more deeply, or their passing is easier and less traumatic.

I made a mental note to offer this service to Maris as soon as an opportunity presented itself, because he looked totally exhausted. As a Guardian living a double life in human form, I manage to get a little time out when I am back in my Earthling container, but ones like Oris and Maris do not. More than a week had passed and they'd been there working almost continuously without a break. With so many people simultaneously transitioning or needing healing, the work load was huge for everyone. Just then Maris's telepathic thoughts touched my mind with a request, "Alarca, when you get back into your human container after work tonight, can you *please* send me some Reiki — I'd really appreciate it! I also picked up on your idea of giving me an aura cleanse, and yes, I'll have one of them too please, before you go home."

"Of course I will," I assured him, "and I'll get Ashka on the job as well with the Reiki. Maris," I went on, "there's something I want to ask you. Did this attack happen because of our surveillance system being put out of action?"

"Yes, Alarca, most definitely. The three-week time delay happened because the time lines don't quite synchronize."

"What do you mean? I don't understand."

"Well, this attack was actually set in motion while our computers were down, but it didn't manifest into physical reality until three weeks afterwards. I had a nasty feeling something like this was happening, and that's why we were so frantic to get the system repaired, but we weren't quick enough. As you know Alarca, there's only so much we can do — some things are beyond us. After all, we are not God!"

"I know, Maris, but it really worries me that some Earthlings think we're on the negative side and out to hurt them. I mean just think of all these people here who would have been left alone and unaided if we hadn't been on hand to give them healing and comfort until they could be reached by the human rescue workers. Entil stayed beside one lady for nearly a week, being careful to show himself in a more angelic form so he wouldn't scare her, giving her healing to ease her pain and to keep her alive until she could be rescued. It's so frustrating, and almost as if some Earth humans don't even *want* to know the truth about us."

"Alarca, what you have to remember is that how an Earth human perceives us depends very much upon where they are in their own consciousness. It's not so much about us but rather more about them. That's the bottom line."

"Okay, fair enough," I sighed. "Maybe I'm letting my own Earthling consciousness get in the way too much. That's also why I got so sick after that first night here, isn't it?"

"Yes. You allowed human emotion to override your Guardian consciousness, and this threw your energy system out of balance. Even human rescue workers have to undergo many hours of rigorous training to learn how not to become too emotionally involved in their work. We are the same, because we also are rescuers — of souls, and so we must remain detached at all times. I know it's hard, but it must be done, particularly by ones such as you and Ashka who occupy Earth human containers as well.

"Remember, Alarca, as Guardians we are very sensitive to lower human emotion. It really affects us deeply, as we are not accustomed to it, so it is most important that we practice nonattachment at all times. Speaking of which, I believe it is time for you to return to your mortal container, and look, the rescue workers have broken through. This one is going to be all right, so you can go home feeling happy that a life has been saved. If you hadn't helped her when you did she would not have made it. Now, before you go, how about that aura cleanse?"

45 ▶ A WALK-IN

I was taking a few minutes' break between shifts, talking to our two Pleiadian crew members, Asara and Solarno, when Maris suddenly appeared. "Alarca, please, I need your container."

"Huh?"

"I said, I need your container, and quickly, but you have to give me permission — please — it's an emergency!"

"Hang on a second, Maris," Solarno intervened. "What's going on? How come you're in astral form? Are you okay? Where's your *own* physical container? Why do you want Alarca's?"

It was only then that the bizarreness of the situation seemed to dawn on Maris. Some of the insubstantial mistiness around his outer astral edges began to clear as he visibly pulled himself together. "Oh dear, I'm sorry," he apologized. "The small disc I was travelling in just got shot down by the Controllers. All three of us on board were ejected quite forcibly from our physical containers, and mine was blown to pieces, so it's of no use to me now anyway, but the problem is, I need one for the work I'm doing."

Solarno put a comforting arm around my Teacher's shoulders. "Come on Maris, you'd better sit down for a minute. You still look a bit shaken. There, that's better. Now what do you mean about needing Alarca's container? Aren't there any spare ones on board? I thought you always kept some for such emergencies."

"No, no, you don't understand! Oh my goodness, I'm sorry! I'm really not explaining myself, am I? I'll start over..." Then, turning to me — "Alarca, I've decided that I need to have an Earth human container for the physical aspect of my work. That way I can be right there, on the spot, during these last few years before the planetary shift, but the problem is, how? I can't just take one over, because we are *not* into possession without permission — that's a real no-no! And even if someone down there were on the way out anyway and willing to allow me to take over the body as a walk-in, it still wouldn't work. As a gray Guardian, my energy signature is just too different. It would take me ages to adapt, and things could go wrong — so that's where you come in, Alarca."

"Huh? But what's it got to do with me? I know I grumble sometimes about life on Planet Earth, but my human container is still healthy, and my work down there is going well. I'm not ready to exit just yet. Don't ask me to do that, Maris — please!"

"No, no, Alarca — you don't understand. I'm not asking you to exit the container. Even though it's yours, it's still an Earth-human one, which I don't think I could manage on my own. No, all I'm asking is, can we share it? After all, as your elder and teacher, we already share a very similar energy signature, so it shouldn't prove too difficult, but I still need your permission."

Waves of intense amusement were radiating from behind me. "Oh dear, Alarca — that's going to 'clip your wings' somewhat, isn't it? Having your Teacher right in there with you, 24/7! You won't get away with *anything* anymore!" Asara and Solarno were having a great chuckle at the prospect.

Seeing the expression on my face, Maris was quick to reassure me. "Oh, don't worry, Alarca. It'll only be during the day. Once our container falls asleep at night and we both come up here onto the disc, we can go our separate ways, no problem. The only difference is that my presence will enhance your consciousness with information about energy that we can teach to many people on Earth."

"But Maris, are you sure? If you come into my container with me, won't it be obvious to others — Paco and my family for example? Won't I seem very different to them?"

Again a ripple of laughter from the Pleiadians. "Alarca, you've *always* seemed a 'little different' to your human family. They'll hardly notice a bit more!"

Then from Maris — "Please, Alarca. I really need your help here, but I also need your full and conscious permission to do a walk-in. You don't have to give me an answer straight away. You can think it through, and if you really don't want to, then so be it — there's no pressure."

"Oh *no* — no pressure at *all!*" I came back at him, maybe a little more forcefully than intended. "But no, it's okay, Maris. I don't need to think it through. Permission granted."

As zero hour approached only one week later, I began feeling very strange indeed. I knew that it was all about preliminary energy shifts in my body, and now I sensed that it was time to prepare myself. I lay down on my bed and soon the familiar paralysis overtook me. I became aware of two figures standing beside me. "It's all right, Alarca — it's only Garnibis and me. We've come to assist with the process." The sound of the Elder Serapis's familiar and kindly voice telepathing inside my head calmed and reassured me.

Then from behind came Maris's voice. "Alarca, don't be scared. This may hurt a little and will be quite uncomfortable, but try to stay as relaxed as you can."

I felt something happening at the top of my head in the area of the crown chakra, and then my head seemed to explode with a deafening, roaring, buzzing noise — but it was more than a noise — it was a sensation that filled my whole being, threatening to blow me asunder. I struggled against it and tried to cry out, but no sound came as Garnibis and Serapis held me down firmly to ensure complete immobility in order to allow Maris's larger and more expansive consciousness to fit itself into my Earth human energy system.

This was a tricky process and not easy for either of us. The sound still reverberated through me, causing my body to shake uncontrollably and my head to throb with pain. I felt as if I were being pulled apart at the seams, as all of my energy centers expanded. Serapis held my hand and Garnibis spoke words of comfort. "Be calm, little one. It is almost done — just a few more seconds."

As Maris's older and wiser mind gently merged and melded with mine, an incredible sense of peace and love suffused my whole being. Deeper awareness and understanding began slowly unfolding within, like the petals of a rosebud opening to the brightness and warmth of the sun at the end of a long, dark night. Lying there, keeping my body as quiet and relaxed as possible, waiting for the unpleasant trembling sensation and the loud noise to gradually subside, I couldn't help but wonder where this new development would lead us. Life would be even more complex now, with Maris working through my physical body, but one thing was certain — the road ahead was going to be interesting.

The following weeks were a learning curve for both of us. My own sense of 'self' was not removed, so a complete memory of who I am and my personal-life experiences was retained in full, but added to this was Maris's own sense of self-awareness and identity. In other words, nothing was removed, but rather added to and expanded upon.

Kaz, of course, picked up straight away on my slightly altered energy field. "What's wrong with you?" she inquired, leaning forward and looking deeply into my eyes. "Something's different!"

"Oh, come on, Kaz, don't you remember me telling you? Maris has done a 'walk-in.' He's here right now, sharing the container."

"Is he? Ah, yes, of course, I'd completely forgotten." A mischievous glint came into her eyes. "This *will* be fun, having a Guardian Teacher down here, on *our* terms! I wonder if I could possibly *tempt* him — with a large block of yummy dark chocolate — or a glass or two of wine — or perhaps even a large, juicy *steak* smothered in onions! In fact," she went on, rubbing her hands together in wicked anticipation, "this will be my *sole mission* in life from now on — to lead him astray. That way maybe he'll stop nagging me to give up smoking and come to a

deeper understanding of how darned *hard* it is for us poor little Guardian workers down here in human form. Too bad he won't experience parent-hood, because it's especially hard for those of us who've chosen to be parents to Star Kids like Ben and Kira, who can be a real challenge to raise, much as you love them dearly. God, this is going to be *fun* — I can't *wait!*"

A telepathic groan and an inner squirm registered inside our shared consciousness, but then I became acutely aware of a wickedly eye-glinting, hand-rubbing thought, which most definitely did not come from me.

"Well, Ashka, we'll see about that! *My* plan is to expand your children's consciousnesses to even *deeper* levels of Guardian awareness, so you'll be kept too busy to even think about leading me astray! Let's see now — what will the *first* step be — deeper trance-states for Ben? Or more conscious recall for Kira? A bit of nice, lively poltergeist activity around the house would liven things up too, wouldn't it! Oh, yes, Ashka, you're *so* right — this *will* be fun!"

EPILOG

As a gray Guardian living on Planet Earth in human form, I find myself caught inextricably between two worlds. While I do understand the terror experienced by Earth humans who are taken on board our discs, I also feel great sadness and frustration at the dread with which my people are regarded. The work we are carrying out is not meant to harm but rather to help in the spiritual awakening process which everyone must come to eventually as part of evolution. We are also attempting to save your beautiful planet from the terrible damage that has been wrought upon her through ignorance and so-called "progress."

During the course of a contact between our people and a female Earthling some years ago, a message was given in a language very close to an ancient tongue of Planet Earth. The words were so similar in fact that it was able to be translated into English. I shall quote this message as it was transcribed:

"The living descendents of the Northern Peoples are groping in universal darkness. Their mother mourns. A dark occasion forebodes when weakness in high places will revive a high cost of living — an interval of mistakes in high places — an interval fit for distressing events."

This message, from several decades ago, is fairly self-explanatory, describing very accurately the state of world affairs today. I will, however, clarify it further, as it is of great importance.

"The living descendents of the Northern Peoples" refers to modern-day Western Society, which is a reincarnation of that ancient civilization known as Atlantis, the northern continent, which was almost entirely annihilated through the greedy and destructive behavior of a number of its inhabitants, brought about by the use of advanced technology without the spiritual maturity to handle it wisely.

The damage being imposed once again on the natural environment of the planet is now glaringly obvious, as man-made pollution and global warming destroy the very lifeblood of your precious Mother Earth. But other more subtle damage is occurring as well, on deeper levels of the human psyche. This damage will eventually lead to the *devolvement* of your species — *as has happened before!* I refer to the destruction of spiritual, ethical and family values, which are the very qualities that set you apart and mark you as "human" as opposed to "animal."

Once again we see some Earth humans returning to a state of bestiality. Animals react purely out of instinct, whereas humans have "tasted the fruit of the Tree of Knowledge." In other words, you have reasoning power and the ability to apply free will in order to choose between right and wrong. Indeed this act of choosing is the key to your evolution as members of the human kingdom.

Some of your modern-day "gurus" attempt to brainwash you by preaching the message that there is no "right" and "wrong," and that free will means that you should be completely free to do as you like, but on Planet Earth this is simply not the case. Earth humans are only on the very first rung of the Human Ladder, and many have not yet evolved to a high enough level to be able to handle such freedom. To attain total freedom, self-discipline must first be mastered, otherwise the planet will soon resemble a classroom full of five-year-olds with no teacher in charge to maintain order.

Unfortunately, that is *exactly* how Planet Earth is seen from the ET perspective! Is it any wonder that, like any parent who sees their children running riot, the ETs are giving warnings through graphic images of the disaster and destruction that will occur if Earthlings persist in their childish and dangerous behavior?

For those humans who refuse to accept that anything exists beyond limited third-dimensional "reality," and who deny the existence of any sort of motivating God-force behind creation, all that can be said is — open your minds! Just as all rivers flow naturally to the sea, as immortal spiritual beings incarnating in physical form for the span of a lifetime, every single one of us yearns on deeper levels of the psyche for a return to that pure state of Oneness and wholeness that is our true home. This applies no matter how hard a person may scoff at or deny this intrinsic need.

One only has to consider the many reports of sightings of otherworldly beings like ghosts and spirit entities, and the uncanny similarity of numerous near-death and out-of-body experiences reported from widely diverse cultures, to know that there is more to life than limited, day-to-day, three-dimensional physical existence. It is simply a deepseated fear of the unknown that causes such vehement denial of such possibilities from certain people.

To explain further — their 'mother who mourns' — refers partly to your beautiful Mother Earth you call home, who is a living, evolving, sentient being just like you, her children. It also refers to our people, the Guardians, who have been responsible for guiding and assisting you on your evolutionary journey.

Like any loving parent, of *course* we feel great sadness to see our human children groping in the darkness of intolerance and fear, simply because of such trivialities as differences of race, color, creed or language. If you cannot accept and get along with members of your own

Earth humankind, then how in the name of the Great Oneness will you ever learn to accept others such as our people, and the many other ET cultures, who look so very different but are, nevertheless, still part of our universal family! This is why we do not come among you openly, and will not, until Earth humans have succeeded in raising their vibrational frequencies to a more spiritually evolved level. We do value our own lives too, you know!

The racial and religious intolerance that humans display is actually a carry-over from your predecessors, in which the marking out of territory by various means was such an all-important part of existence. Any outsider entering this marked area who was not part of the herd or flock was treated with great mistrust, and attacked accordingly. Surely, it is time for humans to move forward from such limiting and fearful behavior, and to come to understand that the color of a person's skin, the language they speak, or the religion they choose to follow, is so very unimportant. All that really counts in the end is the depth of love and compassion in their hearts.

The "weakness in high places" refers to the many immature and less-evolved souls who hold positions of power and control upon your planet — souls whose whole purpose is to incite divisiveness, intolerance and fear rather than unity, understanding and brotherly love. This is of great concern to us, for it is this spiritual ignorance and greed in high places, in the governments and leaders of Earth, which has caused the downfall of the human race in ages past, and will certainly bring about many distressing events in the future of your world. Growth, economy, health, and the whole evolution of humankind will be affected on a planetary level.

We are very much aware of the problems many Earth humans experience in encounters with us, but unfortunately the solution does not lie with us but rather with the humans. It is the nature of the Guardians to act as mirrors for the human psyche, reflecting back whatever is deep in the heart of those who perceive us. This is how we carry out our work of transformation and spiritual awakening — we bring you face to face with your deepest inner being — your own personal "angels" and "devils" as it were.

So many people of Earth are caught up in either fear or egotism, so therefore that is exactly how the Guardians are perceived. In the light of fear we are seen as terrible and evil demons, inflicting pain and humiliation upon innocent human victims; whereas in the light of over-inflated ego we are perceived as gods or great masters, come to save certain "chosen ones" upon your planet. In truth we are neither, for as transmuters of energy we are simply tools in the hands of the Great Oneness, and our job is to transmute the base metal of the lower emotions of humankind into the pure gold of spirituality and unconditional love.

There is a very beautiful future for you, the people of Planet Earth, when you finally learn to put aside the transient physical cravings, fears, emotions and desires that cause you so much pain, suffering and separation. These are the sole cause of your entanglement in the cycle of birth and rebirth, endlessly blocking you from achieving the glorious joy and freedom of higher levels of reality which are your birthright.

There are so many on Earth who experience a sadness, a loneliness and an insatiable thirst on deeper levels of the psyche that cannot be satisfied no matter how much they indulge themselves physically or emotionally. They run in never-ending circles, always seeking out this elusive "something," but never quite finding it. They may forget about it for a while by losing themselves in the acquiring of possessions, or by surrounding themselves with the distractions of work, play, family or friends, but in the end it always comes back to haunt them, gnawing away at their inner being with a hunger that cannot be appeased, a thirst that cannot be quenched, for it is a hunger and thirst of the spirit and of the soul.

This spiritual hunger can only be satisfied by eventually letting go of all physical and emotional cravings and desires. This is the secret behind what is referred to as Nirvana, or heaven. Nirvana is not emptiness or nothingness, as some would have you believe, but rather the pure and glorious blissfulness and peace which fills heart, soul and mind when one finally learns to live one's life in a state of desirelessness — a state which most certainly can be acquired while still living a full and productive life in physical form on Planet Earth. To quote from some ancient teachings known as the Upanishads:

> *When all desires that surge in the heart are renounced,*
> *the mortal becomes immortal.*
> *When all the knots that strangle the heart are loosened,*
> *the mortal becomes immortal.*
> *This sums up the teachings of the Scriptures.*[*]

---

[*] *Katha Upanishad* - chapter 3 verse 4

END NOTE

This book has been presented as a work of fiction to allow you, the reader, to immerse yourself in a completely different world, not as an analytical observer, but a participant. We hope you enjoyed it. This book is based entirely on my non-fiction book, *The Zeta Message — Connecting All Beings in Oneness,* co-authored by Helene Kaye and also published by Wild Flower Press.

The reasons for this story that you have just read and hopefully enjoyed are three-fold — firstly, it has been written to appeal to a wider readership, to include those who have no recollections of ET contact but would like to know a bit more about it; secondly, it has enabled me to express the multilayered complexity of ET reality within a framework that humans can relate to more easily; and thirdly, it is to help people down here come to terms with the idea of ETs, and most especially so-called "Greys," living among you in human form. Hopefully through the adventures of Alarca, Ashka, Maris and the others who live and work on the big disc affectionately known as the "Workshop," you now have a little more understanding and a little less fear in regards to ET contact and all it entails.

The Zeta Message tells the real story of my own lifelong contacts with the gray Guardian Family. It also gives a detailed and moving account of a very normal, average Australian family who suddenly find themselves caught up in full-on contact with the so-called "Greys," involving mysterious flashing lights, black-clad figures appearing in the corner of bedrooms in the middle of the night, and children awakening, screaming in terror.

It then goes on to describe a gradual opening-up process leading to deeper levels of understanding as the "fear barrier" is gradually broken down to reveal incredible depths of love, wisdom and oneness. Helene, the mother of this family, kept meticulous notes on an almost daily basis, on which much of *The Zeta Message* is based.

My own part closely follows "Ali's" story, with a number of inexplicable happenings along with an underlying sense of contact and connection with the strange beings who haunted my entire childhood. Then followed a gradual opening up of conscious awareness and deeper understanding through a number of very full-on encounter experiences during my teens and young adult life.

By the time Helene and her family entered the scene in 2000, introduced to me by a mutual friend who knew of my own experiences, I was completely aware of and in harmony with this "other" side of my reality — Alarca the Guardian. Working from this dual ET/human perspective, I was able to calm and reassure the family, and assist them through their own "awakening" process, which is precisely what contact with the gray Guardians is all about.

The Zeta Message:
Connecting All Beings in Oneness
By Judy Carroll and Helene Kaye
ISBN 978-0-926524-70-5
©2011
Wild Flower Press, an imprint of
Granite Publishing, L.L.C.
POB 1429
Columbus, NC 28722
828-894-8444

http://www.granitepublishing.us
http://www.amazon.com
http://www.thezetamessage.com
http://5thWorldFund.org

The not-to-be-missed companion volume to
Human By Day, Zeta By Night

Made in the USA
Middletown, DE
30 April 2019